Russia and Europe

Russia and Europe:
An End to Confrontation?

edited by
NEIL MALCOLM

Pinter Publishers, London and New York
for
The Royal Institute of International Affairs, London

Distributed exclusively in the USA and Canada by ST. MARTIN'S PRESS

Pinter Publishers
25 Floral Street, Covent Garden, London WC2E 9DS, United Kingdom

First published in Great Britain 1994

Distributed exclusively in the USA and Canada by St Martin's Press, Inc., Room 400, 175 Fifth Avenue, New York, NY10010, USA

British Library Cataloguing in Publication Data
A CIP catalogue record for this book is available from the British Library

ISBN 1-85567-161-1

Library of Congress Cataloging-in-Publication Data
Russia and Europe : an end to confrontation? / edited by Neil Malcolm.
        p.   cm.
Includes bibliographical references and index.
ISBN 1-85567-161-1
    1. Europe—Foreign relations—Soviet Union. 2. Soviet Union—Foreign relations—Europe. 3. Russia (Federation)—Foreign relations—Europe. 4. Europe—Foreign relations—Russia (Federation) I. Malcolm, Neil, 1943–   .
D1065. S65R87   1994
327.4704—dc20   93–27883
                                                                                                        CIP

Typeset by Koinonia Limited
Printed and bound in Great Britain by Biddles Ltd of Guidlford and King's Lynn

Contents

List of tables		vi
List of contributors		vii
Preface		viii
1	Introduction: Russia and Europe	1
	Neil Malcolm	
2	The Atlantic Alliance in Soviet and Russian Perspectives	31
	Hannes Adomeit	
3	The European Community as seen from Moscow: Rival, Partner, Model?	59
	Vladimir Baranovsky	
4	Dismantling the Military Confrontation	79
	Jane M. O. Sharp	
5	The Settlement with Germany	99
	Fred Oldenburg	
6	Relations with Central- and South-Eastern Europe	123
	Alex Pravda	
7	New Thinking and After: Debate in Moscow about Europe	151
	Neil Malcolm	
8	Economic Relations with the Rest of Europe	182
	David Dyker	
9	Russia, the CIS and the European Community: Building a Relationship	199
	Perdita Fraser	
10	Russia and Europe: Possibilities for the Future	224
	Sergei Karaganov	
Index		234

List of tables

Table 4.1 Budapest Agreement of 3 November 1990
on CFE allocations 89

Table 4.2 Treaty-Limited Equipment levels agreed for CIS
states and Georgia at Tashkent, May 1992 91

Table 4.3 CFE–IA Treaty national personnel limits 92

Table 8.1 The commodity structure of Soviet foreign trade 183

Table 8.2 Soviet oil production 183

Table 8.3 The Soviet hard-currency external balance 186

Table 9.1 Summary of Quantitative Restrictions imposed in 1990
by EC member states on Soviet exports by product
category 203

Table 9.2 Summary of the trade balance between the USSR, the
former USSR and the EC 204

Table 9.3 EC trade with the former USSR in the first nine months
of 1992 204

Table 9.4 Share of each member state in Soviet exports to
the EC, 1991 205

Table 9.5 Share of each member state in EC exports to
the USSR, 1991 205

Table 9.6 Breakdown of EC technical assistance programmes to the
former Soviet states in 1992 211

Table 9.7 Distribution of global assistance to the ex-USSR to
March 1993 212

Table 9.8 Membership of the EBRD 214

List of contributors

Hannes Adomeit, Fletcher School of Law and Diplomacy, Tufts University, Boston

Vladimir Baranovsky, Institute of the World Economy and International Relations, Russian Academy of Sciences, Moscow

David Dyker, Science Policy Research Unit, University of Sussex

Perdita Fraser, J. P. Morgan, London

Sergei Karaganov, Institute of Europe, Russian Academy of Sciences, Moscow

Neil Malcolm, Russian and East European Research Centre, University of Wolverhampton

Fred Oldenburg, Bundesinstitut für internationale und ostwissenschaftliche Studien, Cologne

Alex Pravda, St Antony's College, Oxford

Jane M. O. Sharp, King's College, University of London

Preface

Since Mikhail Gorbachev came to power in 1985 and proclaimed his intention of building a 'Common European House', a revolution has come about in European international relations. However it was not the kind of revolution which Gorbachev had in mind, nor was it one which was foreseen by any of the participants. Its consequences are so far reaching and ill-understood that the whole future of Europe, East and West, has become clouded with uncertainties. The greatest uncertainty of all surrounds Russia, the inheritor state of the Soviet Union, now weakened, unsure of its role and marginalized, but potentially one of the main elements in the political and economic balance of the continent.

The purpose of this book is to analyse the origins and the driving forces of the changes which have taken place in relations between Russia and the rest of Europe and to examine the prospects for the future. The first three chapters set Gorbachev's innovations in the context of Russian and recent Soviet history. Chapter 1 describes the uneven course of Russia's long rapprochement with Europe over the last three hundred years, emphasizing the interaction of internal and foreign-policy change. It goes on to summarize the main points made in subsequent chapters. In Chapter 2, Hannes Adomeit traces the history of Soviet and latterly Russian relations with and policy towards the Atlantic alliance, from the unqualified hostility of the 1950s to Yeltsin's bid for eventual membership. He concludes by discussing the current and possible future relationship of Russia with NATO. Chapter 3, by Vladimir Baranovsky, deals with perceptions in Moscow of the other main institution of West European cooperation, the European Community, showing how ignorance and mistrust in Moscow gradually came to be replaced by a desire to emulate and collaborate with the Community.

The next four chapters focus on particularly crucial and sensitive aspects of the dismantling of the Cold War confrontation, and on how the Yeltsin government has followed through with regard to them. In Chapter 4, Jane Sharp analyses Gorbachev's approach to nuclear and conventional disarmament, and discusses the problems created by the demise of the Soviet Union and the emergence of four nuclear-armed states. She explains the interaction of strategic and political changes in Europe in 1990–91, and describes the consequences of subsequent continuing attempts by the Russian military to compensate for the setbacks in their power potential which these changes brought about.

Chapter 5 is devoted to the pivotal relationship between the Soviet Union/ Russia and Germany, and to the working out of a new German settlement, which formed the centrepiece of the 1990 European agreements. Fred Oldenburg's analysis is based partly on the personal testimony of the last ruling SED General Secretary, Egon Krenz.

In Chapter 6, Alex Pravda explains the special part played by the 'socialist bloc' states of Central-Eastern and South-Eastern Europe in closing the circuit between foreign policy changes and domestic politics in the Soviet Union. He shows how misconceptions in Gorbachev's approach to the region led to an accelerating disintegration of Soviet control which prefigured the collapse of the Soviet Union itself. The chapter also considers the effects of the break-up of the Soviet Union on Russia's relations with Central-Eastern Europe, arguing that it pushes Moscow in the direction of flexibility and greater sensitivity to local concerns.

Chapter 7 looks at the internal dimension of foreign policy change and at the debates provoked in Moscow by Shevardnadze's New Political Thinking and the Westernism of the Russian Foreign Ministry under Kozyrev. It traces the gradual growth of 'realism' in late-Soviet and post-Soviet Russian foreign-policy thinking about relations with Europe and analyses its significance.

Chapters 8 and 9 are devoted to the economic issues which have now become central to Russia's relations with the rest of Europe, as instability and uncompetitiveness in the East threaten to cut the region off as effectively as the iron curtain did in the past. In Chapter 8, David Dyker analyses the strengths and weaknesses of Russia as an economic partner and assesses the possibilities for and conceivable paths towards the country's involvement in the European system of micro-specialization. In Chapter 9, Perdita Fraser examines the recent history of Russia's relations with the European Community and associated bodies, such as the EBRD, in respect of institutional relations, trade, aid and investment, and assesses the prospects for a closer relationship.

In the final chapter, Sergei Karaganov outlines four scenarios for Russia's future place in Europe. Although the most important variables which he identifies relate to changes inside the boundaries of Russia and the former Soviet Union, he emphasizes that the rest of the continent will not be able to isolate itself from events in Russia, and will become engaged in its problems in one way or another.

Finally, a few words about terminology. 'Europe' is used throughout the book to describe the region from the Atlantic to the Urals. Russia is thus treated as a European country, and the book deals with its relations with the *rest* of Europe. This does not of course preclude talking about 'Russia and Europe', just as one might talk about 'Britain and Europe', or 'Italy and Europe'. Nor does it imply turning a blind eye to the arguments concerning Russia's cultural or political 'Europeanness': this should be clear enough from the substance of the chapters which follow. Accordingly, the region referred to during the Cold War as 'Eastern Europe' should correctly be called 'Central-Eastern and South-Eastern Europe'. We adhere to this usage as a rule, but in certain contexts 'Eastern Europe' is used in the old sense, where the meaning is clear, for the sake of economy.

The word 'Europe' is used by Russians, too, in a variety of senses. In the eighteenth and nineteenth centuries it was employed most frequently as a synonym for 'the civilized world'. Changes inside Russia in the direction of higher standards of education, respect for the law, democratization, modernization of agriculture and industry, and so on, were perceived there as moves in the direction of 'Europeanization'. This was partly because Europe appeared as the core of the advanced industrialized world. It was also because Russia forms part of Europe as geographically defined and because the rest of Europe was its principal channel of contact with the outside world. This usage of 'Europeanization' returned in the years after 1985.

'Europe' is also treated by Russians in a more specific sense, as one among several parts of the industrialized world. As a number of the contributors to this volume point out, Soviet foreign policy in the decades after 1945, for example, was overwhelmingly oriented towards the United States, often in a way which damaged relations with Western Europe. More recently, some officials and international relations specialists in Moscow have drawn attention to the importance of building closer relations with the Asia-Pacific region, and have criticized what they see as a foreign-policy fixation on the Atlantic world.

However, despite some speculation in Moscow about the kind of conflicts which may break out between Europe, Japan and the United States after the Cold War, most observers there appear to see a fundamental underlying solidarity among the Western powers and Japan. This applies in particular, despite some disagreements inside the Group of Seven, to the broad lines of policy towards Russia and the other former Soviet states. Moreover, the place of Europe in any Russian programme for modernization and greater integration in the community of industrialized nations is so central (because of geographical proximity and the dense pattern of existing ties) that Russian Westernizers as a body are by and large committed to the idea of Russian rapprochement with the rest of Europe.

This means that at times it is difficult to distinguish between, on the one hand, Russian policy towards the rest of Europe and the Russian debate over the country's future role in Europe, and, on the other, Russian policy towards the West as a whole and Russian arguments over Westernization in general. For most of the time, we have to do with one policy and one debate. Thus this book deals with Russian relations with and attitudes towards the rest of Europe *both* as a distinct region *and* as the geographically closest part (and to a degree still an embodiment) of the community of advanced industrialized countries.

The editor and contributors wish to thank all those who participated in the study groups which were held at Chatham House to discuss the separate chapters, and all the others who advised and commented on early drafts. The biggest debt of gratitude is to the Administrator of the Russian and CIS Programme at Chatham House, Shyama Iyer, who worked far beyond the call of duty to keep the project on schedule, and whose expertise made the editor's work far less arduous than it would otherwise have been.

This volume is published under the auspices of the Royal Institute of International Affairs Soviet Foreign Policy Research Programme funded by the Economic and Social Science Research Council (grant no. E 00 22 2011).

The Royal Institute of   Neil Malcolm
International Affairs, London
July 1993

1 Introduction: Russia and Europe

Neil Malcolm

The overwhelming majority of the people of Russia live to the west of the Ural Mountains. They are thus, in a geographical sense, Europeans. What is more, the Russian state has played an important, at times dominating, part in European international politics for more than two centuries. Russian Christianity has recently celebrated its millennium. Russian writers, musicians and artists have been welcomed as contributors to the European cultural tradition since the nineteenth century. In the twentieth century, the Russian Leninist adaptation of German Marxism and the political parties which embraced it have to one degree or another left an imprint on the political life of all the countries of the continent.

And yet, among the multitude of definitions of 'Europe' that have been offered, a large proportion exclude Russia. There is also a strong Russian tradition which emphasizes the nation's cultural distinctiveness and its separate destiny. In terms of area, after all, far more of Russia is in Asia than in Europe. Its Christianity was 'Eastern', Byzantine in origin. From the thirteenth to the fifteenth centuries it was submerged under Mongol and Tartar rule, and thereafter its isolation from the West was only gradually overcome: it did not experience the cultural upheaval of the Renaissance, and it came late to the Enlightenment. Under the Romanov dynasty Russia became a byword in educated European society for backwardness, obscurantism and bureaucratic despotism. By the time of the Cold War the Soviet Union, which exercised control over half the European continent, was widely perceived as an alien force, built on principles fundamentally incompatible with European values. Its apologists, for their part, like those of its imperial predecessors, emphasized the distance which separated Soviet civilization from that of the 'decadent' West.

The uncertain, peripheral status of the country has continually provoked the question: 'whither Russia?' As early as the beginning of the seventeenth century the Muscovite chronicler Ivan Timofeev complained, 'We turn our backs on each other: some look to the East, some look to the West.'[1] In 1966, Denis

1

de Rougemont wrote that, unlike his native Switzerland, 'Russia has the choice, whether or not to be part of Europe, depending on whether or not the latter corresponds to Russian notions of humanity, Christianity and social order'.[2] But of course it is not simply a matter of some kind of once-and-for-all choice made collectively by the nation. Through the centuries Russia has been pushed and pulled by a variety of internal and external pressures, some towards difference and separation from the rest of Europe, some towards rapprochement and similarity. In the process different social groups and parts of the state have been identified at various times with conflicting Westernizing and anti-Westernizing tendencies in home and foreign affairs.

This book focuses on external relations, on the phase of rapprochement with the rest of Europe that got under way in Russia in the middle of the 1980s, and which is still continuing, if less confidently than before. It sets out to analyse its origins, the forces which have driven it ahead and the obstacles which have hampered it, and it tries to estimate how it might develop in the foreseeable future. This introductory chapter outlines the evolution of Russia's relations with the rest of Europe in 1985–93, and draws attention to the central points made in the chapters which follow. First of all, however, it sketches in the broader historical background, and describes the domestic context of external change.

Underlying factors in Russia's relations with Europe

Western writers seeking to identify the roots of Russia's international behaviour often concentrate on explaining why Russia has acted for so long as an 'outsider' in European politics. The most common explanations are to do with geopolitics, with Russia's internal political and economic arrangements, with its cultural specificity and with its relative economic underdevelopment.

As the dominant power of the Eurasian heartland, bounded especially to the west and southwest by wide plains undefined by clear ethnic or geographical boundaries, Russia, it has been argued, feels compelled to expand its frontiers. Its modern history has accordingly reflected a dominant outward thrust, and in particular an 'urge to the sea'. In this conception Russia inevitably clashes with the peripheral, maritime powers of Western Europe and North America, whose role it is to contain Russian expansionism.[3] Russia's drive into Central-Eastern Europe, where it first assimilated the Baltic region, much of Poland and Finland, and later established suffocating control over the Soviet-bloc countries, appeared in the West to reflect this expansionism, and what is more a threatening lack of respect for the European state system.

This source of confrontation has frequently been linked to a second, namely the centralization of political and economic power in the hands of the Russian state which goes back to the emergence of Muscovy.[4] The despotism of the tsars' 'patrimonial state' and the dictatorship of the Bolsheviks have both been seen as congenitally militaristic and aggressive. It is noted that Russian rulers have sponsored messianic ideologies portraying Moscow as a Third Rome, as a champion of the Slav nations of Europe, or as a fortress of world revolution.

Such ideologies rested on a deep-rooted sense of separateness in the Russian population, fed by its long fight for national survival in the Middle Ages, and the centuries of relative isolation which followed. This feeling has expressed itself by turns in exaggerated respect for Western civilization and in vigorous assertions of Russian superiority. Genuine cultural differences, whether revolving around religion in the seventeenth century, or around attitudes to private property and trade in the twentieth century, have been a serious barrier to intercourse with other European societies, and they have helped to form the seed-bed for Russian nationalism.[5]

Finally, Russia's relative technological and economic backwardness on the one hand led its rulers to seek wider contacts with the West, if only to maintain their ability to wage war effectively, and on the other obliged them to maintain barriers against external competition.[6] It also helped to ingrain a pattern of mutual apprehensiveness: partly to compensate for its military-technological inferiority, Russia maintained very large armies, thereby reinforcing Western fears provoked by the sheer size of the country. At the end of the twentieth century, Russia's economic uncompetitiveness continues to cut it off from the world and from integration processes centred on the European Community.

Yet only the first of these factors (the geopolitical one) could be described as immutable, and opinions differ even about its implications in the contemporary world. There is nothing inevitable about Russia's role. Indeed it is the *changing* character of Russia's relations with the rest of Europe over the years that needs emphasizing.

Historians have pointed out that military defeats tended to spark off periods of internal reform and modernization in Russia, accompanied by greater openness to European influences. But these reforms were usually disappointing in their outcome. Varying combinations of government caution and social conservatism eventually choked off radical change. Thus Russia was more successful than Poland, for example, in retaining its independence and its separate cultural identity, but this autonomy was bought at the price of periodic relapses into relative isolation and stagnation, which lasted until some external disaster came along to restart the cycle of adaptation. 'Any regular attack of the Western virus', wrote one author, 'and the resultant spiritual "thaw" were followed by a regular "freeze", invariably accompanied by outbreaks of patriotic xenophobia, struggles against foreign influence, and state expansionism.'[7]

This pattern, however, conceals a larger long-term tendency. Russia has been no exception to that trend to greater internationalization and

Westernizing modernization which in the twentieth century has emerged, for good or ill, as a global phenomenon. The demands of military competition, the attractiveness of European culture to its own educated elites, the pressures of technological change and greater international economic specialization, and the intensifying of cross-frontier communications have all gradually undermined Russia's separateness. It has even been proposed that the processes which have been under way since 1985 are capable of bringing about an epochal breakthrough in Russia's relations with the West, marking the opening of a new stage of Europeanization and radical changes in the content of the old cyclical pattern.[8]

The term Europeanization is used here to refer both to changes in Russia's domestic affairs which bring it closer to European patterns (for example, the development of market institutions and practices, the growth of autonomous social organizations, moves towards a more important role for legal procedures and constitutionality in political life), and also to changes in external policy which bring with them greater openness to Europe and the Western world generally. While there is no tight logical connection between the external and the internal aspects, they do seem to have been connected in practice.[9]

External and internal aspects of Europeanization in Russia: the historical background

The question of Russia's European or non-European destiny has been the central question in Russian politics for centuries. The modern phase of the debate began with Peter the Great. When he came to power three hundred years ago he initiated a sweeping revolution from above, reforming the state administration, improving education, modernizing industry and in general using traditional Russian methods to coerce his subjects into at least a semblance of Western practices. This had a particularly strong effect in St Petersburg (which he had built as his 'window on Europe') and Moscow, and in court circles. By the 1760s, in the reign of Catherine II, the aristocracy had adopted French as their preferred language of conversation, and busts of the *philosophes* stood in the Hermitage palace on the banks of the Neva.

For a moment the illusion appeared that Russia, like America, was a new nation, where human reason could have full sway. 'How happy is the country where nothing has as yet been done', wrote Catherine's correspondent, Diderot. But disillusion soon followed: 'A long tradition of repression has resulted in a general atmosphere of reticence and distrust, a recollection of terror in the mind, as it were, that is in complete contrast to the noble openness characteristic of the free and self-confident mentality of the Frenchman or Englishman.'[10] Catherine herself reacted decisively to the first shoots of an independent Europeanized public opinion, cutting back on reform and throwing her critics into prison.

Especially after the French Revolution, the Romanovs practised a highly qualified, conservative Westernism unpopular both with traditionalists and with the more Europeanized part of society. When Russia emerged after the Napoleonic wars as a major actor in European military affairs it aligned itself with the central European autocracies, but failed to win their trust. Alexander I's draft declaration of 1815 instituting the Holy Alliance bound the emperors of Russia, Prussia and Austria to assist each other in resisting republican sedition, and announced that the three states formed 'one Christian nation'.[11] The end of his reign was followed by a constitutionalist uprising led by a group of army officers and gentry radicalized by exposure to European influences in the first two decades of the century. It was rapidly crushed. Under his successor Nicholas I official ideology took on a more nationalist colouring, and Western influences were more strenuously resisted, but this did not mean isolation from European affairs. In the Convention of Berlin in 1833 the three emperors pledged to act together 'to strengthen the conservative system which constitutes the immutable foundation of their policies'. During 1848 and 1849 Russia intervened politically and militarily in Central Europe to defend the dynastic order. Nicholas sent Russian troops to crush the Hungarian rebellion against Austria and, attempting to stiffen Friedrich Wilhelm IV against democratic pressures, he wrote that if a republic were introduced in Berlin, he would consider it Russia's duty to act to restore the Prussian autocracy.[12]

Inside Russia political and social change was held back. Opportunities for remedying the weak condition of industry and trade were limited by reluctance to change the serf-holding basis of agriculture. The education system had been expanded, but many of those who benefited from it failed to find a function in society: there was hardly any economic base for a middle class, and the scope for open political activity was very limited. The Russian 'intelligentsia', as the educated part of society came to be called, soon gained a reputation for high-mindedness and extremism. Their writings reflected the whole spectrum of contemporary European thought, but with a distinctive Russian tone and emphasis.

Throughout the nineteenth century, the Westernizing part of the intelligentsia, and they were always the majority, agonized over the obstacles posed to their aspirations by autocracy, by the backwardness of the peasantry, and by their own alienation from the people. Some reacted with despair: one notorious statement described Russia as 'a blank on the map of human reason', 'a terrible lesson in the extremes of alienation and slavery'.[13] Some reconciled themselves to official policy, persuaded that progress could only be gradual, and placing their hopes on education and economic advance. Others argued that Russia could jump a historical stage, and adapt the existing peasant communities as the basis for its own kind of socialism. In a Russian setting the scope for prudent liberalism of a West European kind was limited.

There were also those who saw no necessary European destination, however delayed, for Russia. The Slavophils of the 1840s and 1850s drew on German idealist philosophy to construct a theory which implied a special historical mission for their country. They looked back to the pre-Petrine era, when Orthodox Christianity uncontaminated by Western rationality supposedly formed the basis for an organic social harmony. The cult of the individual, private property and the law which Western Europe had inherited from the Roman tradition, they argued, may have produced greater material wealth, but a terrible price was paid in spiritual emptiness and social atomization. Eventually Europe would look to Russian Christianity for its salvation.[14] These ideas subsequently flowed either into official conservatism, or into pan-Slavism, the movement which proclaimed Russian hegemony over the smaller Slav nations, and which called for more energetic Russian action to liberate South-Eastern Europe from the Turks. As Chapter 7 demonstrates, traces of Slavophilism are present in late-twentieth-century Russian nationalism.[15]

Meanwhile, Russia's crushing defeat in the Crimean war of 1854–6 brought home the lesson of its economic and social backwardness and sparked off a wave of Westernizing reform – freeing of the serfs, easing of censorship, a jury system, elected local authorities. But this was still reform from above, dependent on the resolve of enlightened members of the government. The authorities came under strong pressure from the conservative gentry to keep change to a minimum, and they were put on their guard by the revolutionary tone of much intelligentsia discussion. Thus the reforms of the 1860s had disappointing results: rural poverty worsened, the development of industry was delayed, modest proposals for democratic constitutional change were derailed in 1881 by the assassination of Alexander II.

Russia's post-Crimean war policy of cautious activism in the Balkans failed to calm the suspicions of the other European powers, and after the Russo-Turkish war of 1877–8 they forced Russia to accept limitations on its role in the region. In the 1880s the conservative regime of Alexander III adopted an ideology of separateness from a decadent Europe, and proclaimed the empire's mission in Asia, where Russian troops had already penetrated to Afghanistan. The turn of policy this represented was supported by Bismarck, for reasons which are not difficult to understand: 'Russia has nothing to do with the West; she only contracts nihilism and other diseases; her mission is in Asia; there she stands for civilization.'[16]

Yet the underlying forces pushing Russia closer to Europe continued to operate. The closing decades of the nineteenth century saw rapid state-sponsored industrialization designed to substitute for the shortage of native entrepreneurship. The rouble was fixed to the gold standard, tariffs were manipulated to protect developing sectors, and a huge influx of European (mainly French and British) capital was attracted. In 1905 another military humiliation, at the hands of the Japanese, combined with mounting domestic unrest to provoke further reform. The country acquired its first national parliament, and the government began to introduce a system of permanent individual land-holding intended to encourage the growth of a prosperous peasantry. By the second decade of the twentieth century Russia was closer to Europe in cultural and social terms than it had ever been.

Opinion among the more liberal-minded section of the public favoured the notion that Russia should break away from its diplomatic alignment with Germany, and embrace more 'European' policies at home and abroad, including political and economic liberalization, a rapprochement with Britain and France, greater activism (with a pan-Slavist colouring) in the Balkans. The Russian government entered the First World War in 1914 thoroughly split on these issues. The arguments were not decisively resolved by the overthrow of the Tsar in February of 1917. While the liberal Provisional Government aligned itself firmly with the entente powers and declared itself for constitutional democratic reform, the Bolshevik opposition which eventually displaced it called for an end to the war.

The coming of Communist rule in Russia marked the beginning of a long period of alienation from the West. Of course the Russian Marxists had insisted on measuring Russian reality against European benchmarks. They mercilessly criticized illusions among their fellow revolutionaries that the country could bypass the historical era of capitalism and pass unaided to some special Russian kind of socialism. Lenin's plan for insurrection in 1917 rested on the assumption that revolutions would occur soon afterwards in a number of advanced European societies. Even after 1917, Trotsky and the Bolshevik left stuck to the idea that a Russian revolution could not succeed in isolation: it would be dragged down by the country's 'Asiatic' culture. Yet it was not European 'bourgeois' reality which the Bolsheviks admired, but European socialist ideals. When Stalin adopted the policy of 'socialism in one country' he opened the way to a fusing of traditional Russian authoritarianism with Bolshevik contempt for 'parliamentary cretinism'; traditional Russian dislike for commerce with Marxist revulsion against capitalism; traditional Russian xenophobia with Leninist apprehension about the intentions of imperialism.[17] Russian authors now frequently draw attention to continuities between Stalinism and the despotism of the tsars, describing the collectivization of agriculture, for instance, as a reimposing of the serf-holding regime dismantled seventy years earlier.

There were elements of continuity in foreign policy, too. The coming to power of a self-proclaimed revolutionary regime in Russia reinforced the old view in the West that Russia was a country which did not play by the rules of 'international society' and was not to be trusted.[18] The Rapallo Treaty (1922) marked a renewal of the alliance with Germany, as Lenin defensively turned his back on a suspicious and uncooperative Western Europe and sought to manipulate differences of opinion among powerful potential enemies. Lenin's doctrine of a savage, militaristic imperialism, shaped by the experience of the First World War and the Russian Civil War, reinforced the Russian tradition of reliance above all on military strength for security. Stalin, like his predecessors in the Kremlin, imported Western machinery and know-how in order to renew the Russian industrial base, especially the arms industry, but went to extreme lengths to exclude Western influences.

For all the nationalistic, isolationist and quasi-religious characteristics of Stalinism, however, the materialistic Marxist core of Leninist thinking remained intact. Soviet communism set out to beat the West at its own game, to outpace it technologically, to build a more productive economy, and to achieve higher standards of living. Socialism was supposedly a more effective form of social organization derived from a Western 'scientific' analysis of society. Once the failure of the project in material terms became evident, it was difficult to sustain the legitimacy of the regime and preserve belief in its superiority to the Western model. What is more, a huge investment had been put into education, increasing the numbers of those susceptible to infection with Western ideas, and, as the relevant technology developed, it proved impossible to exclude international communications flows. As faith in communism withered, it was natural for the educated part of society to look to Europe and North America for solutions to the country's problems. By the time communism finally collapsed, a large reservoir of enthusiasm for things Western had accumulated among the Soviet intelligentsia. In 1985 the USSR, a complex industrialized, urban society, was in some ways 'further away' from Europe than Russia had been in 1917, but in others much closer.[19]

The Soviet Union and postwar Europe

After the Second World War, as after the First, Moscow turned sharply away from an alliance with the liberal Western powers, and entered a period of relative isolation. The difference was that on this occasion it had participated in the victory, and it faced a transformed international situation in Europe. The dominant powers in the region were now the Soviet Union and the United States. The former was able to shelter behind a buffer zone of satellite states in the east, and to maintain a large military force in the eastern zone of Germany, blocking that country's unification and posing a substantial threat to the western part of the continent.

This brought Russia 'into Europe' willy-nilly, but in a way which reinforced even more strongly its image as an over-powerful, unwelcome intruder. This impression remained over the succeeding four decades, as it strove to exploit its main foreign policy resource, military strength, to influence events. Although the Soviet Union did not as it happened make energetic use of its ties with West European Communist Parties, apprehensions that it could possibly exploit an internal fifth column, and irritation over the way it tried to manipulate public opinion further antagonized West European governments.

Also reinforced was traditional Russian defensiveness about Western subversion. Now there was not only the Soviet population to shield from harmful influences, but also the inhabitants of the Eastern-bloc states, who had less and less enthusiasm for Soviet-style socialism or for the forced alliance with Moscow. Once infection seeped into the outer reaches of the socialist camp, after all, what was to stop degeneration penetrating to its core? Such fears dictated maintaining a sharp dividing line in the centre of Europe and periodically cracking down on revisionism inside the bloc. This in turn strengthened Western antipathy.

During the forty years after 1945, a great deal was written in the West about Soviet goals and intentions in Europe, often in a rather categorical and simplistic style, which failed to distinguish between short-, medium- and long-term aims. As Edwina Moreton and Gerald Segal complained as recently as 1984, 'the difficult grey areas of Soviet foreign policy dilemmas are often forced into unsuitable black and white categories of assertions of straightforward Soviet objectives'.[20] The situation which faced policy-makers in Moscow was not a straightforward one. There persisted the long-standing Russian dilemma of how to maintain the necessary level of economic and cultural interaction with Western Europe while protecting the country against perceived military threats (including, now, that of devastation by nuclear weapons) and political destabilization. In addition, the postwar world posed at least three new dilemmas.

The first was created by the structures which grew up in the western part of Europe in response to the perceived threat from the East, the most important being NATO and the European Community. Should the main priority be to weaken and destroy such entities, or did their existence offer significant advantages to Moscow? Was Atlantic-centred solidarity really a greater threat than West-European-centred (or, worse, German-centred) solidarity?

The second dilemma was posed by the privileged position the Soviet Union had acquired in Germany. What was the balance of advantages between a divided Germany and a united one, if the correct price could be extracted for the latter (neutralization, a wider realignment in Europe, etc.)? How far could the Soviet Union go in building West German hopes of unification without damaging the German Democratic Republic, and its own relations with Berlin?

The third dilemma was posed by the Kremlin's new responsibility for the Eastern bloc. If the Warsaw Pact countries' economies failed to thrive and their leaderships got into political difficulties when they were kept on a tight rein by Moscow, how much autonomy could they safely be permitted in order to work out their own paths to socialism?

Not surprisingly these dilemmas provoked inconsistencies and fluctuations over time in Soviet policy. These in turn have provided plentiful material for dispute among Western scholars, for example concerning Moscow's underlying approach to the NATO alliance. Lawrence Freedman wrote in 1984:

On the one hand the United States is a menacing adversary and anything that weakens it, such as the collapse or serious weakening of its major alliance, is to be welcomed. On the other hand, Europe has a history of turbulence and is, from a Soviet perspective, still politically fragile. The American presence can be seen as an important stabilising influence which, if removed, would open the way for more dangerous forces – especially German revanchism.[21]

Apart from helping to ensure the continued division and military subordination of Germany, in this view, NATO also provided a lever of influence on the United States, inhibited the development of West European military cooperation, and provided a justification of the Soviet presence in Eastern Europe. These aspects are highlighted by Jane Sharp in the early part of Chapter 4.

In Chapter 2, Hannes Adomeit argues forcefully that the advantages listed above were not as weighty as they might seem, and that before 1985 the Soviet Union repeatedly sought to weaken NATO and to decouple the United States from Europe. At the same time, he draws attention to a series of important adjustments of Soviet policy, provoked by successive reassessments of the political situation in Europe; the most striking of these came at the beginning of the 1970s, when Brezhnev switched tack from an increasingly fruitless anti-Americanism to a line emphasizing the bilateral superpower relationship.

Whatever their long-term aspirations, Soviet leaders seemed reluctant to offer a vigorous challenge to the status quo, no doubt for fear of provoking something worse. As a rule they tended to operate in a circumspectly trouble-making way, 'with a permanent wariness,' in Robert Legvold's words, 'of the pendulum swinging too far or not at all'.[22]

A striking feature of Soviet foreign policy after the Second World War was the overwhelming attention given to relations with the principal adversary, the United States. The Soviet Union repeatedly applied pressure in Western Europe, the main site of East–West confrontation, in order to influence Washington, with little apparent concern for the effect on the secondary Soviet–West European relationship. This pattern is evident from the days of the Berlin crises provoked by Stalin and Khrushchev to the deployment of intermediate-range nuclear missiles under Brezhnev.[23] Similarly, Moscow's initiatives of rapprochement with Western Europe never looked likely to lead to a real realignment: they too seemed mainly intended to exert leverage on the United States.

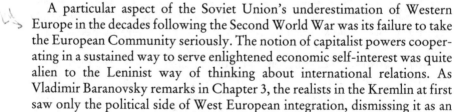

A particular aspect of the Soviet Union's underestimation of Western Europe in the decades following the Second World War was its failure to take the European Community seriously. The notion of capitalist powers cooperating in a sustained way to serve enlightened economic self-interest was quite alien to the Leninist way of thinking about international relations. As Vladimir Baranovsky remarks in Chapter 3, the realists in the Kremlin at first saw only the political side of West European integration, dismissing it as an anti-Soviet ploy initiated in Washington. When, in the 1970s, European political cooperation began to strengthen the European allies' capacity to resist American preferences, interest was sparked off in Moscow. It was speculated that as bipolarity declined Western Europe could join Japan as a powerful challenger to American hegemony. Baranovsky describes how this combined with hopes of gaining recognition for the East European economic cooperation institution, the CMEA, to provoke a tentative diplomatic opening to the EC. The results, however, were negligible.

It is important, nevertheless, to note that by the 1960s a trend had established itself towards closer political and economic relations between the USSR and France, West Germany and Western Europe in general. This closer relationship served a number of Soviet purposes quite apart from gaining leverage on the Western alliance as a whole. It opened up access to a flow of technology and know-how less likely to be hampered by embargoes and restrictions, and it helped to win recognition of the frontiers established in Central and Eastern Europe by the postwar settlement. These gains were highlighted in the Final Act of the Helsinki Conference on Security and Cooperation in Europe in 1975, signed by the United States and Canada as well as all the European states.

The rapprochement did not, as many feared at the time, lead to any significant weakening of NATO. Indeed the main price was to be paid on the Soviet side. It was paid not just in terms of the declarations about human rights included in the 'third basket' of the Helsinki document, but also, more concretely, in terms of the effects on the satellite states and on the USSR itself of detente and closer contacts with the West. As the social, economic and political crisis of the Warsaw Pact countries deepened, the 'Western virus' again began to take hold. This contributed to the collapse of the Communist system and a radical shift in Russia's relations with the rest of Europe.

The end of the Cold War

In an echo of previous arguments over the origins of the Cold War, the reasons why the Cold War came to an end in Europe soon became the subject of violent debate. Possibly too much attention has been paid to deliberate policy moves by the Western powers – whether containment in the long term and military and ideological pressure from the Reagan Administration in the short term, or Ostpolitik, detente and bridge-building – in bringing about change.[24] It would be unrealistic, of course, to expect any resolution of the theoretical arguments over the primacy of developments in the international system, on the one hand, and of internal social and organizational changes, on the other, in explaining innovations in foreign policy.[25] In the Soviet case, however, an approach which focuses on the *interaction* of external and internal processes has proved fruitful.[26]

As we have implied in the preceding pages, where Russia's relations with Europe are concerned such interaction has been particularly intense and diverse in form. The change in policy after 1985 can scarcely be explained simply in terms of shifts in the East–West balance of military and economic strength, however important they may have been. The Soviet Union had willy-nilly become enmeshed in international networks of interdependence and had already begun to be penetrated by external influences. Furthermore, by 1985 the rising generation of policy-makers in Moscow were passing through a phase of revulsion against the isolationism of their predecessors.

That is not to deny the importance of the material factor. By the last decades of the twentieth century the long-standing fundamental contradiction in Russian foreign policy, between the urge to build barriers for security purposes and the need to interact more intensively with the outside world to sustain economic growth, was becoming more and more painful. The link between technological level and military capacity was becoming tighter, and deepening internationalization in research and development made a strategy combining modified autarky with espionage increasingly unworkable. Brezhnev's 'detente' compromise, with its mixture of military-political competition qualified by arms agreements, especially with the United States, and broadening of economic contacts, especially with Western Europe, had failed. Although there had been a certain increase in the level of East–West trade, by 1985 NATO was as solid as ever, the arms race was speeding up, and technology embargoes had been reinforced.

At the same time economic performance continued to decline. Investment was being cut and the rate of return on capital was very low. The windfall benefits from oil and gas exports after 1973 had little long-term impact. Even according to official statistics, the annual increase of GNP had fallen from double figures in the postwar decades to less than 5 per cent in the 1980s, and some Western economists estimated close to zero growth.[27] The technology gap showed no sign of closing. Indeed the decision in Washington to invest heavily in the development of 'space defence' and in advanced conventional weapons threatened to impose a large new drain on available Soviet resources and manpower. In Central- and South-Eastern Europe the unwelcome social and political consequences of economic decline had been demonstrated: in Poland they had already nearly led to a popular revolution, averted only by emergency military rule.

The failure of the Soviet economic system to outdo capitalism was most graphically demonstrated by the contrast between the performance of the resource-rich USSR itself and of its struggling Third World protégés on the one hand, and the performance of the newly industrializing countries on the other. But of more immediate importance, and closer to home, was the contrast between continuing prosperity in Western Europe and stagnation in Eastern Europe (most strikingly evident in the divided Germany). While economic integration moved ahead in the European Community, the CMEA languished, and the socialist bloc became a net burden to the Soviet Union.

As faith in the outcome of the socialist economic experiment faded in Moscow, the Soviet leaders and their advisers had to come to terms with the old underlying economic and cultural gravitational power of the Western part of the continent. If the USSR could no longer be confident of holding its satellite states in its orbit, it was surely a matter of urgency to avoid isolation by establishing its own closer relations with Western Europe. The rhetorical long-term goal of exchanging confrontation in the region for a new pan-continental cooperative system became real and a pressing priority. So pressing, indeed, that by the end of the 1980s Moscow even came to jettison its original central condition, that the United States presence must be removed from the continent first.

Yet as the experience of other countries demonstrates, there was no reason why perceptions of weakness could not have generated a variety of other policy responses of a more inward-looking, defensive kind. The opening up to Europe and the wider world was not inevitable. Important changes in society, politics and ideology had a powerful bearing on the policy choices made in the second half of the 1980s.

By 1985, when Gorbachev became General Secretary of the Soviet Communist Party, Soviet society had undergone a transformation since the days of Stalin: the employment structure was beginning to resemble that of an advanced industrialized country, there were 15 million graduates and 5 million students in higher education. Some sociologists identified a growing network of informal structures, and pointed to 'manifestations of emerging civil society' even in the quintessentially statist Soviet system.[28] Intellectuals began to gain in confidence. The semblance of a 'public opinion' began to find expression in sections of the mass media and through polling activity.

The sense that political modernization was lagging behind economic development became widespread among the intelligentsia as early as the 1960s. The dissidents Andrei Sakharov, Roy Medvedev and Valentin Turchin wrote in a collective letter to the leadership at the end of that decade:

> There is an urgent need to carry out a series of measures directed toward the further democratization of our country's political life. This need stems, in particular, from the very close connection between the problem of economic and technological progress and scientific methods of management, on the one hand, and the problem of freedom of information, the open airing of views, and the free clash of ideas, on the other.[29]

Fifteen years later such views had undoubtedly spread widely among the more cosmopolitan sections of the intelligentsia, which had become increasingly Westernized, listening to international radio broadcasts, reading specialized literature in foreign languages and seizing opportunities to travel abroad and mix with professional colleagues there.[30] The intensifying of international contacts affected governing circles as well.[31] Experience in Central-Eastern Europe seems to have been a particularly potent source of unorthodox thinking.

Many of the new Party leaders and other officials who came to power in the mid-1980s turned out to be conscious of the need for reform and receptive to new ideas. Gorbachev and his closest colleagues also turned for political support to the intelligentsia. Insulted and cold-shouldered under Khrushchev and Brezhnev, they were now too numerous and too indispensable an element in any project for economic and social revitalization to be ignored.[32] Market reforms, freedom of speech, greater openness to the outside world, all answered to their preferences, just as they challenged those of the entrenched bureaucracies which opposed Gorbachev's changes.[33] The Director of the Soviet Institute of Economics, one of a substantial group of academics who were appointed in the late 1980s to high-level advisory and government positions, described the pro-perestroika coalition as 'an alliance of the top political leadership, progressively-thinking scholars and cultural figures, and . . . the mass media'.[34]

In the foreign policy sphere, many in the intelligentsia undoubtedly saw a diplomatic opening to Europe as something inseparable from the 'Europeanization' of their own society. During half a century of enforced isolation, powerful if perhaps sometimes ill-focused pro-Western feelings had accumulated among the intelligentsia. One highly placed Soviet Foreign Ministry official wrote in 1989:

> By Europe we should understand not only the political phenomenon, but also a definite method as to how to live, think, communicate with other people . . . The 'Common European House' is the home of a civilization of which we have been on the periphery for a long time. The processes that are going on today in our country, and in a number of socialist countries in Eastern Europe, have besides everything else a similar historical dimension – the dimension of a movement towards a return to Europe in the civilized meaning of the term.[35]

As these remarks demonstrate, the post-1985 period marked the coming to fruition of long-maturing tendencies in the world of ideas and perceptions. When Gorbachev declared in his 1987 speech on the 70th anniversary of the October Revolution that capitalism was not necessarily linked with aggression he merely set the official seal on a revision of Leninism by Soviet international affairs experts which, as Chapter 7 points out, had been gathering pace since the Second World War. This shift was possible, of course, because the West's policy of containment had indeed been accompanied by a degree of restraint in policy towards the USSR, and even at times by elements of economic and political cooperation; as Fred Oldenburg emphasizes in Chapter 5, Germany's role in this gradual trust-building process was particularly important. The existence of nuclear weapons, moreover, especially after the establishing of 'parity' at the beginning of the 1970s, served to make war in Europe seem unthinkable.[36]

A special part in the reappraisal of international relations carried out by Soviet experts in the postwar period was played by their analyses of developments in Western Europe. The initial scepticism in Moscow about the prospects for economic cooperation and integration had to be abandoned, as the postwar recovery continued and the European Community strengthened and developed. An influential group of Soviet theorists began to argue that Western Europe represented the prototype and the growth point of a more planned and integrated international economy (see Chapters 3 and 7). The acceptance of the idea that in relations between capitalist countries rational cooperation could prevail over destructive competition marked an important step back towards the mainstream of Western international relations thinking.[37]

The 'Common House': Russia in Europe, and Europe in Russia

Under Gorbachev the revolutionary implications of these changes in the world view of certain parts of the Soviet elite gradually made themselves felt. A particularly striking symptom was that 'all-human interests' came to replace the international class struggle as the declared guiding principle of foreign policy. From 1987, parallel and connected tendencies got under way in domestic politics. As Chapter 7 demonstrates, de-ideologization, compromise and an emphasis on the role of international institutions in foreign relations went hand in hand with pragmatism, tolerance of pluralism and aspirations to legal order and constitutionalism in domestic political life. Here is how one reformer described the impact of New Thinking:

> The renunciation of the policy of global antagonism, of the class struggle principle in international affairs, the major breakthroughs in disarmament, the efforts to put an end to economic self-isolation destroyed the 'besieged fortress' way of life in the country. That precisely was the essence of new political thinking, not merely the desire to shift the emphasis from external to internal needs, as it was interpreted abroad. . . . The proclamation of the priority of general human principles immediately put these principles on the agenda of home policy, including the universally recognized democratic freedoms, the pluralism of opinions and the freedom of the press.[38]

It is now amply clear that the approach to implementing reform was itself pragmatic; there was no blueprint, no detailed long-term strategy. As time passed, differences in the strength of resistance meant that advances were made more rapidly in some dimensions of change than in others, which generated a complicated set of interactions between foreign policy and

domestic policy, between economic policy and political reform. New actors –
individual, institutional, even national – appeared on the scene, the language
of politics changed and the leadership was forced to engage in successive
revisions of policy. At first, by showing flexibility, it was able to retain the
initiative. Later it appeared to be trailing in the wake of events. Ultimately it
was swept away by them.

Three important turning points can be distinguished in the period from
1985 to 1991. The first was Gorbachev's initiation of a policy of cautious but
increasingly determined relaxation of tensions with the Western alliance,
backed up by the promulgation of a radical new foreign policy doctrine at the
27th CPSU Congress in February 1986.

The second was the switch, which began to take shape in 1987 and gathered definition in 1988, to a much more intensive rapprochement with
Western Europe, implying large-scale disarmament and an alteration of Moscow's role in Central-Eastern and South-Eastern Europe. This was associated
with a vigorous drive for democratization and with market experiments in the
Soviet economy.

The third was the collapse of Communist power in the satellite states in
1989 and 1990, accompanied by a serious weakening of Communist authority
inside the USSR. At this point Moscow's policy began to appear increasingly
reactive and buffeted by events. External changes aggravated the political,
social and economic turmoil which domestic reform had set going. All this
had reverberations in foreign policy, as Gorbachev, under pressure from
conservative forces, was forced to manoeuvre. Uncertainty about Soviet
policy persisted up to the moment when the failed *coup d'état* of August 1991
brought an end to the regime.[39]

Defusing tensions

Gorbachev's first visit to the West as leader was to Paris, in October 1985.
When he announced that Western Europe was 'at the centre of attention in
Soviet policy', some prepared themselves for a far-reaching reorientation
away from the dominant superpower focus of policy. But it soon became
clear that although there was a new seriousness in the approach to Europe,
Moscow was using diplomatic activism in the region in the classic Soviet
style. As Adomeit expresses it in Chapter 2: 'The notion of the Common
House of Europe was meant primarily to serve as an inducement to Washington to consent to a reordering of its relations with Moscow.' The first priority
was to persuade the United States to come to the arms control negotiating
table.[40] When Washington eventually responded, superpower relations improved very quickly, the process being driven along by a determined Soviet
strategy of concessions. Gorbachev made no further full-scale official visits to
Europe until 1989. Meanwhile he attended four superpower summits, starting

with the meeting in Geneva in November 1985, and there were around thirty US–Soviet meetings at foreign minister/secretary of state level.[41]

Moscow had begun to show a new sensitivity to Western anxieties about plots to drive wedges in the Atlantic alliance. It was careful to stress that, however much it would like to see the end of military blocs in Europe in the long term, for the time being it saw them as necessary for stability; they should even be strengthened. But it failed to anticipate West Europeans' fears that deals were being done between Moscow and Washington behind their backs, and in particular their alarm at the prospect of an early agreement to remove all intermediate-range nuclear missiles from Europe. After the US–Soviet summit meeting in Reykjavik in October 1986, the Soviet press began to express concern that Britain, France and Germany were planning to expand nuclear and conventional defence cooperation to compensate for anticipated American withdrawals.

In this early phase there were some breakthroughs in Soviet–West European relations: in 1985 Moscow finally gave the green light to direct links between the East European states and the European Community, bypassing the CMEA, and in 1986 dramatic progress was made at the CSCE-sponsored talks on military confidence-building in Stockholm when the USSR adopted an unprecedentedly relaxed attitude to verification measures on its territory. Yet West European mistrust of Moscow was understandable enough.[42] There remained three major obstacles to improving relations on the continent. The first was Soviet occupation and control of Central- and South-Eastern Europe. After all, what serious content could the concept of a peaceful Common European House have while half the inhabitants were held at gunpoint by their neighbour? The second was the continuing coolness in relations with the Federal Republic of Germany, still regularly criticized in the Soviet press for its 'militarism and revanchism', as it had been ever since Bonn gave its support in 1979 to NATO's decision to deploy Cruise and Pershing 2 missiles in Europe. The third and most obvious obstacle was the huge accumulation of Soviet armed forces in the centre of Europe.

A European policy

Several factors, we may imagine, pushed the Kremlin to rethink and intensify its European policy after 1987. In the military sphere, European reactions to the INF agreement underlined that the logic of disarmament now demanded radical reductions in the Warsaw Pact's conventional forces. In the economic sphere, perestroika was languishing: if closer integration in the world economy were to play its part in Soviet economic revival, then something had to be done about trade with Western Europe (80 per cent of all the USSR's trade with the capitalist world, but in absolute decline since 1984), and especially with the main partner, the Federal Republic of Germany. In the political sphere, the period between the January 1987 Soviet Communist Party Central Committee meeting and the 19th Party Conference in June 1988 was one of sharp confrontations between reformers and conservatives over plans for extending democracy and reducing the powers of the Communist Party apparat. Here too success abroad could give a boost to Gorbachev's reform process. It is no accident that, as Chapter 7 documents, this was the moment when serious disputes over foreign policy first flared up in Moscow.

In order to implement the grand strategy implied by the precepts of New Political Thinking – to exchange security founded on overwhelming armed strength for security founded on openness, trust and economic integration – a complicated set of parallel changes in the areas mentioned above had to be kept going more or less in step with each other. As far as dismantling the existing confrontation was concerned, the Kremlin could take the initiative and at least at first control the speed of the process. This was the case in conventional arms reductions, in disengagement from Central-Eastern Europe, and in rapprochement with West Germany. But when it came to constructing the new, positive bases of security it was dependent on active and imaginative cooperation on the part of the West. The latter's response was not always as prompt and helpful as Moscow might have desired.

Even more difficult to cope with were the 'internal' processes – in Central- and South-Eastern Europe and inside the Soviet Union – which domestic and foreign policy reform set in motion. However implausible it may seem in retrospect, it does appear that Gorbachev and his advisers seriously expected that a system resting on censorship and coercion could gradually be transformed into one resting on openness and consent. That Russians would use the opportunity of contested elections to return reformed communist governments to power. That the other peoples of the USSR would take advantage of their new rights of self-expression to declare their intention of remaining in the fraternal Russian embrace. That freely elected governments in the satellite states would choose to remain part of a military and economic bloc with the Soviet Union, and in this way participate in a gradual, symmetrical coming together of the two halves of the continent. It was on this rather flimsy basis that the Soviet government proceeded on a broad front to reconstruct relations with the rest of Europe.

Hopes for an accommodation with West Germany began to emerge in 1987. Chancellor Kohl removed a serious obstacle to the INF agreement by retracting his objections to the removal of all ground-based nuclear missiles from Germany, and Soviet spokesmen soon began to suggest that an expansion of contacts between the two Germanies might be in the offing. A rapid intensification of economic cooperation appeared on the agenda. When the first German–Soviet summit meeting in five years took place in Moscow in October 1988, the visiting party included five cabinet ministers and fifty German bankers and businessmen.

The innovative and dramatic approach by Shevardnadze and Gorbachev to confidence-building and arms control is emphasized by Jane Sharp in Chapter 4. The Soviet side put forward radical proposals for disarmament and defensive restructuring of forces in Europe in June and December of 1988, and the opening of the Conventional Forces in Europe talks in Vienna in March 1989 signalled that after decades of shadow boxing genuine cuts were finally on the way. Moscow had made the key concession, that, in order to reach parity at something below current NATO levels, reductions in tanks, armoured vehicles and artillery would have to fall disproportionately heavily on the Warsaw Pact side.

Policy in Central- and South-Eastern Europe was linked to the rapprochement with Germany and to the arms reduction drive. The spectre of West German revanchism and expansionism had repeatedly been used in Soviet propaganda as a device to enforce bloc discipline; now Bonn was acting, with Soviet approval, as advocate in the West for a new East European 'Marshall Plan'. The Soviet armed presence in the satellite states had always been more relevant in practice to internal policing than to waging a European war; by the middle of 1988, defence experts in Moscow were discussing scenarios involving total withdrawal from Czechoslovakia and Hungary.[43]

As Chapter 6 demonstrates, policy in Central- and South-Eastern Europe was intimately intertwined with Soviet domestic affairs. As with internal reform, things began slowly, with hints of non-interventionism coming from Moscow from the autumn of 1986. After the long-delayed 19th CPSU Conference finally confirmed the principle of free electoral choice in June 1988, Gorbachev declared that self-determination applied abroad as well as at home: 'The imposition of a social system, way of life or policies from outside by any means, let alone military, are dangerous trappings of past epochs.'[44] No serious attempt was made to stop the Polish government opening round-table talks with Solidarity participation in August. In the spring of 1989, as Moscow's policy evolved, in Alex Pravda's phrase, into 'reactive permissiveness', partially free elections in Moscow were followed by an announcement from Warsaw that 161 seats in the parliament would be open to free electoral competition. Solidarity won 160 of them, and by August Communist rule in Poland was to all practical purposes at an end. In Hungary, too, Communists were being gradually eased out of power during 1989.

The authorities in Moscow tried to put a good face on events, but it was clear that the disintegration of old security structures was moving ahead more rapidly than the building of replacements, and that a distinctly 'asymmetrical' pattern was emerging in Europe. In August 1989 the Warsaw Pact had declared its intention of evolving into a 'political' institution, but NATO showed no sign of abdicating its military role, far less of dissolving itself in favour of some new structure based on the CSCE. The days of the CMEA, too, were clearly numbered, as more and more of its members established bilateral relations with Brussels. Indeed the Soviet Union itself was already having to bow to the new realities. In July 1989, during his visit to the

Council of Europe, Gorbachev acknowledged that closer economic relations in Europe depended on greater similarity in economic systems, and in particular on his own country making 'the transition to a more open economy'. Soon after the USSR signed its own trade and economic cooperation treaty with the European Community in December 1989, Shevardnadze talked of the pressures for integration 'spreading across the continent in waves' from the West.[45]

When the Berlin Wall fell at the end of 1989 it became clear that a new and more delicate phase in Soviet relations with the rest of Europe had begun.

Improvising a settlement

As the 'German clock' and the 'East European clock' speeded up, commentators began to discuss the prospects for an 'East Europeanization' of the USSR itself, starting with the Baltic states. The Soviet leadership tried to establish linkages which would slow up the process of disintegration of the Eastern bloc, and would speed it up in other areas, such as institution-building and economic assistance, where they might expect some compensating gains. Chapters 2 and 5 give an insight into the tense bargaining which went on around the German settlement, where the relinquishing of four-power rights, the withdrawal of Soviet troops, the acknowledgment of a united Germany's right to membership of NATO were made conditional on strengthening of the CSCE, reductions in the size and limitations on the potential range and type of weapons controlled by the united German armed forces, and financial transfers to the USSR. Bonn also agreed to assist Soviet attempts to establish closer ties with European institutions.

For decades Moscow's position had been that Germany could come together only when Europe came together. Now, if he was to argue that his search for security by political rather than military means had paid off, Gorbachev had to be able to point to some semblance of progress in dismantling East–West confrontation and building all-European structures. As Adomeit notes in Chapter 2, an important contribution in preparing for the agreement reached between Gorbachev and Kohl in the middle of July 1990 was made by the NATO summit in London earlier in the month. Here the participants virtually declared an end to the Cold War, inviting the Warsaw Pact states to sign a formal declaration of peace and announcing a radical change in strategy and redeployment of allied forces on defensive lines. The NATO document also proposed setting up in the CSCE a permanent secretariat, a mechanism to monitor elections, a centre for the prevention of conflict and a parliamentary assembly.

The new dispensation was celebrated at a three-day meeting in Paris in November 1990. The CSCE Charter of Paris, which was signed there, bound members to adhere to the Helsinki principles of peaceful international relations in Europe, self-determination and respect for human rights, including the right to private property and private enterprise. A start was announced on setting up the new CSCE institutions.

NATO's change of strategy was real enough, but the Western alliance was in no hurry to dissolve itself, and it rapidly became clear that the new emphasis on the CSCE's role was in practice mainly a matter of face-saving for Moscow. The ceilings agreed at the Conventional Armed Forces in Europe talks and endorsed in the CFE-1 Treaty signed at the beginning of the Paris summit assumed a balance between NATO and Warsaw Pact forces which was becoming more and more irrelevant as the Eastern bloc disintegrated. After the substantial territorial, political and military retreats of 1990, it is not surprising that Shevardnadze should have come under powerful domestic criticism. Before the year's end he had resigned.

Jane Sharp argues in Chapter 4 that by this time Mikhail Gorbachev had become dangerously out of touch with Soviet military opinion, so that a foreign policy which initially won him praise for courage and decisiveness now began to appear reckless and in danger of reversal. As it turned out, the Soviet leadership successfully avoided catastrophe in Europe in 1989–90, but the pace of change had been forced and a price had to be paid. Conservative forces inside the country were also gaining strength from concern about internal political and economic changes and about calls for secession in the union republics. The last part of 1990 and the first half of 1991 were a period of retrenchment in Moscow, in international as in home affairs. Gorbachev emphasized the USSR's 'socialist choice', sanctioned a harder line in the Baltic states, and proved unable to prevent attempts by the military to evade the provisions of the CFE-1 agreement.

Yet the balance of forces, externally and internally, remained in favour of change. In the summer of 1991 Gorbachev resumed active diplomacy directed at extracting large-scale economic assistance from the European Community and the West in general, and campaigned for the adoption of a decentralising 'Union Treaty', which implied the possibility of secession for individual republics. Vladimir Baranovsky notes in Chapter 3 that at this time conservatives, radicals and centrists in Moscow all cited the experience of integration in Western Europe as a justification for their own vision of the future of the USSR. Soviet attempts to tie Central-East European countries into a special security relationship only served, as Chapters 2 and 6 demonstrate, to hasten the end of the Warsaw Pact. The failure of the Moscow *putsch* of August 1991 only served to boost the reformist cause, and to open the way to power for a Russian government determined to put behind it the ambiguities of Gorbachev.

Yeltsin and Europe

According to the new, post-Communist administration in Moscow, the collapse of Communist rule opened the way for Russia to 'return to Europe'. The rhetoric of the new regime marked a high tide of official Westernism in the country's twentieth-century history (see Chapter 7), and the policy of Andrei Kozyrev's Foreign Ministry appeared to be to achieve as close a relationship as possible with Western institutions.

In December 1991 Yeltsin indicated that Russia sought membership of NATO as a long-term goal. The main purpose of this statement, as Hannes Adomeit comments in Chapter 2, was no doubt to bring home the decisive nature of Russia's realignment in international affairs. NATO responded by extending the scope of cooperation inside the North Atlantic Cooperation Council (NACC), which all the countries of the Commonwealth of Independent States (CIS) belonged to by the spring of 1992. NACC helped to redistribute CFE arms quotas among European CIS members during 1992 and to foster agreement on nuclear weapons issues among the former Soviet states, filling a gap left by the CSCE, whose international visibility was already declining. The complexities of this allocation process are described by Jane Sharp in Chapter 4.

The emphasis placed by the West on tying up loose ends in the arms control area was understandable enough, but it began to cause some dissatisfaction in Russia and the other states. Giscard D'Estaing had already commented in a conversation with Gorbachev in January 1989 that the economic aspect would be the decisive one in determining the nature of East–West relations.[46] By the end of that year the Soviet Union had signed a new trade and cooperation agreement with the European Community. As Perdita Fraser notes in Chapter 9, EC leaders at the end of 1990 were proposing a wider agreement based on Article 238 (on Association) of the Treaty of Rome. In July 1991 the Soviet President was invited to the attend the Group of Seven summit meeting, and in October his country was admitted to associate membership of the IMF. Progress is under way to draw up an EC–Russian Federation cooperation agreement which envisages the eventual opening up of a free-trade area stretching from the Atlantic to the Pacific. Yet the effect of all these steps, and of the aid extended to the USSR and Russia, has been predominantly political. As the barriers of mistrust and military confrontation were removed, the economic barriers to Russia's integration with the world system, and in particular with the rest of Europe, became more and more obvious. The Russian economy is largely uncompetitive in terms of quality and productivity, the financial, trading and communications infrastructure is rudimentary, the currency is unsound, the legal framework is incomplete and not reassuring to potential investors, popular and official attitudes seem ill-adjusted to a market economy and at times hostile to it.

It is true that with its natural resource wealth and large potential consumer-goods market the Russian economy is in important respects complementary with those of Central and Western Europe, but as David Dyker demonstrates in Chapter 8 it is *similar* economies which have made rapid progress in integration based on micro-specialization, and even broad moves towards trade liberalization seem difficult to achieve between economies at different levels of development. Of course, Russia's large potential raw materials and energy exports do not present a serious threat to the EC economies, as cheaply produced manufactured goods and agricultural exports would do. But economic restructuring goals imply a transition to export of manufactures, and it is a disincentive to foreign investment, as Chapter 9 argues, if there is no assurance of eventual access to external and particularly European markets.

Russia, unlike those other former Soviet states which are less well-endowed with natural resources, is quite capable of financing its own restructuring in the medium to long term, but in the near future assistance is required to overcome the problems of transition, which are particularly acute in Russia. The arguments about what kind of aid is appropriate are discussed by David Dyker in Chapter 8 and by Perdita Fraser in Chapter 9 (in the latter with specific reference to the role of the European Community). Both Fraser and Dyker favour careful targeting of financial aid, and stress the crucial role of well-designed educational and technical assistance, which in the latter's judgment could lay the basis for the involvement of Russia in European patterns of micro-specialization in the twenty-first century.

Many factors, Chapter 9 argues, make Russian membership of the European Community look highly unlikely in the foreseeable future. The problem of widening and simultaneously deepening the Community is already complicated enough. There is little desire among the existing members to begin considering how to deal with integrating another state of 150 million people, with such a distinctive economic culture and such a problem-ridden economy. Any discussion of admitting Russia would reawaken difficult boundary-drawing issues: what would be the place, for example, of Turkey, a long-standing supplicant for membership, and also a Eurasian power? More immediately, doubts are strengthened by political instability in Russia, and the many national conflicts already under way inside the boundaries of the former Soviet Union.

In general, there is plenty of material for debate over Russia's future trajectory, and how 'European' it will be. The high-minded internationalism and the hopes for a new world order and a new European order enshrined in the New Political Thinking of Gorbachev and Shevardnadze played a very important part in overcoming the Leninist/Stalinist legacy in Soviet foreign-policy thinking, and in convincing the West that real change in East–West relations was possible. As the painful realities of international retreat and internal transformation began to make themselves felt, there was bound to be a reaction in the direction of greater 'realism' and greater national assertiveness. As Chapter 7 makes clear, this reaction was already evident at the level of specialist debate during the Soviet period, and it gathered pace during 1992. Some of the critics of New Thinking aligned themselves with Shevardnadze's (and subsequently Kozyrev's) neo-communist and nationalist political opponents, and adopted a straightforward anti-Western position. More important, however, was the emergence of a group of writers and political figures who called on the government to abandon its high-minded rhetoric and switch to a more determined defence of national interests, especially on the territory of the former Soviet Union, while preserving, to a greater or lesser extent, its fundamentally pro-Western and European orientation. While certain members of this group identified themselves as a 'Eurasian' tendency, it is arguable that their conscious attempt to, as they put it, 'de-ideologize' foreign affairs discourse in Russia in fact served to Europeanize the atmosphere of discussion. Sergei Karaganov's contribution to this volume, in Chapter 10, provides an example of this 'new realism'.

The main risks of a reversal in Russia's course lie in the domestic political arena. As on so many occasions before, the fate of reform and of rapprochement with the West are intertwined. During 1992 and 1993 economic reform led to a sharp decline in living standards, new and unpopular forms of social differentiation, and the threat of large-scale unemployment. Democratization was widely perceived to have opened the door to chaos, corruption and the free play of individual ambitions. The dismantling of the old Soviet Union was seen as yet a further national humiliation, and an abandonment of Russians abroad to discrimination and persecution.

The outcome is bitter political controversy, in which domestic and international issues are linked together in the traditional way. Liberals press for rapid marketization and assimilation of Western practices; most are prepared to accept, however grudgingly, the sovereignty of the other former Soviet states; they tend to line up with NATO on foreign policy issues. Conservatives call for a rolling back of economic reform and the preservation of native values; most campaign openly for a restoration of the former union; they frequently assume a fundamental clash of interests with the Western powers. Centrists are for more cautious reform, with a powerful role for the state; they advocate the judicious use of pressure and occasionally force in the former Soviet area, which they see as a legitimate sphere of interest and responsibility; they acknowledge that it is in the Russian interest to keep on good terms with the West, but stress that the relationship with Europe, America and Japan must necessarily contain elements of competition as well as cooperation.

By the end of 1992 the honeymoon in Russia's relations with Europe had already come to an end, as the weakness of the liberal wing forced Yeltsin to shift to a more centrist position. Any fundamental threat to the new relationship, however, would come from social and economic breakdown, or the flaring up of serious conflicts with the post-Soviet 'near abroad'. In Chapter

10 Karaganov sketches out four scenarios for the future of the former Soviet area and its relations with the rest of Europe: a) the emergence of a nationalist or fascist regime in Moscow, b) a military coup, c) chaos and civil war, d) hesitant modernization.

The first two scenarios might well prove to be stepping stones to the third, Karaganov suggests. A former Soviet Union seething with national and social conflicts would turn rapidly into a zone of catastrophe. Europe would at first seek to isolate it, by building a Central-East European buffer zone, but later would be forced to intervene. Even in the last scenario, relations with Europe would be complicated. Russia is quite naturally entering a phase of introspection, preoccupation with domestic problems and redefinition and assertion of its national interests.

Russian isolation from Europe, however, seems improbable. Most Russian elites, Karaganov argues, feel an affinity with European values. They are also well aware of their country's economic dependence on the West, and must acknowledge that a strategic alignment with Europe and the USA is dictated by Russia's new relative weakness in relation to China. This forecast receives support from several of the contributions to this volume. In Chapter 6, for example, it is pointed out that the emergence of new states such as Belarus and Ukraine, 'cutting off' Russia from Europe, will have the effect of intensifying Moscow's interest in cultivating the former bloc states in Central-Eastern Europe, to avoid the formation of a *cordon sanitaire* and to build stepping stones to the west of the continent. Chapter 7 argues that even the self-styled 'Eurasian' tendency in Russian foreign-policy thinking has essentially represented a desire to readjust the balance after a period of extreme Euro-Atlanticism in policy, and is not by and large hostile to the general idea of opening up to the West.

Russian foreign policy is at a formative stage, of course, and it would be foolhardy to make firm predictions about its future shape. An important part will be played, as in the past, by Russian perceptions of the international environment. Just as the naked armed confrontation of 1914–18 helped to forge Lenin's bleak view of international relations and to justify the Soviet reliance on massive military power, so the relatively cooperative atmosphere of the post-1945 decades (even, at times, in East–West affairs) made possible Gorbachev's New Thinking and the peaceful rundown of the Cold War. As Chapter 3 demonstrates, Soviet Westernizers were particularly impressed by the experience of the European Community, and the whole flexible system of Western institutions which welded the powers which had fought each other in the Second World War into a single economic, political and security organism.

Despite the disheartening experiences of the early 1990s – economic decline and political disarray in the former Soviet Union, civil war in the former Yugoslavia, Western inability to develop a consistent and effective policy in either area – the case that multipolarity will entail a return to international anarchy and conflict in Europe remains to be proved.[47] A great deal will depend on Western leaders and on their capacity to focus on long-term goals. A controlled and supported exposure of the Russian economy to the pressures of greater openness, and institutional innovation to bind Russia into the European and international system would substantially improve the chances of maintaining the advances towards internal and external Westernization made since 1985.

This is not to deny that internal factors are at present playing the dominant role, forcing a sober reappraisal of the more ambitious hopes of the beginning of the decade. It is being argued more and more widely in Moscow that whatever market economy, whatever democracy, whatever system of relations with the former Soviet states are built, they will have a distinctive 'Russian' character. In particular it is argued that social underdevelopment means that the state cannot afford to abandon its traditionally active role, if chaos and demoralization are to be avoided. Russian reform, it is clear, has again entered the consolidation phase. Indeed a reversion to authoritarianism, economic centralism and isolationism is quite possible. But the long-term tendency to rapprochement with Europe has never been more evident than in the revolutionary years between 1987 and 1993.

Notes

1. Cited in Yu. Borko, A. Zagorsky, S. Karaganov, *Obshchii evropeiskii dom: chto my o nem dumaem* (Moscow, Mezhdunarodnye otnosheniya, 1991), p. 65. See too D. Treadgold, *The West in Russia and China. Russia 1472–1917* (Cambridge, CUP, 1973), ch. 5.
2. D. de Rougemont, *The Idea of Europe* (New York-London, Macmillan, 1966), p. 292.
3. H. Mackinder, 'The Geographical Pivot of History', *The Geographical Journal*, vol. 23, no. 4 (1904), pp. 421–4. See M. Hauner, *What is Asia to Us? Russia's Asian Heartland Yesterday and Today* (London, Unwin Hyman, 1990), for an account of the history of Russian Eurasianism.
4. R. Pipes, *Soviet Strategy in Europe* (New York, Crane, Ruzzak and Co., 1976), pp. 3–11.
5. See Arnold Toynbee's eloquent account of the 'perpetual interplay between the demonic technological process of the Modern Western World and a no less demonic determination in Russian souls to preserve Russia's independence', continuing from the sixteenth to the twentieth century. *A Study of History* (London, Oxford University Press, 1954), vol. 8, pt. IX, p. 130.
6. Pipes cites the poverty of Central Russia as the main stimulus to territorial expansion, with the Russian population expanding into more prosperous neighbouring countries for economic reasons. Loc. cit.
7. G. Derlyugan, 'Was Russia ever a colonial empire?', *International Affairs* (Moscow), 1991, no. 3, p. 87. See too Aleksandr Yanov's analysis of historical cycles of Westernization in Russia, in his *The Russian Challenge and the Year 2000* (Oxford, Basil Blackwell, 1987).

8. Yanov, *The Russian Challenge*, p. 276.
9. For contrasting views on the linkage between domestic reform and foreign policy reform in Russia, see Ts. Hasegawa, A. Pravda (eds), *Perestroika: Soviet Domestic and Foreign Policies* (London, Sage/RIIA, 1990), chs. 1, 9; G. Segal, *Openness and Foreign Policy Reform in Communist States* (London, Routledge/RIIA, 1992).
10. Denis Diderot, cited in A. Walicki, *A History of Russian Thought, from the Enlightenment to Marxism* (Oxford, Clarendon Press, 1980), pp. 3, 5.
11. A. Palmer, *Alexander I. Tsar of War and Peace* (London, Weidenfeld & Nicolson, 1974), p. 334. Walicki, *A History of Russian Thought, from the Enlightenment to Marxism*, p. 72.
12. N. Riazanovsky, *Nicholas I and Official Nationality in Russia, 1825–1855* (Berkeley, CA, University of California Press, 1959), p. 243; B. Pares, *A History of Russia* (London, Jonathan Cape, 1958), p. 384.
13. P. Chaadaev, 'Filisoficheskie pis'ma', *Moskovskii teleskop*, 1836, no. 15.
14. A. Walicki, *A History of Russian Thought, from the Enlightenment to Marxism*, pp. 92–114. Walicki notes the irony that 'seen in historical perspective, Slavophil ideology was clearly only an interesting offshoot of the European conservative romanticism' of authors such as Schelling and Friedrich Schlegel. He suggests that this was connected with similarities in the position of Russia and Germany, in both of which a patriarchal order was threatened by exposure to Western liberalism and developing capitalism (pp. 106–7).
15. For a perceptive survey of Russian writing about Europe during the nineteenth and twentieth centuries, see Iver Neumann, *The Russian Debate About Europe 1800–1991*, Doctoral thesis, University of Oxford, 1993.
16. Pares, *A History of Russia*, p. 464.
17. Karen Dawisha describes the doctrine of 'socialism in one country' as marking 'the final ascendancy of Slavophil reflexes *vis-à-vis* Europe'. 'Soviet Ideology and Western Europe', in E. Moreton, G. Segal (eds), *Soviet Strategy towards Western Europe* (London, George Allen & Unwin, 1984), p. 24. See also Toynbee, *A Study of History*, vol. 8, pt. IX, p. 133; Neumann, *The Russian Debate About Europe*, pp. 141, 162.
18. H. Bull, A. Watson (eds), *The Expansion of International Society* (Oxford, Clarendon Press, 1984); Neumann, *The Russian Debate About Europe*, p. 6.
19. For an eloquent account of the historical-sociological context of perestroika, see M. Lewin, *The Gorbachev Phenomenon. A Historical Interpretation* (London, Hutchinson Radius, 1989).
20. Introduction to Moreton, Segal, *Soviet Strategy towards Western Europe*, p. 2.
21. 'The United States Factor', in Moreton, Segal, *Soviet Strategy towards Western Europe*, p. 87. See too K. Pridham, 'The Soviet View of Current Disagreements between the United States and Western Europe', *International Affairs*, vol. 59, no. 1 (1983). See also M. Light, 'Anglo-Soviet Relations: Political and Diplomatic', in A. Pravda, P. Duncan (eds), *Soviet-British Relations since the 1970s* (Cambridge, Cambridge University Press, 1990), pp. 120–46.
22. R. Legvold, 'The Soviet Union and Western Europe', in W. E. Griffith, (ed.), *The Soviet Empire: Expansion and Detente* (Lexington, MA, Lexington Books, 1976), p. 237.
23. The balance of 'Atlanticism' and 'Europeanism' in Soviet policy is traced in H. Adomeit, 'Capitalist Contradictions and Soviet Policy', *Problems of Communism*,

vol. 33, no. 3 (May–June 1984). For an analysis of the international politics of the SS-20 deployments of the 1980s see J. Haslam, 'Soviets Take Fresh Look at Western Europe', *Bulletin of the Atomic Scientists*, 1988, May, pp. 38–42; and, in greater detail, J. Haslam, *The Soviet Union and the Politics of Nuclear Weapons in Europe, 1969–87* (London, Macmillan, 1989).

24. Cf. R. Perle, 'Military Power and the Passing Cold War', in C. Kegley, K. Schwab (ed), *After the Cold War; Questioning the Morality of Nuclear Deterrence* (Boulder, CO, Westview Press, 1991); T. Risse-Kappen, 'Did "Peace through Strength" End the Cold War? Lessons from INF', *International Security*, vol. 16, no. 1 (1991), pp. 162–88. Cited in D. Deudney, G. J. Ikenberry, 'The International Sources of Soviet Change', *International Security*, vol. 16, no. 3 (1991–2), p. 79. See also M. Cox, 'Beyond the Cold War in Europe: a Review Article', *Soviet Studies*, vol. 44, no. 6 (1992), pp. 1100–01; the symposium in *The Times Literary Supplement*, 6 November 1992.

25. See in relation to this issue R. Taras, M. Zeringue, 'Grand Strategy in a Post-bipolar World: Interpreting the Final Soviet Response', *Review of International Studies*, vol. 18, no. 4 (1992), pp. 355–76; J. Snyder, 'The Gorbachev Revolution: A Waning of Soviet Expansionism', *International Security*, vol. 12, no. 3 (1987/88), pp. 93–131.

26. For an exploration of these interactions in the first years of Gorbachev's perestroika, see A. Pravda, 'Introduction: Linkages between Soviet Domestic and Foreign Policy under Gorbachev', in Ts. Hasegawa, A. Pravda (eds), *Perestroika: Soviet Domestic and Foreign Policies* (London, Sage/RIIA, 1990), pp. 1–24. See too G. Segal, *Openness and Foreign Policy Reform in Communist States* (London, Routledge/RIIA, 1992); M. Light, 'Restructuring Soviet Foreign Policy', in R. Hill, J. A. Dellenbraut (eds), *Gorbachev and Perestroika* (Cheltenham, Edward Elgar, 1989), pp. 171–93.

27. P. Hanson, 'The Economy', in M. McCauley, *The Soviet Union under Gorbachev* (London, Macmillan, 1987), pp. 96–7; C. Friesen, *The Political Economy of East–West Trade* (New York, Praeger, 1976), p. 47; F. Holzman, R. Legvold, 'The Economics and Politics of East-West Relations', in E. Hoffman, F. Fleron (eds), *The Conduct of Soviet Foreign Policy* (New York, Aldine, 1980), p. 431; A. Åslund, *Gorbachev's Struggle for Economic Reform* (London, Pinter, 1991), ch. 1.

28. Lewin, *The Gorbachev Phenomenon*, pp. 49, 80.

29. *Political Diary* (samizdat), March, 1970, cited in C. Merridale, 'Perestroika and Political Pluralism: Past and Prospects', in C. Merridale, C. Ward (eds), *Perestroika. The Historical Perspective* (London, Edward Arnold, 1991), p. 19.

30. D. Wedgwood Benn, *From Glasnost to Freedom of Speech* (London, Pinter/RIIA, 1992); P. Grothe, 'Broadcasting to the USSR and Eastern Europe', *Problems of Communism*, vol. 29, no. 1 (1981).

31. See Deudney and Ikenberry's discussion ('The International Sources of Soviet Change', pp. 108–14) of the socializing effect on Soviet elites of prolonged participation in the work of international institutions and other networks.

32. M. Lewin, *The Gorbachev Phenomenon: a Historical Interpretation*; J. Hough, *The Soviet Leadership in Transition* (Washington, DC, Brookings, 1980).

33. In 1987 Jack Snyder identified Gorbachev's natural supporters as 'Civilian defense intellectuals, reformist ideologues, and supporters of liberalized foreign trade policies', and his opponents as 'the Military-Industrial Complex, old-style

ideologues and autarkic industrial interests': his reforms had the effect of 'empowering new constituencies' from the former categories. 'The Gorbachev Revolution: A Waning of Soviet Expansionism', *International Security*, vol. 12, no. 3 (1987–8), pp. 109, 114.

34. Leonid Abalkin interviewed by L. Pleshakov. 'Strategiya obnovleniya', *Ogonek*, no. 13 (1989), p. 18.

35. V. Lukin, *Moscow News*, 1988, no. 38. Cited in K. Dawisha, *Eastern Europe, Gorbachev and Reform. The Great Challenge* (Cambridge, Cambridge University Press, 1990), p. 22–3. See also I. Neumann (*The Russian Debate About Europe*, p. 288): 'In discussing Europe, the Russians have clearly been discussing themselves, and so the debate is an example of how Russians have forged identities for themselves – how they have talked themselves into existence.'

36. Deudney and Ikenberry ('The International Sources of Soviet Change') make a persuasive case that the shift in Soviet foreign policy followed from a rational recalculation of the nature of the international environment as at once less threatening and less rewarding for military expansionism.

37. N. Malcolm, *Soviet Policy Perspectives on Western Europe* (London, Routledge/RIIA, 1989), ch. 2.

38. Aleksei Arbatov (IMEMO head of department and arms control specialist), 'Three pillars of a besieged fortress', *New Times*, 1991, no. 16, p. 28. On post-1985 domestic-foreign policy linkage see A. Pravda, 'Introduction', in Hasegawa, Pravda (eds), *Perestroika*, pp. 1–24; J. Snyder, 'The Gorbachev Revolution: a Waning of Soviet Expansionism?', *International Security*, vol. 12, no. 3 (1987–8).

39. A similar periodization of Moscow's policy in Central- and South-Eastern Europe is proposed by Alex Pravda, in Chapter 6. Hannes Adomeit sees an additional phase in Gorbachev's policy towards the West, separating out the period from March 1985 until the Soviet-American summit meeting of November 1985, when Moscow's policy still bore a traditional, crude anti-American colouring. See Chapter 2.

40. See Aleksandr Bovin's comment in *Izvestiya*, 25 September, 1985, that Soviet policy was designed 'to make use of Western Europe's potential via the transatlantic channel to meet the evident deficit in common sense on the part of the current administration in the USA'.

41. H. Adomeit, 'The Impact of Perestroika on Soviet European Policy', in Hasegawa, Pravda (eds), *Perestroika: Soviet Domestic and Foreign Policies*, pp. 247–51.

42. For a good example of West European analysis of the relationships between the USSR, Western Europe and the United States at this time, see P. Hassner, 'Europe between the United States and the Soviet Union', *Government and Opposition*, vol. 21, no. 1.

43. M. MccGwire, *Perestroika and Soviet National Security* (Washington, DC, Brookings Institution, 1991), p. 359.

44. *Soviet News*, 6 July 1988.

45. Gorbachev, *Pravda*, 7 July 1989; Shevardnadze, *Izvestiya*, 19 January 1990; Shevardnadze interviewed in *Vecherni Noviny* (Sofia), on 30 January 1990, reported in *BBC Summary of World Broadcasts*, SU/0677, p. A1/2 (1 February 1990).

46. 'Beseda M.S. Gorbacheva s delegatsiei "Trekhstoronnei komissii"', *Mirovaya*

ekonomika i mezhdunarodnye otnosheniya, 1993, no. 2, p. 93.

47. J. Mearsheimer, 'Back to the Future. Instability in Europe after the Cold War', *International Security*, vol. 15, no. 1 (1990), pp. 5–56. See also Jack Snyder, 'Averting Anarchy in the New Europe', *International Security*, vol. 14, no. 4, pp. 5–41.

2 The Atlantic Alliance in Soviet and Russian Perspectives

Hannes Adomeit

Introduction

The member countries of the Atlantic alliance have enjoyed a prolonged, uninterrupted period of political stability, technological progress and economic growth. Of course, there have been differences among these countries in rates of growth and technological advance. Discrepancies in military power and political influence within the European Community and between the EC and the United States have remained, and so have controversies over agricultural subsidies, burden sharing, out of area conflict and the future of the organization. Nevertheless, the processes of integration in the European Community have been compatible with continued coordination of policies in the Atlantic community. The cooperative elements of the relationship between Western Europe and the United States have generally shown themselves to be stronger than the conflicts that have divided the two regions. Even more importantly, the alliance played an important role in managing and safeguarding the fundamental processes of change in Europe, including the collapse of the Soviet Union and the Soviet empire, the emergence of democratic, market-oriented systems in East-Central Europe and German unification.

The contrast between developments in the Atlantic community and the course of events in the eastern half of Europe could hardly be more pronounced. Marxist-Leninist ideology, the glue that had held the 'socialist community' together, has crumbled away and been consigned to the proverbial 'rubbish heap of history'. Once the Brezhnev Doctrine and the threat of military intervention had been removed, the individual communist regimes in that area rapidly disintegrated, and with them the supreme symbol of Soviet domination, the Warsaw Pact. CMEA, the economic counterpart in that domination, disappeared and along with it a large volume of trade in that area, another portion being redirected to Western markets. The extensive contacts that had previously been maintained between ideologues, party leaders, government officials and internal security agents have gone.

Problems of external redirection and realignment have been compounded by the agonies of *domestic* disruption and deterioration. The political order and the socio-economic fabric of Russia and other successor states of the Soviet Union have come under increasing strain as the disintegration of the bureaucratic, centralized one-party system and the command economy has proceeded. Nationalism and ethnic conflicts are proliferating. Concerned by the pattern of unpredictable change in the successor states of the former Soviet Union, Russia's western neighbours in Europe are now looking for new guarantees, alignments and alliances that could enhance their security.

But this search is not limited to Russia's neighbours. The need for reassurance and support is felt in Russia itself as the internal reform process comes under increasing attack from a combination of communists, crypto-communists and conservatives, as well as Russian nationalists and chauvinists.

It is against the background of fundamental change in Russia and the other successor states of the former Soviet Union that Moscow's attitudes and policies in regard to military alliances and collective security in Europe will be analysed.[1] It will be argued here that, despite all the complexity, unevenness and unpredictability of change in Soviet and Russian domestic politics, there is a consistent line in the development of thought concerning the Western alliance. This line can be traced from uncompromising rejection of NATO under Stalin, grudging acknowledgment of this institution as an unpleasant reality under Brezhnev, cautious acceptance of NATO as a stabilizing factor of European security under Gorbachev, to Russia's participation in the North Atlantic Cooperation Council (NACC) and even the declaration of full NATO membership as a long-term foreign policy goal under Yeltsin.

The discussion of these dramatic developments falls into five parts. The first deals with the question of whether, despite incessant propagandistic attacks, the Soviet Union *de facto* regarded NATO and the American military presence in and commitments to Europe as serving Soviet security interests. In order to test this hypothesis, two cases that have played some role in supporting this argument will be considered: Malenkov's bid in 1954 to join NATO and Brezhnev's 'Tbilisi signal' in 1971. The evidence derived from these episodes and other examples, however, will be considered here as insufficient support for the argument. Instead, it will be shown that the desire to get rid of NATO and the American military presence in Europe were dominant in Soviet attitudes and policies from Stalin to Chernenko.

The second part of the discussion deals with the far-reaching revision of Soviet approaches under Gorbachev and the shift to a more positive stance. The idea was finally gaining ground in Moscow that the driving of wedges between one 'power centre of imperialism' and another could perhaps produce some temporary, tactical advantages but that, from a strategic vantage point, it was counterproductive. The United States and the Atlantic alliance, the new reasoning went, had a positive role to play in the construction of the Common European House.

The third part examines German unification as the single most important testing ground for the revised Soviet attitudes and policies which emerged under Gorbachev. Obviously, it was one thing for any Soviet leadership to consent to a unified Germany but quite another to agree to the proposition that East Germany, traditionally one of the Soviet Union's staunchest allies in Europe, should be abandoned altogether and be allowed to add to NATO's military potential. It is not difficult to imagine the acute political conflicts that would have arisen in the Federal Republic of Germany if Gorbachev had consented to German unification but categorically insisted on German neutrality.

The consequences of the collapse of the Warsaw Pact form the subject of the fourth part. Gorbachev's working assumption on the German problem seems to have been the idea that the external aspects of unification would be managed jointly by the two military alliances. The idea, as so many others to which Gorbachev adhered, turned out to be erroneous. All his efforts in late 1989 and the first half of 1990 to transform the Warsaw Pact from an instrument of Soviet domination and control into a political institution respecting the sovereignty and national interests of its members were to no avail. This turn of events had several significant domestic repercussions. It led to the reappearance of some of the more traditional, hard-line Soviet interpretations of the Atlantic community. It was only after the failed coup in August 1991 that this trend was arrested.

The final part of the discussion examines Russia's attitudes and policies after the collapse of the coup attempt and the Soviet Union. It examines the reasons and rationales put forward by the supporters of reform in Russia for active cooperation with NATO on European security issues and even future membership in the alliance. But it also dwells on the dilemmas which are caused by such a comprehensive and fundamental shift in Russian foreign policy priorities and the opposition which this reorientation has caused among nationalist and conservative circles.

The Atlantic alliance: factor of stability or obstacle to Soviet hegemony?

The end of history has by no means arrived. Yet some rewriting of history is already in progress. This is evident, for instance, in the wide acceptance of the idea that, even prior to Gorbachev's consent in July 1990 to Germany's membership of NATO, the Soviet Union had tacitly supported the existence of NATO and the presence of US military forces in Europe.

Supporters of this view argue, first, that the failure of the more narrowly conceived European Defence Community (EDC) and the creation of a wider Atlantic Europe were seen in Moscow to be in its interest, since the brakes were thereby put on any further movement towards a separate Western European defence identity. The Atlantic connection served to limit the size of the West German armed forces and undercut any need for West Germany to become an independent nuclear power.[2]

Second, they maintain that the alliance was seen in Moscow as keeping in place a network of mutual restraints between Europe and the United States. Although they see this as valid throughout the Cold War period they also discern a shift in focus over time. Whereas in the 1950s and 1960s, it is said, the Soviet leaders regarded the American presence in Europe as a means of keeping the Germans in check, in the 1970s they continued their support for NATO because of the added interest of using the Europeans to keep the Americans in check.

Third, the argument continues, NATO and the Warsaw Pact stood for the division of Germany and Europe, which in turn was perceived in Moscow to be in its interest. In its perspective, one part of Germany under direct Soviet control and the other part entangled in NATO formed the cornerstone of security. A united and uninhibited Germany, by contrast, would represent a substantial and all too familiar threat. The immense potential of a united Germany's economy could be mobilized for political ends, and the size and quality of its armed forces worried the Soviet leadership, as it presided over a faltering economy and a disaffected alliance.

Fourth, the point is made that in an important sense the two alliances depended on each other for cohesion. If NATO had broken up in disarray the resulting turbulence would soon have affected the Warsaw Pact and threatened the strategic and ideological buffer between the Soviet Union and the West. Soviet participation in the negotiations on Mutual Balanced Force Reductions (MBFR) in Vienna is said to have demonstrated the validity of the argument, since a successful conclusion of the agreement would have served to legitimize the American military presence in the NATO framework.

While such arguments appear plausible, the evidence adduced to support them is selective, and in some cases erroneous. The historical record is more ambiguous. Thus, at the 23rd CPSU Congress in 1966 Soviet Foreign Minister Gromyko recalled Roosevelt's commitment at the Yalta conference that American troops would be withdrawn from Europe within two years and complained: 'Ten times two years have passed, but the American army is still in Europe and by every indication claims a permanent status here. But the peoples of Europe are having their say and will have their say on this score.'[3] Such complaints were reiterated a decade and a half later by Soviet arms control negotiator Yuly Kvitsinsky. In an outburst to his American counterpart in the Geneva negotiations on intermediate range nuclear forces (INF) he snapped: 'You have no business in Europe.'[4] And in 1990 Soviet Foreign Minister Eduard Shevardnadze was to acknowledge that until 'quite recently our aim was to oust the Americans from Europe at any price'.[5] If this was indeed so, what were the main reasons for this objective?

First, Soviet policy in Europe should be considered as having been designed not only as an attempt to codify but also to *change* the status quo in

Europe. The build-up of US forces in Europe and the addition of the Bundeswehr to the integrated command structure, however, significantly strengthened the military power and political effectiveness of NATO. The Atlantic alliance thereby gave its European members the confidence to stand up to Soviet military pressures and placed stringent limits on any increase in Soviet political influence in Western Europe.

Second, the stability of the Soviet Union's staunchest ally, East Germany, was always in doubt as long as West Berlin acted as a showcase for the Western system and a 'thorn in the flesh' of the GDR. But West Berlin's security and viability depended on the United States retaining its military presence in the city, in Germany and in Europe. This had been the clear lesson of Stalin's Berlin blockade of 1948–9 and Khrushchev's protracted pressure on Berlin from 1958 to 1962.

Third, without the countervailing power of the Atlantic alliance Soviet control over Central-Eastern Europe would in all likelihood have been more complete. Just as a strong NATO and prosperous European Community provided reassurance to its West European members vis-à-vis the USSR, it also gave the Europeans east of the Elbe river reason to believe that the division of Europe and Soviet domination would not last for ever. Differentiation and dissent could more easily develop in such conditions.

Fourth, while from Moscow's perspective an Atlanticist Europe may have had the advantage of discouraging separate German nationalist or revanchist tendencies, the alliance – not least because of rising German international influence – had committed itself time and again to a European settlement that would *end* the division of Germany and Europe.[6] This common position, too, served to limit Soviet options in Europe.

The argument about latent Soviet support prior to Gorbachev for a Europe closely linked with the United States in NATO is predicated on several assumptions. These include the notions that the withdrawal of the United States from Europe would create pressures on the Soviet Union to withdraw from Central-Eastern Europe; make West Germany a more assertive, nationalist and dangerous actor; and induce European defence integration, including even a separate European nuclear force with German participation.

All these developments were possible, but not very probable. Was it really likely that a united Europe with a common defence force and nuclear weapons would have emerged after the withdrawal of US forces? Perhaps. But perhaps not. What must have seemed really unlikely to the Brezhnevs, Andropovs and Chernenkos, however, was the idea that the collapse of NATO would spell the beginning of the end of the Soviet military presence in Central-Eastern Europe. It was precisely to safeguard against such possible pressures for troop withdrawals that the Soviet Union in the course of the 1960s had put in place a complete set of bilateral mutual assistance treaties and stationing of forces agreements with its fellow Warsaw Pact members. The network of treaties also bound the non-Soviet members of the Warsaw Pact to each other. From a practical point of view, therefore, the dissolution of the two military alliances in Europe would have made very little difference. In the end it was not the dissolution or weakness of NATO that contributed to the collapse of the Warsaw Pact but its very strength and viability.

As for the particular cases cited in support of the argument that Soviet leaders perceived NATO and the American presence as a source of stability, we shall first consider Moscow's 1954 bid to join NATO.[7] In the conditions of the time the purposes of the Soviet move would seem to have been fairly obvious. The note was in all probability designed to launch a campaign for international legal recognition of the German Democratic Republic. One week prior to its proposal to join NATO, on March 25, Moscow had declared the GDR to be a sovereign state, and in its subsequent note it described the GDR, like the Federal Republic of Germany, as a possible participant in the proposed European collective security system. Another objective was in all likelihood connected with the European Defence Community (EDC). By mid-March 1954 three of the six countries which had signed the Paris EDC treaty had ratified it, including the Federal Republic. France had signed the treaty but it was uncertain whether the *assemblée nationale* would ratify it. The Soviet initiative, therefore, was indeed most likely meant to influence the parliamentary vote and help defeat the EDC. But it by no means follows from this that Moscow preferred NATO to EDC (or WEU). Any effective Western defence integration remained anathema.

What about the argument that Soviet and Warsaw Pact invitations to pan-European conferences 'consistently' included the United States and Canada?[8] This is in fact not the case. Whereas an initiative by the Polish Foreign Minister, Adam Rapacki, in December 1964 called for the participation of the United States, subsequent Soviet and Warsaw Pact statements did not. In January 1965 the Warsaw Pact Political Consultative Committee (PCC), for instance, expressed 'support' for the Polish initiative. But it also denounced American 'military and political hegemony' in Western Europe and proposed 'the convocation of a conference of European [sic] states to discuss measures ensuring collective security in Europe'.[9] The United States may be a powerful player in Europe but it is not a 'European state'.

Similarly, the July 1966 Bucharest declaration of the PCC invited to a 'general European conference . . . both members of the North Atlantic Treaty and neutrals'.[10] It did not say that *all* NATO members were welcome. In fact, the thrust against the US military presence and political influence in Europe was quite explicit. The declaration called for the cessation 'of flights by foreign aircraft carrying atomic or hydrogen bombs over the territories of European states', an end to 'entry of foreign submarines and surface ships with nuclear arms on board into the ports of such states', the 'withdrawal of all forces from foreign territories to within their national frontiers' and the 'simultaneous abolition' of the two military alliances. Furthermore, Brezhnev extended support to de Gaulle's concept of *l'Europe des patries* and applauded the latter's decision to take France out of the military organization of NATO, apparently hoping that the North Atlantic treaty might not be renewed in 1969.

But what about Brezhnev's consent in 1970 to North American participation in the CSCE and in May 1971 to the MBFR talks (the 'Tbilisi signal')?[11] Given the unimpressive record of Kremlin leaders in understanding American domestic politics it is quite doubtful whether he knew the impact his speech might have on the debate in Washington over Mansfield's proposal to halve the number of American troops in Europe; and not all the 'nay' votes, one might suspect, were cast as a result of Brezhnev's speech.[12] More importantly, in Moscow's perspective a negotiated, multilateral agreement on US troop withdrawals was probably preferable to a unilateral one: unilateral decisions can be rescinded unilaterally but reversals of multilateral decisions need the agreement of all the signatories. Finally, *any* agreement would have legitimized the Soviet military presence in Central-Eastern Europe. But the Soviet position until 1989 was that 'approximate parity' in conventional weapons existed between NATO and the Warsaw Pact. If NATO had agreed to concluding an agreement on that basis it would have enshrined Soviet conventional preponderance in Europe. This, too, would have been a desirable outcome from the Soviet point of view.

In the end, nothing came of the MBFR talks. With the collapse of detente and the onset of the second Cold War, Brezhnev shifted tack again and adopted a more stridently anti-American and anti-Atlanticist stance. Andropov and Chernenko were to follow this course. In fact, all three leaders vigorously opposed the modernization of US nuclear weapons in Western Europe and the stationing of intermediate-range nuclear missiles. The utilization of 'imperialist contradictions' and anti-nuclear campaigns in tandem with European 'peace movements' again revealed the basic underlying goals of Soviet foreign policy of attempting to weaken NATO, singularizing West Germany and separating Western Europe from the United States. It was only under Gorbachev that this basic approach was to change.

Revisions under Gorbachev

The conceptual and practical changes did not occur overnight. As Marshal Akhromeev, the former Chief of Staff of the Soviet armed forces and adviser to Gorbachev on security and arms control issues, was to say in 1990, the new course was elaborated gradually, starting in 1987, by the political leadership in conjunction with the military leadership.[13] 'If someone were to assert', he continued, 'that at the time of Gorbachev's accession to power, in March 1985, it was already evident how things would develop, he would simply be lying.'[14] Genrikh Trofimenko, formerly a leading analyst at the Institute of USA and Canada Studies, asserted that when Gorbachev assumed power in

1985 he shared Andropov's belief that Soviet policy in Europe should be aimed at excluding the United States from any meaningful role in European affairs.[15]

Gorbachev's change of approach towards the Atlantic alliance was a gradual one. The adjustment to new realities occurred in three major phases, which were evident in several dimensions of his policy. In a first period, lasting from March 1985 until October 1985, Gorbachev's theme of the Common European House (*Evropa, nash obshchii dom*) was, in essence, more slogan than substance. In that period, the implications of the theme were that the United States, as a trans-Atlantic power, really had no business in that house. While claiming that the Soviet Union did not intend to drive a wedge between the USA and its NATO allies, Gorbachev nevertheless returned at first to traditional Soviet propaganda themes, deploring that the independent policy of West European states had apparently been 'abducted and deported across the ocean' and that the national interests and destinies of the 700 million inhabitants of the European continent were being 'mortgaged under the pretext of safeguarding security'.[16] Appearing to continue the campaign waged under Brezhnev, Andropov and Chernenko against the stationing of Pershing II and cruise missiles in Western Europe, he and the centrally controlled press claimed that, whereas for Europeans Europe was indeed a home, for Americans it was simply a 'theatre of military operations'[17] and a 'battlefield on the map of their strategists'.[18] European (including Russian and Soviet) political culture and civilization were contrasted favourably with the 'cowboy attitude' to the problems of war and peace allegedly prevalent across the ocean.[19] Such clumsy appeals to Western Europe were capped by Gorbachev's offer, made during his visit to France in October 1985, to enter separately into negotiations on nuclear weapons in Europe with France and Britain.

In retrospect, it seems that the notion of the Common House of Europe was meant primarily to serve as an inducement to Washington to consent to a reordering of its relations with Moscow. By asserting that the Soviet leadership was far from seeing the world through the prism of Soviet–American relations and that it understood very well the weight which other countries had in international affairs,[20] Gorbachev clearly implied that if relations with the United States were to develop unsatisfactorily, the Soviet Union had other options that it could pursue.

In the second phase of Gorbachev's relations with the West, lasting from the Soviet–American summit in Geneva in November 1985 until the visit by Chancellor Kohl to Moscow in October 1988, priority in the Soviet approach to the Atlantic alliance was given to the Soviet–American connection. Improving links with the United States was regarded by Gorbachev and a new generation of civilian advisers on security affairs as vitally necessary to reduce the pace of the arms competition, to curtail the far-flung global commitments of the Soviet Union and its involvement in a host of unstable Third World countries ranging from Afghanistan via Ethiopia and Angola to Nicaragua. Particularly after the Soviet–American summit meeting at Reykjavik in 1986, it appeared as if Gorbachev was going to revert to earlier Brezhnevite ideas of superpower condominium. It was as if the Common European House had never been mentioned.

But the concept continued to be invoked and clarified, and came to be interwoven with two other concepts, the New Thinking (*novoe myshlenie*) in international security affairs and the principle of Freedom of Choice (*svoboda vybora*), applicable primarily to Central- and South-Eastern Europe. Most importantly for the purposes of this inquiry, an end was finally put to the anti-American undercurrents in Gorbachev's approach to the United States and Western Europe.

The practical consequences of this shift became visible in the third phase of Soviet approaches and policies towards the Atlantic community, extending from October 1988 until November 1990 (the Paris CSCE summit conference).[21] In this period, the foreign affairs research institutes of the USSR Academy of Sciences, together with the Soviet Foreign Ministry, were clearly in the ascendancy. They succeeded in defeating military and hard-line political opposition on practically every major issue in defence and arms control policy.[22]

Among the changes in attitudes and policy firmly established by the coalition of *institutchiki* and the Foreign Ministry was a transformation in attitudes and policy on NATO and the US presence in Europe. Indeed the Common House itself was redefined to include the Atlantic dimension. What were the arguments used by this coalition to gain acceptance for such comprehensive changes in policy? Several of the themes are similar to those imputed by Western analysts to previous Soviet leaderships.

First, in contrast to Gorbachev's initial emphasis on a separate continental European identity, the theoreticians of Atlanticism acknowledged that America 'is part of Europe, historically, in religion, culturally, and politically'.[23]

Second, they noted that there are close economic bonds between the USA and Western Europe, which neither of the two entities can afford to sever.[24] One analyst even asserted that 'economically the United States is more a part of Europe than most major European nations'.[25]

Third, the links that had evolved in the security sphere were recognized as being of an equally fundamental nature. Modern weaponry and armed forces, they contended, had narrowed the Atlantic Ocean 'to the size of a gulf' and made the United States as close to the continent militarily 'as England was at the turn of the century'.[26] A significant role for the United States in the current and in any future system of European security was therefore 'logical and necessary'.[27]

Fourth, they reasoned, despite all the talk about shifting its attention to Asia and the Pacific, the United States in reality had no plans to quit Europe and lose influence on the continent. If more attention was being paid to the

Asian-Pacific region in Washington, this was not a substitute for but a supplement to its involvement in Europe.

Fifth, even if it were politically desirable to get the United States out of Europe, from a practical point of view, it would be 'virtually impossible even by the concerted efforts of all European nations'.[28] The driving of wedges between one 'power centre of imperialism' and another, therefore, could perhaps produce some temporary, tactical advantages. But from a strategic vantage point it would be counterproductive.

Sixth, they argued, the part played by the United States in the system of European security would serve to preserve the, in most cases salutary, influence of European powers on American policy and military strategy. European countries had, for instance, helped deter Washington from adventurism in international crises, e.g. during the 1973 Middle East war, and protested when American policy-makers had 'contemplated the use of nuclear weapons' in Korea, Vietnam and the Taiwan straits crisis.[29]

Finally, the point was made that a withdrawal of US forces from Europe could create fears and feelings of insecurity in some of the West European countries. Such anxieties would not necessarily work in favour of the Soviet Union. The Europeans might be driven to strengthen their own defence efforts. Military integration in Western Europe could be enhanced. And such integration would most likely not be in opposition or contradiction to the USA but would run parallel to US defence efforts and enhance the overall military potential of NATO.[30] Thus, in the long run, the effects of a withdrawal of the United States could be 'destabilizing in security terms'.[31]

Such perceptions were endorsed by Gorbachev as early as 1986. In talks with German foreign minister Hans-Dietrich Genscher he said that he had no wish to undermine NATO: 'We are of the opinion that, given all the alliances that have taken shape, it is essential to strengthen those threads whose severance is fraught with the danger of severance of the world fabric.'[32] The Europeans, he told Henry Kissinger in January 1989, needed the participation of the USSR and the USA in the 'all-European process'. Stability in Europe was a 'common interest'.[33] Similarly, during his visit to Bonn, in June 1989, he told his German hosts that the Joint Soviet–German Declaration:

> does not demand that you, or we, should renounce our uniqueness or weaken our allegiance to the alliances. On the contrary, I am confident that adherence to it in our policies will serve to consolidate the contribution of each state to the creation of a peaceful European order as well as to shape a common European outlook.[34]

The unprecedented public acknowledgment by a top Soviet leader of a positive role for the Atlantic alliance in European security almost prejudged Soviet consent to membership of a unified Germany in NATO. But as with so many other domestic and international issues, it is doubtful that Gorbachev was fully aware of the far-reaching implications of his stance.

German unification: application of the revision

The working assumption underlying this section is that Gorbachev, like almost everyone else in East and West, was surprised by the speed with which the East German Communist regime collapsed in 1989 and the subsequent absence of any reform socialist alternatives. After all, the principles of New Thinking, the Common House and Freedom of Choice were clearly intended to provide the conceptual basis for a new European security system which would be acceptable in Moscow. The main prerequisites were to be the withdrawal of Soviet troops from Central-Eastern Europe; abstention from military interference with the processes of change; and acceptance of genuine independence and sovereignty for the countries of that region. Obviously, there was a risk that the communist system would be swept away in some of these countries. But in others, reform socialist regimes would emerge. East Germany, above all, was apparently regarded in Moscow (and not just in that capital) as being among the countries in which a reform socialist regime was likely to be formed.

Indeed, until the summer and autumn of 1989, East Germany had appeared to be relatively stable politically, and relatively efficient and competitive economically. Prior to the Second World War, communist and social democratic traditions had been strong there, notably in Saxony. A reformed East Germany could be part and parcel of a reformed Central-East European state system that included the USSR as a major player. Such reasoning appears strange only in retrospect. Western opinion too did not rule out such possibilities, and envisaged only gradual change. Chancellor Kohl's ten-point plan for unification, for instance, merely envisaged the creation of 'confederate structures' and the gradual establishment of 'new forms of institutionalized cooperation' between the two German states. A 'federal order' (*bundesstaatliche Ordnung*) was declared to be the ultimate aim. But the time frame for its realization remained unclear.[35]

To complete the review of probable assumptions underlying the Soviet design, East Germany and the other socialist and non-socialist countries in Central-Eastern Europe could be persuaded – on the basis of traditional links and their economic dependence on Soviet deliveries of oil, natural gas and other primary products – to remain active participants in a reformed CMEA and Warsaw Pact. The military alliances were seen as necessary instruments for managing the external aspects of German unification, for negotiating and implementing a comprehensive agreement on conventional forces in Europe and for helping to achieve a smooth transition to a new security system in Europe.

It is in all likelihood for these reasons that Gorbachev reiterated themes he had raised, as mentioned, as early as 1986, when he told visiting French Foreign Minister, Roland Dumas, shortly after the opening of the Berlin wall: 'Now is not the time to break up the established international political and economic institutions. Let them be transformed taking into account internal processes, let them find their place in the new situation and work together.'[36] Similarly, in a briefing for the leaders of the Warsaw Pact on the Soviet–American summit meeting on Malta in December 1989, he stated that the two alliances 'will be preserved for the foreseeable future' because they could make a 'contribution to strengthening European security' by becoming a bridge between the two parts of Europe.[37]

From Gorbachev's standpoint, granting a role to the Atlantic alliance in a revised European security system did not perhaps present a major domestic problem. The loss of the GDR, formerly one of the staunchest Soviet allies, however, was more difficult to explain. Even more difficult to advocate domestically was the idea of a united Germany's membership in NATO. This notion was called by Soviet spokesmen, among other things, simply 'a joke'.[38] It was ruled out as 'definitely unacceptable, both politically and psychologically, to the Soviet people'.[39] Gorbachev, too, dampened optimism on that topic. In his interview with *Time* magazine prior to his visit in the United States, in June 1990, Gorbachev expected 'major disagreement' with President Bush on the issue of a united Germany as a member of NATO. He rejected Western arguments that, in a new phase of international relations, NATO would serve the interests of the Soviet Union, as 'just not serious'. For the Soviet people, he continued, 'NATO is associated with the Cold War . . . as an organization designed from the start to be hostile to the Soviet Union, as a force that whipped up the arms race and the danger of war.' Regardless of what was being said about NATO now, that alliance for the Soviet Union remained 'a symbol of the past, a dangerous and confrontational past. And we will never agree to assign it the leading role in building a new Europe.'[40]

The issue of NATO membership for a united Germany became a hotly contested one inside the Soviet Union. Orthodox communist ideologues, Great Russian nationalists, and hard-line political and military leaders regarded the continuing vitality of the Atlantic alliance, the ascendancy of Germany, the withdrawal of the Soviet forces from Central-Eastern Europe and the collapse of the Warsaw Pact as an intolerable national humiliation. To many of the opponents of change it signified not just a loss of prestige, but a loss of world-power status.

The difficulty of justifying a complete reversal of forty years of Soviet policies in Europe probably explains the plethora of proposals on the status of Germany put forward by Moscow in the period from mid-February to mid-July 1990, which are analysed elsewhere in detail.[41] They included: a Europe-wide referendum on the international and security aspects of German unification; the neutralization and demilitarization of Germany; a military-political status for Germany in NATO similar to that of France; continued, though modified, exercise of four-power occupation rights in Germany; the formation of a centre in Berlin to control all military forces in Germany; membership of Germany in both NATO and Warsaw Pact;

membership of the Soviet Union in NATO; and, finally, membership of the Federal Republic in NATO and 'associate' status for the eastern part of Germany in the Warsaw Pact.

It is worth emphasizing that an extraordinarily difficult situation in the two Germanys and the Atlantic alliance would have been created if Gorbachev had stood firm on the principle of 'unification, yes, but no membership of united Germany in NATO'. It was not only unification that depended on the timely resolution of this issue. The size of the German armed forces, the withdrawal of Soviet forces from East Germany, the agreement on CFE and the future shape of European security were all directly linked to it.

Why then did Gorbachev ultimately consent to membership of Germany in NATO? The main answer probably lies in the preceding fundamental reinterpretation of Soviet interests and Moscow's desire to construct a viable, long-term cooperative relationship with Germany. The Soviet consent was helped along also by changes in NATO's declaratory policies and the confidence that substantive changes would occur in the alliance. In fact, the Soviet consent to German NATO membership, on 15 July 1990, given in meetings between Kohl and Gorbachev in the Caucasus, had been preceded by the NATO summit conference in London on 6 July, at which the Western alliance had extended 'the hand of friendship' to the countries of the East and committed itself to enhancing the political component of the alliance. It announced that it intended to field, after the conclusion of the CFE negotiations, smaller and restructured active forces and to move away from 'forward defence' and reliance on nuclear weapons.[42]

Clearly, the NATO declaration greatly facilitated Gorbachev's task of placating his domestic critics and if not gaining their support of, then at least their acquiescence to, membership of Germany in NATO. Gorbachev's concession was also made less difficult by the complete lack of support for alternative solutions in the Warsaw Pact.

Consequences of the collapse of the Warsaw Pact

As argued in the preceding section, in 1989 and the first half of 1990 there was a consensus in Moscow about the need for *both* alliances to continue to exist. One is left to wonder how the Gorbachev leadership would have dealt with the issue of German membership in NATO if, in the spring of 1990, the collapse of the Warsaw Pact had not been regarded in Moscow as a distant possibility but had already been a *fait accompli*. A new Europe with NATO but without the Warsaw Pact surely would have been unacceptable to Soviet decision-makers. But how could they ever have believed that it would be possible to salvage the Pact from the revolution of 1989 in Central-Eastern Europe?

The answer to this may lie in the readiness of the Soviet reformers in 1989 and 1990 to transform the Warsaw Pact from an instrument of Soviet domination and control into a political institution respecting the sovereignty of its member nations. Such a transformation, they thought, would be feasible because even after systemic changes the 'state interests' of the Warsaw Pact member countries would remain essentially unchanged. As the Soviet Chief of Staff Marshal Akhromeev was to explain in November 1989, the member countries would still have to safeguard 'the stability of their territory and state boundaries'. They would also have to take into account the fact that they had been linked for many decades and that 'the economic interests of the states' remained. Furthermore, 'contradictions' between the 'state interests of both alliances' would remain as a result of the continued deployment of 'a certain quantity of arms and armed forces'.[43]

In line with such rationales and rationalizations, the head of a department of the Soviet General Staff, Col-Gen. Nikolai F. Chervov, announced at a meeting of military chiefs from thirty-five nations held to discuss military doctrine in Vienna in January 1990 that the Warsaw Pact would be thoroughly restructured. The Pact's future, as a Soviet Foreign Ministry participant in the meeting explained, would be shaped by political and regional interests rather than ideological solidarity.[44]

The hope that, after an infusion of reform, the moribund Warsaw Pact would survive and return to the life of European politics was initially encouraged by attitudes in Poland in the first months of 1990. Reflecting anxiety about the reconstitution of a potentially powerful Germany at its western borders, Poland at that stage remained firmly committed to cooperation with the Soviet Union in a reformed Pact. The then Polish Prime Minister, Tadeusz Mazowiecki, made this clear when he said that, in its alliance with its eastern neighbour, Poland had passed from the ideological level to the state level. This did 'not mean that at the state level we do not see the importance of this alliance for the problem of security for our borders'.[45] Polish leaders called openly for Soviet troops to remain in Poland because of 'the German problem'.[46]

The Soviet concept for reform of the alliance was presented to the Pact members in June 1990 at two meetings. One was the conference of the Political Consultative Committee in Moscow, the other a gathering of the Military Committee in Stralsund near East Berlin. Despite some differences of position, the trend line that emerged from the final document adopted by the PCC and statements of the participants at both meetings was unambiguous. The 'character, functions, and activities of the Warsaw Pact' were to be thoroughly reviewed.[47] The organization was to change from a political and military alliance to a political alliance with military consultation; the centralized, Soviet-controlled command structure was to be abandoned, which in practice meant that a Soviet Deputy Minister of Defence would no longer be the Pact's commander-in-chief and that perhaps the Supreme Joint

Command would be dissolved; the member states would gain control of their own national forces in accordance with the principle of full national sovereignty; and for the duration of the existence of multilateral institutions, representatives of the member states would fill positions by rotation.

Was there a direct connection between Soviet consent to membership of united Germany in NATO and the continued existence of a reformed Warsaw Pact? The possibility cannot be excluded. Earlier, at the February 1990 'open skies' meeting of the foreign ministers of NATO and the Warsaw Pact in Ottawa, it had become apparent that only two foreign ministers were calling for the neutralization of Germany: Shevardnadze and East German Foreign Minister Oskar Fischer. At the mid-March 1990 Warsaw Pact foreign ministers' conference in Prague, the USSR again found itself in a minority on the issue. At the closing news conference, Czechoslovak Foreign Minister, Jiří Dienstbier, said that neutrality would be 'the worst alternative'.[48] And even the Polish Foreign Minister, Krystof Skubiszewski, stated that a neutral Germany would 'not be good for Europe': it would 'foster some tendencies in Germany to be a great power acting on its own'.[49] Only the East German Foreign Minister, a member of the Communist old guard, still supported his Soviet colleague. But he was to be replaced a few weeks later as a result of free elections.

The declaration adopted by the Warsaw Pact at its June 1990 meeting did not contradict the idea of linkage. It contained the proviso that the member states would review the Warsaw Treaty and 'initiate efforts to transform it into a treaty of sovereign, equal states that is based on democratic principles'.[50] Certainly, nothing was said of a possible dissolution of the Pact.

Whatever the case may be concerning linkage, the course of events yet again created new conditions. The Soviet Union's European allies simply lost interest in the Pact. The Polish government revised its position on the German danger and later in the year began calling for the speedy withdrawal of Soviet forces. These trends were reinforced in the autumn and winter of 1990 as Gorbachev presided over a shift to the right and Shevardnadze resigned from the post of Foreign Minister. The former Warsaw Pact allies were beginning to veer towards a *renversement des alliances*. Hungary and Czechoslovakia in particular began to stretch out feelers to NATO and announced their intention to become full members of the Western alliance. This turn of events decidedly was not part of the original Soviet plan for the establishment of a new European order.

The predictable consequence of the collapse of the Soviet position in Central-Eastern Europe and the demise of the Warsaw Pact was to reinforce conservative tendencies in Soviet foreign policy. Indications of such a shift were the appointment of a bland career diplomat, Aleksandr Bessmertnykh, in December 1990, to the post of Foreign Minister; public expressions of disagreement with the US conduct of the war against Iraq in February 1991; delays in the withdrawal of Soviet forces from Germany; failures to implement the CFE agreement; and complications in the START negotiations. They also included the emergence of an ambiguous and more sceptical attitude towards the Atlantic alliance.

One of the many indications of the revised Soviet attitude was Marshal Akhromeev's interview with *Neues Deutschland* in October 1990. Replying to a question about Germany's membership in NATO he stated, 'Personally, I think that in the new conditions in Europe there is no justification for the existence of NATO.' He 'did not know', he continued, 'why Germany needed NATO'. But he hoped that the Germans would think again so that when they had become used to the fact of a unified country they would reconsider what they should retain from the past.[51]

A return to Cold War images of NATO was evident also in the Soviet Defence Ministry's draft plan on reforming the Soviet armed forces, published in November 1990. Although its authors included some polite references to the principles of New Thinking and noted important changes in international security affairs, they expressed concern that the United States was 'creating a large grouping of non-nuclear strategic offensive arms', 'modernizing its tactical nuclear potential', 'keeping inviolable its positions on naval forces', 'accelerating work on SDI' and 'refusing to stop nuclear testing'. The United States, they charged, was 'resolved to preserve its advantage in Europe no matter what' and to 'adhere to the use of force in international affairs'.[52]

The Foreign Ministry, too, drifted in an ominous direction. In May 1991, CSFR President Václav Havel publicly revealed that Soviet diplomats were raising unacceptable demands in the negotiations on a treaty meant to put Soviet–Czechoslovak relations on a new footing. Moscow insisted on the inclusion of a provision in the treaty that would have ruled out Czechoslovakia's accession to an alliance that the Soviet Union could interpret as being directed against itself. The Soviet negotiators also wanted to include language requiring the respective treaty partners to come to each other's assistance in 'an emergency'.[53] At the same time it became known that Romania had already signed a corresponding treaty with Moscow, and that similar treaties were being negotiated with Poland, Hungary and Bulgaria.[54] In the circumstances, it was obvious that the draft treaty provisions were designed to dissuade Central-Eastern and South-Eastern Europe from aligning itself more closely with NATO.

An unpleasant whiff of the decayed Brezhnev doctrine could also be sensed rising from the Central Committee. In January 1991 its International Department published a document setting out the Party's views on 'Eastern Europe' and the policies to be conducted in this region.[55] The *apparatchik* authors lamented the fact that the traditional postwar European system had broken down and that no new system had been set up to replace it. They deplored the dissolution of the Warsaw Pact and the CMEA, the unification of Germany under NATO auspices, and the desire of their former allies to establish close ties with Atlantic and Western European political and economic institutions. They foresaw the 'Balkanization' of Europe and the emergence of 'a zone of instability along the western borders of the USSR'. In order to forestall this, they too called for *de facto* limitations on sovereignty and demanded that membership of 'our former military allies in other military blocs and groupings, especially in NATO', should be prohibited.[56]

As with other issues of Soviet foreign policy in this period, it is hard to say whether such approaches reflected or contradicted government policy. But certainly, a fundamental rift threatened to open up between the Soviet Union and its former allies in Europe. The danger of such a rift was brought into sharp focus in July 1991 at the Prague summit meeting of the Warsaw Pact that formally ended its existence. Gennady Yanaev, the then Vice-President of the Soviet Union and a future *'putschist'*, said at the meeting that the dismantling of one powerful institution of the Cold War should be followed by the dissolution of its Western counterpart, NATO. The Soviet Union, he stated, 'believes that the existence of instruments that served the policy of confrontation in the Cold War has become obsolete'.[57]

The opposite view was expressed by the Prime Minister of Hungary, Jozsef Antall. In his words: 'The rejuvenated NATO represents a warranty for European security, and the same holds true for the presence of the United States in Europe. European integration and the Atlantic alliance are very compatible.'[58] The clash of interests over NATO could not have been stated more clearly.

After the Soviet Union: Russia's interest and future role in NATO

But by the spring of 1991 the Soviet leadership had begun to shift tack again. Probably as a result of negative Western responses to his attempted crackdown in the Baltic republics, the continuing deterioration of the Soviet economy and the undiminished need for international cooperation and assistance, Gorbachev once again began to steer a reformist course. The April 1991 accord of Novo Ogarevo between the presidents of nine republics and Gorbachev concerning the devolution of power in a new Union treaty is evidence of his shift. It was in all likelihood this very 'betrayal' of the right and the projected publication and signature of the treaty on 20 August that precipitated the right-wing coup.

The failure of the *putsch* created entirely new conditions. It acted like a strong gale, dispersing the dark clouds that had constantly hung over any attempt at radical devolution of power, transition to a market economy and integration of Russia and the other republics into the mainstream of European and Western civilization. The winds of change not only swept away the Soviet Union. They also shifted Russia's stance on the Atlantic alliance so that

Moscow's pennants came to point in the direction of close cooperation with and even full membership in that organization.

The new position was signalled by Yeltsin in a letter addressed in December 1991 to the first meeting between NATO foreign ministers and those of the former Warsaw Pact in Brussels, at which the North Atlantic Cooperation Council (NACC) was created.[59] Russia, he wrote, wished to develop a dialogue between former adversaries 'both on the political and military levels'. He continued: 'Today, we are raising the question of Russia's membership in NATO, regarding it, however, as a long-term political aim.'[60] Similarly, Foreign Minister Andrei Kozyrev stated that Russia does 'not regard NATO as an aggressive military bloc' but views it 'as one of the mechanisms of stability in Europe and in the world as a whole. Our desire to cooperate with this mechanism and to join it is therefore natural.'[61]

Yeltsin and Kozyrev thereby explicitly revised the negative attitude expressed as recently as October 1990 by Marshal Akhromeev in his interview for *Neues Deutschland*. In an obvious allusion to Soviet initiatives in 1954 to undercut the EDC and in early 1990 to forestall membership of united Germany in NATO, he had been asked whether or not, 'despite negative experiences in the past', the Soviet Union would make 'another attempt at becoming a member of NATO'. He replied that in the past: 'There was no direct [Soviet] interest [in such attempts]. We posed this question as a theoretical possibility. And we saw how NATO reacted to it.' He concluded by saying that he did 'not believe that the Soviet Union has a great desire to become a member of NATO'.[62]

What, then, was the reasoning behind Russia's subsequent advocacy of membership in NATO as a long-term option? In late 1991 and early 1992 the following rationales were provided by Foreign Minister Kozyrev and by international relations experts, such as Sergei Karaganov. In economic terms, they argued, there already existed an 'objective semi-isolation' of Russia (and *ceteris paribus* other Soviet successor states) relative to Europe and the West. Contrary to Russia's intentions and hopes for rapid integration in the world economy, the very opposite had occurred: the dismantling of the command economy and the breakdown of central distribution and production had led to a contraction of Russia's external trade relations. Furthermore, administrative confusion and overlap (the 'war of laws'), in conjunction with political instabilities, had made Western investors refrain from accepting commercial risks in Russia and other members of the Commonwealth of Independent States. It would, therefore, be a disaster if the de facto economic isolation were to be reinforced by 'military-political isolation'.[63]

The danger of such isolation, they claimed, was enhanced by the fact that the new democracies of Central-Eastern Europe 'even *today* are gradually aligning themselves with NATO'. Until quite recently measures designed to suppress 'the extension of [NATO] guarantees and bloc structures to Central and Eastern Europe' had been quite appropriate. But now such measures of demarcation were neither possible nor necessary.[64] Furthermore, like Spain after Franco, Russia after the coup had an interest in 'including the military in common European security structures';[65] both NATO and the former members of the Warsaw Pact had to find a 'new place and role for the armed forces of the two sides which were created in order to face each other'.[66] Russian advocates of NATO membership also pointed to a 'sum of problems, threats, let us say, which unfortunately are not disappearing'. Iraq's aggression against Kuwait was mentioned as an example, also 'terrorism and other sources of instability' in general. For these reasons, they endorsed the concept of a 'zone of security and cooperation from Vancouver to Vladivostok' in which NATO is 'playing a role that is positive and by no means insignificant'.[67] Some of the civilian specialists on international relations even went as far as to assert that: 'The North Atlantic alliance is now the guarantor of our security, if you will. And if we could now join it, this would be the best way for us to ensure that security.'[68]

What is one to make of Russia's initiative? How valid are the arguments advanced in its support? Is NATO membership now to be regarded as a firm operational goal of Russian foreign policy? Some caution is appropriate here. As Aleksei Arbatov, a Russian specialist on international security affairs, has pointed out, there is an 'enormous distance between improving relations with former enemies and direct participation in the North Atlantic alliance'. Attempts to cross this gap in a single leap would 'at best put Russia in an awkward situation and at worst create considerable political complications in our relations with the United States and Western Europe'.[69]

In accordance with Article 10 of the North Atlantic treaty, the alliance can of course invite any other European state to join provided it is able to further the principles contained in the treaty and contribute to the security of the North Atlantic area. But, as Arbatov notes, the treaty document is primarily a political declaration. The essence of NATO 'is something far more tangible'. It is to be found in a division of powers and functions, and in the 'sharing of rights and responsibilities'. The United States under historically evolved arrangements provided nuclear guarantees, deployed nuclear and conventional forces on the continent, and established naval and air transport facilities in order to be able to transfer reinforcements across the ocean. The Europeans, on their part, contributed to the collective defence by their own coordinated defence efforts and by permitting the United States to 'use their territory for military bases, garrisons, depots, and other installations'.

The following question therefore had to be answered: 'In what capacity does Russia intend to join NATO?' Arbatov distinguishes three possibilities. First, Russia could join as a guarantor of the security of Western Europe. The West Europeans, however, would most likely say: 'No, thanks.' For the foreseeable future it suited Western Europe perfectly well to have the United States rather than an unstable Russia as its defender. Second, it had been said that NATO was set up not just to deter the Soviet Union but also to control

Germany. So why not involve Russia in this task? This idea too was unrealistic, because the West 'will probably reach some kind of modus vivendi with Germany'. Furthermore, it might be appropriate 'to ask the Germans whether they would mind being controlled with the help of Russia, which receives most of its economic aid from Germany'. Third, 'if one supposes that the United States or Western Europe would guarantee Russia's security, this too is unrealistic. With its armed forces of three million men and tens of thousands of nuclear warheads, Russia faces no serious military threat from the outside ... neither from the Muslim world, nor China, nor Ukraine or any other CIS state, nor any other country'.[70]

Arbatov concludes that one of the main considerations in favour of preserving NATO is 'the instability and unpredictability of the situation in the East'. Given this fact of international life, 'Russia's entry would simply make the alliance fall apart.' If, however, 'the situation in Russia were to normalize and Russia were ready to join NATO, the bloc would immediately lose its raison d'être. To put it bluntly, there would be nothing to join.'[71]

Why, then, to repeat, the initiative that, as Russian observers noted, 'took the West by surprise'?[72] One of the purposes of the dramatic step was certainly a symbolic one. The move was in all likelihood made in order to clarify to critics at home and sceptics abroad that Russia's role in European and world politics had completely and irreversibly changed; that Russia was serious about active cooperation in a new European and global security framework; and that she was intent on finding institutional mechanisms that would convincingly demonstrate her new commitment to international cooperation.[73] Indeed, Foreign Minister Kozyrev stated as much at the foreign ministers meeting of the NACC in March 1992 in Brussels: 'We consider the North Atlantic Cooperation Council to be another mechanism to help us join the international community.'[74]

But symbolic communication was not the only, and probably not even the main, purpose behind the Russian initiative. Another objective was the desire to reap the advantages of practical cooperation with NATO. There is some reason to believe that initially the scope of possible benefits was underestimated in Moscow and in Western capitals. The establishment of the North Atlantic Cooperation Council, for instance, seemed to be little more than a friendly but fairly inconsequential gesture to Poland, Czechoslovakia and Hungary to console them for not having been welcomed as full NATO members, and a nod to Russia that she was not being excluded from European security arrangements. But even before the inclusion of Ukraine and the other members of the Commonwealth of Independent States in NACC in March 1992, the new security arrangement rapidly became more meaningful – for Russia and for her neighbours.[75] NACC, however surprising it may seem, began to play an important role in managing complex intra-CIS security issues.

This development was due to the fact, among others, that Russia had found intra-CIS resolution of controversial issues (e.g. the division of forces and equipment, the status of the Black Sea fleet, and the elimination and redistribution of nuclear weapons) exceedingly difficult. The same difficulty was apparent in Russian efforts at crisis prevention and management (e.g. in the quarrel between Azerbaijan and Armenia over Nagorny Karabakh), which were hampered by deep-seated distrust of Russia's policies on the part of her fellow CIS members. Indeed, the new states suspected, and at times openly accused, Moscow of harbouring 'great-Russian chauvinist' inclinations and wanting to reassert a dominant role in the region.

Such suspicions also affected the disputes over the division of the Soviet Union's large weapons inventory, notably between Russia and Ukraine but also with other former Soviet republics. Kiev charged that Moscow was denying Ukraine the status of great European power it deserved given its size, population and economic potential. It also insisted on receiving a disproportionately greater share of conventional arms if Russia were to emerge as the only nuclear power in the CIS after the redistribution of the Soviet Union's weaponry. International arms control and disarmament treaties, as a consequence, threatened to become casualties of intra-CIS controversies, and even seemed to carry the seeds of future military conflict among some of the Soviet successor states. The November 1990 CFE treaty is a case in point.

The problem with CFE was not ratification pure and simple. Decisions were required as to how the states would divide the 'Soviet' quotas inside the conventional forces balance in accordance with the specific limitations on equipment deployed within various geographical zones. With the exception of the Moscow and the Volga-Urals military districts, all of the zones under CFE (the 'extended' Central European, the 'second echelon' and the 'flank' zones) covered territories of several successor states of the Soviet Union. This meant that these states had to agree among themselves on the number of weapons they should have in each zone, as well as on new deployment patterns. Furthermore, if only one or two of the new states chose not to ratify the agreement, all the others would find themselves in a difficult position. If, say, Kiev failed to ratify, the arms levels in different regions of Russia would depend on the Ukrainian deployments, while Ukraine itself would be exempt from any limitations.[76]

In a formal sense, NACC had not the authority to decide any of these problems. But in practice it appears to have played an important role in resolving them. As early as December 1991, at its inaugural meeting, the founding members of NACC expressed their determination 'to achieve full implementation of the CFE and START treaties'. They also wanted 'to ensure full respect for the Treaty on the Non-Proliferation of Nuclear Weapons' (NPT) and 'to prevent the unauthorized export of nuclear or other destabilizing military technologies'.[77] In the end, the West succeeded in extracting definite commitments from the CIS members, Georgia and the Baltic states, who agreed not only to ratification but also to the reallocation of

military equipment across the specified zones of limitation in conformity
with the CFE treaty provisions. Formal resolution of these matters was
announced at the Tashkent summit of the CIS in May 1992, but the decision
was predetermined by several meetings under NACC auspices at various
levels, including ministerial and ambassadorial meetings from January to
March 1992, and the conference of NACC defence ministers and other high
level defence officials in April 1992.[78] An account of this aspect of relations
between the former Soviet states is given in Chapter 4.

The NACC also helped to bring about progress on other security issues,
including the transfer of tactical nuclear weapons to Russia; destruction of
such weapons under CIS auspices and with international cooperation; prospects for START ratification; adherence to the Non-Proliferation Treaty; and
efforts to ensure that scientists formerly engaged in research on weapons of
mass destruction would find opportunities for work in civilian institutions.

The Cooperation Council made less progress with regard to intra-CIS
crisis prevention and conflict management. But Russia was at least able to
elicit NATO interest in these matters. It subsequently reacted favourably to
suggestions made by Dutch Foreign Minister van den Broek, and supported
by the United States Secretary of State, James Baker, and NATO General
Secretary Manfred Wörner, that NATO could act under the auspices of the
CSCE or the United Nations after political instruments of conflict resolution had been exhausted.[79] But, as in the case of the Russian initiative to join
NATO in the long term, the significance of such suggestions by individual
Western leaders and alliance officials should not be exaggerated: they should
not be taken as proof of NATO plans for intervention in intra-CIS conflicts
but as symbolic statements outlining possible directions of European and
global security cooperation and the future role of the North Atlantic
alliance.

It is useful to recall in this context that the alliance originated as an open,
not a closed system. As a perceptive Western analyst of Atlantic affairs has
written, the legal and political premises on which NATO was built in the late
1940s allowed and even encouraged a change of the alliance into a broad
ordering system; the structure and processes of the alliance, as they actually
developed since 1949, had demonstrated a capacity for such an international
ordering role; and the condition of global affairs urgently necessitated a bold
effort to use the alliance to promote a more comprehensive international
order.[80] His conclusions are also worth repeating: 'Although [NATO's]
potential as a model for a larger pattern of security and peace may never fully
be realized, the very idea enables us to address the problem of regional
alliances and world order in a new way: not alliance versus order, but alliance
as order itself.'[81]

These conclusions are congruent with those advanced by Aleksei
Arbatov. If Russia, as he 'would like to believe', were to overcome its present
predicament and turn into a stable, democratic country, 'the time would

come to set up a real system of collective security incorporating the United States, the Western European countries, Russia and its current neighbours, Japan, and other states. If the North Atlantic alliance turns into this sort of new security system, then only the NATO name will remain. And even this is unlikely.'[82]

Notes

1. The primary focus of this analysis is on the political rather than the military aspects of Moscow's conceptual and practical approaches towards the alliance. For a treatment of the military aspects see Robbin F. Laird and Susan L. Clark (eds), *The USSR and the Western Alliance* (Boston, Unwin and Hyman, 1990).
2. This and the following three arguments are an almost verbatim summary of Lawrence Freedman, 'The United States Factor', in Edwina Moreton and Gerald Segal (eds), *Soviet Strategy Towards Western Europe* (London, Allen & Unwin, 1984), pp. 94–5, 108, and Jane M. O. Sharp 'Why Discuss US Withdrawal?', in Jane Sharp (ed), *Europe After an American Withdrawal: Economic and Military Issues* (Oxford, Oxford University Press, 1990), pp. 20–23.
3. 'Rech' tovarishcha Gromyko', *Pravda*, 3 April 1966.
4. Strobe Talbot, *Deadly Gambits* (New York, Knopf, 1984), p. 113.
5. Eduard Shevardnadze, 'V mire vse menyaetsya s golovokruzhitel'noi bystrotoi', *Izvestiya*, 19 February 1990.
6. One of the many instances is the report on the 'Future Tasks of the Alliance' (Harmel Report), adopted at the December 1967 NATO ministerial meeting in Brussels. The 'German Question' is defined there as the 'first and foremost' of the 'central political issues in Europe'. It asserted that no lasting settlement in Europe was possible unless the division of Germany and Europe were overcome.
7. For the text of the note see *Foreign Relations of the United States*, vol. 7 (1952–4), pp. 1190–92. The analysis here follows Robert Charles, 'The 1954 Soviet Bid to Join NATO', The Fletcher School of Law and Diplomacy, unpublished MALD (Master of Arts in Law and Diplomacy) thesis, December 1988.
8. Sharp, 'Why Discuss US Withdrawal?', p. 21.
9. PCC communiqué of 20 January 1965, *Pravda*, 22 January 1965. The Commander in Chief of the Warsaw Pact, Marshal Grechko, reiterated this line when he referred a few months later to that organization's proposals 'for the convocation of a conference of European [sic] states to discuss measures ensuring collective security'. See *Pravda*, 13 May 1965.
10. PCC Bucharest declaration of 5 July 1966, *Pravda*, 8 July 1966. The invitation extended to 'members of the North Atlantic Treaty' does not mean, as one writer proposes, that the PCC was 'thereby including the USA and Canada' (Sharp, 'Why Discuss US Withdrawal?', p. 21). It deliberately did not state that 'all' members of NATO were invited. Furthermore, the PCC meeting of March 1969 reverted to the 1965 formula of 'all the European states' and 'all the countries of Europe'; PCC Budapest communiqué, *Pravda*, 18 March 1969.
11. On 14 May 1971, in Tbilisi, Brezhnev publicly agreed to the MBFR conventional arms talks. His consent came on the very eve of a proposal introduced by Senate

majority leader Mike Mansfield unilaterally to reduce by one-half the number of US troops in Europe. Brezhnev's speech is alleged to have been a deliberate attempt to influence the Senate vote and is said to have 'tipped the balance' against the amendment; see Sharp, 'Why Discuss US Withdrawal?', p. 21.

12. This interpretation is supported by the fact that the margin of rejection of the Mansfield amendment on 19 May 1971 was quite large, with 61 Senators opposing and only 36 Senators (almost all of them Democrats) endorsing it. *Congressional Almanac*, vol. 27 (1971), p. 274.

13. Akhromeev interview with the newspaper of the Party of Democratic Socialism (PDS, formerly SED), *Neues Deutschland*, 4 October 1990. The year 1987 as a starting point is mentioned twice by him, once in relation to the Soviet military doctrine ('elaborated approximately in mid-1987'), the other instance being in the German context ('starting from 1987 the GDR itself decided which state and social order it would have').

14. Ibid. Someone, as Akhromeev undoubtedly knew, had made such a claim. Talking about the collapse of the communist regimes in Central- and South-Eastern Europe, Shevardnadze said at the 28th CPSU congress that, 'in principle we had predicted all this'. 'Otchety chlenov i kandidatov v chleny Politbyuro, sekretarei TsK KPSS. E.A. Shevardnadze', *Pravda*, 5 July 1990.

15. 'The Soviet Union: Ejected From Europe, Rejected in Asia', *At the Harriman Institute* (seminar report, Columbia University, New York), vol. 4, no. 2. Trofimenko made these comments at the Harriman Institute on 31 January 1991.

16. *Izvestiya*, 1 July 1986.

17. Gorbachev's speech to the British Parliament, *Pravda*, 19 December 1984.

18. *Pravda* editorial, 13 November 1985.

19. Aleksandr Bovin, *Izvestiya*, 25 September 1985.

20. Gorbachev interview with *Pravda*, April 8 1985. Similar formulations were used by Gorbachev in his speech to the 27th CPSU Congress in February 1986.

21. For details on these phases see Hannes Adomeit, 'The Impact of Perestroika on Soviet European Policy', in Tsuyoshi Hasegawa, Alex Pravda (eds), *Perestroika: Soviet Domestic and Foreign Policies* (London, Sage/RIIA, 1990), pp. 242-66.

22. See John Van Oudenaren, *The Role of Shevardnadze and the Ministry of Foreign Affairs in the Making of Soviet Defense and Arms Control Policy*, Santa Monica, CA, Rand Report, R-3898-USDP, July 1990; see also Suzanne Crow, 'International Department and Foreign Ministry Disagree on Eastern Europe', *Report on the USSR*, vol. 3, no. 25 (June 1991), pp. 4–8.

23. Sergei Karaganov, 'Amerika v obshcheevropeiskom dome', *Moskovskie novosti*, no. 46, 13 November 1988, p. 3 (italics mine).

24. Ibid.

25. Yury Davydov, 'The Soviet Vision of a Common European House', Paper Delivered to the International Studies Association (ISA) conference in London, 29 March–1 April 1989, p. 10. The author is a deputy director of the USA and Canada Institute of the Academy of Sciences.

26. Karaganov, 'Amerika v obshcheevropeiskom dome'. In almost the same words another Soviet analyst writes: 'The nuclear age has drastically shrunk the Atlantic, and now America is as close to Europe in security terms as Great Britain was at the beginning of this century, or even closer.' Davydov, 'The Soviet Vision of a Common European House', p. 10.

27. Karaganov, 'Amerika v obshcheevropeiskom dome'.
28. Davydov, 'The Soviet Vision of a Common European House', p. 10; similarly Karaganov, 'Amerika v obshcheevropeiskom dome'.
29. Karaganov, 'Amerika v obshcheevropeiskom dome'. The author restated this argument at a conference held at the Centre for European Policy Studies (CEPS), in Brussels, as quoted in *Süddeutsche Zeitung*, 25 November 1988, and at the 86th round of the Bergedorfer Gesprächskreis. See *Das gemeinsame europäische Haus aus der Sicht der Sowjetunion und der Bundesrepublik Deutschland*, Protocol of the 86th round of talks of the Bergedorfer Gesprächskreis, a politically and economically independent forum initiated by industrialist Hans A. Körber, held in Bonn-Bad Godesberg, 3–4 December 1988 (Hamburg, Körber Stiftung, 1989), p. 78.
30. Thus Vladimir Baranovsky argued that, in the past, West European military-political integration had proceeded parallel and in tandem with US military efforts in Europe; see his *Zapadnaya Evropa. Voenno-politicheskaya integratsiya* (Moscow, Mezhdunarodnye otnosheniia, 1988), pp. 180–84.
31. Davydov, 'The Soviet Vision of a Common European House', p. 10. Karaganov, Bergedorfer Gesprächskreis, 86th session, *Das gemeinsame europäische Haus*, p. 78.
32. *Soviet News*, no. 23 (July 1986). I am indebted to Neil Malcolm for providing this citation.
33. In talks with former Western political leaders and current members of the Trilateral Commission, including former French President Giscard d'Estaing, Japanese Prime Minister Nakasone and US Secretary of State Henry Kissinger, in January 1989 (in response to a question by Kissinger). *Pravda*, 19 January 1989.
34. 'Vizit M. S. Gorbacheva v FRG. Rech' M. S. Gorbacheva,' *Pravda*, 13 June 1989.
35. *Bulletin des Presse- und Informationsamts der Bundesregierung* (Bonn), 29 November 1989. Initially, even this modest aim was rejected in Moscow. Portugalov, for instance, said that he believed that the two German states had 'the right to a special relationship'. But he added that 'under today's geopolitical conditions Europe cannot bear a confederation'; as quoted by Ferdinand Protzman, 'Kohl Offers an Outline to Create Confederation of the 2 Germanys', *The New York Times*, 29 November 1989.
36. Bill Keller, 'Gorbachev Urges West to Show Restraint on Turmoil in Eastern Europe', *The New York Times*, 15 November 1989 (italics mine).
37. *Pravda* and *Izvestiya*, 5 December 1989. Similarly, reporting to the Supreme Soviet on the results of the Soviet-American summit of early June 1990 in Washington, Gorbachev conceded that the two alliances would continue to exist 'for longer than might be imagined'. 'Vystuplenie M. S. Gorbacheva na tret'ei sessii Verkhovnogo Soveta SSSR', *Pravda*, 13 June 1990.
38. Soviet Communist Party Central Committee expert on German affairs, Nikolai Portugalov, in February 1990, *The Economist* (London), 10 February 1990, p. 49. For a detailed treatment of the evolution of Soviet thinking on the issue of united Germany's membership in NATO see Hannes Adomeit, 'Gorbachev and German Unification: Revision of Thinking, Realignment of Power', *Problems of Communism*, vol. 39, no. 4 (July–August 1990), pp. 1–23.
39. Col-Gen. Nikolai Chervov, 'United Germany Should Not Be NATO Member,' *Svenska Dagbladet* (Stockholm), in Swedish, 1 July 1990, quoted in *Foreign*

Broadcast Information Service Daily Report, Soviet Union, FBIS-SOV-90-129, pp. 4–5.

40. *Time,* 4 June 1990.
41. For details see Adomeit, 'Gorbachev and German Unification'.
42. Text of the London declaration of NATO, *The New York Times,* 7 July 1990.
43. Interview with Bill Keller, 'Gorbachev's Hope for Future: "A Common European Home"', *The New York Times,* 30 November 1989. After his resignation in late 1988, Marshal Sergei Akhromeev became adviser to Gorbachev on arms control issues. He was also a member of the Supreme Soviet.
44. Alan Riding, *The New York Times,* 18 January 1990.
45. In a news conference in Warsaw, Associated Press (from Warsaw), 21 February 1990.
46. Ibid.
47. According to the text of the final communiqué of the PCC meeting, *Pravda,* 8 June 1990.
48. Celestine Bohlen, in *The New York Times,* 18 March 1990.
49. Ibid.
50. Text of the declaration as published in *Pravda,* 8 June 1990.
51. *Neues Deutschland,* 4 October 1990.
52. Soviet Defence Ministry's draft plan for reforming the Soviet armed forces in November 1990, *Pravitel'stvennyi vestnik,* no. 48 (November 1990), p. 5.
53. Ladislav Valek, 'Havel widersetzt sich Vertrag mit Moskau', *Süddeutsche Zeitung* (Munich), 4 May 1991.
54. For an analysis of the Soviet demands see Gerhard Wettig, 'Ostmitteleuropa und Balkan zwischen NATO und UdSSR', *Aktuelle Analysen* (Cologne, Bundesinstitut), 28 May 1991.
55. 'O razvitii obstanovki v Vostochnoi Evrope i nashei politike v etom regione', *Izvestiya TsK KPSS,* no. 3 (January 1991). For an analysis of the significance of this document see Suzanne Crow, 'International Department and Foreign Ministry Disagree on Eastern Europe'.
56. For suggestions that the catastrophic drop in Soviet trade with Eastern Europe and the refusal by Soviet officials to restore barter trade were due to political considerations in Moscow, see Stephen Engelberg, in *The New York Times,* 6 May 1991.
57. Stephen Greenhouse, 'Death Knell Rings for Warsaw Pact', *The New York Times,* 2 July 1991.
58. Ibid.
59. The inaugural meeting of the NACC took place on 20 December, that is, only one day prior to the foundation (for a second time) of the Commonwealth of Independent States, in Alma Ata. The course of events in the East prompted the 'Soviet' delegate to the meeting, the ambassador to Belgium, Nikolai N. Afanasevsky, to state that he had been instructed by the Russian Foreign Ministry to request that 'all references to the Soviet Union be deleted from the text of the Statement [on Dialogue, Partnership and Cooperation issued by NACC]'. See *NATO Review* (Brussels), vol. 40, no. 1 (February 1992), pp. 29–30.
60. Yeltsin's letter as quoted by staff correspondent, Vladimir Persada, in his report from Brussels, *Pravda,* 23 December 1991.
61. Andrei Kozyrev, on Radio Mayak (Moscow), in Russian, on 23 December 1991,

Foreign Broadcast Information Service, Daily Report, Soviet Union, FBIS-SOV-91-247, 24 December 1991, p. 41.

62. Akhromeev interview in *Neues Deutschland*, 4 October 1990.

63. S. A. Karaganov, 'Die Aussenpolitik Russlands nach dem Putsch', *Auslandsinformationen*, Konrad Adenauer-Stiftung, Bonn/Sankt Augustin, no. 11 (1991), p. 14; also personal communication.

64. Ibid.

65. Ibid. The translation from the German is not quite literal but in all likelihood closer to the Russian original. The confidence of the author is based on an interview with Karaganov on 15 November 1991 in Amsterdam, where he essentially made the same point.

66. Kozyrev on Radio Mayak (Moscow), in Russian, on 23 December 1991.

67. Ibid.

68. Sergei Blagovolin in an interview conducted by Sergei Guk, 'NATO mozhet byt' garant bezopaznosti Rossii', *Izvestiya*, 22 January 1992.

69. Aleksei Arbatov, 'Rossiya i NATO', *Nezavisimaya gazeta*, 11 March 1992. The author is director of the Center for Disarmament and Strategic Stability at Russia's Foreign Policy Association.

70. Ibid.

71. Ibid.

72. Yu. Kovalenko, 'Obrashchenie Rossii zastalo NATO vrasplokh', *Izvestiya*, 23 December 1992.

73. There are, of course, still voices which vociferously and violently oppose the new Russian security orientation. As one of the opponents of the course put it, 'Those in Russia who are urging us to join NATO under the pretext of consolidating democracy are in reality prepared to seal the collapse of the country and its armed forces . . . . The calls to join the North Atlantic pact and to carry out a kind of "Atlanticization" of Russia or the CIS could have very dangerous consequences for all our peoples.' B. Zanegin, *Pravda*, 18 January 1992; see the similar diatribe by Captain First Rank A. Demchenko, in *Krasnaya zvezda*, 5 March 1992.

74. TASS in Russian, 10 March 1992.

75. At the NACC inaugural meeting in December 1991 the participants, in addition to the NATO countries, included only Russia, the Baltic states and the former 'East European' (non-Soviet) members of the former Warsaw Pact. The other member states of CIS joined in March and Georgia in April.

76. This analysis of problems connected with CFE draws on Andrei Kortunov, 'Strategic Relations Between the Former Soviet Republics', *The Heritage Foundation Backgrounder*, no. 892, 17 April 1992.

77. NACC Statement on Dialogue, Partnership and Cooperation.

78. Personal conversations with NATO officials; communications by the Institute for Defense and Disarmament Studies, Cambridge, Massachusetts; Reuter reports of 3 February and 9 May 1992; and Aleksandr Sychev in *Izvestiya*, 2 April 1992.

79. See the report by Yury Kovalenko and Aleksandr Sychev, *Izvestiya*, 11 March 1992.

80. All three points were made almost verbatim by Alan K. Henrikson, 'The North Atlantic Alliance as a Form of World Order', in Alan K. Henrikson, (ed.), *Negotiating World Order: The Artisanship and Architecture of Global Diplomacy* (Wilmington, DE, Scholarly Resources Inc. 1986), p. 113. Henrikson wrote this

article in 1984 as part of a series of public lectures and working group meetings of the Negotiating World Order Project, which took place under his chairmanship during the academic year 1983–4 at the Fletcher School of Law and Diplomacy.

81. Ibid., p. 134.
82. Arbatov, 'Rossiya i NATO'.

3 The European Community as seen from Moscow: Rival, Partner, Model?

Vladimir Baranovsky

This chapter deals with changing perceptions of West European integration in Moscow. The author does not pretend to give a comprehensive analysis of relations with the EC on the level of practical policy. The goal is rather to understand the internal logic of Moscow's approach, contrasting the pre-1985 period with the years of the New Political Thinking. In many respects this logic – with all its limits, inconsistencies and contradictions, but also with its emerging rationalism and even new ethical considerations – reflected more general trends in foreign-policy thinking.

Either impossible or reactionary

The initial attitude of the Soviet Union towards the integration process in Western Europe was unequivocally negative. This attitude was based not only on traditional ideological dogmatism but also on a postwar 'political realist' assessment of the bipolarity that had emerged in Europe and in the global international system. These two sources, however incompatible they may seem, have in fact a great deal of affinity.

The very phenomenon of integration was perceived first of all as the result of purely political manoeuvres by the West European ruling classes. This intellectual tradition was deeply rooted in the Soviet mentality, going back to the declaration of Lenin in 1915 that a United States of Europe would be 'either impossible or reactionary'.[1] Impossible because of deep insurmountable and unresolvable contradictions between the imperialists themselves; reactionary because it could only be 'an agreement of the European capitalists ... on what? On ways together to put pressure on socialism in Europe and together to defend their colonies'.[2]

The elegant simplicity of these formulae did not prevent their application to postwar reality. West European rulers attempting to unify their efforts on a transnational basis were accused of pursuing two main goals. First,

59

preventing the collapse of the social order inside the West European countries. Second, reinforcing the positions of 'world capitalism' vis-à-vis the 'socialist camp' which had emerged in the eastern part of the continent after the 'people's democratic revolutions'. At that time both these interpretations seemed realistic. In the years immediately after the Second World War a radical socio-political shift to the left, at least in some countries of Western Europe, was by no means simply a theoretical possibility. Traditionally oriented political elites perceived such a prospect as something to be avoided at any price, and this in itself created a substantial incentive for common action. Even more powerful as a stimulus was the perception of the 'Soviet military threat'. As the USSR could not be matched militarily by any single country in Western Europe, consolidation seemed to be the only effective way to ensure security. It is only natural that the Soviet Union – in mirror-image fashion – was not very enthusiastic about West European defence cooperation.

Elements of 'political memory' also played their part. Between the two world wars pan-European ideas (of the kind promoted by R. Coudenhove-Kalergi and others) had been flatly rejected by Moscow, which described them as oriented against the Soviet Union and the revolutionary workers' movement. This ideological legacy was a significant factor at a time of growing East–West antagonism.

The attitude of the Soviet Union was also deeply influenced by the fact that integration in Western Europe almost from the start had a substantial military dimension, whereas the prospects for economic unification seemed very modest.

The Schumann Plan, for example, could conceivably have been perceived in the Soviet Union as something of uncertain significance – dangerous, of course, but not necessarily requiring immediate counter-actions. One could even suppose that the Soviet response could have gone not very far beyond energetic but essentially symbolic and propagandistic condemnation. But the treaty establishing the European Defence Community changed the situation drastically. There was no longer merely a theoretical 'danger' of West European unification somewhere in the distant future; there was a quite clear-cut decision to create a military alliance that would inevitably be hostile to 'world socialism'. This attempt at defence integration became the original sin of West European integration in the eyes of the Soviet Union. It was repeatedly referred to in Moscow, both openly and in 'internal' deliberations, even as late as the Gorbachev period.

There were other grounds for Soviet concern. Early integration plans were closely associated with the attempt to include the western part of Germany in the Western security system. In Soviet eyes even sophisticated schemes for achieving this goal without reinstating the 'German danger' were unacceptable because of concern over the consequences of any future rearmament of the defeated enemy.

This background was not particularly favourable for objective impartial analysis of the centripetal trends developing in Western Europe, and even less so for devising an adequate political response to the phenomenon of integration itself. In contrast to the anxiety about the implications of West European integration, its prospects and its real scope were assessed rather sceptically. The main reason for this scepticism was a dogmatic interpretation of the notion of 'inter-imperialist contradictions' as something irreconcilable and permanently intensifying. The European Coal and Steel Community and later the Common Market were dismissed, for example, as short-lived attempts at cooperation doomed to failure.[3] Soviet policy-makers were inclined to underestimate the real achievements of the EC, proceeding from the assumption that they were only temporary. For some time even the word 'integration' was used only in inverted commas.

Moving towards a more realistic assessment

Elements of more realistic approaches to the new trends in Western Europe were almost non-existent in the 1950s. But the very development of the process was creating incentives for rethinking the phenomenon of integration. A part was also played by the first (albeit symbolic) steps being taken along the path of de-Stalinization inside the USSR. In the 1960s this resulted in animated debates in academic circles, which later – though with a certain delay (in some respects rather a substantial one) – contributed to changes at the level of practical policy.

A less orthodox vision was developed first of all by those academic economists who analysed the phenomenon of 'internationalization'. Its more advanced stage, involving energetic government participation, was held to assume a special character, which justified the use of the term 'integration' to describe it.[4] It is important to note that the trend towards 'internationalization' was traditionally understood in Marxist analysis as a positive and progressive one. This in itself – despite the accompanying pseudo-dialectical exercises condemning 'imperialist integration' – could not but bring about changes in the structure of Soviet thinking about the EC and its development.

Particularly important was the conclusion which flowed from this kind of assessment, that integration was an objectively determined process.[5] A substantial three-volume study published by the Academy of Sciences Institute of the World Economy and International Relations (IMEMO) stated in 1965 that 'integration is not just a new manoeuvre of the governments of several capitalist countries of Western Europe. The policy and the practice of European integration represent a step further in the development of state-monopoly capitalism, a new phenomenon in the development of imperialism. [It is an attempt] to find a constructive answer to the objective requirements of the contemporary productive forces.'[6] In other words, integration began in response to concrete challenges, and not in a purely political way as a result of decisions taken by the ruling classes of the West European countries.

This was not only a blow to the conspiracy theory of European integration. It also led to a policy-oriented conclusion: if integration in the western part of the continent is the result of some 'natural' development, then it would be utopian to think of preventing it or halting it. However, this theoretical advance remained incomplete. Political aspects of integration were interpreted in a traditional way. Besides, the 'new vision' was still to be implemented in practical policy. Both of these problems slowed down reassessment of the Soviet approach to West European integration.

Even recognizing that the latter had its own sources and its own logic, Soviet writers continued to blame those who participated in the process for 'using' it for subversive political purposes. It is difficult to say now to what extent this was a matter of propagandistic routine, and to what extent a genuine (even if mistaken) perception of the international role played by the emerging integrated entity. But even the quotation from the IMEMO study cited above went on as follows: 'European integration creates an economic basis for imperialist military blocs, oriented against socialist states and the national-liberation movement.'[7]

Having accepted the idea of the 'objective character' of economic integration in Western Europe, the academic community was in particular rather reluctant to develop a similar approach to the process of political unification. This prudence can be partly explained by the force of inertia hampering the 'depoliticization' of political analysis. The absence of movement towards political integration in the EC, as well as the predominance of sceptical approaches in Western debates in the 1960s also played a part.

Paradoxically enough, the traditional Marxist approach, which stipulated a strong influence of economic aspects of social development on political ones, would have described the centripetal processes in both spheres as deeply interconnected. However, it took more than a decade before the objective character of the process of integration not only in economics but also in politics was acknowledged.[8] It was only at the turn of the 1970s that Soviet researchers started to analyse systematically and in depth the driving forces of political consolidation in Western Europe,[9] instead of denouncing the process itself as a conspiracy of 'reactionary forces' against the USSR and its allies or against national sovereignty *per se*.

The main incentive for developing a fresh look at political integration in Western Europe was the visible intensification of this process after the turbulent developments of the 1960s. The increase in EC membership, the establishment of the European Council, direct elections to the European Parliament, cooperation of the participating states in the field of foreign policy, all these new realities demanded the attention of analysts in the Soviet Union.

Official relations: pros and cons

On the level of practical policy the changes developed much more slowly. No doubt there was a tacit assumption that it was in the best interests of the Soviet Union to deal with each of the Western countries separately, not only because of the specific character of the content of bilateral relationships but also because the Soviet Union hoped to play on their divergent approaches to international issues. In this sense the very phenomenon of a common position on the part of the EC countries – be it on external trade policy or anything else – was perceived as damaging to the interests of the USSR.

Moscow was well aware that common positions in the framework of the EC had already become a fact of life by the 1960s. But the scope of such synchronization was as a rule very limited, and especially in respect of the Ostpolitik of the member states. Their bilateral contacts with the socialist countries continued to develop primarily on a strictly individual basis, which corresponded to Soviet preferences regarding the structure of East–West relations in Europe. This lack of enthusiasm for developing direct contacts with the EC was not overcome even with the first official statement (by Brezhnev, in 1972) concerning the desirability of building 'businesslike relations' between the CMEA and the Common Market,[10] which turned out to have no immediate practical consequences.

When practice did change it seems that it did so primarily in reaction to the emergence of European Political Cooperation: this new element in the development of integration in Western Europe altered Soviet perceptions of the whole process. The consequences of foreign policy coordination, even if rather limited at the initial stage, were more 'visible' from Moscow than the results of the economic integration. As the phenomenon of integration began to expand into the realm of traditional diplomatic activity, it became a tangible issue for the Soviet Ministry of Foreign Affairs. It was clear that this phenomenon, if it was not taken into account, could damage Soviet interests in the international arena; this pushed Moscow to search for some mode of interaction with the Community.

An even more important factor affecting attitudes towards the EC related to the USSR's global political competition with the United States. Policy in respect of the EC was affected more and more by calculations concerning its perceived role in the distribution of power in the world. West European integration could be perceived either as an additional instrument reinforcing the global potential of 'American imperialism', or as a process undermining its position. The Soviet Union should accordingly either oppose it (as a pro-American political force), or develop more cooperative relations (in order to disadvantage Washington). This understanding of the possible options for the Soviet Union in respect of the EC reflected more general trends in the thinking of the foreign policy community, its gradual movement away from a black-and-white vision of the world towards more realistic and multidimensional perceptions.

However it seems that the goal of the new policy was not only to normalize relations with the EC but also (perhaps even primarily) to win recognition of the CMEA as an international actor, to make it 'accepted' by the West as a body representing the socialist states. The idea that it was important to deal with the Western countries only on the basis of 'mutual concessions' also played a part: Soviet movement towards the EC should be *sine qua non* reciprocated by similar steps on the part of the Common Market states in respect of the CMEA. The notion of 'equal relations' was emphasized especially strongly. This reflected not so much some perceived risk of discrimination, but rather illusions about increasing the international status of the socialist community. The argument that direct CMEA–EC relations were impossible because of the differing capabilities of the two organizations was simply not politically acceptable. The changes that had been introduced into the CMEA's regulations enabling it to conclude external agreements were considered all that was needed.

It is an open question what the importance of legalistic considerations was in the response which came from the EC. Its approach was in fact rather similar to that of the Soviet Union and proceeded from similar assumptions. The CMEA was perceived as a political structure created in order to ensure the dominance of the USSR; to recognize this organization would actually mean to legitimize the Soviet sphere of influence – an unacceptable option for the West. A politically motivated desire to build differentiated relations with separate East-European countries was also responsible for the lack of enthusiasm in the EC attitude towards negotiations with the CMEA.

All these factors created a kind of deadlock by the mid-1980s. There were growing incentives for both sides to normalize relations; but political factors blocked the way. In order to make a new start it was first necessary to overcome old assumptions and to get rid of unrealistic expectations.

Breakthrough

It was in the context of Gorbachev's New Political Thinking that a breakthrough finally became possible.[11] The reassessment of Soviet foreign policy goals and priorities which took place after 1985 proceeded from a much more realistic vision of the contemporary world. The economic potential of the capitalist system, the viability of its political organization, the foreign policy behaviour of the Western countries, the character and intensity of 'inter-imperialist contradictions', all these notions structuring the traditional Soviet vision of the international environment were reconsidered.

The Soviet perception of the EC could not but change in a radical way once a more adequate analysis of the integration process in Western Europe had been accepted. It was no longer seen as a hopeless attempt to 'prolong the agony' of capitalism, but rather as a demonstration of the latter's internal economic and political resources; not a reproduction of the irreconcilable contradictions between the Western states at a new level, but a more effective instrument for defining and defending their common interests; not an offensive of the West European monopolies against the working class, but a negotiated process of social accommodation, which in some respects could be beneficial for large sections of the population; not necessarily a system designed solely to ensure the dominance of the bigger states, but also a mechanism for upgrading the smaller ones.[12]

All these new formulas – even if they were not introduced into Soviet political thinking without hesitation – contributed to a much less suspicious view of integration in Western Europe. What is more, rejecting the notion of 'class struggle' in the international arena and endorsing the idea of the integrity of the world, Soviet official thinking began to stress the necessity for East–West cooperation. In this context the EC had to be regarded as an entity with common or complementary rather than hostile interests; it was no longer a competing power pole challenging the Soviet Union, but a partner for mutual accommodation.

More controversial was the relationship to the emerging positive attitude towards the EC of the notion of the 'Common European House' that became the cornerstone of the Soviet Union's post-1985 foreign policy activity. It is obvious that the idea itself represented a strong appeal to overcome the division of Europe and the antagonism between the political and institutional structures existing on the continent. From this point of view it was only logical to envisage a more cooperative attitude towards the EC. However, some analysts and politicians, both in the East and in the West, were inclined to consider this project as an attempt to counteract the growing role of the EC and in this sense as oriented against it.

Some more concrete considerations affected the Soviet attitude towards the European Community. In as much as overcoming alienation from and returning back into the world community was *de facto* proclaimed as one of the most important objectives of the Soviet Union in the international arena, to achieve this goal 'through the European window' seemed the most easy and the most natural way, due to a number of obvious reasons related to historical experience, cultural traditions, economic rationale, geographic realities, etc. From this point of view the EC could be seen as one of the most promising international partners of the Soviet Union.

The question could also be approached the other way round. In the framework of New Political Thinking Moscow became much more cautious and was visibly reducing its international non-diplomatic activism, trying to ease the burden of redundant external obligations. The future foreign policy of the Soviet Union might well be envisaged as predominantly focused upon its immediate environment, in which the EC occupied a prominent place.

All the above-mentioned changes influenced not just Soviet theoretical thinking. They also had very concrete effects at the level of practical policy. It is significant that one of the first public declarations from Moscow made in the spirit of New Political Thinking was Mikhail Gorbachev's statement (during a meeting with Benedetto Craxi in May 1985) that the Soviet Union was ready to treat the EC as 'a political entity'.[13]

Subsequently relations with the EC were raised from virtually zero point to a level that before 1985 would have been unimaginable. In a relatively short period an EC–CMEA 'Common Declaration' was agreed upon and signed (June 1988). At the end of 1989 the USSR and the EC concluded an agreement on trade, commercial and economic cooperation. Gorbachev defined it as 'an innovative document',[14] and Soviet official commentators were particularly keen to underline its much broader scope than in any other case of the Community's relations with single countries.[15] Later the intention was declared to replace this agreement with a new treaty which would further upgrade relations between the EC and the USSR, and increase the political component.

Thus the Soviet Union recognized the Community, and official relations were developed. Shevardnadze visited the EC headquarters in December 1989[16] and Jacques Delors arrived in Moscow on an official visit in July 1990; exchanges at the level of high-ranking officials on both sides became normal practice.[17] A qualitatively new framework emerged for relations between the USSR and the EC. Obstacles to interaction were removed; a legal foundation was established; ideologically-based suspicions gave way to pragmatic realism.

Beyond 1992: not a challenge any more?

In Soviet academic and political circles, as well as in public opinion, there emerged an increasingly realistic assessment of the latest phase in the development of West European integration. In his speech in Strasbourg in July 1989, Gorbachev said explicitly: 'We have no doubt that the process of integration in Western Europe is acquiring a new quality.'[18] The signing of the Single European Act, which at first was perceived rather sceptically, came to be understood as a major step towards ensuring deeper integration in the Community and substantially reinforcing its position. The project to create a single twelve-nation-wide market by the year 1992 was taken more and more seriously.

This was reflected in numerous articles in the mass media, and in numerous analyses prepared by research institutes as well as by government agencies concerned with external relations. In contrast not only to the first years of West European integration but even to the recent past, there was much less scepticism about the outcome of the whole enterprise. To illustrate this one need only compare two articles in the newspaper *Izvestiya* written by its correspondent in Paris and separated by an interval of two and a half years. In 1988 the emphasis was on difficulties on the path to the internal market and on the fact that it would serve primarily 'big business' interests.[19] In 1991, on the other hand, the doubts had evaporated and the predominant tone had become approving.[20]

At the same time there was much more concrete interest in the implications of the 'Europe 1992' project for the USSR. The most obvious 'minuses' were expected in the economic field. Soviet concerns resembled those felt by many partners of the EC, who feared that it would turn into a 'Fortress Europe' and make penetration of its internal market much more difficult. The scale of such apprehensions was qualitatively different in comparison with those felt in the USA or Japan, since the absolute size of the economic flows between the USSR and the Community was much smaller. But the EC was the major trade partner of the Soviet Union in the West; more complicated terms for exports from the USSR threatened substantially to reduce its import possibilities and thus hamper the technological modernization of the country.

Soviet industrial products were still almost totally absent from West European markets; export prospects were made even more gloomy by the likely growing competitiveness of industrial production inside the emerging single market as well as by plans to introduce more rigid technical standards, environmental protection regulations and other new legislation. It is true that the immediate negative effects would be lessened by the fact that industrial goods formed a very low percentage of Soviet exports to the West. But the archaic structure of Soviet exports was widely regarded as a serious shortcoming and the emergence of new market conditions in the EC was perceived as something which would make it more difficult to remedy the situation.

At the same time, a number of studies carried out at Moscow research institutes[21] demonstrated a certain shift of opinion away from considering the new trends in the EC as mainly unfavourable to Soviet economic interests. There was a widespread understanding that integration in the EC would in any case go ahead quite independently of the Soviet reaction. And pure logic as well as the New Political Thinking required that the Soviet Union should try to adapt to the emerging realities in the Community rather than try to prevent or to neutralize them.

However this understanding does not seem to have been translated into a coherent political line. Policy, it is true, increasingly proceeded from the assumption that the EC was playing the part of a major international political as well as economic actor and that this role was by and large a positive one. Political interaction with the Community was becoming more important. One example was the USSR–EC common statement on the situation in the Near East and in the Gulf adopted by Eduard Shevardnadze and the foreign ministers of the twelve EC countries in September 1990.[22] This statement went far beyond the stating of generalities: it could even be seen as evidence of a kind of ad hoc participation by the Soviet Union in the EPC process. Further possibilities for foreign policy cooperation were considered in the Soviet Union to be quite likely, for instance, in order to organize a conference on security in the Mediterranean.[23] Meanwhile Soviet officials met from time to time, albeit not on a regular basis, with representatives of the EC 'troika'. Participation by President Gorbachev was a sign of the importance attached to such meetings by the Soviet side.[24]

Yet the new line did not receive the emphasis that the Community's importance dictated. It is clear from major foreign policy statements made by high-ranking Soviet officials, and presumably defining the country's main perceptions, goals and priorities in international affairs, that the EC was still very often treated simply as an 'international organization' of relatively secondary importance, one among many others existing in the world.

For instance, although Gorbachev mentioned the EC in his speech at the Paris CSCE summit in November 1990 this reference was somewhat cursory: the Community was listed along with 'international economic organizations, public, scientific and information centres and inter-party and inter-trade union associations'.[25] And when the Soviet president reported to the Supreme Soviet about the results of the summit the EC did not even rate a mention.[26] Similar revealing negligence cropped up in other cases as, for example, during the Gorbachev–Kohl negotiations on the future of Germany in Stavropol in July 1990.[27] Even during his meeting, at around the same time, with Jacques Delors, the Soviet President seemed much more inclined to discuss the economic assistance which the EC could provide, rather than its wider role.[28]

The post-confrontation pattern: Europe from Brest to Brest?

Before the collapse of the communist regimes in Eastern Europe the future of the European international system was perceived in the post-1985 Soviet Union as one embracing the progressive development of less confrontational, more 'civilized' East–West relations. In such a scenario there was every reason to expect that the EC would become an element of the emerging system alongside the CMEA, both cooperating with each other though retaining their fundamentally different characters.

The New Political Thinking made the Soviet Union much more flexible and open-minded in regard to the practical implementation of this script. Moscow did not insist any longer, for example, that the socialist countries delegate to the CMEA all their competence to deal with the Community. According to Gorbachev, relations with the EC could be both 'collective' and individual.[29]

What is more, there was a recognition of the worsening problems of the CMEA, and of the need to reform it in a radical way. The success of the European Community and the prospect of '1992' were apparently taken as a stimulus for serious efforts to carry out substantial changes in the style of cooperation between the socialist countries. 'Socialist integration' having proved ineffective, the EC pattern was considered more and more as a possible model for the CMEA. But without deep reforms of the internal economies of the countries concerned any modifications on the international level were doomed to failure. The dramatic events of 1989–90 in all the countries of the continent that had been the partners of the Soviet Union in the 'socialist community' forced a radical adjustment in Soviet perceptions of the international implications of West European integration. The reassessment was not always explicit but there is no doubt that it influenced Soviet foreign-policy thinking.

The most radical (and possibly the most painful) element in this reassessment concerned the erosion of bipolarity in Europe. This process affected not only the EC itself but also its image in the Soviet Union. As the international context was transformed West European integration came to be analysed and perceived in a new light. Partly because of the new political values, but partly also because of a sense that 'the game had been lost' hostility was gradually overcome with regard to certain aspects of the EC's development that had been regarded as unacceptable only a couple of years earlier.

Thus the plans for political union in the EC failed to evoke any serious expressions of concern in the USSR, either on the official level or in the mass media. This was in sharp contrast to Moscow's earlier nervous reaction to any talk of political union on the basis of the EC. Significantly, even the debates about future military integration in the framework of the EC (pan-European multinational forces, fusion with the Western European Union, etc) provoked only muted and rather neutral comment in the Soviet press.[30] In the past the official Soviet line had been to condemn any development in this direction as an attempt to increase the military might of the West, and as a blatant manifestation of militarism. Politicians as well as the majority of researchers were obsessed by the spectre of a new military bloc which would serve purely to forward the 'aggressive intentions' of the North Atlantic alliance.

Thus gradual overcoming of simplified 'Cold War' stereotypes as well as favourable changes in international relations helped to make the Soviet response more relaxed. This was encouraged by the hope that with the substantial reductions of conventional forces which were under way the very basis for military integration in Western Europe would be eroded.

Another major change in Europe affecting the Soviet perception of the Community was connected with the unification of Germany, something which Moscow insisted from the very beginning should be matched in time with the formation of common European structures.[31] After the futility of this approach became clear, more attention came to be paid to the idea of ensuring Germany's participation in *existing* structures (including the EC), in order to restrict its ability to exercise a free hand in the international arena.

However, traditional anti-German suspicions were also present in Soviet political thinking, and these generated scepticism concerning the ability of the EC or any other structures to prevent 'excessive' dynamism and self-confidence in the enlarged German state, as it acquired major international status. It is true that the question 'Who is going to control whom?' was raised not only (and not first) in Moscow, but it was an important one for Moscow. Gorbachev found it necessary to remind his German negotiating partners that unification had created 'a new situation in NATO, in the EEC, and in the other European structures'.[32]

It was difficult to detect any sign of uneasiness in the Soviet Union concerning the prospect of enlargement of the EC. This also marked a radical break with the concern that had been expressed in the past because of the neutral status of potential new member states. In the case of Austria Soviet diplomacy had been especially intransigent. It was considered that the USSR possessed certain political (if not legal) rights due to the circumstances surrounding the establishment of the Austrian state in the postwar period, and it was hoped to prevent a kind of 'domino process' involving Sweden, Finland and Switzerland being drawn into the EC and thus supposedly 'reinforcing the Western bloc'. As it overcame a confrontational vision of the European scene and developed a more positive attitude towards integration in the western part of the continent, the Soviet Union was less inclined to see arguments for opposing Austrian participation in the EC. There were no official comments (and only neutral ones in the mass media) in response to the announcement that Sweden was going to apply for membership of the Community.[33]

The problem of enlargement of the EC threatened to become much more sensitive for the Soviet Union, however, because of the Central- and South-East European countries' desire to join the Community. One of the most tangible recent effects of 'capitalist integration' as viewed from Moscow had been precisely its influence on those countries. The EC's increasing attractiveness to them – actual or potential – provided the most serious reason for Soviet suspicion regarding centripetal developments in Western Europe. Ironically, it was in the period of the deepest relaxation of tension that the old fear of its disintegrating consequences for the Eastern bloc proved to be justified (though it was obviously not the only reason for the CMEA/WTO collapse, or even the main one).

Even if it was disappointed by the open reorientation of its ex-allies, who all proclaimed their intention of joining the European Community sooner or later, the Soviet Union did not make a single move to prevent this development. The main reason was most probably the clear impossibility of breathing new life into the CMEA. Moscow was in any case also becoming more inward-oriented.

Paradoxically enough, calls to preserve the CMEA were most commonly to be heard from those in the West who were trying to convince the Central and South-East Europeans that 'unilateral attempts to join the European Community as soon as possible would mean misunderstanding of the processes which are under way and nourishing political illusions'.[34] *Pravda*, by contrast, referring in December 1990 to negotiations between Gorbachev and Jozsef Antall, Prime Minister of Hungary, stated: 'The desire of Hungary to become an associate member of the EC by 1992 can only be welcomed.'[35]

The real problem for the USSR was not so much 'losing' its satellites as the prospect of being cut off from the rest of Europe. It was in this sense that the movement of its former allies towards the EC could damage Soviet interests. Such an evolution would only underline the fact that they were being 'westernized' in a more dynamic manner and with more far-reaching results than the Soviet Union. If the tendency was maintained, the European 'dividing line' could well be displaced from the centre of the continent to the western borders of the Soviet Union. Of course the best way of preventing such an undesirable development was for the Soviet Union to speed up its own internal reform processes. Meanwhile, on the level of foreign policy, Moscow was faced with the task of convincing its partners – and most particularly the EC – that the assistance which they were giving to the newly born democracies in the post-socialist countries should be extended further to the East.

The EC became an issue in relations between the Soviet Union and the East European countries in another context. In negotiations for new bilateral treaties to be concluded with the ex-WTO member states, Moscow insisted on introducing a special clause referring to non-participation in alliances that could be directed against the other partner. Reactions to the proposal varied. Romania went along with the condition, whereas Czechoslovakia resolutely rejected it as an intolerable limitation on its freedom of action. The argument put by Václav Havel was quite explicit: the clause is unacceptable because the country wants to join a European Community which intends to transform itself into a political union, one with elements of common policy in the field of military security.[36]

The outcome was rather peculiar: what was most likely intended by Moscow to prevent an expansion of NATO provoked the articulation of a certain perception of the EC as a body potentially oriented against the Soviet Union. Regrettably, this perception was expressed not by some 'old thinking' orthodox figure in Moscow but by one of the best known and popular leaders of the democratic movement in Eastern Europe.

The EC as a factor in Soviet and Russian internal affairs

Assessing the 1989 agreement between the Soviet Union and the European Community, Shevardnadze declared that it represented an important landmark of perestroika as well as demonstrated a degree of international recognition of the viability of the emerging economic system in the USSR.[37]

In other words, the state of relations with the EC was treated by the Soviet Foreign Minister as an indicator of progress in internal evolution. But in the end it was the unfolding Soviet economic crisis – or rather the dismantling of its economic system – which highlighted most clearly the importance of relations with the EC. By the end of 1990 it was obvious that the country was facing the prospect of an economic collapse which it would not be able to prevent without external assistance. The EC played a prominent role in organizing emergency aid to the Soviet Union and in shaping a positive attitude on the part of West European public opinion on the issue. (For a detailed account of the recent course of relations between the European Community, the USSR and Russia, see Chapter 9.)

Even more vital for the Soviet Union was the ability and the readiness of the Community to go beyond 'ordinary' help. One example is the EC's initiating role in setting up the European Bank for Reconstruction and Development and in extending an invitation for the Soviet Union to take part, something which Shevardnadze drew attention to during his visit to Brussels in January 1990.[38] Another promising idea launched by the EC was the plan for a European Energy Community. Though not widely covered by the Soviet media, this project provoked great interest both in academic and political circles in the country, because of the broad potential scope of the project and because of its appropriateness to Soviet capabilities – the energy market was probably the only one where the role of the Soviet Union would not be the humiliating one of unilateral recipient.[39]

During 1990 and 1991 relations with the EC became linked with Soviet internal developments not only in economic, but also in political terms. Competing political forces were intensifying their activity in the field of external relations not so much because of foreign policy considerations *per se* as in order to strengthen their positions inside the country. It was more and more important for them to have political partners outside the Soviet Union. For Gorbachev and the 'centre' it was a question of preserving a monopoly on official relations with other international actors, whereas his challengers were looking to develop independent channels of interaction with the same actors. And those actors, including the EC, began to face a serious problem of choice.

Mikhail Gorbachev was perceived in Western Europe as the most reliable politician in the Soviet Union. As Federal German Chancellor Helmut Kohl expressed it, 'We trust in him more than anyone who could take his place.'[40] Moreover, he was considered to be a guarantor of the continuation of the Soviet Union as a single state. The EC had set its face against disintegration in the Soviet Union, as indeed in the eastern part of the continent in general. In the case of Yugoslavia the Community even tried to exert direct pressure to avoid open internal military conflict: the EC Luxembourg summit in April 1991 stated that the country could hope for association and financial assistance only if its territorial integrity were preserved.[41]

As far as the Soviet Union was concerned, the EC leaders were more cautious and appeared to consider that it was important to avoid being accused of interference in the country's internal affairs. But on the whole the Community demonstrated a predominantly status quo approach. The latter played into the hands of Gorbachev, who was able to argue strongly (even if indirectly) that foreign aid and foreign assistance depended on him. EC officials in particular were unequivocal in their preference for Gorbachev. Early attempts by 'dissident' republican leaders to set up ties with Community structures consequently did not show very impressive results. This was so, for example, in the case of the Russian Federation leader Boris Yeltsin, when he visited Strasbourg in April 1991 with the intention of establishing 'some form of official relationship' but was received at the European Parliament with a distinct lack of enthusiasm.[42]

But the weakness of any status quo approach consists in the possibility of the existing situation eroding, as it indeed was in the Soviet Union. The centre was progressively losing legitimacy and becoming unable to control the country, while the republics were *de facto* acquiring more and more power. The question 'whom to deal with?' was arising more and more often in practical contexts, for example when the Community was considering the effectiveness of its assistance to the Soviet Union.

The abortive *coup d'état* in August 1991 propelled the Soviet Union to its final disintegration. The EC could only pursue a reactive policy, as the headlong transformation of the country into a qualitatively new entity gathered speed. Even the collective decision of the EC member countries to recognize the independence of the Baltic states in no way influenced the situation in the Soviet Union.

However the EC (and the Western countries in general) did have the capacity to influence internal developments in the Soviet Union and they retained that capacity in relation to the post-Soviet states. To preserve democratic trends, to make the authorities more respectful of civil and human rights, to prevent (or at least to soften) any totalitarian backsliding, etc., for all such purposes important (if not irresistible) leverage could be exerted by control over the economic assistance that had become vital for Moscow and the other capitals as well as by control over the whole positive potential of non-confrontational relations. An example was provided at the beginning of 1991, when the Community reacted to the pressure and violence exerted by the 'centre' against the Baltic republics with a decision to freeze temporarily the supply of credits to the Soviet Union that had been agreed upon at the EC summit in Rome in December 1990, and to delay a planned meeting of the Joint EC–USSR Commission.[43] Some observers consider that this clear signal was one of the factors that made Moscow more compromise-oriented[44] and, in particular, persuaded it to refrain from blocking forthcoming referenda in these republics.[45]

Learning from the experience of the EC

The increasing attention which was being devoted by (and in) the Soviet Union to West European integration was stimulated not just by the EC's perceived role as a partner or as a rival in the international system. Growing interest was coming to be focused on the experience of the Community and how it could be applied in regard to the USSR's internal political and economic problems (how to organize relations between the republics, how much sovereignty they should delegate to the central authorities, etc.). Gorbachev demonstrated this during his meeting with Jacques Delors in Moscow in July 1990: 'We obviously need the experience [of others], especially of the kind that has produced substantial positive results – as in the case of the Common Market.'[46]

In the acute internal debates which were under way over the future of the country the EC's experience was more and more often referred to, for example, as an argument against exaggerated demands for autonomy on the part of the national republics. Such demands, it was claimed, ran contrary to an objective worldwide trend to 'internationalization'.[47] This position was bolstered by Jacques Delors, when he stated while he was in Moscow that he was 'frightened' by the intention of some republican parliaments to introduce their own currency.[48] Those in favour of greater republican autonomy stressed the other side of integration in Western Europe: it was successful because the main actors in the process were fully independent states and, even when they accepted some limitation on their sovereignty, their relations had a voluntary character.

The experience of the EC was, not surprisingly, interpreted in very different ways, and was used to justify quite specific policy perspectives. In the last months of 1990 (when demands for a radical transformation of the structures of power at the highest level provoked a political crisis) Gorbachev seemed ready to increase the role of the Federation Council, which represented the republics, but he insisted on majority voting for reasons of efficiency, as unanimous voting had, he said, been renounced 'even by the European Community'. Advocates of preserving a centralized Soviet state were, however, also prone to refer to EC experience as something to be avoided. *Pravda*, the official newspaper of the Communist Party, declared in December 1990: 'Attempts to turn the Centre into a consultative body similar to the European Parliament are fraught with unpredictable consequences.'[49]

But most common was a positive assessment of EC experience and confidence about its applicability to the Soviet Union, both on the part of centrist-conservative politicians and on the part of their reformist opponents. The EC was held up as a model for the country even at the plenum of the Central Committee of the Soviet Communist Party in December 1990 – and not by the most liberal-minded speakers.[50] Its experience was also recommended by prominent economists and politicians, such as N. Shmelev, representing the liberal extreme of the spectrum of Soviet public opinion.[51]

As time passed, the debate acquired a more technical character. In April 1991 the Institute of Europe of the USSR Academy of Sciences held a seminar on the subject 'Prospects for integration in Europe and the Soviet Union' which attracted the participation of many prominent specialists in Moscow, both from academic circles and from government decision-making bodies.[52] The first paper was presented by Michael Emerson, Head of Delegation and Ambassador of the Commission of the European Communities to the USSR. 'While the two cases of the EC and the USSR are of course very different', he remarked, 'the framework of analysis used by economists in the EC may help stimulate and organize economic researches in the USSR too.'[53]

Academician Bronstein from Estonia, a member of the Supreme Soviet Commission on economic reform, suggested establishing a number of general-purpose economic bodies with representation from all the republics and endowing them with adequate financial resources and instruments of the kind provided in the Community. These bodies might include, he proposed, a Regional Development Fund or a Reserve Banking System.[54] Criticizing legislative drafts intended to ensure the economic integrity of the Soviet Union, the parliamentarian Yu. Sharipov and the economist A. Sadykov compared them with the treaty establishing the European Economic Community. They emphasized that in the draft Union Treaty only five articles were devoted to economic relations whereas the 1957 Rome Treaty had approximately 200 articles designed to promote efficient integration.[55]

In the first weeks after the August 1991 *putsch*, with the political paralysis of the Soviet 'centre', a feverish search began for new formulae to organize relations between the scattering republics. The discussions were inspired to a very substantial degree by the EC experience. Only recently considered unacceptable by the majority of faithful believers in the Soviet Union's sustainability, the EC model now represented a kind of maximalist strategy for preserving the union.

Explicit or implicit references to the EC appeared also at the level of the newly independent republics. For example, there was broad understanding that the trend towards self-encapsulation could damage the economic capacity of those smaller republics which would have difficulties in responding to the demands of the world market. In the case of the newly sovereign Baltic republics, one of the remedies proposed was to set up a Baltic Common Market. Its participants would coordinate their production process and set up a single mechanism to deal with other Soviet republics and outside countries. In principle such a development seemed to be within the realm of the possible in the foreseeable future, although the process would undoubtedly be complicated and time consuming. It was unclear, for example, whether trade barriers against other Soviet republics would be erected and what currency would be used.

The notion of 'variable geometry' integration also looked like one that could be usefully transferred from a West European to a Soviet setting. According to one line of argument the emergence of a more consolidated area inside the former Soviet economic complex could create additional problems for the integration of the country as a whole. This thesis was challenged by those who regarded a differentiated approach as beneficial for the interests of the whole post-Soviet area and likely to get the process of internal integration started in those regions with the best conditions for it.

Subsequently it became clear that the only practical goal was a very 'soft' integration of the former Soviet states, probably with differentiated arrangements for each state. But it is difficult to be any more precise when talking about the future evolution of relations in the former Soviet space. The turmoil in the East makes continuity and consolidation in the West all the more important. There are three areas in particular where the EC may play an important role.

In the first place, a strong and powerful European Community can be a factor of stability and predictability in a Europe at a time of change. This is of special relevance in respect of the Central-East European and South-East European countries. Russia has no interest in destabilizing them, but it has scarcely any instruments for influencing them – at least in the near future. If these countries are included in the EC sphere of influence it would lead to an increase in stability in the region, something which would be very welcome in Moscow.

The EC could also play an important geopolitical role, operating as a kind of a counterweight to large entities such as Russia. For the latter this would mean not so much the emergence of a threat, but rather a necessary condition for being accepted by the other European countries, if not as 'members of the family' then at least as reliable partners. In other words, a more powerful EC could minimize uneasiness in respect of the size and potential capabilities of Russia and reduce the likelihood of it being excluded from European affairs.

Finally, we must recognize the important achievement of the EC in creating a sub-regional security system that has reduced virtually to zero centuries-old antagonisms between the participants, notably in the case of France and Germany. To create a pan-European security system (of the kind advocated by Soviet diplomats) what may be necessary is to reproduce the EC experience on a larger scale. In any case it seems reasonable to think more seriously not just about the EC itself, as a core area of the emerging international system in Europe, but also about including in schemes for a new all-European architecture those elements that have been successfully tested in the EC.

The emergence of new states and new uncertainties in the space formerly occupied by the USSR places new demands on all Moscow's international partners. The European Community in particular faces important challenges to its capacity for coordination, innovation and flexibility. Whether or not it is able to make the sizeable contribution that is required of it in assisting the transition to a stable post-communist order in the region will have the most serious repercussions not only for its own member states but for the world community as a whole.

Notes

1. V. I. Lenin, *Polnoe sobranie sochinenii* (Moscow, Izdatel'stvo politicheskoi literatury, 1958–65), vol. 26, p. 354.
2. Ibid.
3. See '"Obschii rynok" i rabochii klass', *Mirovaya ekonomika i mezhdunarodnye otnosheniya*, 1959, no. 7.
4. M. M. Maksimova, *Osnovnye problemy imperialisticheskoi integratsii. Ekonomicheskii aspekt* (Moscow, Mysl', 1971).
5. 'Ob imperialisticheskoi integratsii v Zapadnoi Evrope', *Mirovaya ekonomika i mezhdunarodnye otnosheniya*, 1962, no. 9.
6. *Mezhdunarodnye otnosheniya posle vtoroi mirovoi voiny*, vol. 3, 1956–64 (Moscow, Izdatel'stvo politicheskoi literatury, 1965), p. 27.
7. Ibid.
8. S. Madzoevsky, D. Mel'nikov, Yu. Rubinsky, 'O politicheskikh aspektakh zapadnoevropeiskoi integratsii', *Mirovaya ekonomika i mezhdunarodnye otnosheniya*, 1974, no. 9.
9. N. S. Kishilov (ed.), *Zapadnoevropeiskaya integratsiya: politicheskie aspekty* (Moscow, Nauka, 1985).
10. *Pravda*, 19 March 1972.
11. See N. Malcolm, 'De-Stalinization and Soviet Foreign Policy: The Roots of "New Thinking"', in Ts. Hasegawa and A. Pravda (eds), *Perestroika: Soviet Domestic and Foreign Policies* (London, Sage/RIIA, 1990), pp. 178–205.
12. See 'Evropeiskoe soobshchestvo segodnya. Tezisy Instituta mirovoi ekonomiki i mezhdunarodnykh otnoshenii AN SSSR', *Mirovaya ekonomika i mezhdunarodnye otnosheniya*, 1988, no. 12, pp. 8–9; *The European Community*, IMEMO Discussion Paper, Moscow, 1989.
13. *Pravda*, 30 May 1985.
14. *Vizit M. S. Gorbacheva v Italiyu i Vatikan* (Moscow, Izdatel'stvo politicheskoi literatury, 1990), p. 60.
15. *Pravda*, 6 August 1990.
16. *Pravda*, 20 December 1989.
17. *Pravda*, 20 July 1990.
18. *Vizit M. S. Gorbacheva vo Frantsiyu* (Moscow, Izdatel'stvo politicheskoi literatury, 1989), p. 138.
19. Yu. Kovalenko, 'EES: plyusy i minusy integratsii', *Izvestiya*, 16 August 1988.
20. Yu. Kovalenko, 'Bez Gerakla ne oboytis'. Evropa na puti k "sverkhderzhave"', *Izvestiya*, 19 February 1991.
21. See 'Posledstviya formirovaniya edinogo rynka Evropeiskogo soobschestva', *Mirovaya ekonomika i mezhdunarodnye otnosheniya*, 1989. no. 4, pp. 38–44.
22. *Izvestiya*, 27 September 1990.
23. *Izvestiya*, 20 May 1990.

24. *Izvestiya*, 14 March 1991.
25. *Izvestiya*, 20 November 1990.
26. *Pravda*, 27 November 1990.
27. *Izvestiya*, 18 July 1990.
28. *Pravda*, 20 July 1990.
29. *Vizit M. S. Gorbacheva vo Frantsiyu*, p. 138.
30. *Izvestiya*, 4 July 1990; *Izvestiya*, 21 March 1991; *Izvestiya*, 27 March 1991.
31. In February 1990 Eduard Shevardnadze stated: 'We are anxious that the process of German unification is moving faster than the process of European integration' (the latter was referred to in terms of 'constructing the Common European House').
32. *Vizit M. S. Gorbacheva v FRG* (Moscow, Izdatel'stvo politicheskoi literatury, 1990), p. 29.
33. *Pravda*, 17 December 1990.
34. *Delovoi mir*, December 1990, p. 3.
35. *Pravda*, 19 December 1990.
36. *Izvestiya*, 30 April 1991.
37. *Izvestiya*, 17 December 1989.
38. *Izvestiya*, 18 January 1990.
39. According to *Izvestiya* (22 February 1991), 'The future common energy market will correspond to the interests of both the Soviet Union and the European Community. The USSR will be able to get the hard currency that it needs so much at the present time, as well as more sophisticated Western technologies. In return the West could have guaranteed Soviet oil supplies, which would represent a serious alternative to Middle East oil and enable the Europeans to diversify their sources of energy.'
40. *Izvestiya*, 25 April 1991.
41. *Nezavisimaya gazeta*, 13 April 1991.
42. *Kuranty*, 16 April 1991; *Izvestiya*, 16 April 1991.
43. *Kommersant*, 21–28 January 1991; *Izvestiya*, 23 January 1991.
44. *Kommersant*, 18–25 February 1991.
45. *Kommersant*, 4–11 March 1991.
46. *Izvestiya*, 20 July 1990.
47. *Literaturnaya gazeta*, 30 January 1991.
48. *Izvestiya*, 20 July 1990.
49. *Pravda*, 21 December 1990.
50. *Pravda*, 13 December 1990.
51. *Izvestiya*, 17 December 1990.
52 *Izvestiya*, 20 April 1991.
53. Michael Emerson, 'Why Economic and Monetary Union? Current Thinking in the European Community, with Some Comments on the USSR', Moscow, March 1991. Unpublished.
54. *Izvestiya*, 20 February 1990.
55. 'Antikrizisnaya programma: Soyuz i respubliki', *Izvestiya*, 30 April 1991.

4 Dismantling the Military Confrontation

Jane M. O. Sharp

Introduction

This chapter explores the role of arms control in achieving Soviet security goals in Europe under the leadership of Mikhail Gorbachev from 1985 to 1991, and assesses the current and likely place in European arms control diplomacy of Russia and the other former Soviet states.

In Brezhnev's time Soviet policy in Europe was designed to defend the Soviet Union against nuclear and conventional military attacks from NATO.[1] A second Soviet goal was to consolidate 'the gains of the Second World War', a euphemism employed to justify the preservation of communist governments in Central- and South-Eastern Europe. It was a policy designed to secure the political, territorial and military status quo. Thus Soviet policy at the Conference on Security and Cooperation in Europe (CSCE) during the 1970s and early 1980s was directed above all at preserving and codifying control over its Warsaw Treaty Organization (WTO) allies. Moscow's goal at the Mutual and Balanced Force Reductions (MBFR) negotiations was essentially to prevent any meaningful reductions at all on the Soviet side.

A third goal was to guard against the resurgence of German power. In the 1950s and 1960s Soviet policy appeared to oscillate between a desire to expel American influence from Europe and a desire to maintain American troops on the continent as a hedge against German revanchism. In the first of a number of draft treaties for collective security in Europe, submitted in 1954, the USSR excluded the USA.[2] And during the recurrent crises over Berlin both Party First Secretary Nikita Khrushchev and Foreign Minister Andrei Gromyko sometimes suggested that they would like to see all US troops out of Germany. But from 1955 onwards Soviet invitations to their proposed pan-European security conferences usually included all the NATO allies, i.e. the United States and Canada as well as the West Europeans.[3] If there was some ambiguity about this question in the 1950s and 1960s, by the early 1970s it was quite clear that United States troops were not only acceptable but welcome. At the Vienna negotiations from 1973 to 1989 Soviet delegates repeatedly told their Western partners that keeping US troops in the Federal Republic of Germany was an important goal of Soviet policy in Europe in general, and at the Mutual and Balanced Force Reduction talks in particular.[4]

A fourth goal of Soviet arms control policy in the pre-Gorbachev era, in both bilateral and multilateral forums, was the maintenance of a bipolar international security system. This required constant efforts to codify equal status with the United States, not only in numbers of strategic nuclear missiles and deployed forces in Europe, but also as a co-equal manager of the international system.

Once the Warsaw Treaty Organization collapsed and the USSR devolved into its constituent republics, the notion of parity with the West also collapsed, and with it much of the self-respect of the Soviet military establishment. The political leaders of the former Soviet republics were more concerned to reassure the West that they were ready to cooperate on military issues, that they were responsible partners and worthy recipients of financial and technical assistance. The Soviet and former Soviet General Staff and other senior military officers, however, found their reduced status difficult to accept. The discomfort of the military manifested itself in opposition to the disarmament initiatives of the politicians, in attempts to evade the provisions of the Conventional Armed Forces in Europe (CFE) disarmament treaty before it was signed in November 1990, in foot-dragging on the ratification of CFE during 1991 and 1992; in slowing troop withdrawals from Eastern Europe and the Baltic states; and, in May 1992, reversion to a military doctrine that was unambiguously offensive.[5] In January 1993 conservatives in the Supreme Soviet complained that the START I and START II treaties had 'brought a great nation to its knees'.[6]

The Gorbachev era

In the late 1980s, Gorbachev was clearly impatient with the emphasis on parity and the status quo, but he was just as apprehensive as his predecessors about the security implications of the unification of Germany, and he was keen to retain an American presence on the continent. Anxiety about German unification manifestly hampered Soviet policy at the CFE talks during the summer of 1990.[7]

Gorbachev started his term in office with radical arms control proposals designed to transform relations with neighbouring countries. Motivated in part by the need to make capital available for the civilian economy and to make the USSR a more attractive trading partner, Gorbachev democratized, demilitarized and de-ideologized Soviet relations with the international community. Despite considerable resistance from the General Staff, he cut the overall size of the armed forces and tried to impose a more defensive doctrine on Soviet military policy. He not only renounced the Brezhnev doctrine that rationalized the use of military force to impose communist orthodoxy, but also accelerated the dissolution of the Warsaw Treaty Organization by starting to withdraw Soviet troops from Eastern Europe. The decision, announced in December 1988, to cut forces unilaterally and the agreements in early 1990 to withdraw all Soviet forces from Hungary and Czechoslovakia by mid-1991 convinced most Western publics and governments that the Soviet Union no longer posed a serious military threat. Gorbachev's conciliatory policy also provoked radical changes in NATO's rhetoric towards the former WTO countries and in NATO's own force planning.[8]

In his arms control diplomacy Gorbachev broke with Soviet tradition in several ways. In contrast to his predecessors' obsessive secretiveness, Gorbachev was willing to allow intrusive on-site inspections of Soviet territory, which opened the way to the CSCE Stockholm Agreement on Confidence and Security Building Measures in September 1986 and the Intermediate-Range Nuclear Forces in Europe (INF) Treaty in December 1987. His willingness to make data available and to undertake asymmetrically large cuts, where Soviet forces were superior to those of the West, facilitated the signing of the CFE Treaty in November 1990.

Nuclear priorities

In January 1986 Gorbachev proposed a schedule of cuts leading to complete denuclearization by the year 2000.[9] This was later modified by his security advisers to a goal of minimum deterrence.[10] Indeed, by the early 1990s both civilian and military analysts in Moscow were stressing the risks of a nuclear-free world and the need to maintain a strong, if minimal, nuclear deterrent given the cuts imposed on conventional forces by the CFE treaty.[11] Nevertheless, Gorbachev persisted with efforts to make deep cuts in nuclear forces right up to his departure from office at the end of 1991. Whereas his predecessors saw nuclear parity with the United States as the *sine qua non* of superpower status, Gorbachev argued that status related primarily to economic power and political legitimacy and that nuclear weapons were best kept to a minimum, then eliminated. In late 1986 at the Reykjavik summit, Gorbachev came close to persuading President Ronald Reagan of the wisdom of both the USA and the USSR eliminating all their intercontinental ballistic missiles.

In late 1987 Gorbachev succeeded where his predecessors had failed, in achieving an agreement to eliminate all Soviet and American intermediate-range nuclear missiles.[12] Gorbachev was much less successful, however, in persuading his General Staff to renounce long-range strategic nuclear weapons. Parallel to the negotiations for a Strategic Arms Reduction Treaty (START), the USSR continued to deploy new strategic missiles, adding new rail-mobile SS-24 and SS-25 rockets during 1990–91, for example. A modest START agreement was signed in July 1991, but not ratified during Gorbachev's last six months in office.

Of more relevance to the security of Europeans was Gorbachev's interest in eliminating short-range nuclear weapons (SNF). During the late 1980s Western analysts claimed that one reason NATO should develop a follow-on to the nuclear armed Lance missile (FOTOL) was that Soviet SNF were being modernized. In a speech to the Council of Europe on 6 July 1989 Gorbachev proposed East–West talks to establish the requirements for stable minimum deterrence forces, and offered to remove all SNF from Europe if the US would reciprocate.[13] The USSR began to withdraw SNF from Europe unilaterally in mid-1989. In addition to the 500 warhead cuts announced by Gorbachev in May 1989, Eduard Shevardnadze announced on 5 June 1990 that by the end of 1990 the USSR would have withdrawn an additional 140 missile launchers and 3,200 nuclear artillery pieces from Europe.[14]

Nuclear arms control after the August 1991 coup

The nature of Soviet–American nuclear arms control diplomacy changed dramatically in the second half of 1991.[15] Mikhail Gorbachev's approach was more dynamic and more cooperative than that of his predecessors, but it still took him more than six years to negotiate the Strategic Arms Reduction Treaty (START agreement) with the US, which was finally signed in late July that year. After the failed coup in August, however, came a rapid succession of unilateral measures. This was largely because as the Soviet Union unravelled the Western powers grew increasingly alarmed about the safety and security of the Soviet nuclear arsenal. Little was known about how these weapons were guarded.[16] In addition, Western analysts were uncertain about the Soviet ability to store and dismantle nuclear warheads safely.[17] Apart from the safety issue, NATO countries feared that if the USSR collapsed the risk of nuclear proliferation could increase. The successor states might become independent nuclear powers, and redundant Soviet nuclear technicians might be hired by other states with aspirations to acquire nuclear weapons.

In 1991 long-range nuclear weapons were deployed in four of the Soviet republics. Seventy per cent (9,650 warheads) were in Russia; 1,656 in Ukraine (460 on SS-24 missiles, 780 on SS-19s, 416 on 30 strategic bombers); 1,360 warheads were in Kazakhstan (1,040 on SS-18 missiles, 320 on Bear H bombers); and 54 in Belarus on SS-25 missiles. The United States naturally worried most about those systems with ranges long enough to target North America, while Europeans worried more about the tactical nuclear weapons; not only because there were more of them targeted on Europe but also because they did not appear to be as tightly controlled as the strategic systems. Tactical weapons were deployed in all fifteen republics and divided among four different services: army, air force, air defence and naval.[18]

The United States and its NATO allies took a series of steps to reduce these risks. In late September, President Bush announced the destruction of 3,000 tactical nuclear weapons, and put another 1,275 into storage. He took all strategic bombers off alert status as well as all ICBMs scheduled for reduction once the START treaty entered into force. He also proposed a negotiated elimination of all multiple-warhead (MIRVed) missiles, and offered technical help to the USSR in reducing and dismantling its nuclear systems.[19]

Gorbachev's response came just over a week later, on 5 October. He too cut tactical nuclear weapons, took strategic systems off alert and committed the USSR to reduce strategic warheads to 1,000 less than the ceiling agreed in the START treaty.[20] NATO defence ministers followed this with a decision on 17 October to remove all ground-based nuclear weapons from Europe, and to cut by half the number of nuclear gravity bombs deployed on dual-capable aircraft.[21] In November, the US Congress passed the Soviet Nuclear Threat Reduction Act of 1991, which allocated $400 million to help the Soviet Union to dismantle its nuclear arsenal.

The NATO allies (especially the United States) were reluctant to take any steps that might undermine Gorbachev. One former US secretary of defence argued that nuclear deterrence would be strengthened if the republics retained control of the nuclear systems on their territories.[22] But the clear Western preference was for a unitary state and a single force under Gorbachev's leadership.[23]

From the USSR to CIS: the nuclear problem

On 1 December, however, Ukraine voted for independence and a week later Ukraine, Russia and Belarus signed an agreement to form a new Commonwealth of Independent States (CIS).[24] The three leaders agreed to respect each other's borders (Article 5) and to seek the complete elimination of all nuclear weapons under strict international control (Article 6). Pending complete nuclear disarmament, however, the Slav leaders agreed to maintain unified control over their armed forces in a single strategic space. Faced by these rather vague undertakings, Western leaders reacted by expressing concern about the danger of nuclear proliferation and asserting the need for tight central control over the former Soviet nuclear arsenal.[25]

On 21 December, the five central Asian states, Moldova, Armenia and Azerbaijan, joined the three founding CIS states at a meeting of the new entity in Alma Ata. The eleven agreed that the former permanent Soviet seat on the United Nations Security Council should go to Russia.[26] They also agreed that all short-range nuclear weapons should be transferred to Russia by 1 July 1992 and dismantled.[27] But strategic nuclear weapons were to be placed under unified CIS, not Russian, command. Mikhail Gorbachev formally handed the codes which gave him control over the nuclear arsenal to Boris Yeltsin on 25 December, but it was not clear how much independent control was exercised by the Soviet General Staff and the Strategic Rocket Forces.[28] Moreover, it was not clear how, with all their political disagreements, the former republics would be able to exercise a joint command and control regime.

Responding to repeated expressions of Western concern, the eleven CIS leaders further refined their nuclear agreements at a second summit in Minsk on 30 December, with a new Agreement on Strategic Forces. Article 4 stated that decisions about nuclear use would be made by the president of Russia with the *agreement* of Belarus, Ukraine and Kazakhstan and in *consultation* with all the CIS states. The four 'nuclear republics' (Russia, Ukraine, Belarus and Kazakh-stan) differed, however, in their commitment to dismantling their arsenals.[29] For example, in Article 5 of the Agreement on Joint Measures on Nuclear Weapons, signed in Alma Ata on 21 December 1991, Ukraine and Belarus undertook to join the 1968 Nuclear Non-Proliferation Treaty (NPT) as non-nuclear states. But Kazakhstan made no such commitment. In early January 1992, President Nazarbayev of Kazakhstan told French Foreign Minister Roland Dumas that his country would join the NPT as a nuclear weapon state like France.[30] Nazarbayev claimed nuclear status because nuclear devices had been tested in Kazakhstan before 1967.[31] In Article 4 of the Minsk Agreement Ukraine, which earlier had given mixed signals about its long-term nuclear status, now explicitly agreed to dismantle not only all tactical nuclear weapons by 1 July 1992, but all nuclear weapons by the end of 1994. Belarus and Kazakhstan made no such commitment, although Belarus had earlier stated its intention of becoming non-nuclear and neutral.[32]

Once the USSR had collapsed, Western leaders sought to encourage the transfer of all former Soviet nuclear weapons, and responsibility for nuclear matters, to the Russian government at the expense of the other republics. This was not a policy universally popular either in Russia or in the other republics. Some experts in Moscow argued that Russia would collapse if it had to assume the full burden of a nuclear superpower.[33] In the other nuclear republics, President Kravchuk and President Nazarbayev in particular resented the fact that Boris Yeltsin presumed to speak on their behalf in bilateral talks with the United States.[34] Tactical nuclear weapons were withdrawn from the non-Russian republics ahead of schedule. The process was completed by May 1992,[36] but things did not go smoothly in regard to longer-range weapons. Ukraine, Kazakhstan and Belarus all insisted on adhering to the START treaty as independent parties. In May 1992 the United States and the four CIS nuclear states negotiated a protocol to the treaty that made Ukraine, Kazakhstan and Belarus parties to START, in exchange for pledges that all three would join the NPT as non-nuclear-weapon states.[35] Paradoxically this Protocol appears to delay the denuclearization of Ukraine, which had earlier pledged to denuclearize by the end of 1994, because under START I Ukraine would be allowed seven years from entry into force of the treaty to denuclearize. More worrying are the interpretations by Ukraine that although START, if ratified, would oblige them to give up the 130 SS-19 missiles on their territory, they could retain both the 46 SS-24 missiles and the 30 strategic bombers with accompanying nuclear warheads. This suggests that Ukraine does not intend to honour its pledge in the Lisbon Protocol to adhere to the NPT as a non-nuclear state. And indeed in July 1993 the defence minister General Konstantin Morozov suggested that Ukraine join the NPT as a nuclear state in transition to non-nuclear status.[35a]

The START ratification process was accompanied in the first half of 1992 by further Russian and American unilateral initiatives, and a new Joint Understanding, that went far beyond START, was signed by George Bush and Boris Yeltsin in mid-June 1992.[37] This evolved into the START II treaty signed by Bush and Yeltsin in Moscow in early January 1993. Under START II strategic warheads will be reduced to 3,000–3,500 per side by the year 2003 (or earlier if the US provides additional financial assistance to dismantle Soviet systems), all MIRVed systems will be eliminated, and submarine launched ballistic missiles (SLBMs) will be reduced to 1,750 on each side.[38]

Apart from these agreed cuts in force levels, and Western technical and financial assistance to help the former Soviet republics dismantle their excess nuclear weapons, the other major effort in nuclear diplomacy in early 1992 was to stem the nuclear brain drain from the former Soviet republics. The Western powers were worried that Soviet technicians might be lured away as nuclear mercenaries by Third World countries.[39] Accordingly, $35 million of the $400 million allocated by the US in November 1991 (see above) was earmarked for two research institutes, in Moscow and Kiev, to provide employment for nuclear experts.[40]

The other Western allies also provided financial and technical assistance for disarmament on a smaller scale in early 1992. Britain for example, offered 250 special containers for the secure transport of nuclear warheads and 20 special armoured transport vehicles.[41]

For all their encouraging rhetoric, however, by the end of 1992 none of the CIS states (apart from Russia) had signed the Non-Proliferation Treaty. Moreover, relations were deteriorating among and within the CIS republics, especially within the Russian Federation, in Tajikistan and between the states of the Transcaucasus. Relations between Russia and Ukraine were tense for most of 1992, although there was some improvement in mid-1992, at least in the dispute over control of the Black Sea Fleet.[42] While none of the CIS conflicts were as serious as those in Yugoslavia, there was nevertheless concern in the West that conflicts in the next few years could disrupt the agreed schedule of nuclear reductions.

Gorbachev's approach to conventional arms control

When Mikhail Gorbachev assumed leadership of the Soviet Union in 1985 he was manifestly impatient with Cold War politics and the plodding incrementalism that had dominated the inter-alliance talks on Mutual and Balanced Force Reductions through the Brezhnev years. Thus instead of responding to NATO efforts to move the talks forward in late 1985, Gorbachev proposed much more radical reductions than those on the MBFR agenda. As early as October 1985, Mikhail Gorbachev and his Chief of Staff Sergei Akhromeev began to talk of asymmetries in the conventional balance and to admit that in some areas the Warsaw Treaty Organization was ahead of NATO.[43] Over the next year and a half both men repeatedly stated that these asymmetries should be resolved by levelling down, rather than by levelling up.

For Gorbachev in the 1980s, as for Khrushchev three decades earlier, an important motivation for Soviet cuts was to reallocate resources to the civilian economy. Another was to curb NATO's capability to strike targets deep in Warsaw Pact territory.[44] Gorbachev's calculation appeared to be, as it had been in the INF agreement, that the USSR should make asymmetrical quantitative concessions to curb NATO's qualitatively superior technologies. In the case of conventional arms in Europe, he was willing to cut Soviet armoured forces in exchange for modest limits on superior NATO air power. In addition he hoped to persuade NATO leaders to join the WTO in changing their military doctrine to emphasize defence over offense. To this end in speeches in East Berlin and Prague in the Spring of 1987 he pressed NATO to enter expert-level talks on military doctrine, so that each side could explain what it found offensive and provocative about the other. Two seminars on military doctrine were held under the auspices of the Conference on Security and Cooperation in Europe, the first in January–February 1990, the second in October 1991.[45]

The Treaty on Conventional Armed Forces in Europe

In February 1987, at the third CSCE follow-up conference in Vienna, delegates from the sixteen NATO and seven Warsaw Treaty countries began a series of informal meetings to negotiate a mandate for negotiations on Conventional Armed Forces in Europe. The primary questions that had to be settled were: who should participate, which categories of force to limit, how to dispose of excess forces, how wide a geographical zone to cover, and what kind of verification and stabilizing measures should be applied.

In the CFE mandate signed on 10 January, 1989, the twenty-three participating states agreed that their objectives were to establish a stable and secure balance of conventional armed forces, to remove disparities prejudicial to stability and security, and to eliminate as a matter of priority the capability to launch surprise attacks and to initiate large-scale offensive action. They agreed to include conventional armed forces and equipment based on the territory of the participants in Europe from the Atlantic to the Urals (the ATTU zone). They also agreed, contrary to early Soviet preferences, that nuclear weapons would not be a subject of CFE, nor would naval and chemical weapons be addressed.[46]

The CFE treaty was negotiated remarkably quickly, in less than two years. The CFE-1 agreement, signed in November 1990, codified a balance within five categories (main battle tanks, armed combat vehicles, artillery, combat aircraft and combat helicopters) between the group of sixteen states that belong to NATO and the group of six (later thirteen) states that used to belong to the WTO.[47] Anticipation of Western aid to rebuild the collapsed economies of former communist states was a powerful stimulus to compromise, particularly on the Soviet side. Agreements on troop withdrawals were signed in the late 1980s and early 1990s between the Gorbachev government and Hungary, Czechoslovakia, Poland and Germany. Soviet troops left Hungary and Czechoslovakia by mid-1991 and are scheduled to leave Poland by the end of 1993 and Germany by the end of 1994.[48]

Intra-WTO negotiations

In the non-Soviet WTO states the euphoria of getting rid of oppressive communist regimes in late 1989 soon gave way to anxiety in 1990, adrift as these countries were between NATO and the Soviet Union with no security guarantees from either. The newly democratic countries strove to reduce Soviet allocations of treaty-limited military equipment (TLE), and to increase their own allocations. They also applied to Germany for surplus equipment that used to belong to the National Volksarmee (NVA) of the GDR. These negotiations among the 'group of six' ex-WTO states produced an agreement signed in Budapest in early November 1990, and further refined in June 1991.[49]

Soviet attempts to renegotiate the terms of CFE

Codification of the NATO–WTO balance became meaningless once the WTO was abolished, leaving Europe with a new set of asymmetries that were anything but reassuring to the Soviet military establishment. The USSR remained militarily superior to its former allies in the WTO, but NATO forces were now quantitatively as well as qualitatively superior to those of the Soviet Union west of the Urals.

The Soviet General Staff began to try to compensate for, and in some cases evade, what they saw as unacceptable limits imposed by the treaty. Some of these measures undermined the spirit of CFE, and others threatened to breach the letter of the agreement, but all had the effect of eroding the confidence painstakingly built up by Shevardnadze. Clashes between Shevardnadze's Foreign Ministry and the Defence Ministry became quite overt after his resignation in December 1990. Gorbachev too appeared politically vulnerable, and refrained from intervening in the dispute.

After CFE was signed in November 1990, three categories of issues which were causing problems were discussed in the Joint Consultative Group (JCG) established to oversee treaty implementation:

- the transfer of Soviet equipment east of the Urals, i.e. outside the jurisdiction of the treaty;
- discrepancies between US intelligence estimates of Soviet treaty limited equipment in the Atlantic to Urals zone of application and data reported by the USSR on November 18, 1990;
- Soviet claims that TLE with coastal defence, naval infantry and strategic rocket forces was exempt under Article III of the treaty.

Between July 1988 and November 1990 almost 80,000 pieces of treaty limited equipment were transferred east of the Urals out of the ATTU zone. Conservative military spokesmen in Moscow made no bones about their opposition to the treaty and to the concessions made to it in Vienna.[50] To the extent that the transfers were made before treaty signature, they were of course a breach of the spirit but not the letter of the agreement. This was acknowledged by US Secretary of State Baker after the NATO ministerial meeting in Brussels in December.[51] Nevertheless, the other twenty-one CFE signatory states demanded that the Soviet Union continue to provide information about the future disposition of the equipment east of the Urals and asked for assurances that the Soviet military would not generate a new strategic reserve out of the transferred equipment. The other data discrepancies were eventually resolved by the summer of 1991, but not without exacerbating relations further between the Soviet Foreign Ministry and the Soviet General Staff.

From USSR to CIS: restructuring of conventional forces

Once the USSR had split up into its constituent republics, the CFE compliance regime helped to smooth the process of allocation of equipment to the non-Russian republics, although the Soviet General Staff went to some lengths to compensate for and evade the limits imposed by the CFE agreement, and were reluctant to bring in the other republics as full parties to international agreements. In late 1991, the eight independent successor states with territory west of the Urals (Armenia, Azerbaijan, Belarus, Georgia, Kazakhstan, Moldova, Ukraine and Russia) indicated their willingness to

Table 4.1 Budapest Agreement of 3 November 1990 on CFE allocations

State	Battle tanks	Artillery	ACVs*	Combat air†	Att. hlcpt‡
'Group of 6'	20,000	20,000	30,000	6,800	2,000
USSR	13,150[1]	13,175[2]	20,000[3]	5,150	1,500
Bulgaria	1,457	1,750	2,000	235	67
Czechoslovakia	1,435	1,150	2,050	345	75
Hungary	835	840	1,700	180	108
Poland	1,730	1,610	2,150	460	130
Romania	1,376	1,475	2,100	430	120

Notes
* ACVs Artillery armoured combat vehicles
† Combat air Combat aircraft
‡ Att. hlcpt Attack helicopters
1 933 tanks deployed with Soviet naval infantry (120) and coastal defence forces (813) counted against this allowance of 13,150. NB. the total tank allocation of 20,000 was not taken up: country allocations amount to 19,983.
2 1,080 artillery pieces deployed with Soviet naval infantry (234) and coastal defence forces (846) counted against this allowance of 13,175.
3 1,725 ACVs deployed with Soviet naval infantry (753) and coastal defence forces (972) counted against this allowance of 20,000.

implement all the arms control agreements signed by the former USSR, including confidence-building measures agreed in the 1986 Stockholm and 1990 Vienna Documents, and the CFE-1 treaty signed in November 1990. The CFE treaty could not be ratified or implemented, however, until all the former Soviet states had resolved their differences over the allocation of Soviet military assets. This proved painful for the Russian military leadership, because during the Cold War years it had deployed its most up to date offensive weapons on its western border facing NATO, and a painfully large share of them accordingly went to Belarus and Ukraine.

The NATO powers were reluctant to apply heavy pressure to the former Soviet republics, but they pointed out that foot-dragging over reaching agreement with each other and accepting the CFE regime would slow up the process of financial and technical assistance. (NATO's role in helping to reach a settlement is described in Chapter 2). The biggest obstacle was resistance by the Russian military establishment to allotting the relatively high share of equipment demanded by Ukraine and Belarus. Eventually, however, force ceilings were agreed for the European former Soviet states at a meeting in Tashkent in May 1992.[52]

After the Tashkent agreement, the entire twenty-nine-state JCG in Vienna negotiated the language changes required in the 1990 text to accommodate the newly independent republics. The adopted treaty was formally signed by all twenty-nine CFE state parties in Oslo on 5 June.[53]

On 10 July 1992 sixteen NATO countries, six former non-Soviet Warsaw Pact countries and seven former Soviet republics met in Helsinki to sign two accords. The first was the Provisional Application of the CFE-1 Treaty, which in effect brought the treaty into force despite the fact that four of the twenty-nine parties (Armenia, Belarus, Portugal and Russia) had not yet deposited instruments of ratification.

The second was an agreement (CFE-1A), which set ceilings on various categories of military personnel in the territory of the twenty-nine states within the zone of application defined by CFE-1, i.e. the Atlantic-to-Urals zone.[54] Two states are assigned zero forces: Iceland, which has no armed forces, and Kazakhstan, whose territory lies almost wholly east of the Urals. In the treaty text as published on 10 July four states, all currently at war, had not yet agreed to any limits on personnel: Armenia, Azerbaijan, Georgia and Moldova.

As well as dividing up military assets in compliance with international arms control obligations, the CIS states also had to restructure and reallocate responsibility for the former Soviet forces now spread among fifteen different republics. In some cases this was difficult to resolve. For example, Ukraine initially claimed sole control of the Black Sea Fleet and all Soviet forces on its territory. Eventually President Kravchuk agreed to share the Black Sea Fleet with Russia, and servicemen were given the opportunity to sign loyalty oaths to the republic of their choice.[55] Yet differences over whether Ukrainian or Russian troops should be responsible for security at the strategic missile sites in Ukraine were still unresolved in 1993.

Decisions about other former Soviet deployments varied according to the degree of independence the different republics wanted from Moscow as well as their desire and their ability to raise their own national armies. Where conflicts had erupted over border disputes or ethnic rivalries, some governments asked for Russian troops to serve as peace-keeping forces.

Two of the Central Asian republics (Tajikistan and Turkmenistan) could not yet afford to raise their own armed forces and agreed that Russia should take control of former Soviet units and accept responsibility for defence of their territories. The other three Central Asian republics (Kazakhstan, Kyrgyzstan and Uzbekistan) put the former Soviet units on their soil under national control once the Turkmenistan Military District ceased to exist on 1 July.

The reassignment of authority for former Soviet troops was most easily arranged in Belarus where in July 1992 the government in Minsk signed over twenty agreements with Russia relating to the assignment of former Soviet forces to Belarussian command and the sharing of former Soviet military assets.

In the former Baltic and Transcaucasus Military Districts (covering the territory of Estonia–Latvia–Lithuania and Armenia–Azerbaijan–Georgia respectively) Russia designated former Soviet forces as Groups of Russian Forces stationed abroad, to be withdrawn as soon as was feasible, as they had been from the territory of the non-Soviet WTO allies.[56] Withdrawal schedules proved difficult to negotiate with the Baltic states because the latter

Table 4.2 Treaty-Limited Equipment levels agreed for CIS states and Georgia at Tashkent, May 1992

	Tanks	Artillery	ACVs	Combat aircraft	Combat helicopters
Zone 2					
Russia					
active	4,275	3,825	9,945		
stored	825	910	155		
total	5,100	4,735	10,000	3,450	890
Ukraine					
active	2,850	2,850	4,000		
stored	550	300	700		
total	3,400	3,150	4,700	1,090	330
Belarus					
active	1,525	1,375	2,175		
stored	275	240	425		
total	1,800	1,615	2,600	260	80
Subtotal Zone 2					
active	8,650	8,050	16,120		
stored	1,650	1,450	1,280		
total	10,300	9,500	17,400	4,800	1,300
Flank					
Russia					
active	700	1,280	580	0	0
stored	600	400	800	0	0
total	1,300	1,680	1,380	0	0
Ukraine					
active	280	390	350	0	0
stored	400	500	0	0	0
total	680	890	350	0	0
Moldova					
active	210	250	210	50	50
stored	0	0	0	0	0
total	210	250	210	50	50
Georgia					
active	220	285	220	100	50
stored	0	0	0	0	0
total	220	285	220	100	50
Armenia					
active	220	285	220	100	50
stored	0	0	0	0	0
total	220	285	220	100	50
Azerbaijan					
active	220	285	220	100	50
stored	0	0	0	0	0
total	220	285	220	100	50
Subtotal Flank					
active	1,850	2,775	1,800	350	200
stored	1,000	900	800	0	0
total	2,850	3,675	2,600	350	200
Total Atlantic-to-Urals area					
active	10,500	10,825	17,920		
stored	2,650	2,350	2,080		
total	13,150	13,175	20,000	5,150	1,500

Table 4.3   CFE–IA Treaty national personnel limits

Armenia	N/A
Azerbaijan	N/A
Belarus	100,000
Belgium	70,000
Bulgaria	104,000
Canada	10,660
Czechoslovakia	140,000
Denmark	39,000
France	325,000
Georgia	N/A
Germany	345,000
Greece	158,621
Hungary	100,000
Iceland	0
Italy	315,000
Kazakhstan	0
Luxembourg	900
Moldova	N/A
Netherlands	80,000
Norway	32,000
Poland	234,000
Portugal	75,000
Romania	230,248
Russia	1,450,000
Spain	300,000
Turkey	530,000
Ukraine	450,000
UK	260,000
USA	250,000

Source: Concluding Act of the Negotiation on Personnel Strength of Conventional Armed Forces in Europe signed in Helsinki, 10 July 1992, Section II, para. 1, p. 5

wanted the Russian troops to leave immediately, while the Russians were short of housing for returning army families. Through the summer of 1992, Baltic governments appealed to the CSCE and the UN to pressure the Russians to withdraw more quickly and to provide observers to monitor the withdrawals. The Russians signed an agreement to withdraw troops from Lithuania by August 1993 in early September 1992, but agreements with Estonia and Latvia proved more difficult to reach. In October President Yeltsin temporarily suspended withdrawals from the Baltics, citing the lack of housing in Russia and denial of basic rights to Russian nationals in the Baltic states.[57]

In the context of the CFE agreement the equipment in the former Transcaucasian Military district of the USSR, comprising Georgia, Armenia and Azerbaijan, was divided on the basis of parity, but Russian troop withdrawals from the region were complicated by local conflicts: between Abkhazia and Georgia, between North Ossetia (in Georgia) and South

Ossetia (in Russia), and between Armenia and Azerbaijan over the disputed territory of Nagorny Karabakh. By 1993 the role of the Russian troops which dominated CIS peace-keeping operations in the region was looking more and more post-imperial in character, dedicated to the protection of Russian nationals and Russian national interests.[58]

The new Russian military doctrine articulated in May 1992 appeared to reflect a serious backsliding from Gorbachevian new thinking on defence issues. No longer invoking common security and defensive defence concepts, Russian doctrine now emphasized the growing threat from Islamic powers like Turkey and Iran, and potentially from former Soviet adversaries like Japan and Germany. It also expressed concern about the American military presence overseas and NATO's growing technological sophistication. The new doctrine identified an internal threat within the CIS, and defined the rules under which force might be applied in the successor states or in the Russian federation, namely, when the civil rights of Russians are threatened or when a foreign military power projects force close to Russian borders. Nevertheless, the September 1992 Russian Law on Defence decreed that the current 2.8 million Russian armed forces would be cut to 1.5 million (1% of the population) by 1995.[59]

Conclusion

In the late 1980s Gorbachev established a Politburo Arms Control Coordinating Committee.[60] Lev Zaykov, who initially chaired the group, explained its function as coordinating the activities of the Foreign Ministry, the Defence Ministry, the General Staff, the KGB, the military industrial council of the Council of Ministers and various other departments.[61] Zaykov claimed as important results of this coordination the ending of the war in Afghanistan, improved relations with other nations, the INF agreement, proposals for a 50 per cent cut in strategic armaments, the ending of secrecy about military data and unilateral cuts in Soviet forces. By mid-1991, however, it appeared that the coordinating group was functioning badly, if at all. One explanation might be the fluctuations in Gorbachev's attention to arms control issues as opposed to domestic problems. Certainly from November 1990 until April 1991 no one appeared to be seriously engaged in the CFE debate except military critics of the agreement. The CFE experience suggests that if the arms control diplomacy of the new Commonwealth of Independent States (or of the individual Russian, Ukrainian or other former Soviet republics) is to produce stabilizing agreements in the new Europe, the various branches of government in each state will have to coordinate their positions more carefully before beginning to negotiate with others.

In Gorbachev's time, many senior Soviet military officers claimed that too many concessions were made to the West at the expense of Soviet prestige and military security. Once the Conventional Armed Forces in Europe treaty was signed, the military expressed resentment about the greater material sacrifice made by the USSR to achieve an agreement and questioned whether they had been left with adequate resources to defend the political and territorial integrity of the country.[62] Opposition to Gorbachev among the General Staff was further exacerbated by the reduced status of the military in Soviet society, and of the USSR in the world, and finally as the USSR collapsed by the even more diminished state of Russia. From the military perspective, there were three serious problems, two of which related directly to Russia's position in Europe: the unification of Germany, especially the loss of GDR territory and assets to NATO; the collapse of the WTO and the turning of former allies to Western institutions for political, economic and military security; and the technological superiority of the US-led coalition forces in the 1991 Gulf war.

From 1985 to 1990, Gorbachev's arms control policy appeared highly successful in improving Soviet relations with the rest of Europe. Western commentators applauded Soviet negotiating tactics as open, cooperative and conciliatory, in contrast to the secret, confrontational and incremental policies of the Brezhnev years. But when it became clear in late 1990 and early 1991 that the terms of the CFE treaty were unacceptable to the General Staff, Soviet policy in Vienna began to appear inept rather than far-sighted. It was hardly useful for Foreign Ministry officials to negotiate an agreement with former adversaries that its own military found difficult to accept. Intra-governmental differences then had to be resolved under public, confidence-eroding scrutiny. If the CFE process was confidence-building from January 1989 until November 1990, it was certainly the opposite from November 1990 until June 1991.

Once the USSR broke up into its constituent republics, conventional arms control became increasingly irrelevant to the security problems that were erupting across Europe. And the Russian military resented the fact that the CFE treaty pushed them into sharing out the assets of the former Soviet armed forces and withdrawing troops not only from their former bloc allies but also from the territory of the other Soviet republics, the territory now known as the near abroad. Although the CFE treaty was eventually ratified by all parties in late October 1992 and came into force *de jure* in mid-November, doubts remain as to how strictly the provisions will be implemented by those former Soviet states heavily involved in local conflicts.

Notes

1. A Soviet posture to defend against NATO could of course be perceived as offensive by NATO. Documents discovered by the Bundeswehr in NVA files after German unification suggested to one German analyst highly offensive contingency plans for a WTO takeover of western Europe if a NATO attack looked

imminent. See Lothar Ruehl, 'Offensive defence in the Warsaw Pact', *Survival* vol. 33, no. 5 (September/October 1991), pp. 442–50.

2. US Senate Committee on Foreign Relations, *Documents on Germany 1944–1961* (Washington DC, December 1961), pp. 152–4. For a different perspective, see the discussion of this question by Hannes Adomeit in Chapter 2.

3. See for example draft treaties proposed on 29 July and 28 October 1955 in Senate Foreign Relations Committee, *Documents on Germany 1944–1961*, pp. 181, 195, 202.

4. Interviews with Canadian, US and British delegates to Vienna talks on MBFR. Leonid Brezhnev's acceptance of NATO's invitation to begin MBFR talks when it looked as if the Mansfield amendment might pass the Senate in 1971 was consistent with this view. On the conventional build-up in Europe in the late 1960s, see Michael MccGwire, *Military Objectives in Soviet Foreign Policy* (Washington DC, The Brookings Institution, 1987) p. 245.

5. The new Russian draft doctrine is outlined in *Voennya Mysl'* (*Military Thought*), May 1992. See Natalie Gross, 'Reflections on Russia's New Military Doctrine', *Jane's Intelligence Review*, August 1992, pp. 339–41.

6. Iona Andronov, deputy chairman of the Russian Supreme Soviet foreign affairs committee, cited by John Lloyd, 'Arms Treaty is a hostage to fortune', *Financial Times*, 4 January 1993.

7. On anxiety about German unification, see remarks by Dmitry Yazov reported in *The Daily Telegraph*, 15 May 1990; *Arms Control Reporter*, 1990, p. 407–B.367.

8. NATO communiqués, London, July 1990; Copenhagen, May–June 1991; Rome, December 1991.

9. Gorbachev's speech of 15 January 1986, reprinted in *Pravda*, 16 January 1986.

10. For Soviet thinking on nuclear weapons in the early Gorbachev years, see Stephen Shenfield, *The Nuclear Predicament: Explorations in Soviet Ideology* (London, Routledge and Kegan Paul/RIIA, 1987); for the later years see: Pavel Bayev, Sergei Karaganov, Victor Shein and Vitaly Zhurkin, *Tactical Nuclear Weapons in Europe: The Problem of Reduction and Elimination* (Moscow, NPA Publishing House, 1990), and 'Is a third zero attainable?', *International Affairs*, Moscow, 1990, no 4, pp. 3–12; Sergei Kortunov, 'Negotiating on Nuclear Weapons in Europe', *Survival*, vol. XXXIII, no. 1 (January–February 1991); Andrei A. Kokoshin, 'Arms Control: The View from Moscow', 'Arms Control: Thirty Years On', *Daedulus*, Cambridge, winter 1991, pp. 133–43; Michael MccGwire, *Perestroika and Soviet National Security* (Washington DC, The Brookings Institution, 1991); Rose Gotemoeller, *Future Options for the Soviet Nuclear Arsenal*, Rand Corporation, 1991.

11. Stephen Shenfield, *Minimum Nuclear Deterrence: The Debate Among Soviet Civilian Analysts* (Providence, Brown University Center for Foreign Policy Development, 1989); M. Moiseev, *Izvestiya*, 6 April 1991 (Union Edition), in *Foreign Broadcast Information Service* (hereafter *FBIS*) *Daily Report: Soviet Union*, no. 067, 8 April 1991, pp. 1–4; Boris Pyadyshev, 'View from Moscow: A Security Concept is Needed', *Pravda*, 12 January 1991, in *FBIS, Daily Report: Soviet Union*, no. 011, 16 January 1991, pp. 3–5.

12. For a comprehensive account of the INF negotiations, see Jonathan Dean, 'The INF Treaty Negotiations', *SIPRI Yearbook, 1988* (Oxford, Oxford University Press, 1988) pp. 377–406.

13. Gorbachev Council of Europe Speech, *Pravda*, 7 July 1989.
14. 'Text of Shevardnadze speech' Moscow, Tass, 5 June 1990, in *FBIS, Daily Report: Soviet Union*, no. 109, 6 June 1990, p. 5.
15. Steven E. Miller, 'Western Diplomacy and the Soviet Nuclear Legacy', *Survival*, vol. 34, no. 2 (Autumn 1992), pp. 3–27.
16. On Western understanding of how Soviet controls worked before the coup, see Bruce G. Blair, *The Logic of Accidental War*, Washington DC, The Brookings Institution, forthcoming; see also other sources in *Soviet Nuclear Fission*, no. 3, p. 5; on the loss of control by Gorbachev during the August 1991 coup, see World Briefs, 'Moscow Book Insists Gorbachev Lost Control of Nuclear Suitcase in Coup', *International Herald Tribune*, 24 August 1992.
17. Their concerns were heightened by alarming reports in the Russian press. Boris Gorbachev, *Komsomol'skaya pravda*, 4 February 1992; see also Jonathan Lyons, 'Moscow's Atom Bombs Built by Staff with Rubber Gloves', *Independent*, 7 February 1992.
18. Robert S. Norris, 'Where the Weapons are', *Bulletin of the Atomic Scientists*, November 1991, p. 49.
19. Text of Bush announcement, 27 September 1991, reprinted in *SIPRI Yearbook, 1992*, pp. 85–7.
20. Gorbachev statement, 5 October, reprinted in *SIPRI Yearbook, 1992*, pp. 87–8.
21. NATO Nuclear Planning Group communiqué, 18 October 1991, reprinted in *NATO Review*, December 1991.
22. Caspar Weinberger, cited in *Arms Control Today*, December 1992, p. 28.
23. The pros and cons of having to deal with one or more nuclear successor states are assessed in Kurt M. Campbell, Ashton B. Carter, Steven E. Miller and Charles A. Zraket, *Soviet Nuclear Fission: Control of the Nuclear Arsenal in a Disintegrating Soviet Union*, Harvard University, 1991, pp. 48–116.
24. Text of the Minsk Agreement establishing a Commonwealth of Independent States, 8 December 1991, reprinted in the *SIPRI Yearbook, 1992*, pp. 558–9.
25. John Palmer, 'EC Demands Slav Pledges', *Guardian*, 10 December 1991; James A. Baker, *America and the Collapse of the Soviet Empire: What has to be done*, Speech at Princeton University, 12 December 1991; Thomas Friedman, 'Baker Presents Steps to Aid Transition by Soviets', *New York Times*, 13 December 1991.
26. This is not stated in the Alma Ata agreement but was reported by several sources after that meeting. See David Remnick, 'Russia in the New Order: Still Unequal Equal', and 'Gorbachev Warns US on Transition', both in *International Herald Tribune*, 23 December 1991.
27. *SIPRI Yearbook, 1992*, pp. 560–62.
28. For speculation on how controls work since the collapse of the USSR, see Frank Umbach, 'Who Controls the Nuclear Arsenal of the CIS', unpublished paper, June 1992; Richard Garwin, 'Post-Soviet Nuclear Command and Security', *Arms Control Today*, January–February 1992, pp. 18–23.
29. Graham Allison, Ash Carter, Steven E. Miller, and Philip Zelikow (eds), *Cooperative Denuclearization: From Pledges to Deeds*, Harvard University (CSIA), 1993, pp. 46–8, n. 7.
30. Jacques Amalric, 'Le Kazakhstan conteste le monopole nucléaire de la Russie', *Le Monde*, 28 January 1992.

31. This is the definition of a nuclear weapons state in the 1968 NPT, Article IX para. 3. See *Treaty Series, Volume 729*, United Nations, New York.
32. Minsk Agreement on Strategic Forces, 30 December 1991, reprinted in *Arms Control Today*, January–February 1992, p. 39.
33. Valeri Davydov, 'Nyet to Full Battle Dress', *The Bulletin of the Atomic Scientists*, July–August 1992, pp. 33–7.
34. 'Ukrainian Criticizes Yeltsin for Negotiating on A-Arms', *New York Times*, 20 February 1992; Paul Quinn-Judge, 'Republics Want Own Arms Talks', *The Boston Globe*, 20 February 1992; Stephen Foye, 'Kazakh President on Disarmament', *Radio Free Europe/Radio Liberty Research Report*, 21 February 1992, p. 55.
35. *The Arms Control Reporter 1992*, pp. 611–D, 91–4.
35a. Jane Perlez 'Ukraine offers nuclear deal' *International Herald Tribune*, 27 July 1993.
36. Robert S. Norris, William M. Arkin, 'Nuclear Notebook: Estimated (Soviet) Nuclear Stockpile (July 1992)', *The Bulletin of the Atomic Scientists*, July–August 1992, p. 49.
37. For the texts of President Bush's State of the Union address on 28 January 1992 and President Yeltsin's response on 29 January, see *Survival*, Summer 1992, pp. 121–4.
38. *Joint Understanding*, office of the Press secretary, The White House, 17 June 1992. See also 'Impact of Bush–Yeltsin Strategic Arms Accord', *The Arms Control Association Fact Sheet*, 18 June 1992.
39. William C. Potter, 'Russia's Nuclear Entrepreneurs', *New York Times*, 7 November 1991.
40. Leyla Boulton, David Buchan and Patrick Blum, 'US to Fund Redundant Scientists in Russia', *Financial Times*, 18 February 1992.
41. 'Britain to Help Russians Dispose of Nuclear Arms', *Financial Times*, 28 February 1992.
42. Celeste Bohlen, *International Herald Tribune*, 4 August 1992.
43. For Akhromeev's view on asymmetries in the NATO–WTO balance, see Leslie Gelb, *New York Times*, 18 October 1985, cited in the *Arms Control Reporter*, 1985, p. 401–B–B.95.
44. General Yury Lebedev, in an interview with *Corriere della Sera*, 2 March 1987, cited in *NATO Report*, no. 2, March 1987.
45. For an account of the CSCE seminar on military doctrine held in Vienna, January–February 1990, see Appendix 13D, *SIPRI Yearbook, 1991*, pp. 501–11. On the October 1991 seminar, see: Austrian Committee for European Security and Cooperation, *Focus on Vienna*, no. 25 (November 1991); no. 26 (December 1991).
46. Mandate For Negotiation on Conventional Armed Forces in Europe, Annex II of the Concluding Document of the 1986–89 Vienna Meeting of Representatives of the Participating States of the Conference on Security and Cooperation in Europe; for a discussion of the contentious issues at the mandate talks see 'Conventional Arms Control in Europe: Problems and Prospects', *SIPRI Yearbook, 1988*, pp. 315–37; 'Conventional Arms Control in Europe', *SIPRI Yearbook, 1989*, pp. 369–402.
47. The groups of states at CFE coincide with the 1990 membership of NATO and of the former WTO, but will remain intact for the life of the treaty regardless of the

subsequent collapse of the WTO and the transformation of the USSR into fifteen independent states, ten of which lay within the Atlantic to Urals zone defined by the CFE mandate. Of these ten the three Baltic states opted for complete independence, and are not parties to CFE. The remaining seven adhered to CFE under a special agreement signed in mid-1992. See below.

48. *SIPRI Yearbook, 1991*, pp. 433–9.
49. On the 1990 intra–WTO negotiations see Pal Dunay, *The CFE Treaty History, Achievements and Shortcomings*, Peace Research Institute, Frankfurt, PRIF Reports, no. 24, 1991, pp. 15–23 *et passim*.
50. See for example Soviet military officers' reactions to Shevardnadze's resignation and the CFE treaty in 'Officers react to Shevardnadze resignation', *Krasnaya zvezda*, 22 December 1990, in *FBIS, Daily Report: Soviet Union*, no. 247, 24 December 1990, pp. 81–2.
51. Robert Mauthner, 'NATO Warns Soviets on Conventional Pact', *Financial Times*, 19 December 1990.
52. *Agreement on the Principles and Procedures of Implementation of the Treaty on Conventional Armed Forces in Europe*, with four protocols, and a *Joint Declaration in Relation to the Treaty on Conventional Armed Forces in Europe*, signed in Tashkent 15 May 1992 by Armenia, Azerbaijan, Belarus, Kazakhstan, Moldova, Russia, Ukraine and Georgia.
53. *Final Document of the Extraordinary Conference of the States Parties to the Treaty on Conventional Armed Forces in Europe*, 10 July 1992, Helsinki.
54. *The Concluding Act of the Negotiation on Personnel Strength of Conventional Armed Forces in Europe (CFE–1A)*, 10 July 1992, Helsinki. List of national personnel limits, Section II, para 1, p. 5.
55. On sharing the fleet, see *Financial Times*, 18 August 1992.
56. 'Transcaucasus Military District Transformed: New Commander Named', *RFE/RL Research Report*, 11 September 1992.
57. Tony Barber, 'Fury in Baltics over Yeltsin Troop Decree', *Independent*, 31 October 1992.
58. See 'Russia's Monroe Doctrine', in *The Economist Foreign Report*, 17 October 1992, pp. 2–3.
59. *Rossiiskaya gazeta*, 9 October 1992.
60. Harry Gelman, *Gorbachev and the Future of the Soviet Military Institution*, Adelphi Paper, no. 258, London, IISS, Spring 1991.
61. L. Zaykov in *Pravda*, 4 July 1990. Cited in *FBIS, Daily Report: Soviet Union*, no. 129–S, July 1990, pp. 2–4.
62. See in particular General Vladimir Lobov, *Voennaya mysl'*, 1991, no. 2.

5 The Settlement with Germany
Fred Oldenburg

The aims of Soviet policy towards Germany, 1945–84

The difficulty of determining the foreign policy intentions of the Soviet leadership was especially evident in regard to its policy towards Germany.[1] Its aims were formulated by a small circle of actors and obscured by a smokescreen of propaganda, and they remain a matter for debate to this day. It is only possible to guess at them in the light of events and outcomes. The latter, it must be said, seldom accorded with the intentions proclaimed by the foreign policy actors concerned.[2]

During the decade after 1945, it seems clear, however, that Moscow's first priority was almost certainly to control the whole of Germany, or at least not to surrender it to the West.[3] After the East German uprising in June 1953 and the Federal Republic's voluntary alignment with the Western bloc in 1955, this goal became patently unrealistic. Stalin's successors switched to a strategy that gambled on the advantages of a divided Germany, evidently hoping thereby to preserve the status quo in Europe, and especially Germany, until a new opportunity for expansion of influence presented itself. A second key goal of Soviet diplomacy during the entire postwar period was to ensure that Germany, whether united or divided, never again became a military threat.

The division of Germany into two separate states presented Moscow with new challenges and opportunities. The Soviet Union did everything it could to bind East Germany tightly into the bloc-wide party and state system, into the CMEA and into the Warsaw Pact; it endeavoured to counteract the magnetic attraction of the Federal Republic for the GDR by means of propaganda designed to isolate and attack the former, portraying it as a revanchist, revisionist successor to the Third Reich. This tactic was particularly marked in the period up to the late 1960s, and at the beginning of the 1980s. In general, the situation afforded the Soviet Union certain advantages in its relations with Germany and with the West. It was able to play on the desire of the German population to be united as a nation, and on the precarious position of a divided Berlin. Through propaganda and pressure on Bonn, Moscow continually strove to aggravate conflicts inside the Atlantic Alliance.

The legacy of the Brezhnev era

By the time Gorbachev became General Secretary of the Soviet Communist Party on 11 March 1985, the European members of the NATO alliance had been thoroughly alienated by Moscow, partly as a result of the deployment of Soviet medium-range missiles on the continent and the overall Soviet military build-up. The special relationship between the Soviet Union and West Germany that had been established by the Moscow treaty of 12 August 1970 had faded away.

Inside the Soviet bloc, discipline was becoming more difficult to maintain. At the end of November 1983, when Andropov's emissaries walked out of the East–West arms control negotiations in Geneva, the GDR began to distance itself from the Kremlin's position on political and security issues in a way it had never done before. The main explanation for its audacity was that East Berlin had become accustomed to depend on a life-support system provided by West Germany. At the beginning of the 1980s the GDR faced a series of severe balance-of-payments crises; without guarantees from the West German government it risked insolvency.[4] Along with Hungary, therefore, it resisted Soviet pressure and tacitly embraced the priority of national interests over bloc interests.[5] The Kremlin, distracted by three successive leadership crises, was incapable, before 1985, either of shaking free from its own fortress mentality and ending its isolation from the West, or of forcing its rebellious allies back into line.

Soviet relations with Germany had for a long time been organized on a firmly bilateral basis, linking Moscow separately with the two German states. Nevertheless, Soviet policy-makers were conscious of the peculiar intensity of intra-German relations, and their importance for the standing of the coalition government in Bonn from the end of the 1960s. Moscow, moreover, consistently asserted its rights and responsibilities in relation to Berlin and Germany as a whole in all the treaties it signed concerning central Europe.[6]

Gorbachev's new approach to Germany, 1985–6: old wine in new bottles

When Gorbachev took power, he did not at first appear to have in mind a fundamentally new approach to Germany. He set out to deal with the problems facing the socialist system step by step, modifying Moscow's style of control and cutting the costs of confrontation. The Kremlin was aware of the significance of the Federal Republic in its long-term reform strategy. Since the 1970s it had been the Soviet Union's most important Western trade partner and source of foreign currency. However, at the initial stage little diplomatic effort was directed at Bonn.

After several unsuccessful overtures had been made to West European capitals it became clear that the top priority in Gorbachev's foreign policy was to repair the relationship with the United States. The policy of the Federal Republic appeared in a number of respects close to the preferences of hawkish elements in the Reagan administration. Bonn had given its support to the Strategic Defence Initiative (SDI) programme – a further challenge to the already over-burdened Soviet economy – and it had begun to emphasize the need for a more active West German security policy. The trend to Europeanization in defence policy, which first became evident in closer Franco-German military cooperation, also strained relations between Moscow and Bonn.[7] Thus Soviet policy towards Germany in the first phase of Gorbachev's period in office, from 1985 until the middle of 1987, represented for the most part a continuation of the policy of neglect, or even punishment, that had been introduced in 1984.[8] The Soviet media in general reflected this coolness. The German question, journalists in Moscow continued to insist, was closed.[9] In the spring of 1986 Gorbachev refused to take part in any summit meetings with the Federal German leaders before the West German elections. There was reluctance in Moscow to lend any support to the CDU/CSU government, whose policy was perceived as subversive of the GDR and the existing European order. But by March 1986 Gorbachev appeared to have understood that Bonn could be a valuable partner for his reform plans, and he set about a gradual improvement of relations. Towards the end of 1986, several leading Soviet politicians were even, it seems, coming to understand that the division of Germany was unsustainable.[10]

The first signs of a thaw in relations with the Federal Republic were already visible at Foreign Minister Hans-Dietrich Genscher's July 1986 meeting with the Soviet leaders. But the initiative had come from the German side. Moscow's readiness to initial various agreements on this occasion may be attributed mainly to its interest in increasing imports of West German advanced engineering equipment in the aftermath of the Chernobyl disaster. In October 1986 Helmut Kohl publicly compared Gorbachev's propaganda skills to those of Joseph Goebbels, and claimed that the Kremlin was planning to interfere in the Federal Republic's internal politics before the Bundestag elections in January 1987, in order to prevent the CSU/CDU coalition gaining an absolute majority.[11]

There was another side to it. In 1985 Gorbachev had launched a drive to reinforce the crumbling socialist bloc. At first he seemed to be having some success, renovating the Warsaw Pact and revitalizing bilateral contacts. His strategy of intensified consultation, in which the smaller states had an increasingly important voice, served to make policy differences and ideological divergences less noticeable. For the USSR a socialist *Kleindeutschland* was only a second-best solution, but it was at least proof that Marxist-Leninist policies were sustainable in a developed industrial nation. The GDR was, moreover, the country's most important trading partner in the CMEA by far, and it provided a channel through which Western technology could filter eastwards: thanks to inter-German arrangements, the GDR was practically the eleventh member state of the European Community. Finally, East Berlin had been particularly energetic in fulfilling 'internationalist' commitments in the Third World, thereby relieving the USSR of some of the costs incurred there. If the situation is looked at in the perspective still dominant at that time in decision-making circles in Moscow, the GDR was undoubtedly a net asset for the Kremlin, in foreign policy terms and particularly as a geostrategic factor.

At the beginning of his period in office, Gorbachev himself apparently saw the GDR fulfilling an important function in the European architecture. Even before he took over as General Secretary, speaking at the CMEA summit in June 1984, he had spoken of the value of East German assistance to the USSR. The economic recovery concepts promoted by the East Germans seemed ready-made for his own initial strategy of 'discipline' and 'acceleration'.

East Berlin at first greeted Gorbachev's domestic and foreign policies with unconcealed relief. Yet it reacted nervously to the first signs of glasnost.[12] Discord between the allies was already apparent during the 11th SED party congress in April 1986: Honecker confidently denied any desire to imitate the Soviet reforms, limited though they were at that time.[13]

The beginning of the end, 1987–9

From the middle of 1987, electrified by Gorbachev's new style and his embracing of democratizing reform, West Germany was cautiously and gradually drawn into the developing East–West rapprochement. The Federal Republic began to commit itself to strengthening perestroika, to the policy advocated by Foreign Minister Genscher at Davos at the beginning of the year, when he argued for 'taking the first man of the USSR at his word'.[14]

It was the state visit of President Weizsäcker to the Soviet Union, from 6 to 11 July 1987 – the first visit by a German head of state for thirteen years – which signalled most clearly Moscow's readiness to lift bilateral relations out of the doldrums. A number of agreements that had been signed twelve months earlier were finally ratified in 1987. Both during his meeting with Weizsäcker and in his book *Perestroika*, published in that year, Gorbachev retracted the long-standing Soviet doctrine that the German states were destined to follow 'divergent paths'.[15] There were no concrete concessions on unification, but the Soviet leader acknowledged that in the long term ('a hundred years') history would decide the matter. Moreoever it became clear that Moscow was ready to make a new start in relations, and to put recent clashes behind it.

During the late summer of 1987 differences emerged between Moscow and Bonn over the intermediate-range nuclear forces in Europe (INF) negotiations.[16] It was when Bonn finally announced, on 26 August, that it was prepared to give up the German-owned Pershing missiles on its territory, that a decisive change seems to have occurred in Soviet perceptions of German policy.[17] The decision was greeted with unconcealed pleasure by the Soviet foreign ministry. Even conservative German politicians like Späth and Strauss began to be referred to in increasingly respectful terms in the Soviet press. At the end of 1987 they were invited to Moscow.

The atmosphere during Chancellor Kohl's working visit to Moscow from 24 to 27 October 1988, the first for five years, reflected the breakthrough that had occurred.[18] It was preceded by the awarding of 3 billion DM of credits to the USSR by a consortium of German banks. Some progress was made on the Berlin issue: already in June the Soviet side had finally conceded that the EC's area of competence extended as far as West Berlin. One year later, during his visit to Bonn, Gorbachev warned yet again against turning the Berlin question into a touchstone for bilateral relations. He was still not prepared, probably out of deference to the GDR, to endorse any formal change of status for West Berlin. However, the four days which Gorbachev spent in the Federal Republic from 12 to 15 June 1989 set the seal on the return of the special relationship. Indeed the agreements which were signed in Bonn, and especially the 'Joint Declaration' issued on 13 July 1989, established a completely new framework for German–Soviet relations.

All this created a corresponding unease in East Berlin, despite the efforts made to reassure it that the GDR's future was not in question. Moscow's pragmatic new foreign policy line, it was beginning to seem, would necessarily lead to a declining priority for the socialist bloc and in particular for the GDR. Internal changes such as the democratization moves announced at the January 1987 plenary session of the CPSU Central Committee had already aroused Honecker's concern.[19] From February 1987 the SED leadership was mobilizing opposition to Soviet perestroika in its regional and local organizations. At the same time Honecker demonstrated his sympathy for Gorbachev's opponents in the Soviet politburo. Neues Deutschland reprinted and endorsed Nina Andreeva's sensational attack on perestroika, published with Ligachev's backing in the conservative Moscow newspaper Sovetskaya Rossiya in March 1988.[20] When Gorbachev reasserted control, and progressive intellectuals began the process of reappraising the history of communism, the SED leadership reacted by banning liberal Soviet journals, and arranged to have copies of Gorbachev's speeches bought up by local Party organizations. From the spring of 1989 SED fears about the consequences of New Thinking increased dramatically. The leadership bluntly criticized Gorbachev's visit to West Germany in June 1989 and the 'Joint Declaration' signed during that visit as marking a deviation from his earlier strict insistence on the equal status of the two Germanies and a betrayal of 'the close socialist

links' that had existed up to then between Moscow and East Berlin – all for
the sake of economic and financial benefits from West Germany.[21]

These fears were not unjustified. When Gorbachev spoke out in April 1989
in favour of open multi-partyism in Hungary, and, at the end of August, lent
his approval to the non-communist-led government in Poland, he sealed the
fate of that apparent bulwark of late totalitarian stability, the GDR. Towards
the end of the summer of 1989 the pace of destabilization there accelerated.
Although the International Department of the CPSU Central Committee had
for a long time foreseen trouble, it had assumed that unrest in the GDR need
not be anticipated before the spring of 1991.[22] The Kremlin was probably just
as surprised as the West by what happened next.

After Hungary opened its border with Austria to the first wave of 7,000
East German refugees on 11 September 1989 without notifying Moscow in
advance, Soviet diplomats made it clear to the GDR leadership that Budapest
could not be brought to heel.[23] The situation quickly reached crisis point.
Thousands more GDR citizens began to emigrate by way of the Federal
German embassies in Prague and Warsaw, and many more joined the demon-
strations calling for radical changes inside their country. This all occurred
against the backdrop of a decision by the Soviet Defence Council in August
1989 to keep Soviet troops out of domestic political conflicts in Central-East
European countries.[24] During the disturbances on the streets of the GDR, for
example during the mass demonstration in Leipzig on 9 October 1989,
corresponding instructions were given to Soviet military and KGB units.[25]

By the autumn of 1989 the Brezhnev Doctrine was thus to all intents and
purposes dead, even for the strategically important GDR.[26] Horst Teltschik,
Helmut Kohl's foreign policy adviser, believes that Gorbachev assured the
German Chancellor in October 1988 and June 1989 that he would hold back
from any military intervention in Germany.[27] It is striking that Egon Krenz,
who succeeded Honecker on 18 October 1989, and who previously held the
post of Central Committee Secretary for Defence Matters, claims that the
GDR leadership was not aware of any such order for Soviet restraint.[28]

On 7 October, after attending the GDR's fortieth-anniversary celebrations, Gorbachev held talks with the SED Politburo behind closed doors at
Niederschönhausen Castle. For the first time, the CPSU General Secretary
explicitly distanced himself from Honecker's policies and declared: 'Reality
punishes latecomers.'[29] Gorbachev apparently believed that the SED could
retain power if it renovated its leadership with perestroika supporters. Now
at last radical change came onto the agenda even of the SED Politburo. The
ailing Honecker was deposed on 18 October 1989.

Krenz subsequently claimed that at his meeting with Gorbachev in Moscow on 1 November 1989, after Honecker's fall, both of them still considered
the GDR reformable, contrary to what Shevardnadze and others later asserted concerning Gorbachev's view at the time.[30] Krenz pointed out to
Gorbachev that 'the GDR was a child of the Soviet Union' and that it was

important to know whether the USSR would continue to acknowledge its paternity. 'Gorbachev agreed', Krenz reported, 'and said that "all his counterparts abroad had emphasized that no serious politician in the world could envisage a united Germany".'[31] Krenz's notes of his conversation with Gorbachev record that the Soviet leader expressly called for 'better coordination of the triangular relationship between the GDR, FRG and USSR'.

Krenz related that in the course of their conversation Gorbachev also stressed, however, that the GDR should find a way of enabling people to visit their relatives. The government in Berlin, which was under pressure not only from the streets, but also from a party organization that was by now in complete turmoil, not to mention from the Czech Foreign Ministry because of the besieging of the embassies in Prague, felt it necessary to open a safety-valve. By drastically easing East–West travel restrictions, it hoped to blunt the edge of unrest among the population. On 9 November 1989 the Berlin wall was opened.

There is evidence to suggest that this step was unintentional, and that it flowed from confusion among the leadership. Apparently neither the Soviet embassy nor the Soviet leaders were informed in advance.[32] Krenz, however, had proceeded on the assumption that by opening the wall he was merely anticipating the travel regulations agreed with the Soviet authorities. He was all the more surprised when, on the morning of 10 November 1989, shortly after 9 o'clock, the Soviet ambassador Kochemasov rang to inform him of Moscow's concern 'about how the situation at the Berlin Wall developed last night'.[33] When Krenz retorted that the opening of the border in Berlin could only have been prevented by military means, Kochemasov at first hesitated, and then agreed.

Despite the dramatic shift of mood among the GDR population – people cherished only one, albeit impractical goal: to live like their West German 'brothers and sisters' – a significant part of the official world in Moscow still appeared to harbour the illusion that a reformed socialist GDR could remain, anchored in a continuing socialist community.[34] Thus Shevardnadze understood that the German question was on the move, but at first he brusquely rejected even the gradualist ten-point plan put forward by Chancellor Kohl, which assumed that German unification would take five to ten years to come about. At the beginning of December Gorbachev stated at a meeting with Genscher that the Soviet Union regarded the GDR as 'a reliable ally and an important guarantor of freedom and stability in Europe'.[35] The Soviet leadership even tried to reassert its four-power rights, together with France and the United Kingdom, who were also made uneasy by the speed of change in Germany. It managed to convoke a meeting of ambassadors from the four powers in the control commission building, in order, as TASS put it, to consult over the 'control mechanisms that had been created by the former members of the anti-Hitler coalition'.[36] However the Western powers limited the scope of the talks from the outset, focusing strictly on the Berlin problem.

On the streets of the GDR, socialist renewal slogans increasingly gave way after the end of November 1989 to the slogan 'We are one people'. This forced Moscow to reassess the situation radically and to adopt a policy of active crisis management.[37]

'Agreement in principle' to German unity, January to July 1990

The opening of the border with the West had rendered the situation in the GDR hopelessly unstable by the beginning of 1990.[38] Making a virtue of necessity, Gorbachev adopted the role of promoter of German unity. On 30 January, immediately before his talks with the new GDR Prime Minister Hans Modrow, he publicly announced that the Soviet Union had nothing 'in principle' against German unification.[39] Another breakthrough occurred at his meeting with Chancellor Kohl on 10 February 1990 when the Soviet Union conceded to the Germans the unconditional right to unification. They themselves, moreover, had the job of deciding, Gorbachev declared, on 'the constitutional forms, the time, the pace and the conditions for bringing about their unity'.[40] At the same time, however, Gorbachev linked the solution of the German question to external conditions. European unity must be forwarded, account must be taken of 'the security and interests not only of Germany's neighbours but also of all the other European states and of the whole world'. In addition, the Soviet Union pressed for Bonn to take on the GDR's existing export commitments.

Cooperation in overcoming supply bottlenecks, and compensation for economic losses incurred by giving up the GDR,[41] were important themes in the talks with Bonn, but at first Moscow's primary concerns were political and security ones. The Soviet leadership was not prepared to accept any dramatic shift in the balance of power in favour of the West as a result of unification; as well as sizeable financial benefits, it sought help from Bonn in safeguarding its position in Europe. In both bilateral and multilateral forums the main Soviet priorities were: preventing the extension of NATO to East German territory; ensuring that a united Germany abided by the nuclear non-proliferation treaty and renounced all nuclear, chemical and biological weapons; drastically reducing the strength of the federal German army; drawing up a treaty to settle the western and thus also indirectly the eastern borders of Poland; having the GDR's economic commitments taken over wholesale by the Federal Republic; and asking the new Germany to subsidize generously the withdrawal of Soviet troops over a five-year period.

After February 1990 it became increasingly evident that the Soviet leadership wanted to use the German desire for unification as a lever to construct a pan-European security system, although it appeared to have no clear conception of the Federal Republic's future relationship to the existing alliances, far less of the shape of a comprehensive security arrangement. Some leading

Soviet spokesmen, particularly in the Central Committee and the armed forces, promoted the idea of neutralization, others favoured dual membership for Germany in both alliances, or at least keeping East Germany's territory under the jurisdiction of the Warsaw Pact. At meetings with Genscher in Windhoek and Lisbon, Shevardnadze suggested that Germany and the USSR conclude a peace treaty and that they jointly revise the forty-five-year-old Potsdam agreement.[42] In public he continued to declare his resistance to the idea of the whole of Germany being included in NATO. By the time of the Warsaw Pact foreign ministers' conference in Prague at the end of March, however, it was clear that even Germany's eastern neighbours were interested in binding the new Germany into the Western alliance.[43] The decisive victory of the CDU in the East German elections on 18 March 1990 must have brought home to Moscow just how bad a hand it held in the unification poker game. It reacted, first, by seeking ways of slowing up unification, and, second, by redoubling its efforts to extract benefits for the Soviet Union from the process.[44] Even in April and May 1990 certain Soviet military leaders – the armed forces stationed in East Germany amounted to over 337,000 men – still felt that they could dictate conditions for unification. There were those in the CPSU Central Committee, too, who hoped that the GDR could be saved by combining the efforts of the SPD and the Greens in the West, and the PDS (Party of Democratic Socialism, the reformed SED) and civic movements in the East.

The external aspects of German unification were the subject of the Two-plus-Four talks involving the two German states, the USA, UK, France and the USSR, proposed by the United States and agreed on in Ottawa in mid-February 1990. At the first full session of the talks, in Bonn on 5 May 1990, Shevardnadze suggested a temporary decoupling of the internal and external aspects of unification, implying a prolongation of the allies' four-power rights.[45] However, he had backed down by the time of his meeting with Genscher in Geneva on 24 May. At that time the Soviet Union was already on the verge of bankruptcy, and on 5 May it asked for 20 billion dollars from the Federal Republic of Germany. During negotiations with Prime Minister Ryzhkov in Moscow on 13 May,[46] the Federal Chancellor's adviser, Horst Teltschik, was handed Soviet requests for an unsecured credit of around 1.5 to 2 billion roubles and a long-term credit of around 10 to 15 fifteen billion roubles. Teltschik responded that the Federal Republic was already prepared to take over the GDR's existing economic obligations. Any further support for the USSR, he argued, had to be understood as part of the total package for the resolving the German question. Thus on 24 May the process of constructing that package took another implicit step forward.

A more difficult issue was the future alliance status of Germany. It was only after intense diplomatic activity on the part of the United States and its allies that Soviet resistance to the enlarged Federal Republic's inclusion in NATO was finally overcome. On 18 May 1990, in Moscow, Baker presented a nine-point plan for a settlement. At first it was received with little enthusi-asm, although Baker, with Bonn's agreement, held out important concessions to Moscow. Gorbachev was coming under increasing pressure from domestic critics, particularly in the Soviet military, and he evidently wished to exploit last-minute opportunities to gain whatever advantages could be extracted. At first he remained outwardly unyielding. Even at a summit meeting with George Bush at the end of May, there was no public sign of a breakthrough on the German question. Nevertheless, in Washington both sides agreed that progress on the internal and external aspects of German unification should be synchronized, and it was the American Secretary of State's nine-point plan for a settlement that was to form the basis of the position adopted by a NATO conference held in London at the beginning of July 1990. Indeed it underpinned the final compromises struck with Gorbachev in Moscow and Arkhyz.

At the second round of Two-plus-Four talks, held in East Berlin on 22 June, Shevardnadze once again put the Western side's firmness of purpose to the test, proposing a detailed Soviet draft, agreed in the Politburo, for a final international settlement. He now insisted on a five-year transition period, during which any previous obligations entered into by the two German states – for example regarding their respective memberships of NATO and the Warsaw Pact, and regarding the rights of the four powers – should continue in force. In addition, the Soviet Foreign Minister proposed limiting German armed forces to a maximum of 250,000. The Western states unanimously rejected these suggestions, and for a time it looked as if the possibility of agreement was slipping away.

It was in these circumstances that the Soviet President decided to try for a breakthrough in the form of a direct understanding with Germany. This was only possible because at the 28th CPSU Congress held during the first half of July he and his supporters had managed to weather a barrage of criticism provoked by the 'loss' of Eastern Europe and East Germany. In addition, Gorbachev had succeeded in temporarily paralysing the Party leadership by almost completely replacing it.[47] The Gorbachev line received a further boost when NATO leaders, meeting in London on 5–6 July, agreed on further disarmament initiatives and a revision of military strategy that implied the end of East–West confrontation.[48] What is more, at the conference of Euro-pean Community heads of state and government in Dublin (25–6 June), and at the world economic summit in Houston (9–11 July), the leaders of the advanced industrialized countries, urged on by President Mitterrand and Chancellor Kohl, lent their support to the idea of providing large-scale assistance to the Soviet economy. At the beginning of July Kohl also took steps to ensure that the USSR was granted an unsecured credit of 5 billion DM from German banks, guaranteed by the German government. Moscow laid claim to the full amount only a few days later.

The Arkhyz compromise

Gorbachev's meetings with Chancellor Kohl on 15–16 July 1990, in Moscow and immediately afterwards in the Caucasus, marked the culmination of the negotiating process.[49] In an unexpected concession, made during the first session in the Kremlin, the Soviet President agreed that Germany could after all remain in NATO. In addition he agreed that the final document of the Two-plus-Four negotiations should cancel forthwith all four-power rights. In exchange Gorbachev requested agreement on a separate bilateral treaty with Bonn concerning the Soviet troops still remaining in East Germany. During the second session of talks, in Arkhyz, he proposed a departure deadline three to four years away for some of the Soviet troops and five to seven years away for the remainder. The Germans, for their part, promised to pay a share of the transport and resettlement costs of the Soviet units. Gorbachev emphasized that, even in the future, NATO structures, and especially nuclear systems, should not be located on former GDR territory. The Germans, however, at first resisted any special conditions being applied to their country.

The Soviet–German compromise that was finally negotiated meant that a united, sovereign Germany could be a member of NATO and that Soviet troops would pull out of the former East Germany within four years at the most. In return the Germans promised that they would reduce their forces by 42–45 per cent; that no NATO installations would be located on former East German territory; that only German troops would be stationed on former East German territory, no foreign troops or nuclear weapons. Gorbachev called this last promise a precondition for 'maintaining the trust which had grown up'. The agreement was endorsed by the other Two-plus-Four states on the following day, 17 July, in the presence of Polish Foreign Minister Skubiszewski. The latter expressed satisfaction with the agreement that a German–Polish border treaty should be concluded immediately after German unity was achieved.[50] From the start, it was agreed that any settlement would have to fit into a continent-wide framework: it would be incorporated in a European 'charter' to be ratified at the next CSCE conference in Paris. German unification, it was understood, would take place within a new European architecture.

After Arkhyz hard negotiations got under way over the details of the treaty on partnership, the agreement on troop stationing and the transition arrangements. At times it seemed as if Gorbachev would retract the compromise already reached if the Germans did not comply with his financial proposals. Moscow even raised the issue of four-power rights on the day of unification.[51] Shevardnadze, who referred on several occasions to the pressure that was being applied to him by the Soviet military, was clearly playing on German interest in a rapid settlement. The Soviet side insisted that a non-aggression clause be included in the partnership treaty, ruling out active

German participation on the side of the Western alliance in the event of war against the USSR. The Germans gave way on this point in view of the presence of similar undertakings in existing treaties, and in view of the defensive character of NATO military strategy.[52] However, when at the last minute Soviet diplomats tried to persuade the Germans to renounce the stationing of heavy artillery and aircraft on East German territory, this was refused.

A further point of disagreement was the size of the compensation to be given for Soviet troop withdrawals. As late as 7 September Gorbachev spoke on the telephone to Chancellor Kohl (for the first time since their July meeting), requesting approximately 11 billion DM to build living accommodation for returning officers, and additional payments for maintaining and resettling troops whose departure was delayed.[53] Two days before the final meeting of the six foreign ministers in September, Gorbachev again telephoned the Federal Chancellor to indicate that the negotiation process would have to begin all over again if Bonn could not come up with 15 billion DM for the withdrawal of Soviet troops. In the face of pressure, Kohl offered an interest-free credit of 3 billion DM,[54] in addition to the 12 billion DM already promised. This was sufficient to save the agreement.

The final settlement

At the last Two-plus-Four meeting, in Moscow on 12 September 1990, the 'treaty on the final settlement for Germany' was signed. In it a united Germany renounced all territorial claims and declared itself ready to sign a corresponding treaty with Poland. It confirmed its existing undertakings not to manufacture, possess or deploy nuclear, biological and chemical weapons. German troops were to be cut by over 42 per cent, to a total of 370,000, of which a maximum of 345,000 were to be ground and air forces. Until the pullout of Soviet troops was completed, only forces from the German territorial army not integrated into alliance structures would be stationed on former East German territory. Once all Soviet troops had been withdrawn, German forces that had been integrated into NATO could also be deployed there, but without nuclear-weapon delivery systems. Foreign forces could not be transferred to the new federal Länder. The conclusion of the treaty brought an end to four-power rights, and Germany received accordingly 'full sovereignty over its internal and external affairs' (Article 7).[55]

The unification of the two German states finally took place on 3 October. Additional agreements were signed between Bonn and Moscow: the Treaty on Good-neighbourliness, Partnership and Cooperation; the Treaty on the Stationing and Withdrawal of Troops; the Transition Treaty; and a Treaty on Wide- ranging Economic, Industrial, Scientific and Technological Cooperation.[56]

The Good-neighbourliness Treaty, signed on 9 November, contained passages similar to the Two-plus-Four documents. Germany also committed itself to help the Soviet Union to develop cooperation with 'international, especially European, organizations',[57] and the first practical effects of this were to be seen during the preparations for the Group of Seven economic summit in London in 1991. From a political and security point of view, the most important part was Article 3, where the two sides comprehensively renounced the use of force in relations with each other. Nine articles in the Transition Treaty concluded on 9 October settled, among other things, responsibility for the costs of keeping Soviet soldiers on the territory of the five new Länder until the withdrawal deadline, finally set for the end of 1994, as well as the costs of transporting them home and of reintegrating them into society.[58]

Difficulties in the ratification process

In July 1990 Gorbachev still seems to have been able to cope with domestic political pressures. He no doubt hoped that German financial assistance would at least help him to cope with the hardships of the coming winter. Conservative elements, however, redoubled their efforts to obstruct attempts at reform, especially moves towards a market economy. The faltering of perestroika was already evident in the autumn of 1990, when the Soviet–German agreements were being concluded. Even before Gorbachev signed the Good-neighbourliness and Partnership Treaty in Bonn in November, Shevardnadze was forced into an emotional defence of his policy in the face of mounting criticism from the army.[59] Despite Moscow's earlier official announcement that this problem had been resolved, several military deputies resurrected the reparations issue. In the Foreign Relations Committee of the Supreme Soviet a number of conservative representatives of the armed forces, backed behind the scenes by Central Committee Secretary Valentin Falin and others, sought to have the German treaties rejected. Deputy Foreign Minister Kvitsinsky was obliged to issue warnings about the consequences of non-ratification of the agreements; the negotiations would have to be conducted all over again, he argued, and in circumstances far less advantageous to the Soviet Union. Even so, the Supreme Soviet at first ratified only the Two-plus-Four and the Partnership treaties, on 4 March 1991. The Transition Treaty and the Troops Treaty were only approved in principle, because it was hoped, particularly in military circles, that renewed pressure on the West German government might lead to it offering improved financial terms.[60]

In mid-March 1991 the German Foreign Minister flew to Moscow to bolster Gorbachev's position. Genscher promised that Germany would argue the case for building cooperation between the USSR and the European Community, and other European institutions. This was followed by a meeting between Chancellor Kohl and the Soviet President in Kiev to prepare for the London economic summit. In a personal letter to the Chancellor in

March, President Gorbachev had requested an additional credit of 20 billion DM, without success. Nevertheless, the Supreme Soviet finally ratified the two remaining treaties, on 2 April 1991. (See the Appendix to this chapter, 'The Price of Unity'.)

Soviet–German relations between the Moscow coup and the dissolution of the USSR

In the period following Gorbachev's first visit to the Federal Republic, in June 1989, better relations between Moscow and Bonn were reinforced by shifts in the Soviet Union's perceptions of its interests, by changes in the international context, and by the developing personal relationships between Gorbachev and Kohl, Shevardnadze and Genscher. After the collapse of the GDR, Gorbachev increasingly looked to the Federal Republic for help in his efforts to sustain gradual change in the Soviet system, while staving off its collapse, and preventing the disintegration of the USSR. The Germans for their part preferred a transformation that was at least calculable to the break-up of the union. After the attempted *coup d'état* in August 1991, Bonn was forced to recognize very swiftly that it would have to deal with the republics as well as the Union. Genscher set out on a fact-finding mission in autumn 1991 which took him first to Kiev and Alma-Ata, and only then to Moscow. Germany was by now pursuing a double strategy: not neglecting the centre, but according a new importance to the increasingly independent new centres of power. Nevertheless, Bonn was reluctant to abandon the union. It refused at first to acknowledge officially that the December 1991 agreement in Brest between the Slavic republics, setting up the Commonwealth of Independent States, marked the demise of the Soviet state. It insisted on waiting until Gorbachev and Yeltsin met and agreed the end of the Soviet Union.

The relationship between Russia and Germany: a contradictory new start

As he set out on his first foreign trip since the failed August coup, in November 1991, Yeltsin looked to Germany as Russia's most important European partner. Yet his visit to Bonn left an ambivalent impression. Apart from Moscow's uncooperative reaction to the issuing of a warrant for the arrest of former SED General Secretary Erich Honecker by the Berlin Supreme Court – Yeltsin insisted that the final responsibility was still Gorbachev's – there was friction over treatment of the Volga Germans. The other immediate outstanding issue was that of troop withdrawals.

The fate of the Volga Germans

At the beginning of the Second World War, Stalin abruptly deported beyond the Urals the German communities settled along the Volga and in the Crimea. In the years of detente the fate of these people had become a permanent issue in Soviet–German diplomacy. Under Brezhnev and Gorbachev, the number of emigration permits issued to Soviet Germans was always regarded as an indicator of the warmth of relations between Moscow and Bonn. At the lowest point, in 1985, only 460 Germans were permitted to emigrate to the Federal Republic, as against 148,000 in 1990 and 142,000 in 1991.

On various occasions after 1987 the German Foreign Minister was told that the Soviet Germans would be permitted to resettle along the Volga, in order to keep them within the country. Indeed, in Bonn in November 1991, Yeltsin even suggested setting up an autonomous Volga republic (albeit partly on land previously used for military exercises). At the beginning of 1992, however, as the Russian president's popularity began to wane, so his position shifted. When he visited Saratov and Engels on the Volga, former centres of German settlement, he was met by protestors bearing the slogans 'Germans yes, autonomy no!'. Subsequently Yeltsin stated that only areas in which not less that 90 per cent of the population were of German nationality should be eligible for autonomy, and that Germans should only settle in uninhabited regions or in regions where no protest was anticipated. Foreign Minister Kozyrev confirmed during a visit to Bonn on 15 January 1992 that autonomous areas would be set up gradually. It seems safe to assume that the Russian government will be in no position to satisfy the hopes which have been kindled in Bonn and in the regions of the former USSR where Germans live in exile.

As early as the end of 1991 hundreds of thousands of Soviet Germans had applied for exit visas. In the Federal Republic of Germany, not surprisingly, there was great apprehension about a possible massive wave of immigration. In 1990–91, 600,000 German settlers had already arrived from the USSR and Eastern Europe. Bonn's policy was to encourage the development of areas of settlement for Germans in Russia, and more than 100 separate locations were identified. It provided 100 million DM to support the establishing of these settlements in 1991 and around 200 million DM in 1992. Yeltsin, on the other hand, seemed to be tending towards the setting up of larger 'German national regions' near Saratov and Volgograd. The ongoing economic decline of Russia and the national tensions there and in Kazakhstan and Kyrgyzstan subsequently gave rise to the expectation that more than one million Germans in the former Soviet Union would leave for Germany in the near future.

Troop withdrawals

The withdrawal of Soviet soldiers stationed on former GDR territory, by contrast, went relatively smoothly and according to plan: 337,800 soldiers were involved, along with 44,700 civilian employees and 163,000 dependants. Around 160,000 soldiers and officers, as well as dependants and civilians, left the five new federal Länder during 1991. Problems had arisen in the early phase of the withdrawals, because Warsaw suddenly demanded financial compensation for allowing transport across Polish territory,[61] and because, for reasons of cost, the Soviet authorities had passed over German contractors when commissioning work on the German-financed building of homes for returning troops.

Complications were also caused by the break-up of the Soviet Union, since the agreements reached in 1990 assumed that the forces would withdraw mainly to Belarus and Ukraine. According to the 1990 agreements, 36,000 homes for returning families were to be built, with German financial support of 7.8 billion DM. At the beginning of January 1992 only one of the thirty-three planned accommodation complexes was ready for occupation. The separate former Soviet republics seemed to be ill-equipped to take on the resettlement role; disputes also broke out over the distribution of scarce materials.

The Soviet military authorities did manage to limit the problem of desertion among troops stationed in Germany, a problem which had grown to alarming proportions in the spring of 1991, by enforcing stricter supervision and by confining troops to barracks. In the period up to the end of December 1991 there were a mere 250 known cases of desertion.[62] There was, however, an increase in arms-dealing by poorly paid Soviet soldiers. Already in December 1990 the military department office of the public prosecution service had drawn attention to an upsurge in crime in army supply units.[63] As ethnic tensions worsened and the material prospects of the ex-Soviet military deteriorated, conditions were created for greater friction between the remaining ex-Soviet forces and the local population.

Summary and prospects

The spread and the collapse of the Soviet empire were inseparable from the division and the reuniting of Europe, and the division and reuniting of Germany was at the centre of the process. Moreover, there is no doubt that after unification Germany was central to Moscow's hopes for finding a new role in Europe.

In this chapter the emphasis has been on the interplay of Soviet domestic and foreign policy: Gorbachev's policy towards Germany between 1985 and 1991 was clearly primarily determined by the growing internal problems of the regime.[64] But the Soviet Union's external behaviour cannot be conceived of simply as an inevitable consequence of the crisis of its social system. The conciliatory (often, some said, excessively conciliatory) stance adopted towards Moscow during the Brezhnev period by the West European states, and especially by the Federal Republic of Germany, had the effect of eroding the sense of a threat from their direction, and in particular breaking down the image of a hostile, aggressive Germany. The Ostpolitik of Brandt and his successors, the signing of the 1970 Moscow Treaty, the relative consistency of the West German approach, and Bonn's willingness to back up its assurances with solid economic support, all gave Gorbachev grounds to hope that he could count on a powerful source of external backing for his domestic and foreign policy reforms.[65] Concern remained, of course, about the fate of the GDR, but there was a tendency in Moscow to make that less of an overriding preoccupation than in the past, and to put more responsibility for it on the shoulders of Honecker and Krenz.

Equally important, of course, was the vigorous strategy adopted by the Reagan and Bush administrations and more widely by the Western alliance: on the one hand they wielded sticks which intensified the Soviet economic crisis; on the other they subsequently offered enough carrots to provide an incentive for 'civilized' behaviour. In the final analysis, the strength of the West, not least its nuclear strength, meant that compromise was the only way forward for Moscow.

Finally, the assurances given to the Soviet Union about its new place in the European architecture during the Two-plus-Four talks, and the declarations made in the Charter of Paris at the end of 1990 made it easier for the country to accept the loss of the outer empire and the reunification of Germany. Its leaders could even accept that a united Germany's new economic potential might be more advantageous to the Soviet economy than that of the GDR on its own.

Conservative elements in the Soviet Communist Party, the military and the KGB were politicized and divided by the new foreign policy. Their resistance to German unity came to a head just at the moment when Gorbachev had given his blessing, in September 1990, to the new settlement. But the counter-revolution that began in autumn 1990 cannot really be blamed primarily on Moscow's foreign policy concessions. Gorbachev's 'swing to the right' was brought about principally by internal political setbacks, by the failure of economic reform and by the growing crisis over the nationality question. The collapse and break-up of the USSR was certainly not a goal of Western strategy. Indeed the West, in particular the United States and the Federal Republic of Germany, had supported the preservation of an albeit thoroughly reformed USSR right up to the end, for fear of the consequences of dissolution. In the case of Germany, concern over the fate of the treaties that had been concluded with Moscow, over the orderly withdrawal of Soviet troops and over debt problems played a major role.

Russia and Germany have once again returned as autonomous actors in history. This evokes mixed feelings in Europe. But national interests coincide: the emergence of a democratic, economically successful Russia will be to the benefit of all the countries on the continent.[66] Now that bipolarity, which repressed old historical conflicts, has been replaced by an unstable multipolarity, which is capable of allowing these conflicts and contradictions to break out again in a destructive form, the challenge is to maintain a united and constructive policy towards the East. Here Germany's role will continue to be a central one.

Appendix: The price of unity

While official statements from Moscow set the total of German payments to the Soviet Union associated with the settlement at 15 billion DM,[67] Bonn's payments and commitments since 1989, and its planned commitments until 1994, probably come to over 75 billion DM. It would be misleading, of course, to treat all this simply as 'payment for unification': there was undoubtedly a pressing concern in Bonn, for instance, to bolster the threatened market for East German goods. In calculating the price paid by Germany for its settlement with Moscow, care must be taken to distinguish between direct, indirect and consequential costs, and between financial, humanitarian and technical assistance on the one hand, and normal Soviet–German economic relations on the other.[68]

1 The 'direct costs' of German unity included:
    (a) Grants or gratis goods of 13.5 billion DM. The largest item was 7.8 billion DM, in the framework of the Transition Treaty, for the building of 36,000 homes for returning military personnel. Three billion DM were to be paid for the maintenance and withdrawal of Soviet troops. Two hundred million DM were agreed for retraining and education. The 13.5 billion DM also included a cost to the German budget of 1.5 billion DM for interest forgone on a five-year credit of 3 billion DM for financing the Soviet part of the costs of maintenance and withdrawal.
    (b) Over and above this, Bonn paid 0.7 billion DM in 1990 for maintenance of Soviet troops. A further 2 billion DM (not included in the 13.5 billion DM direct costs mentioned above) were to be spent during the next four years on maintenance of Soviet army property.
2 To these payments had to be added the credit guarantees and Hermes guarantees (government guarantees for public credits) indirectly connected with reunification. It would be fair to regard them as directed towards promoting exports to the USSR in order to sustain the viability of East German businesses.
    (a) Bonn took over the GDR's commitment to balance a 6.5 billion

rouble (15.2 billion DM) trade deficit with the USSR, including accrued interest costs of 1.9 billion DM. This meant a credit stretching over four or five years. Orders to the value of 10 billion DM were placed under this heading during 1991; and to the value of 7.2 billion DM during the first part of 1992. Around 150,000 jobs in the former GDR were estimated to depend on exports to the former Soviet Union.

(b) The indirect costs also included a 5 billion DM guarantee for unsecured debt granted in July 1990 (in connection with Kohl's trip to Moscow and Arkhyz), which allowed a twelve-year extension, of which six years were interest-free.[69]

3 A clear distinction must be made between these payments and the export guarantees given since 1989 to the USSR in the framework of normal German–Soviet economic relations, a total of 11.7 billion DM for capital and 4.9 billion DM to cover interest payments; 3.4 billion DM was also set aside for the continued development of natural gas and mineral deposits. As for wider German support for the Soviet economy, including humanitarian and technical aid, this amounted to around 27.7 billion ecus. German payments accounted for more than 57 per cent of total Western financial commitments up to the end of 1991.

Notes

1. For the first thorough analysis of recent Soviet policy towards Germany, linking domestic and foreign policy aspects, see H. Adomeit, 'Gorbachev and German Unification: Revision of Thinking', *Problems of Communism*, vol. 39, no. 4 (July–August 1990), pp. 1–23; F.S. Larrabee, 'The New Soviet Approach to Europe', in Nils H. Wessels (ed.), *The New Europe: Revolutions in East–West Relations* (New York, The Academy of Political Sciences, 1991), pp. 1–25; B. Meissner, 'Das "neue Denken" Gorbatschows und die Wende in der sowjetischen Deutschlandpolitik', in Werner Weidenfeld (ed.), *Die Deutschen und die Architektur des europäischen Hauses*, (Cologne, Wissenschaft und Politik, 1990), pp. 53–79; B. Meissner, 'Die Wechselbeziehungen zwischen der Innen– und Außenpolitik Gorbatschows', in *Sowjetpolitik unter Gorbatschow. Die Innen– und Außenpolitik der UdSSR 1985–1990* Proceedings of the Göttingen Working Group, vol. 7, with contributions by H. Brahm et al., (Berlin, Duncker und Humbolt, 1991), pp. 87–114; G. Wettig, *Changes in Soviet Policy towards the West* (London, Pinter, 1991).

2. On Soviet foreign policy in general, see especially F. J. Fleron, E. P. Hoffman, R.F. Laird (eds), *Soviet Foreign Policy: Classic and Contemporary Issues* (Aldine de Gruyter, New York, 1991); on the factors determining Soviet foreign policy, see E. Schulz, 'Kontinuität und Wandel in der sowjetischen Politik gegenüber Westeuropa und den USA', in K. D. Bracher, M. Funke, H.-P. Schwarz, *Deutschland zwischen Krieg und Frieden* (Bonn, Bundeszentrale für politische Bildung, 1990), pp. 166–80; good recent works on the history of Soviet policy

towards Germany include H.-A. Jacobsen, 'Deutsch–sowjetische Beziehungen: Kontinuität und Wandel 1945–1987', *Aus Politik und Zeitgeschichte*, vol. 3 (1988), 15 January, pp. 28–44; M. J. Sodaro, *Moscow, Germany, and the West from Khrushchev to Gorbachev* (Ithaca, NY, Cornell University Press, 1990).

3. On Soviet policy towards the Soviet zone of occupation/GDR in the first postwar decade, see A. L. Phillips, *Soviet Policy Toward East Germany Reconsidered: The Postwar Decade* (New York, Westport, Conn.; London, Greenwood Press, 1986); on the different motives and options for Soviet policy towards Germany, see W. Pfeiler, *Deutschlandpolitische Optionen der Sowjetunion* (Melle, E. Knoth, 1988).

4. According to former currency dealer A. Schalck-Golodkowski, *Die Zeit* (Hamburg), no. 3 (1991), p. 10, confirmed by the then Central Committee department head C.-H. Janson, *Totengräber der DDR*, (Düsseldorf, Vienna, New York, Econ, 1991), p. 67ff.

5. As early as the mid-1970s the KGB and officials in the Soviet embassy in East Berlin had been concerned that dependence of East Germany on the FRG would undermine socialist values in the former. From the beginning of the 1980s Moscow had feared that Honecker's pursuit of his own country's interests was likely to interfere with the overall bloc strategy towards the West. He was seen as being at the mercy of strategists in Bonn.

6. W. Pfeiler, *Deutschlandpolitische Optionen*; see also Pfeiler, 'Moskau und die deutsche Frage,' in K.-D. Bracher et al., *Deutschland zwischen Krieg und Frieden* (Bonn, Bundeszentrale für politische Bildung, 1990), pp. 182–97.

7. See *Pravda*, 26 August 1985, 19 April 1986; *Sovetskaya Rossiya*, 15 February 1986.

8. Kohl was made aware of the negative view of his policy at his first meeting with Gorbachev on the occasion of Chernenko's funeral; see *Pravda*, 15 March 1985.

9. See also J. P. Dawydow, D. W. Trenin, 'Die Haltung der Sowjetunion gegenüber der deutschen Frage', *Europa Archiv*, 1990, no. 8, pp. 251ff.

10. E. Shevardnadze, *Die Zukunft gehört der Freiheit* (Reinbeck, Rowohlt, 1991), p. 233; Yakovlev, too, had already become uncertain about the stability of the GDR, according to a former consultant of the CPSU Central Committee, Aleksandr Tsipko, in conversations with the author in June 1991.

11. *Newsweek*, 27 October 1986, p. 29.

12. Report of the 11th party congress of the SED, 17–21 April 1986, vol. 1 (Berlin, Dietz–Verlag, 1986, p. 160ff. See, among others, R. Andert, W. Herzberg, *Der Sturz. Erich Honecker im Kreuzverhör*, 2nd edn (Berlin, Weimar, Aufbau–Verlag, 1991), pp. 60ff.

13. G. Schabowski, *Das Politbüro, Eine Befragung*, F. Sieren, L. Koehne (eds), (Reinbeck, Rowohlt Aktuell, 1990), p. 35ff; G. Schabowski, *Der Absturz* (Berlin, Rowohlt, 1991), p. 217; E. Krenz, *Wenn Mauern fallen* (Vienna, Neff, 1990).

14. For a personal and political assessment of the head of the Foreign Ministry by two German journalists, see W. Filmer, H. Schwan, *Hans Dietrich Genscher* (Düsseldorf, Vienna, New York, Econ, 1988) (with contributions from various authors).

15. M.S. Gorbachev, *Perestroika i novoe myshlenie dlya nashei strany i dlya vsego mira* (Moscow, Politizdat, 1987), p. 209; on this, see B. Meissner, 'Das "neue Denken" Gorbatschows und die Wende in der sowjetischen Deutschlandpolitik', p. 70ff.; from Soviet specialist point of view, Dawydow and Trenin, op. cit., p. 252.

16. *Pravda*, 7 August 1987.

17. *Izvestiya*, 20 September 1987; *Pravda*, 19 January 1988, p. 4.

18. *Pravda*, 25 October 1988.

19. This was the judgment of the former GDR diplomat J. Kaiser after talking to staff of the Central Committee, 'Zwischen angestrebter Eigenständigkeit und traditioneller Unterordnung', *Deutschland Archiv*, 1991, no. 5, note 20.

20. *Sovetskaya Rossiya*, 13 March 1988; *Neues Deutschland*, 2/3 April 1988; 9/10 April 1988.

21. Kaiser, op. cit., p. 490 and note 11.

22. According to information from the German federal intelligence agency (BND), *Die Welt*, 15 September 1989, Falin, Kopteltsev and the by then retired head of the GDR secret service, Markus Wolf, who held talks in Moscow, might have been able to dispel the illusion of the Soviet Central Committee. Pre–publication extracts from M. Wolf, *In eigenem Auftrag*, (München, Schneekluth, 1991), in *Stern*, no. 49 (29 November 1990), p. 178.

23. Schabowski, *Der Absturz*, p. 222.

24. V. Dashichev, 'The Diplomacy of German Unity', Lecture to the American Institute of Contemporary German Studies, 17 July 1991, unpublished paper, p. 21.

25. V. Kochemasov, quoted by S. Kondrashov, *Izvestiya*, 29 April 1990, p. 7; *idem*, 'Wir haben das als Wahl des Volkes akzeptiert', *Tribüne*, 8 May 1990, p. 5; two colleagues of the Soviet ambassador said that the SED leadership had been informed about the military non–intervention of the troops of the Western Group; see I. Maksimichev, P. Men'shikov, 'Edinoe germanskoe otechestvo', *Mezhdunarodnaya zhizn'*, 1990, no. 6, p. 45; see also the interview given to F. Burlatsky by E. Shevardnadze in *Literaturnaya gazeta*, 10 April 1991. See. H. Engelhardt's testimony: 'They quickly abandoned us', *Norddeutsche Neueste Nachrichten*, 24/25 May 1991, p. 8.

26. See also the article by Central Committee consultant V. Aleksandrov, 'Vneshnyaya politika – algoritmy perekhoda', *Mezhdunarodnaya zhizn'*, 1991, no. 5, p. 21, in which he mentions a memorandum from Gorbachev to the Politburo of the CPSU, cancelling the Brezhnev doctrine. Unfortunately Aleksandrov does not mention *when* this 'zapiska M. S. Gorbacheva' was sent.

27. H. Teltschik, *329 Tage. Innenansichten der Einigung* (Berlin, Siedler), 1991, p. 144.

28. From written comments by Egon Krenz on the article by F. Oldenburg, 'Sowjetische Europa–Politik und die Lösung der deutschen Frage', *Osteuropa*, vol. 41, no. 8 (1991), pp. 751–73, especially pp. 758ff. See E. Krenz, 'Anmerkungen zur Öffnung der Berliner Mauer im Herbst 1989', *Osteuropa*, vol. 42, no. 4 (1992), pp. 365–9.

29. See the report on Gorbachev's speech during the celebrations in *Pravda*, 7 October 1990. Schabowski does not believe that Gorbachev encouraged Krenz to 'Take action, take action!'

30. Krenz, op. cit., pp. 365ff. For the official report of the meeting, see Tass (in Russian), 1 November 1989.

31. Comments by Egon Krenz, op. cit., p. 367.

32. This view is confirmed by former GDR Prime Minister Modrow; see H. Modrow, *Aufbruch und Ende*, 2nd edn (Hamburg, Konkretliteratur Verlag, 1991), pp. 25ff. Foreign ministry spokesman Gerasimov stated as early as November 1989 that the

green light had not come from Gorbachev but from Krenz. See his interview with the television channel Antenne 2, quoted by the German Press Agency (DPA), 13 November 1989.

33. Quoted from E. Krenz, op. cit., pp. 368ff.

34. See Shevardnadze's speech to the Supreme Soviet on 17 November 1989, *Pravda*, 18 November 1989; interview with Deputy Foreign Minister V. Petrovsky, *Le Figaro*, 2 December 1989.

35. *Pravda*, 3 and 5 December 1989; *Süddeutsche Zeitung*, 1 December 1989; *Frankfurter Allgemeine Zeitung*, 7 December 1989.

36. Tass (Russian), 12 December 1989.

37. In mid–December 1989 a joint conference was held by the Soviet Communist Party Central Committee and the Ministry of Foreign Affairs, at which experts on Germany asserted that the GDR was at an end. They proposed that Moscow take the lead in the unification process so as to salvage what advantage it could from this unavoidable situation (this information came from the author's own conversations with a number of those who attended this conference). An initial tentative move in this direction can be seen in Shevardnadze's conditions for German unification, expressed in the form of a question on 19 December 1989. See his speech to the political assembly of the European Parliament, *Pravda*, 20 December 1989.

38. In 1989 343,854 GDR citizens left East Germany. In the first week of 1990 2,298 left daily, and in the whole month of January 1990 a total of 58,000.

39. GDR Press Agency (ADN), 30 January 1990; *Pravda*, 31 January 1990; 3 February 1990. At first Gorbachev's far–reaching remarks were not reported in the TASS summary of his talks with H. Modrow. On this meeting, see also Modrow, *Aufbruch und Ende*, pp. 120ff.

40. *Izvestiya*, 11 February 1990.

41. According to a study completed in 1988, the GDR already represented a net economic burden for Moscow. For more detail on this, see L. Tsedilin, 'Torgovat' tsiivilizovanno – znachit vsaimovygodno', in *Kommunist*, no. 9 (1990), pp. 115ff.

42. Interview given by E. Shevardnadze to M. Yushin, in *Izvestiya*, 19 February 1990; Gorbachev in *Pravda*, 21 February 1990; 16 March 1990; Shevardnadze, *Pravda*, 7 March 1990.

43. Shevardnadze is assumed to have thanked the foreign ministers of the Pact for their declarations, because they provided ammunition to answer internal political critics of Soviet foreign policy. See H. Teltschik, *329 Tage*, pp. 184, 201.

44. See the declaration of the Soviet government that the expropriations that occurred between 1945 and 1949 had been legitimate according to the Soviet Military Administration in Germany (*Pravda*, 29 March 1990), as well as Soviet declarations describing union according to Article 23 of the Basic Law as usurpation by the FRG, *Pravda*, 14 March 1990. At the end of March Central Committee consultant Portugalov signalled, like Gorbachev's adviser Chernayev, that Moscow could come to terms with the adherence of the GDR according to Article 23 of the Basic Law.

45. Confidentiality had been agreed, but the speech was nevertheless published. See *Pravda*, 6 May 1990.

46. For an analysis see G. Wettig, 'Die sowjetische Rolle beim Umsturz in der DDR und bei der Einleitung des deutschen Einigungsprozesses', in J. Elvert, M. Salewski

(eds), *Der Umbruch, Osteuropa*, supplement 14 of the *Historische Mitteilungen der Ranke Gesellschaft* (Stuttgart, Franz Steiner Verlag, 1993), pp. 39–63; R. F. Laird, *The Soviets, Germany, and the New Europe* (Boulder, CO, Westview Press, 1991); F. Oldenburg, 'Sowjetische Deutschlandpolitik und die Lösung der deutschen Frage', *Osteuropa*, 1991, no. 8, pp. 751–73; F. Oldenburg, *Die Implosion des SED–Regimes*, Reports of the Bundesinstitut, Cologne, 1991.

47. Critics of the government's foreign policy at the February 1990 plenum already included Central Committee Secretary Egor Ligachev; at the Russian Communist Party founding congress in June 1990 the commander of the Volga–Urals Military District, General Albert Makashov (*Sovetskaya Rossiya*, 21 June 1990, pp. 3–4); and at a conference of the working group on foreign policy of the 28th CPSU Congress in July 1990 the head of the Main Political Administration of the Southern Group of the armed forces, Major–General Mikulin and the Commander of the Pacific fleet, Admiral Zhvatov. See on this L. Mletshchin, 'Streit um Osteuropa', *Neue Zeit*, 8 (1990), p. 9; also S. Foye, 'Defence Issues at the Party Congress', *Radio Liberty Report*, no. 30 (1990), pp. 1ff; for an analysis of the 28th Party Congress see B. Meissner, 'KPdSU zwischen Macht und Ohnmacht', *Osteuropa*, 1991, no. 1, pp. 15–45.

48. See the declaration issued by the NATO conference of July 1990, in *Europa–Archiv*, 1990, no. 17, pp. 456–60.

49. *Pravda*, 18 July 1990; also *Izvestiya*'s report on the results of Arkhyz, 19 July 1990. For the course of the talks, see the book by then government spokesman H. Klein, *Es begann im Kaukasus*, 2nd edn (Berlin, Frankfurt am Main, Ullstein, 1991). For an assessment of the events, see especially W. Pfeiler, 'Moskau und die deutsche Frage', in *Deutschland zwischen Krieg und Frieden*, pp. 181–96, as well as G. Wettig, 'Die sowjetische Rolle'.

50. On 14 November a treaty was concluded between the FRG and Poland confirming the borders already existing between them.

51. See H. Teltschik, *329 Tage*, pp. 348 and 352.

52. Deputy Soviet Foreign Minister Kvitsinsky described this particular paragraph of the treaty as a significant victory for Soviet diplomacy, since the Germans had undertaken 'not to use any kind of weapon apart from for the purposes of self–defence and never to be the first to use their forces. However, if one of the partners of the great Soviet–German treaty is attacked, the other side is committed not to give any military or other kind of help to the attacker.' In Kvitsinsky's opinion, 'Basically this is not just a non–aggression treaty, it is more than that. Don't forget that this treaty was signed by a NATO member state.' Tass (in Russian), 15 February 1991.

53. Teltschik, *329 Tage*, p. 360.

54. Teltschik, *329 Tage*, pp. 362ff.

55. *Deutsche Außenpolitik 1990/1991. Dokumentation* (Federal German Foreign Ministry, Bonn, 1991), pp. 167–71.

56. *Izvestiya*, 21 September 1990; for the texts of the treaties in German, see *Bulletin of the Federal Government*, no. 123, 17 October 1990; no. 133, 15 November 1990. See also *Europa–Archiv*, 'Dokumentation', Series 19, 1990, no. 3, 1991.

57. *Pravda*, 10 November 1990.

58. *Bulletin of the Federal Government*, no. 123, 17 October 1990, pp. 1281ff.

59. *Izvestiya*, 16 October 1990.

60. Thus the then commander–in–chief of the Soviet troops stationed in the GDR demanded sums of between 10.5 and 20 billion DM for leaving Soviet property. *Izvestiya*, 12 February 1991; AFP, 6 March 1991.

61. *Neue Zürcher Zeitung*, 23 March 1991.

62. German Press Agency (DPA), 19 February 1991.

63. *Izvestiya*, 31 December 1990.

64. On this, see G. Józsa et al., 'The Heart of Gorbachev's Reform Package: Rebuilding the Party Apparatus', *The Soviet Union 1988/89* (Boulder, Westview Press, 1990), pp. 23–9, especially pp. 25ff.

65. For a more recent fundamental approach to 'sources and responses' in Soviet foreign policy, see especially D. Deudney, G. J. Ikenberry, 'The International Sources of Soviet Change', *International Security*, vol. 16, no. 3 (winter 1991/92), pp. 74–118; and also V. Rittberger, 'Transformation der Konflikte in den Ost–West–Beziehungen. Versuch einer institutionalistischen Bestandsaufnahme', *Politische Vierteljahresschrift*, vol. 32, no. 3 (1991), pp. 399–424.

66. See the first analyses: *Russia and Today's Challenges*, Report by a Group of IMEMO Analysts, headed by V. A. Martynov, Moscow, Institute of the World Economy and International Relations, 1992; from a Western viewpoint V. V. Aspaturian, 'Farewell to Soviet Foreign Policy', *Problems of Communism*, vol. 40, no. 6 (November–December 1991), pp. 53–62, especially pp. 54–7; S. Bialer, 'The Death of Soviet Communism', *Foreign Affairs*, vol. 70, no. 5 (winter 1991/92), pp. 166–81; H. Brahm, 'Der historische Holzweg der KPdSU', *Osteuropa*, vol. 42, no. 2 (1992), pp. 99–109; I. Kljamkin, 'Der sowjetische Weg zu Markt und Demokratie', *Aus Politik und Zeitgeschichte*, vol. 52, no. 3 (20 December 1991), pp. 3–15; D. Simes, 'Russia Reborn', *Foreign Policy*, no. 85 (winter 1991/92), pp. 41–62; G. Simon, 'Von der Sowjetunion zur "Union Souveräner Staaten"', *Europäische Rundschau*, 1991, vol. 19, no. 4, pp. 13–19.

67. 'Vneshnepoliticheskaya i diplomaticheskaya deyatel'nost' SSSR. Obzor MID SSSR (noyabr' 1989–dekabr' 1990)', *Mezhdunarodnaya zhizn'*, 1991, no. 3, p. 42.

68. See Chr. Meier, *Deutsch–sowjetische (russische) Wirtschaftsbeziehungen: Bestimmungsfaktoren, Bereiche und Potentiale* (forthcoming); see also H. Meyer, *Die Sowjetunion zur Jahresmitte 1991*, Federal Office for Foreign Trade Information, July 1991, pp. 6ff.; *The Financial Times*, 27 June 1991.

69. *Handelsblatt*, 20 February 1991.

6 Relations with Central- and South-Eastern Europe
Alex Pravda

The eastern part of Europe has long represented both a source of threat and a channel of influence for Moscow in its relations with the west of the continent. The effort to combine a *cordon sanitaire* and a channel of possible Russian influence with territorial control was a feature of tsarist policy towards Eastern Europe which Soviet leaders developed in unprecedented measure. Stalin's Sovietization of the region turned it into a redoubt as well as a putative platform for extending Moscow's influence further west. However a concern to reduce the threat from Western Europe, rather than to further influence over it, has predominated in Russian and Soviet policies towards the countries of Central- and South-Eastern Europe.* Controlling their territory for military purposes has formed only part of Moscow's security objectives. Controlling access to Russia, managing the flow of Europeanization, has always formed an important part of security policy in the region.

At the height of the Cold War the East European empire made sense both as a barrier and as a springboard. As Western Europe stabilized and Cold War tensions eased and policies were tempered by ideas of peaceful coexistence, so notions of Eastern Europe as a jumping off point for continental influence diminished. The nature of its security role also changed. The normalization of relations between Moscow and Bonn as well as between the FRG and the East European states lessened tensions in the region. Detente in Europe and between the superpowers would, the Brezhnev leadership hoped, 'normalize' Soviet hegemony in Eastern Europe and make it less of an obstacle to improving relations with the West. Indeed, there was greater recognition of the region as a Soviet sphere of influence, an acceptance that facilitated and was reinforced by the invasion of Czechoslovakia in 1968. Even so, tension remained between Moscow's aims of building better relations with the West and maintaining an imperial hold over the European socialist camp. This

*In this chapter the term 'Eastern Europe' is used in the traditional sense, to refer to the (former) 'Socialist bloc' countries of Central- and South-Eastern Europe, in order to avoid cumbersome repetition.

tension was both eased and exacerbated by the Helsinki Final Act. Its legiti-
mation of the territorial status quo blunted the edge of the contradiction
between the two halves of Soviet European policy. The Helsinki process,
however, brought its own problems. Human rights proved more salient in
East–West relations and more disruptive within Eastern Europe than the
Kremlin had anticipated. To cope with persistent political problems as well as
growing economic difficulties, East European leaders adopted increasingly
varied national strategies.

National differentiation within the socialist camp further complicated
Soviet management tasks at a time when the overall balance of economic and
military costs was moving in an unfavourable direction. The 1970s and early
1980s saw growing awareness of the high costs of energy subsidies and the
low quality of East European manufactures. Efforts to make economic relations with the region more productive through cooperation and
specialization within the CMEA proved ineffectual. The material costs of the
empire loomed larger against a backdrop of stagnation and increasing dislocation in the Soviet economy.

The economic costs of military competition also made themselves increasingly felt. The very large Soviet portion of the Warsaw Pact budget became
less acceptable. From the 1970s Moscow pressed, without much success, for
greater burden-sharing. However, despite the costs, Brezhnev and his interim
successors continued to see Eastern Europe as fundamental to Soviet security.
This generation of Soviet leaders regarded the region as an irreducible gain of
the Second World War and a vital safeguard against Western aggression.

For the Brezhnev generation the security value of the region was inextrica-
bly linked with the maintenance of the socialist camp as a political as well as
military bulwark against capitalism, as the ideological frontline of socialism.
Notwithstanding the West Europeans' strong attachment to detente through
the tensions of the later 1970s and early 1980s, the Brezhnev generation
continued to view their motives with deep suspicion. The FRG, in particular,
was still distrusted and the GDR was seen as the pillar of Soviet European
policy. The issues surrounding the two Germanys lay at the core of the
security role of the socialist camp, whose additional economic, ideological
and political weight helped to make Eastern Europe the bulwark of established Soviet foreign policy.

What made the East European pillar so firm was its deep setting in the
foundations of Soviet domestic as well as foreign policy. As the outer ring of
the Russian empire, Eastern Europe penetrated further than any other non-
Soviet area into developments within the USSR. Lying at the intersection of
Moscow's internal and international policy concerns, the region reflected, as
well as to some extent affected, policy shifts in both spheres. It was reassessment under Gorbachev of Moscow's priorities in both areas that produced
the radical changes in intra-bloc relations and opened the way to the demise
of the empire.

At first glance, the dramatic shift in Soviet priorities in the late 1980s seems to provide a perfectly adequate explanation for the revolutionary changes in the relationship with Eastern Europe. It is one that Soviet decision-makers' own accounts favour. Once Gorbachev had made 'new thinking' the basis of policy and extended the principle of freedom of choice to all states, Moscow had little choice, they would say, but to allow its allies to go their own way. Natural developments took their revolutionary course. Using force, as Shevardnadze reminded his critics in 1990, would have undermined perestroika and risked serious international conflict.[1] The end of the empire was the ineluctable result of perestroika and New Thinking.

In retrospect, perhaps, it all looked unavoidable to those who had been in charge of Soviet policy. Yet at the time the promoters of New Thinking and new foreign policy appeared to view East European prospects in rather different terms. The revolutionary transformation of Soviet–East European relations was more complicated than the application of new policy principles, more confused than any programme of liberalization. If new policy priorities did stimulate change, they did so in a largely unintended and messy fashion, as is usually the case in politics. Gorbachev's initial idea seems to have been to transform the empire into a Soviet–led alliance of reformed communist states. This notion corresponded to domestic and foreign policy requirements. At home, Gorbachev needed an Eastern Europe that would help demonstrate the viability of perestroika. Abroad he needed more equal relations within the socialist alliance to facilitate more open relations with Western Europe.

In the event, achieving reform in the East European states without revolution, and democratization of relations without their demolition, proved extremely difficult and, ultimately, impossible. Unwilling to use force to prevent disintegration, Gorbachev allowed political revolutions to run their course in late 1989. Despite efforts to retain loose economic and military ties with the region, both the CMEA and the Warsaw Pact came to an end, again more rapidly than Moscow anticipated. A turn towards tougher policies, designed to tie the region minimally into a new Soviet security zone, ended with the failure of the August 1991 coup.

Since the coup Moscow has sought to unravel old military ties and establish new economic and political contacts. For independent states strongly oriented to the West the highest priority in the East is to normalize relations so as to reduce the danger of any new Russian threat. Relations with non-Russian former Soviet states are often seen from this perspective. For a Russia now separated geostrategically from Eastern Europe, relations with the region are less pressing than those with former Soviet neighbours. If Eastern Europe now appears to Moscow as a second-rank tier of states, its very distance should make stable relations easier. Given the likelihood that at least some of the East European states will become part of the European Community by the end of the century, the region will retain an importance for Russian European policy, less as a *cordon sanitaire* and more as a channel for the European influence and access to Russia which the Russian political establishment still seems to favour.

The first and more substantial part of this chapter sketches the evolution of Soviet policy towards Eastern Europe through the Gorbachev years and seeks to assess the leadership priorities as well as domestic, foreign policy and regional factors that shaped its course to the revolutions of 1989.[2] The second part considers the post-revolutionary development of policy and relations between Russia and the region.

New policy values and priorities under Gorbachev

The Gorbachev leadership approached Eastern Europe, along with most policy areas, determined above all to avoid their predecessors' errors and to make good their losses. The new leaders saw past crises in relations with Eastern Europe largely as the result of heavy-handed imposition of an imperial system. They intended to put the relationship on a more modern, sophisticated and equal footing. They assessed the value and role of Eastern Europe as well as its management by Moscow in a different way from their Second World War generation predecessors. As far as the value of the region was concerned, these new leaders laid far greater emphasis on building a viable and prosperous area rather than maintaining a militarily and ideologically regimented *cordon sanitaire*. Not that they were indifferent to the ideological and security alignment of the region. Gorbachev, Shevardnadze and Yakovlev still saw Eastern Europe as the core of a socialist sphere of Soviet influence, though one that was less important militarily than in economic and political terms.

The salience of economic considerations in Moscow's perceptions reflected Gorbachev's anxiety to use all available resources to ease the severe crisis in the Soviet economy. Soviet energy subsidies to the region were by now past their peak. Moscow was keen to make relations more cost effective by improving technological and specialized production cooperation within the CMEA. A better division of labour plus cooperation, it was hoped, would not only raise productivity; it would also increase interaction with the developed capitalist economies.

If in the economic sphere Gorbachev's thinking projected rather than rejected that of his predecessors, in the military realm the new leadership's approach marked an important departure. The prominence of arms control and disarmament in Gorbachev's foreign policy initiatives, and the critical importance of European Intermediate-Range Nuclear Force negotiations in realizing them, affected Soviet perceptions of the strategic role of the region. The new stress on 'reasonable sufficiency' and defensive deployment also had far-reaching implications. As an area of forward deployment, Eastern Europe became a prime source of reductions in nuclear and in conventional arms.

More broadly, considerations of Westpolitik and the promise of economic savings pushed Gorbachev to make radical cuts in Soviet forces in Eastern Europe.

Soviet troop withdrawals, contemplated early in the Gorbachev period, made building a firmer, more dependable Warsaw Pact alliance a high priority. Rather than being satisfied with a Pact that acted merely as a framework for extended Soviet command, Gorbachev wanted something approximating a real alliance which would share economic burdens and, to some degree, policy responsibility. The Soviet Union was of course still to remain the dominant partner, but its leadership was to be more like that of the US in NATO, exercised through consultation rather than diktat. The Warsaw Pact would thus appear as less of a Soviet bloc and more of a collective negotiating partner for the Western Alliance. As head of what appeared to be turning into a genuine alliance, Moscow hoped it would be easier to achieve a better working relationship with NATO while retaining influence within the region.

The politicization of the Warsaw Pact was envisaged as part of a diplomatic activation of the region. Rather than viewing any East European move to foster ties with Western Europe with the suspicion displayed by his predecessors, Gorbachev encouraged direct contacts, such as those with the EC, as something complementary to Moscow's own efforts. Greater diplomatic autonomy for all members of the socialist alliance was seen as potentially increasing the overall influence of the grouping and of its leading state, the USSR. As leader of a powerful, more genuine alliance Gorbachev hoped that he would be able to speak to Western Europe more effectively and, on fundamental issues, speak for allies who would play a more active role in European affairs.

A more active role for Eastern Europe, and the reconstruction of the Pact involved a radical shift in Soviet notions of how to manage relations with Eastern Europe. There were, as we have noted, good pragmatic economic, military and diplomatic reasons for changing the imperial bloc or camp into an alliance. The main drive behind the anti-imperialist thrust of Gorbachevian thinking about Eastern Europe, however, was provided by lessons newly drawn from forty years of Soviet rule over the region.

Many in the Gorbachev generation saw the history of Soviet power and the major crises it had faced in a very different light from their elders. Brezhnev, Grechko and Andropov saw Eastern Europe as an inalienable gain of the Second World War, an effective extension of the Soviet realm. They also viewed it as an area of resilient nationalism pressing on fragile communist regimes imposed by Soviet power and maintained by tight organization, ideology and, ultimately, force. If Moscow wished to keep Eastern Europe as its extended security sphere it had to be prepared to give local leaders strong support and, on occasion, to restore order. For those who ruled the Kremlin until 1985 these principles were pointed up by the crises in Hungary, Poland

and Czechoslovakia; for most, Hungary 1956 was the seminal crisis which demonstrated the strength of anti-Russian nationalism and the efficacy of forceful intervention.

For the Gorbachev cohort, Prague 1968 was closer and loomed politically larger than Budapest 1956. A remarkable number of policy-makers and advisers, who participated in fashioning New Thinking and the new European policy, had spent time in Prague in the 1960s. They included Chernyaev, Shakhnazarov, Frolov, Arbatov and Zagladin, all of whom worked at the journal *Questions of Peace and Socialism*. Many more, including Gorbachev, had close contacts with Prague Spring reformers and regarded their activities essentially as an extension of the de-Stalinization reforms started under Khrushchev. Perestroika had much in common with Dubček's attempts to democratize communist rule. The crushing of reform socialism in Czechoslovakia, which coincided with increasing conservatism in Moscow, appeared as a retrograde step of which many perestroika leaders felt deeply ashamed.[3] For them the 1968 invasion, along with that of Hungary thirteen years earlier, represented a use of force as counterproductive as it was morally reprehensible. Shevardnadze's particularly strong antipathy to the use of force stemmed in part from his memory of the suppression of Georgian nationalist protests in 1956.[4] Reinforcing the 1956 and 1968 'complexes' was the experience of Afghanistan. Disgruntled members of the party elite, such as Gorbachev, Shevardnadze and Yakovlev, shared with a far wider circle of the political establishment a highly critical attitude towards the Afghan war. They saw it as by far the most damaging instance of the imperial syndrome and the 'tank philosophy'[5] so characteristic of the management of Eastern Europe. The high costs and low political returns of the Afghan intervention made the new leadership all the more determined to reject the use of force as a means of maintaining influence in neighbouring states.

This self-denying ordinance on the use of imperial force removed the keystone of the traditional management of Eastern Europe without substituting a new one. In so far as a novel management strategy seemed to exist in these leaders' minds it was predicated on East European regimes becoming more capable of self-management. They realized that the regimes had little popular legitimacy but believed that local leaders could be found capable of undertaking democratizing reforms and building firmer, self-sustaining systems. This would make it possible for Moscow to exercise an effective influence through indirect, softer methods. Such a strategy would enable Moscow to shift from enforced hegemony to leadership, thus reconciling the old conflicts between 'viability' and 'control' and between dominance over Eastern Europe and good relations with the rest of the continent.

Policy flaws and factors

This strategy, or vision, of more equal allied relations with the region rested on questionable hopes and assumptions. The Gorbachev leadership hoped that local political elites were willing and able to carry through reforms along perestroika lines. The assumption was that such democratizing reforms could make these states viable without destroying Communist Party influence or the Soviet alliance. Gorbachev and Shevardnadze were aware that controlled change would be far from easy, yet they thought it the natural way for Eastern Europe to evolve. In any case they expected such change to take place in a gradual fashion, supported by reforms in the Soviet Union and a favourable international environment. Their expectation of gradual change proved unrealistic, their hopes of able reformers forlorn and their assumptions about democratized communist rule mistaken.

Few if any decision-makers, in Moscow or elsewhere, in 1985 could have foreseen the speed and revolutionary nature of change. The weakness of Gorbachev's policy, however, also lay in its vagueness and impracticability. If Gorbachev wanted from the outset, as was apparently the case, to move from hegemony to primacy[6] he failed to formulate the kind of Soviet influence primacy would entail. More important was the failure to elaborate a strategy for achieving the shift. Gorbachev and his colleagues expected to have a domestic, regional and international environment which allowed for gradual transition within the framework of a minimalist, laissez-faire approach. When developments started to accelerate, they could not resolve the policy dilemma created by their self-denying ordinance on the use of force or even the use of forceful political intervention. 'Since we had rejected "the export of ideas", (the) interference in the affairs of neighbours and allies', Shevardnadze recalled, 'we could not invoke the old methods to push them vigorously toward reforms.'[7] Advice and encouragement proved inadequate, especially as differences within the policy establishment in Moscow weakened its impact.

Structural policy flaws were compounded by poor information and bureaucratic conflicts. Active support for radically changing relations with Eastern Europe was largely confined to the top political leadership and their aides, some of whom, such as Shakhnazarov, had influence in the Central Committee departments which handled policy towards the region. Few in these departments and in the Party and security bureaucracy dealing with Eastern Europe were as progressive. Many of the Party officials who traditionally held ambassadorial positions in socialist capitals sent back assessments that favoured the status quo. Their conservatism on Eastern Europe reflected a critical stance towards change at home.

Indeed, while the new policy towards Eastern Europe owed almost everything to the changes in Soviet internal politics, this very entanglement in domestic affairs did much to hamper its execution. Not only were officials opposed to Gorbachev's new line often in a position to distort decisions and sabotage their implementation. Close political ties across the empire also meant that politicians banded together to combat change.[8] These cross-border alignments, and the political sensitivity of Eastern Europe in Moscow made Gorbachev all the more determined neither to use traditional methods nor to push reforms where they might produce the instability in the region that would give succour to his domestic opponents. Domestic pressures thus account in part for the strange combination of radicalism and caution that coloured his policy in Eastern Europe.

Coping with domestic pressures made deploying a consistent and effective East European policy complicated enough. Adjusting to broader foreign policy requirements and, especially, to developments in the region itself, made keeping the process within manageable bounds extremely difficult.

The foreign policy effects were both environmental and directly policy-linked. Changes in the climate of East–West relations, especially in Europe, had a major impact on the political environment in Eastern Europe. While Gorbachev may have calculated that an active Westpolitik would make it possible to take a more passive, laissez-faire approach towards Eastern Europe, the reverse proved to be the case. Moves towards entente with the West helped foster popular demands for rapid change which went beyond reformist bounds.

The policy effects of Westpolitik priorities are obvious. Anxious first and foremost to set the pace in demilitarizing Europe, Gorbachev took disarmament initiatives which accelerated the timetable of military withdrawals from Eastern Europe. Concerned to improve the political climate on the continent, to further the notion of a Common European House, the Soviet leader undertook commitments on freedom of choice that accelerated the process of change in Eastern Europe far beyond the pace originally anticipated in the Kremlin. Gorbachev sought to construct a pan-European scaffolding in order to accommodate and manage radical change in the east. As it transpired, he found that the process of trying to put up the scaffolding itself helped to undermine the East European side of the structure before it could be remodelled.

The shifts in the international environment and the difficult course of perestroika in the USSR had destabilizing effects on the situation within Eastern Europe. Gorbachev's policies had a disruptive impact on relations inside the political elite, and between rulers and ruled as well as between states. The promotion of reform in Moscow encouraged public pressure for similar changes in the empire. For the first time ever, a Soviet leader was genuinely feted by East European crowds. Such popularity did little to endear Gorbachev to conservative local politicians. In Warsaw and Budapest, where reforms fared well, leaders welcomed the new scope for autonomy. Elsewhere perestroika and Gorbachev's advice to follow suit made rulers nervous. In Berlin, Prague, Bucharest and Sofia they refused to risk any change, especially as Moscow made clear that it would no longer provide a safety net in case of major protest. This shift in Soviet policy did weaken the conservatives' positions, though not strongly or rapidly enough. By stubbornly digging in their heels, conservative leaders dug their regimes' political graves. Without political intervention from Moscow, which its new hands-off policy now ruled out, effective challenges from local reformers failed to materialize in time. Conservative immobilism contrasted ever more sharply with the gathering pace of reform in Poland and Hungary. Polarization between states made the process of change more dislocated, unstable and difficult to manage. Even Polish and Hungarian leaders, who managed to take advantage of Soviet permissiveness to push forward reform, failed to keep pace with the pressure for change from below. That pressure was far stronger, far more radical and erupted far more rapidly than anyone had anticipated.

The depth and sheer pace of change clearly accounts in large part for the failure of any policy of managed transformation of imperial relations into alliance ones. None of the decision-makers in the Kremlin calculated on anything near the right time-scale. They reckoned on something like a ten to fifteen year period of managed regional perestroika rather than on a revolutionary upheaval over as many months.[9] Any assessment of Soviet conduct must take such chronological miscalculations in conjunction with two inherent policy weaknesses. One related to the derivative nature of policy, the other to its deficiency of means.

For a region of continuing, albeit diminished, strategic, economic and political importance, Eastern Europe was given little direct and active policy consideration. Too much of East European policy derived from policy priorities at home and in Western Europe, without being sufficiently coordinated with either area. Decision-makers focused on what their domestic and wider foreign policy priorities required of Eastern Europe rather than on the policy responses regional developments demanded. Gorbachev was concerned primarily that Eastern Europe should not hamper either his Westpolitik or his domestic struggle for reform. This external focus made it easier to accept over-sanguine assessments of the stability of regimes in the region. The Soviet leadership perhaps wanted to believe that East European leaders could manage on their own, since any intervention threatened to jeopardize higher-priority projects. For domestic reasons, the Kremlin was reluctant either to accelerate change in conservative-led states or to moderate its speed elsewhere. Foreign policy and especially European concerns reinforced a reluctance to intervene which also reflected uncertainty as to how to make an effective impact on developments in the region. Non-intervention and stability were thus the watchwords.

Encouraging careful change was of course an eminently sensible policy. However, there is little evidence that Moscow fashioned any coherent strategy, with means adjusted to ends, to deal with a political crisis in one or more of the East European states. As changes became more far-reaching, so the bounds of Soviet tolerance seemed to stretch, suggesting an open, adjustable policy of response rather than one of well considered management. The means by which to manage developments that threatened Soviet interests turned out to be severely limited. The self-denying ordinance on the use of force removed the keystone of the traditional structure of control. Other parts of the control and management system, such as personnel leverage, were emasculated by Gorbachev's determination not to use traditional interventionist means. Economic instruments were blunt at the best of times as means of exercising political influence. So what remained for a Soviet leader intent on managing allies more sensitively were authority and persuasion. Gorbachev perhaps overestimated the capacity of his authority to induce East European conservatives to risk reform and to encourage the reform-minded to risk challenging incumbents. And where change was initiated, Gorbachev seemingly had exaggerated expectations that communist reformers would prove equal to managing gradual change. He apparently assumed that their task would be made easier by the gratitude of East European populations for perestroika and a consequent tendency to refrain from pushing change too far or too fast. In the event, more favourable popular attitudes towards Moscow sharpened rather than mollified criticism of local regimes.

Three stages

In retrospect it is easy to highlight the mistaken assumptions which made the policy of non-interventionist gradual change an unworkable one. In practice, it took some time for its lack of viability to become evident. Not until early 1989 did developments in the region begin to deviate seriously from the broad range of the course envisaged, and Moscow's policy start to deteriorate into a series of improvised responses. This was the broad pattern. Closer examination of Soviet policy in these years reveals three distinct stages: a preliminary one of alliance invigoration, followed by a longer phase of reformist dispensation (late 1986 to late 1988) brought to an end by a turbulent period of reactive permissiveness (1989 to early 1990). The broad direction of Soviet policy towards a looser alliance relationship remained similar throughout. The rapid pace of events drove it so much further than planned that in the last phase differences of degree between the various stages became ones of kind.[10]

Alliance invigoration

In the first eighteen months of Gorbachev's leadership the thrust of his East European policy was to strip away the inefficient rigidities of the Brezhnev era. By setting a new, less arrogant and more open tone, Moscow hoped to achieve reform of its East European relations without destabilizing them. These months therefore saw a policy of rather cautious yet increasingly clear resolve to modernize relations and place military and economic ones in particular on a more 'intensive' footing.[11] The keynote was gradual invigoration, greater efficiency, rather than radical departures or rapid restructuring. This was the note which Gorbachev struck on his stock-taking visits to the GDR, Hungary and Poland. He encouraged efforts to get higher returns from existing ties, as from the domestic socialist system, while stressing the need for steady and stable development. East European leaders, looking for signs of policy change in Moscow, saw reformist views apparently gaining ground. At the 27th Party Congress in February 1986 the message was still a mixed one, but by May 1986 Gorbachev was making plain his disapproval of old policies towards the region and his support for new ways of handling relations.[12] Addressing a Foreign Ministry conference, he hit out at the 'prejudice, arbitrariness and rigidity' Soviet officials had tended to show in the past and questioned the right of the USSR to tell other socialist states what they should do. Rather than laying down the law, Moscow had to behave 'modestly' and enlist allied support through a process of consultation.[13]

The aim of stripping away the rigid, bureaucratic imperialist practices of preceding generations fitted in well with the need to increase the efficiency of the East European connection, to improve the performance of economic and military organizations linking the Soviet Union with the region. Placing cooperation in the CMEA on a more effective basis reflected the same kind of thinking that lay behind the domestic economic agenda of 'acceleration'. Building a more genuine alliance consensus on burden-sharing and arms control served Moscow's wider military objectives. Some progress was made along these 'invigoration' lines, even if the changes were largely ones of style. In the CMEA, and particularly in the Warsaw Pact, Soviet behaviour reportedly became less overbearing, discussions less orchestrated and consultation less cosmetic.[14] In this way Gorbachev hoped to bring about a gradual change, first in the form and, eventually, in the nature of the relationship. To translate this objective into reality, reformers in the Kremlin had to break through traditional attitudes in Moscow and the capitals of Eastern Europe. Conservatives in all these locations proved resistant to change in greater measure and in different ways than the reformers anticipated.

Reformist dispensation, autumn 1986 to winter 1988–9

A determined effort to break through conservative inertia came in the autumn of 1986. While Shevardnadze may claim that he and Gorbachev wanted a fundamental change in East European relations from as early as spring 1985, it was only in the following autumn that the domestic and international environment came to favour an upward shift of policy gear. This was a remarkable period for major policy initiatives, notably the announcement of initial troop withdrawals from Afghanistan, the agreement to intrusive verification at Stockholm and the attempted breakthrough in arms control talks at Reykjavik. Such initiatives reflected and reinforced the ascendancy of New Thinking over the kind of ideologically entrenched conservatism that obstructed change in policy towards Eastern Europe. The ascendancy of New Thinking in foreign policy paralleled progressive moves in the winter of 1986–7 on the domestic front, including the return of Sakharov to Moscow and a new emphasis on political democratization. Reformist positions were reinforced inside the Party foreign policy establishment by individuals such as Georgy Shakhnazarov who were critical of the traditional approach exemplified by the Brezhnev doctrine of limited sovereignty.

Two pillars of the Brezhnev doctrine came under fire from Gorbachev during these months: Moscow's right to lay down lines and limits of 'socialist' development and its right to intervene forcefully to prevent their violation. In increasingly explicit statements Gorbachev declared that all socialist states were free to determine their own policies free from outside interference.[15] For East European leaders, who could recall previous Soviet pledges to the same effect, two kinds of message delivered by Gorbachev's statements struck a new chord. The first, delivered at bilateral and multilateral leadership meetings from late 1986, was that East European allies could no longer count on Moscow using economic and military resources to salvage regimes that proved incapable of sustaining themselves.[16] The decision to remove the intervention sanction formed part of a wider determination to downgrade military control over Eastern Europe. In line with the decision to withdraw from Afghanistan, the Kremlin decided at this point to cut troop numbers in Eastern Europe. Not only would this move catalyse conventional arms reductions throughout Central Europe, it might also pre-empt popular anti-Soviet pressure and strengthen the position of local regimes.[17] Gorbachev clearly hoped that removing the interventionist safety net would make East European regimes more viable by concentrating their leaders' minds on the need for economic and political reform. The first message thus contained a threat as well as a promise: it left conservative regimes on their own, exposed to domestic pressures. For reformers, assurances about the end of Brezhnevite imperial intervention amounted to a new dispensation to carry through domestic reforms.

What this dispensation meant, beyond a rejection of crude intervention, was partly clarified by the second set of messages Moscow delivered in a set of statements throughout these months. These were clearer in rejecting past norms than establishing new guidelines. Their thrust was one of deregulating East European development. There was to be no monopoly on truth, no one model of development. The criteria for socialist development underwent the kind of de-ideologization which was being applied to foreign policy and, increasingly, to Soviet domestic issues. The important Soviet–Yugoslav declaration of March 1988 defined the success of any socialist course in terms of 'practice and concrete results'.[18] That such pragmatism meant a free hand on the domestic front was suggested by Moscow's growing emphasis on pluralism and choice. From the Washington summit in May 1988 to his United Nations speech in December, Gorbachev highlighted the 'freedom of social choice' as a cardinal principle of policy.[19]

Whether such choice extended to a change of social system and international alignment remained unclear.[20] East European leaders knew that Moscow now gave them dispensation to do whatever was needed to change the system in a stable fashion without destroying it, to develop their own versions of perestroika. Their reactions varied widely. Warsaw and Budapest took full advantage of the new scope for reform. The response in the other capitals ranged from what one Soviet official called 'hypocritical approval to total disagreement'.[21] Bulgarian and Czechoslovak leaders responded by 'trimming', adjusting cosmetically to perestroika. Their Romanian and East German counterparts behaved in recalcitrant fashion, asserting they had no need of perestroika.

Gorbachev took a benign stance towards the reformers, backing moderate rather than radical plans for change. As for the 'trimmers', he tried to persuade rather than cajole them. And when faced with conservative recalcitrance he maintained a strictly non-interventionist stance. Such a stance showed greater appreciation than past Soviet leaders had demonstrated of the need to allow for national differentiation. It also showed a basic uncertainty about Soviet desiderata for the region, which mirrored a constantly shifting domestic agenda. Most of all, non-intervention reflected a keen concern to avoid any move that might further destabilize the situation in the region and jeopardize progress in East–West relations. Non-interference, verging on benign neglect, was felt to be safer than any kind of pressure. At a time when Moscow still had some steering power over the region, Gorbachev made little or no use of this either to build new alliance relations or to help reformers to replace trimmers and conservatives. His tolerance of a widening diversity of developments sent mixed signals to East European elites which reinforced caution among radical reformers and obduracy among conservatives. By cautiously avoiding political intervention supporting radical change Gorbachev perhaps contributed to the very pace and depth of the destabilization he sought to avoid.

Cautious endorsement of moderate reform was evident in policy towards Poland and Hungary. Gorbachev clearly admired the skill with which General Jaruzelski had achieved growing international rehabilitation and what appeared to be domestic stability in extremely difficult conditions. Given the traditional fragility of Communist support and the pivotal importance of Poland for the German question, Gorbachev seemed content to endorse any policy Warsaw wished to pursue as long as it maintained 'national concord, stability and socialism',[22] a combination which smacked of wishful thinking.

Hungary offered somewhat more room for policy manoeuvre. It had long been in many ways a pathbreaker for perestroika, and for the wider process of Europeanization that lay at the heart of Gorbachev's policy. With its ageing leader, Kádár, presiding over arguably the most competent party elite in the region, Hungary seemed set for what Gorbachev sought: stable, vigorous and Communist-led reform. The fact that Moscow seemed happy to see Grósz, rather than a more dynamic reformer such as Poszgay, replace Kádár in May 1988 highlighted the nature of Gorbachev's stance on political change in the region. It showed a predilection for a leader who commanded wide support within the party establishment and sought elite consensus. It also displayed a preference for a strategy of moderate reform, of 'defensive liberalization'[23] rather than radical change that might jeopardize communist control.[24]

Similar features were evident in Gorbachev's handling of Bulgaria and Czechoslovakia, whose leaders paid lip service to perestroika. In Sofia the ageing Zhivkov introduced pseudo-perestroika reforms which only confused the Bulgarian Party. They brought no more than private reprimands from a Kremlin unwilling to risk political action to help replace the region's oldest ruler.

Policy towards Czechoslovakia demonstrated the extent to which fear of instability overrode the wish to foster reform. The very susceptibility of the Husák leadership to any Soviet public reassessment of 1968 increased a political vulnerability that induced Soviet restraint in promoting reform. During his April 1987 visit Gorbachev refrained from public criticism of 'normalization', hoping presumably that his very presence as the leader of a reform that echoed the Prague Spring would catalyse change. There was no active Soviet encouragement of a real reformer to replace Husák; Moscow accepted Jakeš as the choice of the local party barons.[25]

Similar short-termism, compounded by particularly difficult local circumstances, shaped Soviet policy towards obdurate conservatives in Bucharest and East Berlin. Ceauşescu, dependent on sustaining a show of national defiance of Moscow, predictably rejected perestroika. If the Gorbachev leadership, along with most observers, saw his rule as plainly dictatorial, they underestimated the regime's fragility. Such was the extent of repression, however, that the Romanian elite included few if any reformers capable of ousting Ceauşescu and introducing reform. Apart from giving ritual encouragement to reform, Moscow made little effort to try to change Romania, a country which was in any case of secondary political and strategic importance.

The vital importance of the GDR made it the object of far greater, if scarcely more effective, Soviet attention.[26] The combination of strategic indispensability, regime fragility and leadership intransigence made East Germany a peculiarly intractable target for Moscow. Confident that he could cling to power by maintaining a hard line, Honecker arrogantly rebuffed any advice from Gorbachev.[27] Such haughty behaviour served to heighten antipathy towards Honecker in Moscow. Suspicion on Honecker's part was increased by the marked improvement which occurred in relations between Moscow and Bonn in the course of 1988. Anxiety about a deal being done over his head reinforced the stubborn resistance of Honecker and the old party guard to any reform; they insisted that they were 'on the right path'.[28] Confronted by such intransigence Moscow continued tactfully to counsel change[29] rather than risk destabilizing the situation by taking action to hasten Honecker's demise. Here, as elsewhere, Gorbachev considered that no reform was better than too much. Had the reform dispensation been less passive and Soviet political action more decisive, the conservative states could have undergone earlier change that might have tempered the cataclysmic course of subsequent developments in the region. Even Shevardnadze later reflected that this was a period when more might have been done.[30]

Reactive permissiveness

The policy of reform dispensation sought to encourage socialist evolution, a gradual process of change managed autonomously by local leaders that enabled the region to stay within the bounds of a socialist system, Communist control and Soviet influence. In the course of 1989 assurances of autonomy became firmer and the bounds of permissible, socialist development wider. So great was the latitude afforded and so ad hoc the manner in which it expanded that the Soviet policy, or rather pattern of response, became one of reactive permissiveness.

Assurances about the political autonomy of Eastern Europe became firmer as Gorbachev's policy towards Western Europe made greater progress towards building entente. The growing links between the two facets of Moscow's European policy were strengthened by the December 1988 unilateral declaration on troop reductions. This move signalled Gorbachev's seriousness about demilitarizing relations with both parts of Europe and underscored the need to make the socialist alliance a more suitable partner in the structure of entente Gorbachev sought to build. Similarly, as part of its own economic strategy towards Western Europe, Moscow had since 1985 actively encouraged closer ties between the European Community and the CMEA. The joint EC–CMEA declaration of October 1988 was soon followed by an EC agreement with Hungary. This, along with subsequent bilateral EC accords, highlighted the difficulty of reconciling two strands of Soviet policy. On the one hand Gorbachev wanted to thicken economic links between the two halves of Europe, which could be done most easily on a bilateral basis. Bilateral contacts tended, however, to weaken the viability of the CMEA which Moscow needed to develop the multilateral cooperation strand of its policy towards Western Europe.

Similar problems plagued the political dimension of Soviet policy. To create anything approaching a balance in a new relationship of entente in

Europe, the gap between integration in the western part of the continent and growing fragmentation in the east had to be narrowed. The only way Gorbachev saw to sustain commitment to entente and promote a more viable Eastern Europe was by allowing national leaders to go their own way. Indeed, the more successful his West European policy, the more committed Gorbachev became to absolute freedom of choice. In the first half of 1989, Moscow applied such freedom specifically to the socialist states and agreed to the principle being anchored in pan-European declarations. The right of self-determination, 'to choose one's political and social system' was described in the joint Soviet–West German statement of July 1989 as a 'building block of peace and cooperation'.[31] In a speech at the Council of Europe in the same month Gorbachev stated: 'Social and political orders of one or another country changed in the past and may change in the future as well. However, that is exclusively the affair of the people themselves. It is their choice.'[32]

Gorbachev and his colleagues still apparently hoped, or even thought, that popular choice, suitably managed by national elites, would lead to more democratic socialist members of an alliance capable of building a pan-European entente, a Common European House. When in the course of 1989 Poland and Hungary took radical reform paths that went somewhat beyond Gorbachev's desiderata, he acted permissively to accommodate the prevailing tide of developments. When, in the other states, cracks became clearly visible in the dams of conservative obduracy, Moscow stood by and saw them broken by the pressure of popular choice, in the hope that reformers could keep change within socialist bounds. However, the changes soon exceeded in pace and reach the kind of reform envisaged in Gorbachev's dispensation.

Developments in Poland from late 1988 saw a managed process of reform change, stage by stage, into revolutionary political transformation. The Polish party leadership allowed the legalization of Solidarity, agreed to Round Table talks and competitive elections which produced a Solidarity victory and the first non-communist government in the 'socialist' camp. At each stage it was the Poles who determined the nature and timing of change. Moscow kept a close and often critical eye on developments and, in the few instances where it participated at all, seemed to seek to remove obstacles to prevailing trends to minimize instability. Gorbachev's prime concern was to try to preserve what, in April 1989, he described as 'a dynamic balance' on a 'socialist basis'.[33] If it was unpleasantly surprised by the size of the Solidarity electoral victory in June 1989, Moscow nevertheless accepted the need for a coalition government.[34] Once the possibility of a Communist-led government had passed, Gorbachev reportedly used his influence with Party leaders to smooth the way to a power-sharing solution. With Communists in key security posts and Jaruzelski at the presidential helm, Moscow saw the Mazowiecki government as a bearable if disagreeable outcome of popular freedom of choice. The hope was that it would remain a peculiarly Polish choice.[35]

Developments in Hungary, however, took a comparably radical, if less dramatic, course. Moscow responded with a similar mix of public permissiveness and private concern about stability and control. It took somewhat longer for Budapest to cause the same concern as Warsaw. The Hungarian Party managed to maintain more visible control, and developments followed a perestroika direction, even if at a faster pace. In February 1989 the Party abjured its 'leading role' and agreed to competitive elections for the following year. Gorbachev reportedly showed considerable understanding – the Soviet Party abandoned its own leading role a year later – accepting the usefulness of such steps in defusing pressure for more extreme change.[36] What troubled Moscow was doubt concerning the ability of the Grósz leadership to keep in check radical communists, such as Poszgay, who lent their support to the rehabilitation of the 1956 revolution. By the summer of 1989 Gorbachev began to have serious doubts about the capacity of the Hungarian leadership to hold a neo-perestroika line. Such doubts were confirmed in October when the Party acquired a more social democratic leadership, programme and name. If Moscow viewed such shifts with apprehension, this did not affect its non-interventionist stance. Gorbachev, at this stage, rightly judged that interference of any kind, beyond advice, could only further destabilize a fragile situation and bring anti-communists to power.

The broad, pragmatic permissiveness shown towards domestic developments also extended to Hungary's external policy. In mid-August, Budapest decided to allow East Germans to cross its newly opened border with Austria in transit to the West. This critical step, made public in September, was reportedly taken by the Hungarians without specific prior Soviet approval. Budapest rightly supposed that Moscow would not oppose a move that fitted in well with its entente strategy and promised to reduce pressure for mass emigration in the GDR while possibly catalysing leadership change in East Berlin.

Mounting Soviet frustration with the obstinacy of the Honecker leadership was compounded in the summer by growing alarm in Moscow about the mass protests and regime collapse such immobilism seemed likely to precipitate in a matter of months.[37] At this very late stage Moscow therefore redoubled public and private pressure. Gorbachev issued clear public warnings during his visit in October. His private discussions with all members of the Politburo undoubtedly helped Krenz to unseat Honecker shortly afterwards.[38] It is likely that Moscow supported the decision to open the Berlin Wall.[39] At the very least the new East German leaders knew that Gorbachev wanted measures taken to relieve popular discontent and took this as 'outline approval' for a move designed to give the regime some credibility. Even after the mass protests of November, Gorbachev and his colleagues probably believed that Modrow could salvage something resembling a socialist regime. They seemed to have entertained similar hopes for Czechoslovakia after developments in the GDR helped accelerate Jakeš's fall. First in Prague and then in East Berlin such hopes were quickly exposed as illusions, when freedom of choice, exercised through the ballot box, brought non-socialist governments to power.

Salvaging efforts

The end of the 'socialist camp' precipitated the first major attack on Gorbachev's and Shevardnadze's foreign policy. Their conservative opponents used the 'loss of Eastern Europe' as a stick with which to hit out at New Thinking and the 'romantic' notion of a Common European House. Shevardnadze responded by defending the way they had handled the crises and emphasizing the potential advantages of the new situation. None of the critics publicly suggested that forceful intervention would have resolved the problem. However, they viewed justifications based on the priority of rapprochement with the West as merely underscoring the mistaken nature of that wider policy. The leadership's assumption that whatever the political complexion of the new East European regimes they would be more genuine allies became less credible through the first half of 1990.

In the early months of that year Moscow sought to salvage something of value from the wreckage of its East European relations. On the economic side this took the form of reducing costs by deciding to switch all trade to hard currency transactions at world prices from 1991. In the meantime, lower priority was given to maintaining oil exports to the region than selling to Western hard-currency customers. This, together with declining production, resulted in sharp falls in deliveries (amounting to nearly a third over the year) which contributed little to bolstering East European allegiance.

In the political and security sphere, however, allegiance is precisely what Moscow tried to engender. Preserving some kind of multilateral alliance was made urgent by the unexpectedly rapid process of German unification and pressure for the absorption of the GDR into NATO. Many of the improvised schemes thrown up hastily by Shevardnadze to stem the tide of German developments depended on the continued existence of a Warsaw Pact to preserve the appearance of a security symmetry in Europe.[40]

Trying to maintain some semblance of a continuing alliance with an Eastern Europe rapidly distancing itself from the Soviet system, Moscow used a combination of concession, obstruction and prevarication in negotiations on troop withdrawals and the future of the Warsaw Pact. It is difficult to discern a strategy in what seems to have been little more than a series of responses to a rapidly evolving situation. Deploying a consistent policy was made more difficult by differences within the security and foreign policy establishment about relations with Eastern Europe and the West in general.

Given these circumstances, the Soviet line on troop withdrawals proved to be relatively consistent and pragmatic. Moscow initially considered slowing the process by linking it with broader conventional forces talks. Faced with East European insistence that the two remain separate and that delays might provoke popular pressure to sever all ties, Moscow adopted a more accommodating stance. After some differences over timetables, the talks with Czechoslovakia produced a schedule in February 1990 that envisaged complete withdrawal by June 1991. Summer (July) 1991 was also the deadline agreed in remarkably smooth negotiations with Budapest which concluded in March. The key strategic position of Poland made withdrawal from that country a more complicated matter. Transit arrangements and payments were among the contentious issues that were to prolong negotiations for two years. At this early stage, however, Warsaw seemed in far less hurry than Prague or Budapest to see rapid withdrawal. The relatively soft line of the Mazowiecki government on the whole question reflected unease about the security implications of German unification.[41]

By endorsing Polish concerns for safeguards on the Oder–Neisse border Moscow hoped to induce Warsaw to agree to remain in a reformed Warsaw Pact. It hoped that other East European capitals would also be willing to remain allies of a Soviet Union which had shown itself to be reasonable on troop withdrawals. Initially it seemed as if the East European members might stay within a looser, more political Warsaw Treaty Organization. By March 1990, however, Hungary, Czechoslovakia and even Poland were taking an independent line on the Conventional Armed Forces in Europe disarmament accords and, more significantly, had supported NATO membership for a united Germany.[42]

Rather than showing interest in negotiating more acceptable multilateral arrangements with Moscow, these three states began actively to coordinate efforts to leave the Warsaw Pact.[43] At the June 1990 Political Consultative Committee meeting in Moscow, Hungarian and Czechoslovak representatives made clear that they would withdraw unilaterally from the command structure unless early steps were taken to wind up the Pact.[44] Moscow responded by reiterating its hopes that the Pact still had a political future and employing delaying tactics, including the postponement of meetings in late 1990.[45] This prompted the Polish, Czechoslovak and Hungarian foreign ministers, at their January 1991 meeting, to call for an end to the military functions of the Warsaw alliance within two months and the winding up of its political role by March 1992. In order to pre-empt this unilateral withdrawal, and the humiliation it would bring Moscow, Gorbachev accepted the proposed timetable, which was formally endorsed at the Political Consultative Committee meeting in Budapest in February 1991.[46] The last meeting of the Committee, in July 1991, formally brought the Warsaw Pact to an end.[47]

When in late 1990 Moscow saw the old multilateral military links inexorably coming to an end, it tried to fill the imminent vacuum with a network of new bilateral treaties. Talks were started on accords which included security provisions of two kinds. The first involved cooperation on military policy.

The draft treaty with Bulgaria, for instance, stipulated collaboration in defence policy and military-technical matters.[48] The second kind of security provision pledged mutual support against aggression and, most importantly, undertakings 'not to conclude alliances and not to participate in coalitions directed against the other country'. Although negotiations with Bulgaria had reached an advanced stage by February 1991, Sofia finally pulled back under the pressure of domestic criticism. Less headway was made with Prague, Budapest and Warsaw, which rejected such conditions as unacceptable limitations on their national sovereignty. Only in the case of Romania was a treaty along these lines signed in April 1991.

These efforts to tie former socialist 'allies' into new security undertakings reflected the growth in policy influence in Moscow in late 1990 of military, foreign ministry and party apparatus groups associated with what Neil Malcolm, in discussing views of Europe in general, calls Defensive Realist thinking (see Chapter 7). As far as Eastern Europe was concerned, their priorities were made most explicit in an International Department memorandum sent to the Central Committee Secretariat in January 1991.[49] Their overriding concern was to prevent the region from becoming what the memorandum depicted as a three-fold threat to Soviet security. General instability arising from 'Balkanization' and nationalist regimes was the first form they saw this threat taking. More specifically, they were apprehensive about such regimes and the general turmoil continuing to catalyse national separatism and 'centrifugal tendencies' within the USSR. Finally, they viewed the region as being vulnerable to what they still saw as hostile Western 'penetration'. The memorandum therefore stressed the need to oppose East European attempts to join NATO (or eventually the WEU) or to become a party to any agreements that could result in the deployment of foreign troops. It was this kind of reasoning that lay behind the restrictive clauses in the new treaties which aimed at re-establishing a security *droit de regard* over the region.

This approach to Eastern Europe formed part of a wider conservative critique of Shevardnadze's foreign policy which focused on Soviet mistakes in relation to Germany and the Gulf. It was to protest against such views and warn against their influence that Shevardnadze resigned as Foreign Minister in December 1990. As the conservative ascendancy continued through the first months of 1991, the new East European governments became increasingly apprehensive about the negative effects this tougher stance could have on their domestic situation as well as their external security. Developments in Moscow, and especially the use of force in the Baltic, contributed in large part to the consultations between Poland, Czechoslovakia and Hungary in February 1991 which gave birth to the Višegrad triangle grouping. Its members clearly saw the Moscow coup as a direct threat, and actively supported Gorbachev and Yeltsin. With almost 50,000 Soviet troops on its soil, Warsaw had to act more cautiously than others; so, for domestic political reasons, did Bucharest.[50]

After the coup

Just as the coup attempt marked the lowest point of a cooling in relations between Moscow and Eastern Europe since autumn 1990, so its collapse made possible a rapid breakthrough. This was evident in Moscow's policies towards the region as well as in East European ties with the now sovereign republics.

The most important change in Soviet policy was the almost immediate abandonment of the insistence on restrictive security clauses which had blocked progress on bilateral agreements.[51] This shift was the result of the political defeat of those groups in the Communist Party apparatus and the Foreign Ministry who had been able to put a brake on the progress of East European negotiations in 1990–91. The speed with which Soviet policy shifted perhaps partly reflected the East European experience of the new Foreign Minister, Boris Pankin, who, having served in Prague immediately before his appointment, was well acquainted with the political machinations over the treaties. The new Soviet willingness to grant full security sovereignty to the East Europeans led to agreements on bilateral accords between October and December 1991. All were formulated along similar lines, affirming cooperation on a basis of equality and guaranteeing the observance of minority rights according to CSCE principles. Where, as in Poland, troop withdrawal issues still remained unresolved, the new climate in Moscow brought speedy agreement on the timetable of the process.[52]

The importance of this stage was of course questionable from the outset, given the evident fragility of the all-Union structures and the growing duplication of East European ties with Moscow by ties with republics which were becoming de facto independent states. The Soviet republics' separate relations with the region long predated the coup. The sympathy dissident groups in Eastern Europe had felt for nationalist movements within the USSR was transformed into declarations of solidarity and active support when non-communists came to power. Economic interest reinforced political affinity in promoting links. The breakdown of the Soviet economy and of energy deliveries, on top of the collapse of CMEA trade, made direct contacts with republics increasingly attractive. Poland, for instance, had signed economic agreements with Uzbekistan, Kazakhstan and Ukraine by autumn 1990.[53] The transfer to hard-currency transactions in 1991 made it mutually advantageous for East European states and republics and regions to make special trading arrangements, including a mix of payments and barter. Parallelism in economic relations between the Soviet space and Eastern Europe had acquired a powerful momentum by the time of the coup and continued to gather pace in its wake.

At a political level the coup had substantial effects. The fillip it gave to disintegration removed previous East European circumspection about openly recognizing the republics' independence lest this complicate relations with the USSR. This particularly affected the Baltic states, whose independence was now readily recognized throughout the region. Moves from declared sovereignty to full statehood in Ukraine and other republics led to almost immediate recognition from Eastern Europe. The parallel, two-track policy pursued by the East Europeans was most evident in their fostering of relations with the RSFSR. This was aided by Yeltsin's readiness to take more radical positions than Gorbachev on sensitive bilateral issues, such as 1968 for Czechoslovakia or 1956 for Hungary. Encouraged by such flexibility, East Europeans took steps to insure themselves against what appeared increasingly to be the inexorable demise of the Soviet Union. Hungary, ever quick-footed in such matters, signed near-simultaneous agreements with the Union, Ukraine and the RSFSR.[54]

Russia and Eastern Europe

When the broken scaffolding of all-Union structures fell apart, East European relations with Russia and the other new states were self-supporting if undeveloped. Developing relations with Eastern Europe has appeared to Moscow as a necessary if somewhat distant priority. Yeltsin has occasionally paid lip service to the importance of fostering good relations with the region in its own right.[55] Yet the new CIS configuration has quite simply placed Eastern Europe at one remove from Russia. More than ever before, Moscow views the region in the context of the two priority areas that figure most prominently in Russian foreign policy: the developed West and the new ex-Soviet states.

The movement of the Eastern, and particularly the Central-East European states closer to Western institutions, with which Russia also seeks to foster involvement, has made it important that Moscow be seen to observe European, CSCE standards in conducting its relations with the region. Hence the emphasis on such standards in all the bilateral treaties. To some extent Russia sees the East European (especially the Polish, Czechoslovak and Hungarian) paths to association with Western organizations as paving the way for its own efforts.

As models or pathfinders, however, the East Europeans are perhaps of greater importance for Belarus, the Baltic and Ukraine than for Russia. Kiev has, for instance, described Hungary as a 'special bridge' to the European Community.[56] To Russia the East European states appear important in the new geostrategic situation as secondary neighbours, as the neighbours of those ex-republics now bordering the Russian Federation. It is often through the prism of relations with Ukraine, Belarus or Moldova and their ties with East European states that Moscow sees the region. This mediated view of relations is reciprocated by the East Europeans, whose recent Ostpolitik has been focused largely on establishing stable relations with immediate neighbours. Relations with mutual neighbours have had some impact on direct relations between Russia and the East European states. This is most evident in the case of Romania, whose public support for Moldova over the Dniestr conflict has contributed to the slow development of relations between Bucharest and Moscow.[57]

The most important 'link' between Russia and Eastern Europe is of course Ukraine, which has established good relations with virtually all states in the region (Romania being a partial exception). Among the best are with Budapest, which has much appreciated Kiev's willingness to stand by its commitment to safeguard the collective rights of the 163,000 Hungarian minority and to consider granting autonomous status to the Subcarpathian region where they live.[58] The most important East European relationship for Ukraine, and indeed for Russia, is that with Poland. Both Kiev and Warsaw have moved effectively to build on the cordial relations established in the late Soviet period, partly because of a shared anxiety about Russia. This has undoubtedly helped to prevent minority issues from hampering progress in relations, as has been the case with Belarus and Poland. Ukraine was the first CIS state to sign a treaty of Friendship and Cooperation with Poland (May 1992).[59] It remains the CIS state with the closest links with Eastern Europe and has sought to become associated with regional groupings such as the Višegrad Triangle (Czechoslovakia, Poland and Hungary).[60]

The negative response which such overtures have elicited reflects the concern of the Central Europeans to avoid any moves that might make them appear as a 'bloc' against either East or West. It also points up an understandable anxiety about the possibility that Ukraine might try to dominate security arrangements in the region.[61] Similar concerns act as incentives for Moscow to try to foster good relations, particularly with Warsaw, to balance Ukrainian influence. In seeking to do so, Russia can capitalize on the fact that physical proximity, potential minority disputes and the nuclear and conventional military might of Ukraine cast a longer and darker shadow over the region than does Russia. Elites in Czechoslovakia and Poland seem to view Ukraine as posing the greater threat to national security.[62] Good relations with Russia are seen by Poles in particular as a necessary complement to those with Ukraine. As Polish and indeed East European security requires an equilibrium between the two, Wałęsa has even offered to act as a mediator in Russian–Ukrainian relations.[63]

If Poland is unlikely to play such a mediating role, it does constitute a critical pivot in Russian efforts to foster what Yeltsin has termed 'stable and substantive relations' with states in the region.[64] Hungary and Czechoslovakia, as smaller and strategically less important states with somewhat less traumatic historical memories of Russia, have presented fewer problems than Poland. Czechoslovakia was the first East European country with which the Russian Federation signed a Treaty of Friendship of the new type. Budapest has proved as adept at establishing good relations with the new Moscow as it did at untying multilateral bonds with the old.[65] Achieving this new kind of relationship with Poland has proved more troublesome. Particular problems were posed by the arrangements surrounding the withdrawal and transit of Soviet/CIS troops. While the schedule was agreed in October 1991, the financial settlement was the subject of prolonged and acrimonious negotiation made more tortuous by the volatility of Polish domestic politics. The final agreement was reached only during Wałęsa's May 1992 visit to Moscow.[66]

The final settlement of the financial aspects of troop withdrawals from Hungary and Czechoslovakia in spring 1992 opened the way for Russian military cooperation agreements with states throughout the region. Progress along this path has been most evident in relations with Bulgaria, which has signed a technical exchange accord that gives it access to supplies of spare parts and other Russian equipment vital to the maintenance of its armed forces.[67] Warsaw has plans to include Moscow in its growing network of bilateral military accords, which embrace other members of the CIS as well as East European neighbours. None of these accords seems likely to lead to policy coordination, since all the states in the region are loath to jeopardize their chances of closer association with Western security structures. They want to use their membership of consultative forums such as NACC to gain access to NATO. Meanwhile they stress the need to settle conflicts within the CSCE framework, rather than within any narrower regional arrangement.

If regional security arrangements with Eastern Europe appear unlikely in the near future, the outlook for economic cooperation seems somewhat less gloomy. Eastern Europe remains economically significant for Russia in terms of reform models as well as for trade. Russian economic reformers have looked to Central Europe for guidance on how to Westernize post-command economies.[68] As the 'shock therapy' treatment, advocated by Polish advisers such as Dombrowski, in 1992 came to appear less appropriate to a Russia going from recession to collapse and slowing the pace of reform, so restoring trade with Eastern Europe appeared more important.

Only gradually did the scale of the collapse of trade within the old CMEA area seem to make an impact on decision-makers. The first half of 1991 saw trade between the Soviet Union and Eastern Europe halve; in the first six months of 1992 it plummeted by a further third.[69] Many East European leaders regarded the collapse as an unavoidable consequence of the switch to hard-currency transactions coupled with the disintegration of the Soviet economy. Despite its considerable negative impact on East European production, some of the most ardent reformers, such as Václav Klaus, consider the collapse of the old Soviet trade a useful part of shock therapy. None the less all East European states have sought to secure stable deliveries of oil and gas, albeit at reduced levels and at world prices, in deals based on complicated, part-barter arrangements.[70]

The major problem with all these agreements remains Russian capability to deliver and to pay outstanding debts. Officials in Moscow now increasingly place blame for the collapse of trade with Eastern Europe on the way in which their predecessors made the move to hard-currency transactions in 1991. At the same time, they highlight the need for imaginative, barter-based deals to try and recover some of the lost ground. Projections of regaining the trade volume of the mid-1980s by the end of 1993[71] seem excessively sanguine in view of the continuing dislocation of Russian production and a determined East European orientation to world markets. Penetrating Western markets, however, is proving far from easy and this may necessitate a partial return to 'softer' if less rewarding ones in the East. The recent growth in bilateral accords and inter-enterprise agreements may thus provide a framework for some thickening of economic links between Russia and the region.

Russia can make a reasonable case for such a development. Leaving to one side the critical and vexed question of Russian capacity to engage in such trade, the political environment is relatively favourable. Whatever the political coloration of Russian governments in the near future, Moscow is unlikely to seek to reassert domination over Eastern Europe. Those nationalists and patriots who favour 'Russia first' policies concentrate their Finlandizing plans on Baltic and CIS neighbours rather than on the former outer empire. Even hard-headed nationalist realists will tend to view Eastern Europe as a region to court rather than to pressure. In security terms, it is important for Moscow to avoid the region becoming a *cordon sanitaire* for NATO or, worse, a Ukraine-based alliance. Good economic relations with Eastern Europe might help to prevent what Mitterrand has called the 'silver curtain' descending in the region to cut Russia off from Europe. In post-Soviet conditions Eastern Europe may have lost much of its old significance as an area for the projection of Russian influence; it still retains its importance as a point of Russian access to developed Europe.

Notes

1. Interview with Radio Moscow, 21 April 1990, *Foreign Broadcast Information Service*, Daily Report. Soviet Union (hereafter FBIS), no. 78, p. 7. For comparisons with the China witch-hunt see Shevardnadze, *Pravda*, 26 June 1990, p. 3.
2. For a fuller account of these years see Alex Pravda (ed.), *The End of the Outer Empire. Soviet–East European Relations in Transition 1985–90* (London, Sage/RIIA, 1992), ch. 1.
3. Aleksandr Yakovlev, *Ce que nous voulons faire de l'Union Soviétique. Entretien avec Moscou* (Paris, Seuil, 1991), p. 101.
4. E. Shevardnadze, *The Future Belongs to Freedom* (London, Sinclair-Stevenson, 1991), pp. 20–21.
5. Shevardnadze, *The Future*, p. xii.
6. For an interesting discussion of hegemony and primacy in this context see M. Skak, 'The Changing Soviet–East European Relationship', paper presented at the IV World Congress for Soviet and East European Studies, Harrogate, 21–6 July 1990.

7. Shevardnadze, *The Future*, p. 115.

8. Shevardnadze, *The Future*, pp. 115–16.

9. See V. Zhurkin, *Izvestiya*, 27 May 1990, p. 5.

10. For assessments of this period within the context of broader historical surveys of East European developments, see K. Dawisha, *Eastern Europe, Gorbachev and Reform. The Great Challenge* (Cambridge, Cambridge University Press, 1990); C. Gati, *The Bloc that Failed* (London, I. B. Tauris, 1990); and R. de Nevers, *The Soviet Union and Eastern Europe: the End of an Era*, Adelphi Paper no. 249 (London, Brasseys, March 1990). A thorough and perceptive analysis of developments to mid-1989 is M. Kramer, 'Beyond the Brezhnev Doctrine: A New Era in Soviet and East European Relations?', *International Security*, vol. 14, no. 3 (winter 1989–90), pp. 25–67.

11. See Gorbachev, *Pravda*, 10 June 1986.

12. See K. Dawisha, J. Valdez, 'Socialist Internationalism in Eastern Europe', *Problems of Communism*, vol. 36, no. 2 (April 1987), pp. 1–14.

13. See speech at the Ministry of Foreign Affairs, 23 May 1986, *Vestnik Ministerstva inostrannykh del SSSR*, 1987, no. 1, p. 5.

14. Interviews with Polish, Czechoslovak and Hungarian officials who participated in Warsaw Pact meetings during this period.

15. See *Pravda*, 11 April 1987.

16. Aboimov, the Deputy Foreign Minister in charge of East European affairs, referred in his speech at the July 1988 Ministry conference to a key Politburo decision being communicated at this meeting, see *International Affairs*, 1988, no. 10, p. 38; also see O. Bogomolov interview in *Komsomol'skaya pravda*, 23 July 1988, p. 3; and V. L. Musatov, *Pravda*, 14 May 1990, p. 7.

17. Shevardnadze, *The Future*, p. 122.

18. *Pravda*, 19 March 1988, p. 1.

19. Gorbachev interviewed in *Newsweek*, M. S. Gorbachev, *Izbrannye rechi i stat'i*, tom 6 (Moscow, Izdatel'stvo politicheskoi literatury, 1989), p. 245.

20. Radical statements about non-intervention even in the case of counter-revolution came from second-rank officials. See V. Loginov, a member of the International Department of the Central Committee, interviewed in *Neue Kronen Zeiting*, 23 July 1988, *FBIS*, no. 143 (1988), p. 3. Assertive statements were still being made about the Soviet Union retaining dominant influence in the region. See G. Arbatov, interviewed in *Politika* (Warsaw), 26 March 1988.

21. V. L. Musatov, in *Pravda*, 14 May 1990, p. 7.

22. Gorbachev's speech in Warsaw, *Pravda*, 12 July 1988, p. 2.

23. For this term see L. Bruszt, '1989: the Negotiated Revolution in Hungary', *Social Research*, vol. 57, no. 2 (summer 1990), cited in J. Batt, *East Central Europe from Reform to Transformation* (London, Pinter/RIIA, 1991), ch. 2.

24. According to Grósz, Gorbachev saw the Hungarian path as the 'closest' to that of perestroika. *Magyar Hirlap*, 6 July 1988.

25. See *Listy* (Rome), vol. 18, no. 1 (February 1988).

26. W. E. Griffith, 'The German Democratic Republic' in W. E. Griffith (ed.), *Central and Eastern Europe: the Opening Curtain* (Boulder, CO, Westview Press, 1989).

27. For documentary evidence on the exchanges, see *Spiegel*, 16 April 1990, p. 85.

28. *Izvestiya*, 20 February 1990.

29. Shevardnadze, *The Future*, p. 117.

30. Shevardnadze, *The Future*, p. 41; Modrow, *Pravda*, 30 June 1990, p. 6.
31. Joint statement of 13 June 1989, *Soviet News*, 21 June 1989, p. 202.
32. Soviet television, 6 July 1989, *FBIS*, no. 129, (1989), p. 29.
33. *Pravda*, 29 April 1989, p. 3.
34. See comments by V. Karpov cited by Flora Lewis, *International Herald Tribune*, 8 June 1989.
35. See Shevardnadze interview in *Gazeta Wyborcza*, 27–9 October 1989, pp. 4, 5; *FBIS*, no. 209 (1989), pp. 23–5; N. Shishlin, *Libération*, 22 September 1989, p. 4.
36. See Nemeth's account of his 2–3 March discussions, MTI, Budapest, 3 March 1989, *FBIS*, no. 42 (1989), pp. 31–2; and Grósz's press conference after his 23–4 March visit, MTI, Budapest, 24 March 1989, *FBIS*, no. 57 (1989), pp. 25–30.
37. See an account of a West German Federal Intelligence Report dated 16 August outlining an assessment of the situation by Falin, *Die Welt*, 15 September 1989, *FBIS*, no. 179 (1989), p. 34; and Shevardnadze's assertion that they were well aware of the problems, 'Ubezhdat' pravdoi', *Ogonek*, 11 March 1990, p. 4.
38. See A. Yakovlev, *Ce que nous voulons faire de l'Union Soviétique* (Paris, Seuil, 1991), p. 99 (interviews by L. Marcou); and I. Maximychev, P. Menshikov, 'The German Fatherland', *International Affairs*, 1990, no. 7, p. 37.
39. See S. Kondrashov, *Izvestiya*, 30 April 1990, p. 5.
40. For their ideas of the role a more politicized Pact might play, see, for instance, Shevardnadze, *Izvestiya*, 18 March 1990; and D. Yazov, *Izvestiya*, 14 May 1990.
41. See V. V. Kusin, 'Security Concerns in Central Europe', RFE/RL Research Institute, *Report on Eastern Europe*, vol. 2, no. 10 (8 March 1991), p. 31, and pp. 25–40 for a good review of security developments.
42. For one account of the Warsaw Pact Foreign Ministers meeting in Prague at which this independent line was taken, see *The Independent*, 19 March 1990.
43. See Rudolf L. Tökés, 'From Visegrad to Krakow: Cooperation, Competition, and Coexistence in Central Europe', *Problems of Communism*, vol. XL, no. 6 (November–December 1991), pp. 103–4 and *passim* for the trilateral cooperation that ensued.
44. MTI, 7 June 1990, *FBIS*, vol. 111, (1990), pp. 9–10.
45. For an example of the conservative Soviet line of argument, see Yu. Kvitsinsky, in *Sel'skaya zhizn'*, 9 June 1990, *FBIS*, no. 112, (1990), p. 3.
46. *Izvestiya*, 26 February 1991; Kusin, 'Security Concerns', pp. 27–9.
47. See *Izvestiya*, 3 July 1991.
48. This and other details are taken from a typescript of the draft treaty, leaked to the West together with a report from the Bulgarian Foreign and Defence Ministers dated 27 February 1991.
49. 'O razvitii obstanovki v Vostochnoi Evrope i nashei politike v etom periode', *Izvestiya TsK KPSS*, 1991, no. 3, pp. 13–17.
50. See D. Perry et al., 'The Attempted Coup in the USSR: East European Reactions', Radio Free Europe, *Report on Eastern Europe*, 30 August 1991, pp. 1–16.
51. According to P. Dunai, leader of the Hungarian delegation negotiating with Moscow, MTI, 13 September 1991, in *BBC Summary of World Broadcasts, Eastern Europe* (hereafter *SWB EE*), no. 1182, p. A2/4.
52. See *Gazeta Wyborcza*, 28 October 1991. The outline accords marked a genuinely new stage in Soviet–East European relations.
53. According to Skubiszewski, interviewed in *New Times*, 1990, no. 43, pp. 24–5.

54. See J. Antall, Hungarian television, 13 December 1991, in *SWB EE*, no. 1259, p. A2/2.
55. For instance in a speech to the diplomatic corps, see *Diplomaticheskii Vestnik*, 1992, nos. 4–5, pp. 77–9.
56. See Fokin (Ukrainian Foreign Minister), Kiev Radio, 22 May 1992, *SWB EE*, no. 1392, A2/1–2.
57. See, for instance, the comments of M. Pogorelyi, the Romanian chargé d'affaires in Moscow, in *Krasnaya zvezda*, 8 August 1992.
58. See Antall comments, MTI, 21 and 22 May 1992, *FBIS East Europe Daily Report*, no. 101 (1992), pp. 17–18.
59. PAP reports, 18, 19 May 1992, *SWB EE*, no. 1388, A2/1–2.
60. For a good review of Ukraine's relations with Eastern Europe, see L. Roucek, *After the Bloc: The New International Relations in Eastern Europe* (London, RIIA Discussion Paper, no. 40, 1992), pp. 14–15.
61. See *Le Monde*, 8–9 March 1992 on fears of Ukrainian efforts to build a Baltic–Black Sea axis.
62. According to one poll conducted in spring 1992. See *Warsaw Voice*, 21 June 1992.
63. Interview in *Kuranty*, 10 June 1992, *FBIS*, no. 113 (1992), p. 21.
64. Interview in *Rzeczpospolita*, 22 May 1992.
65. See, for instance, Antall, Kossuth Radio, 16 September 1992, *FBIS East Europe Daily Report*, no. 181 (1992), p. 16.
66. A. Didusenko, *New Times*, 1992, no. 22, p. 12; and PAP, 22 May 1992, *FBIS East Europe Daily Report*, no. 101, (1992), p. 19.
67. See *Rossiiskaya gazeta*, 8 August 1992.
68. On Gaidar's visit to Czechoslovakia, see A. Kuranov, *Nezavisimaya gazeta*, 14 May 1992.
69. See *PlanEcon Report*, vol. VIII, nos. 30–31 (7 August 1992), p. 1; and Roucek, *After the Bloc*, p. 9.
70. See for example that between Russia and Czechoslovakia, ITAR-TASS, 11 May 1992, *SWB EE*, no. 1380, A2/1–2.
71. P. Aven, Russian Foreign Trade Minister, in *Rossiiskie vesti*, 18 August 1992, *FBIS*, no. 162 (1992), pp. 12–13.

7 New Thinking and After: Debate in Moscow about Europe
Neil Malcolm

When Mikhail Gorbachev began to expound the New Political Thinking about international relations he did not just signal the end of neo–Stalinism in Soviet foreign policy. In the longer perspective of Russian history he also heralded a period of unusual openness, and willingness to conceive of Russia as an integral part of Europe. It would have been unrealistic, therefore, to expect that the new approach would prove uncontroversial, or that its domestic implications would be easy to manage. The arguments which it provoked were all the stronger because the break with 'Leninist' ideological orthodoxy came first and most obviously in the area of foreign affairs. Once conservative groups grasped the importance of the New Political Thinking, and its radical domestic implications, it became a central issue in the internal political struggles which erupted at the end of the 1980s.

After the collapse of Soviet communism in 1991 the debate refused to die away. Indeed it re-emerged with new force as intellectuals and politicians fought over new definitions of Russian identity and Russian national interest.

This chapter concentrates on the clash of ideologies and attitudes which surrounded Soviet, and subsequently Russian European policy during the eight years after 1985, placing these arguments in the context of the internal political struggle. The account is divided into three parts on a chronological basis: the enunciation of New Political Thinking, and attempts to implement a new policy in Europe (1985–90); the crisis of New Political Thinking (1990–91); the debate on Russian national interests (1991–93).

New Political Thinking and the 'Common European House'

The New Thinking as it was announced in a series of statements by Mikhail Gorbachev and his colleagues, and elaborated by specialist writers, put forward a conception of national security quite different from the one embraced by their predecessors, and it was grounded in an equally heretical conception of international relations.[1] Security, it maintained, could not be ensured by military strength, or by a favourable 'balance of forces' in which military strength played the main part. Security depended ultimately on good political relations with potential enemies: arming against them was more likely to increase the external danger than to reduce it. The way forward was therefore to do everything possible to build trust and to reduce the level of confrontation. The capitalist West, which Lenin had described as innately aggressive and militaristic, was in reality capable of reaching reasonable compromises and of cooperating to reduce the danger of war, which in a nuclear age had become unthinkable. Both sides should seize opportunities for confidence-building, disarming by unilateral steps when appropriate, redeploying their forces in defensive configurations, striving for maximum transparency and regular consultation.

As the world became more and more interdependent, according to the New Thinking, cooperation was indeed becoming imperative in all spheres of international relations. Global problems – the danger of nuclear war, economic instability, poverty, environmental degradation and disease – threw into relief 'all-human interests', which for the sake of mankind's survival must prevail over lower-order (national or class) interests. The future reference point should be not the axioms of historical materialism, but what were described as all-human values, peace, justice, self-determination. International relations should no longer be envisaged as an expression of class struggle, but rather as a process of working out a just 'balance of interests'.

In a striking inversion of old Leninist assumptions about deepening inequalities and tensions in the capitalist world, international interdependence was presented principally as a unifying force and as a stimulus to enlightened collaboration.[2] Instead of two competing socialist and capitalist world economies, Soviet reformist writers depicted an increasingly integrated whole, in which all nations stood to benefit from increasing internationalization. The task was set of using international institutions to achieve more equitable patterns of development.

In this new vision of the world, as Vladimir Baranovsky demonstrates in Chapter 3, Western Europe, and especially the European Community, came to play an important part. It was described as a model and a point of crystallization for the new collaborative pattern of international relations.[3] Its economic and political achievements could, it was suggested, be replicated in a wider Common European House.[4]

Origins of the New Thinking

The New Thinking appeared to combine revisionist Soviet approaches dating back to the immediate postwar years with liberal and social democratic ideas current in the West in the 1970s and 1980s.

Even Stalin had been obliged to allow some scope for real debate on international affairs among a small group of specialists, and as the years passed his successors encouraged the development of a sizeable community of researchers. Throughout the 1960s and 1970s the latter worked patiently to wear away the established doctrine of imperialism at the edges, providing rationalizations for the policies of peaceful coexistence and detente.[5] Research institute directors such as Nikolai Inozemtsev and Georgy Arbatov became well known as advisers to Khrushchev and Brezhnev. A network of ties grew up linking institutes to the Foreign Ministry and to less benighted elements in the Communist Party bureaucracy.

The Soviet community of *mezhdunarodniki* (international affairs specialists) tended to be recruited from more cosmopolitan-inclined members of the intelligentsia. While much of their work represented routine elaboration of official doctrine, the more independent-minded among them were able to smuggle in new ideas from the West behind the obligatory ideological smokescreen. During the thirty years before 1985 the traditional image of a hostile and crumbling West, from which the Soviet Union could and should remain aloof, had been gradually eroded.[6]

Experts and officials were regularly sent abroad to try to manipulate the peace movement, to strengthen ties with potential fifth columnists abroad, or to enforce ideological and political control in the outer empire in Central- and South-Eastern Europe. This could have subversive effects at home. By sending representatives to the Palme Commission, for example, at the beginning of the 1980s, to participate in its discussions of 'common security', the Soviet government helped to legitimate in its own country doctrines which Lenin had dismissed with contempt as 'bourgeois pacifism'. Gorbachev later stated that the New Thinking 'took into account and absorbed the conclusions and demands of the non-aligned movement, of the public and scientific community, of the movements of physicians, scientists and ecologists, and of various anti-war organizations'.[7]

Also present in Soviet writing were traces of British and American thinking about 'international society' and peaceful conflict resolution, about economic internationalization and about interdependence as a force for cooperation. The common element in all these currents was a determined turning away from the crudely power-political perspectives embraced by Stalin and his successors, a turn which was reflected in a sometimes almost quixotic idealism. This iconoclasm was the expression of a strong underlying conflict between forces of innovation and forces of resistance inside the Soviet Union.

At first, however, things went relatively smoothly. Athough conservative figures continued to stress the need for 'vigilance' and military strength, the new line found expression in a reasonably full form in Gorbachev's address to the February 1986 27th Party Congress. Even when serious talks got under way with the United States the debate remained subdued.[8] After all, as a reform-inclined official in the Communist Party International Department was to comment in 1991, New Thinking in its early stages could be interpreted in different ways. It could be seen on the one hand simply 'as a political and propaganda framework for a policy of forced retreats on the part of the Soviet leadership', while on the other it could be seen as part of a genuine attempt 'to change the world by changing ourselves'.[9]

Another reason for early lack of opposition was probably Gorbachev's vigorous personnel policy. He was undoubtedly involved in the appointment of a new Minister of Defence and a new Chief of the General Staff (Marshal Sergei Akhromeev) in the final months of 1984. A year after he took office as General Secretary he had also installed new men at the top of the Foreign Ministry and the Communist Party International Department. Eduard Shevardnadze in turn replaced both first deputy foreign ministers and appointed six new deputy ministers who could be relied on to forward New Thinking with more enthusiasm. At the Party International Department the orthodox Boris Ponomarev was replaced as head by ex-ambassador to Washington Anatoly Dobrynin. Like the Foreign Ministry, the International Department acquired a new subdivision dealing with arms control issues: it appeared destined to change its role from that of heir to the Comintern and ideological watchdog to one of foreign policy think tank. Along with arms control specialists in the research institutes, these two bodies were set to erode the Ministry of Defence's monopoly in preparing decisions affecting the military.[10] Foreign Ministry spokesmen called openly for a 'demilitarization' of security policy-making. Shevardnadze appealed for the area to be opened up to 'democratization, full primacy of the law and elective bodies expressing the will of the people, greater openness, and better interaction with the public'.[11]

Certainly the new doctrine was useful to the leadership. It helped it to execute a more or less dignified escape from their obsolescent and indeed by then rather implausible role as vanguard of a world revolutionary movement, and from the unsustainable strategic competition with the United States. The appeal to 'higher' all-human values and to moral absolutes masked what might have been thought a betrayal of class interests. The crypto-social democratic stance facilitated reconciliation with the West while maintaining a degree of ideological continuity and while salvaging as much as possible of existing goodwill among the Western left and in the Third World. The slogans about a common wider-European destiny harmonized with certain currents of thinking in the rest of the continent, particularly in Central-Eastern Europe and in Germany. For the most practical reasons, Moscow was increasingly interested in encouraging the broadest possible geographical definition of 'Europe', as integration and continuing prosperity in the West came to be matched by accelerating disintegration and economic decline in the East.

All this does not necessarily support a cynical interpretation of the behaviour of the main exponents of New Thinking. What it does do is help to explain why there was remarkably little open dissent from it inside the USSR in the early years. Conservatives could accept the new course as a useful ingredient in a policy of lowering the costs of confrontation and of exploiting cooperation in order to strengthen the established order. For the military a slackening of the technological arms race and the opportunity to refurbish the economic base were no doubt welcome. Radical reformists, for their part, preferred to see it as the first step in a sustained revolutionary process of Westernization. The political debate gathered pace slowly.

Implementing New Thinking: internal and external Europeanization

The downgrading of 'class' criteria which was central to New Political Thinking heralded, nevertheless, a momentous shift in the leadership's approach to domestic as well as international politics. Again and again the Communist Party had justified its total political dominance in the country by reference to a historic class mission. Any opposition to the Party was by definition 'bourgeois' and reactionary, if not in intent, then in effect. Thus when he asserted in the autumn of 1986, with reference to international relations, that 'the interests of societal development and pan-human values take priority over the interests of any particular class',[12] Gorbachev indirectly cast in doubt the whole system of Communist Party rule.

Shortly afterwards, at an important session of the Party Central Committee in January 1987, the General Secretary launched a campaign for 'democratization' which culminated in proposals for radical constitutional innovations at the June 1988 19th Party Conference, and the first contested elections in March 1989. It was no accident that the argument over foreign policy doctrine flared up with special acuteness in the summer of 1988. By declaring in *Pravda* that 'coexistence . . . cannot be identified with class struggle. The struggle between the two systems is no longer the prevailing trend of the present era', Eduard Shevardnadze stung the main conservative spokesman in the leadership, Egor Ligachev, into a vigorous response. 'We proceed from the fact', the latter insisted, 'that international relations are particularly class in character . . . Any other way of putting this question introduces confusion into the minds of our people and our friends abroad.' In the debate which followed, Gorbachev's ally Aleksandr Yakovlev threw his weight behind the Foreign Minister's position, while Valentin Falin, future head of the Party International Department, backed the conservative line.[13]

More generally, the new principle of legitimacy on the basis of popular vote came in harness with a new conception of politics less as a matter of leadership, discipline and struggle, and more as a matter of reconciliation of plural and equally valid interests. All this harmonized with the new image of 'democratized' international relations. It helped to justify the East–West negotiating process, and it made success in that process more likely, by reducing fear and mistrust in other countries of a totalitarian Soviet Union.

The most sensitive area of foreign policy was of course relations with the socialist bloc states of Central- and South-Eastern Europe. As Chapter 6 explains, the internal affairs of the Soviet Union and its satellites were closely interconnected. Conservatives in Moscow were concerned that any substantial loosening of control over these countries would open up a Pandora's box. Once a spontaneous process of change was allowed to begin in the region, it would be costly to stop, as 1953, 1956, 1968 and 1980 had demonstrated. A reunified Germany would rapidly extend its influence over its Eastern neighbours. The Red Army might well come under pressure to abandon its forward positions. Moreover, were they to witness the fraternal nations enjoying genuine self-determination, would not the peoples of the Baltic states and other Soviet republics aspire to independence for themselves? Worse still, if a number of socialist states were to revert to capitalism, what message would that give to the Russian population about the durability of their own regime, and about the determination of the Communist Party to preserve it?

These political linkages between Central- and South-East European and Soviet affairs were supplemented by connections in the biographies of key political leaders and advisers. Gorbachev's patron, Yury Andropov, had served in the Soviet embassy to Hungary during 1956 and had headed the Central Committee Department for Liaison with Ruling Communist Parties from 1957 to 1967. The department's 'consultant group' included a group of men who were to emerge as key foreign policy intellectuals in the 1970s and 1980s: Georgy Arbatov (later head of the USA Institute), Fedor Burlatsky (later deputy head of the Soviet Political Science Association and editor of the influential weekly *Literaturnaya gazeta*), Oleg Bogomolov (later head of the Institute for the Study of the Economics of the World Socialist System), Aleksandr Bovin (chief *Izvestiya* political correspondent) and Georgy Shakhnazarov (head of the Soviet Political Science Association, first deputy head of the Party Department for Liaison with Ruling Communist Parties from 1986, and adviser to Gorbachev from 1988). Gorbachev himself had briefly been responsible for bloc affairs in the Party secretariat before becoming leader.[14]

Events soon demonstrated that this group of individuals held quite different views from the preceding generation of Central Committee officials about the connected issues of the future of Eastern Europe and of the Soviet Union. Oleg Rakhmanin, whom Shakhnazarov replaced in the Communist Party apparatus in 1986, triggered a dispute as early as 1985 when he claimed in *Pravda* that 'anti-Communist theoreticians and opportunists, slandering proletarian internationalism, declare it to be "outdated", and try to pose as trailblazers of some kind of "new unity"', thereby 'betraying the interests of the struggle against international imperialism'. Bogomolov and his academic colleagues, with support from Aleksandr Yakovlev's Party propaganda department, responded with calls to respect sovereignty and 'the specific national and state interests' of the Central- and South-East Europeans.[15]

In the years that followed, members of Bogomolov's institute continued to press the case that neo-Stalinism in Central- and South-Eastern Europe was on its last legs, and that the countries concerned had to be allowed to find their own solutions. Vyacheslav Dashichev, head of its Foreign Relations Department, argued in 1987 that even German unification would have to be accepted as part of the building of a genuine Common European House.[16] These individuals were also among the most forceful campaigners for radical reform *inside* the Soviet Union. Dashichev, for instance, argued that both his own country and its satellite states had experienced Stalinist socialism as 'suppression of individual freedom, with material and spiritual vegetation, with inefficiency of production, economic and technological backwardness, moral degradation, with the tyrannical dictatorship of individual leaders or a party oligarchy, with lawlessness and arbitrary rule'.[17]

The crisis of New Political Thinking

The events which unfolded with increasing speed in 1989 and 1990 seemed to confirm the worst fears of conservatives. The assumption implicit in the plans for a Common European House set out by Gorbachev in 1987 that there could be a normalization of relations in Europe which left the existing East–West balance unimpaired was thoroughly falsified. Germany was reunited on the West's terms. NATO failed to respond to the collapse of the Warsaw Treaty Organization by dissolving itself, and only the sketchiest outline of an all-European security system emerged in the framework of the CSCE. Processes of disintegration in the outer empire spread rapidly to the USSR itself, beginning in the Baltic states. Modifications in the Soviet political and economic systems and changes in the cultural sphere alarmed powerful groups in society. In the counter-offensive against moves to 'internal Europeanization', which got under way in 1990, complaints about failures in foreign policy turned out to be a useful stick with which to beat the reformers. The debate around New Political Thinking flared up with new strength.

The attack on New Thinking: Defensive Realism

The discussion was not between two tightly defined positions, nor could the sides be identified neatly with particular institutions. Criticism of Shevard-nadze, for example, came from within the ranks of the Foreign Ministry. The armed forces, too, were divided; there was a vocal group of dissident, radi-cally minded military deputies in the Supreme Soviet. Different voices could be heard in the Party International Department. Conservatives had a variety of priorities. For some (a shrinking number) the main priority was to preserve the old anti-imperialist traditions. For others it was to maintain a powerful defence. For yet others it was to protect Russian culture and natural resources from foreign contamination and exploitation.

For the sake of simplicity, the summary which follows concentrates on three important clusters of opinion, which formed in the final years of Soviet power, and which we shall call Defensive Realism, Radicalized New Political Thinking, and New Realism.[18] The contested term, 'realism', is used here simply because critics of the Gorbachev–Shevardnadze line repeatedly described themselves as 'realists'.[19]

From the beginning of 1990, as the bloc crumbled, attacks began to be made in public on 'the sentimental theory of the "Common European House"', and on the policy of concessions in Germany and Eastern Europe.[20] At the Russian Communist Party Congress in June, future Russian presidential candidate General Albert Makashov attacked 'the Arbatovs, Korotiches, Sobchaks, Gelmans, Egor Yakovlevs' and the academics 'who twitter on about the fact that no-one intends to attack us'.[21] The most frequent contributions came from representatives of the military who shared the view of General Lobov, ex-Chief of Staff of the Warsaw Treaty Organization, that 'political means of ensuring security are good only in so far as they are backed up by effective military power'.[22] The Gulf War was frequently cited in the military and conservative press as evidence that the NATO countries were continuing to use force where it seemed appropriate to them in order to forward their international plans, 'while we were fooling around with slogans about de-ideologization, universal nuclear emasculation, and the "European Home", which no-one took seriously', as one characteristic statement put it.[23] This was not necessarily said in a doctrinaire or violently anti-Western spirit. Gorbachev's senior military adviser, Akhromeev, appeared to reflect a widespread view among his colleagues when he argued that Western-style pragmatism in foreign affairs would be much more effective than the Soviet practice of veering from one ideological extreme to another.[24] A point frequently made by military authors was that while the external threat had indeed diminished, it was folly to speak as if it had vanished altogether. National interests diverged, and were interpreted differently. Keeping a rough balance of forces was the best guarantee of peace.[25]

Much of this writing could be described as professional soldiers defending a soldierly world view. There were also, however, more comprehensive appeals to redefine Soviet national interests, and to place them above all others, whether 'global' or class-related. 'The concept of New Political Thinking put forward at the dawn of perestroika', wrote Mikhail Aleksandrov in the conservative newspaper *Literaturnaya Rossiya* in February 1991, 'has come into blatant contradiction with the processes of real life.' Developments in Central- and South-Eastern Europe had demonstrated that 'contrary to widespread belief' other countries are not guided in their actions by all human values: 'We can have either the *all-planetary* approach, in which national security does not come into it, or the classical *nation-state* approach, in which case we have to reject the principles of all-planetary universalism. There can be no middle position – otherwise we have eclecticism, logical contradictions and, as a result, confusion and muddle in foreign policy.' The Soviet Union should recognize that interdependence is an uneven affair, and itself generates new conflicts. It should 'return to the canons of traditional diplomacy, which reflect the objective laws of international relations'.[26] In his *Postperestroika*, published towards the end of 1990, the conservative theorist Sergei Kurginyan, head of a research institute generously supported by the Pavlov government, painted a similar picture, criticising the benign representation of interdependence given in official statements, and focusing on what he saw as an intensification of international conflict and competition.[27]

Conservatives frequently referred to 'pressure' (military, political and economic) being exerted on the country by the West: pressure to abandon 'the socialist choice', to sacrifice the integrity of the Union, or to permit destructive exploitation of its resources.[28] Several were sceptical, or downright dismissive, of the assumption implicit in Common European House rhetoric that the USSR would be welcomed (or assisted) into the community of industrialized nations, as world politics resolved itself into a North–South pattern. Cultural distinctions and economic backwardness, it was argued, meant that Moscow was neither a have nor a have-not: it would have to fight with all the means at its disposal to establish the role of a 'subject' rather than an enserfed and exploited 'object' in world affairs.[29]

Several authors pointed, with some justification, to a damaging lack of definition in Soviet policy in Central- and South-Eastern Europe. Whereas in the first part of 1990 the main concern which was voiced was over the spread of German power, later more anxiety was aroused by events in the ex-socialist states. It was warned that they could become a base for subversive, separatist movements, or that they could provoke border disputes involving the USSR. In an only lightly veiled assault on the Foreign Ministry's record, the Party International Department called for a new concept of Soviet interests, goals and strategy in the region to be worked out. There was a risk, it warned, that Soviet behaviour might be interpreted as 'an irrational withdrawal from previous partnership, a neglecting of our previous material and spiritual investments'. The levers at Moscow's disposal (energy supplies, fear of Germany, Western apprehensions about instability) should be vigorously deployed to defend Soviet interests.[30]

The most striking feature of this material, especially from the beginning of 1991, is the virtual absence of pre-New Political Thinking Marxist-Leninist rhetoric about international issues. Conservatives put their case in the language of power politics and national interest. These were, after all, no doubt the categories many of them had always privately seen the world in. There was little chance, moreover, of mobilizing the public around socialist ideals. The Westernizing side, however, responded *both* in terms of ideals and in the 'practical' language of their opponents.

The defence: New Political Thinking radicalized

From the beginning of 1990, as conservatives attacked those they blamed for the 'loss' of the socialist bloc more and more openly, a number of writers from the Ministry of Foreign Affairs and the research institutes mounted a vigorous defence of the principles underlying the Soviet Union's recent policies. It was not a shift of the balance in Europe which was under way, they argued, but an overcoming of its divisions, the creation of a single community. 'Today one can confidently predict', wrote Vyacheslav Dashichev, 'that unification and cooperation will supersede rifts and enmity, that a balance of interests will replace the balance of fear, that the security of individual states will replace bloc security, while freedom of development and tolerance will supersede hegemony and ideological messianism.'[31] The defence was sustained into 1991. In the March issue of the Ministry of Foreign Affairs journal, *International Affairs*, Deputy Minister Vladimir Petrovsky declared that by building a European House the continent was vindicating Kantian principles of international relations, 'discarding stereotypes of disunity as it shapes a new system of human relations on the principles of non-violence, solidarity and cooperation'. Echoing the first documents of the New Thinking, the minister described the security system being built in Europe as only a first step ('the component and prototype') towards the kind of global security system envisaged by the United Nations Charter.[32]

During this period the interconnectedness of changes in internal and international affairs became an especially prominent theme. A community of rule-of-law states of the kind envisaged in the CSCE, the Foreign Ministry journal asserted in January 1991, is likely to shun violence at an international level just as it avoids using violence against the people. The atmosphere of openness and cooperation which is likely to prevail among the participants will tend to stabilize international relations and to make them more predictable.[33] The writers who made such points repeatedly warned that any slowing up or regress in the process of domestic reform would aggravate the problems of 'compatibility' between the Soviet Union and the rest of Europe that were already emerging as a serious obstacle to closer rapprochement. In contrast to the Defensive Realists, who warned that Russia was being shut out of the European club, they declared that everything depended on whether it could meet the universally recognized standards for membership. As Shevardnadze expressed it in March 1991, the only danger of isolation the country faced was the danger of self-isolation:

> If we manage to settle our national, economic and political problems and continue the construction of a law-ruled and democratic state, we will continue to participate in the creation of an integral European economic, legal, humanitarian, cultural and ecological space. Its foundation has already been built . . . If we want to be a civilized country we should have the same laws and standards as all other civilized countries.[34]

This kind of writing reflected the views of that part of the original New Thinking coalition whose motivation was a highly committed Westernizing one, and who after 1989–90 were able to shed their political camouflage. One specialist in European affairs wrote in March 1991, for example, that the changes in Eastern Europe 'are part of a progressive process – the collapse of totalitarian "real socialism" and the disintegration of a "socialist common-wealth" bound together by the iron hoops of Soviet tank divisions'. Soviet citizens, he argued, must see the changes not in geopolitical/strategic terms, 'but in terms of a socio-political choice – "for" or "against" radical perestroika of Soviet society, the transition to a mixed economy, multi-party democracy, a law-governed state, a renewed community of the peoples that make up our country'.[35]

Defying their conservative critics, the New Thinking Radicals forebore from discussing events in terms of 'national interests' narrowly defined. The future could only be assured, they claimed, by concentrating on absolute values and on the project of building a European House as the first stage towards the creation of a global international society. They could thus offer no convincing response to the specific warnings issued by their opponents. This was left to those associated with the third current of opinion, those who sought to present more immediate and concrete justifications for the policies initiated in 1985.

New Realism

In the post-1989 climate of debate this sizeable group of officials and specialists felt obliged to distance itself from what they described as the idealist aspect of New Thinking. In March 1991 Andrei Kozyrev, RSFSR Foreign Minister and ex-Soviet Foreign Ministry employee, offered a fairly detailed evaluation of the doctrine that he himself had helped to formulate five years earlier. In order to overcome one, harmful ideology, he explained, it had been necessary to propagate an alternative one, one that may have been 'utopian to a degree, but had a measure of positive quality just the same'. Now, however, in order to avoid being vulnerable to conservative criticism, it was necessary 'to move on as fast as possible to a policy of common sense'. Other New Realists like Andrei Kortunov were less tactful. New Thinking, he wrote, had been useful in a 'destructive' way, for the purpose of breaking down old confrontational assumptions; now, however, it was completely outdated. It had, indeed, ossified into a new dogma: 'Current leaders harp on about "the priority of the interests of humanity", about the goal of "universal harmony" supposedly attainable in a "non-nuclear", non-violent world . . . The slogans of the New Thinking must again be coordinated with real world problems and the coun-try's capabilities, while the good of mankind has to be dovetailed with national interests; political idealism has to be replaced by sober realism.'[36]

In common with the conservatives this group made a point of the need to elaborate an adequate concept of Soviet national interests and to defend them energetically in a world order which was still hierarchical and conflict-ridden despite the spread of interdependence.[37] But having dismissed the notion of interdependence as a guarantee in itself of international harmony and equity, they nevertheless argued for continuing the process of opening up to the West and joining European networks. Asymmetrical interdependence, it was commented in one article published in October 1991, exacts a political and economic price from weaker participants, but the Soviet Union, by virtue of its very weakness, has no choice but to strive for 'inclusion in existing subsystems of interdependence': such a policy had already yielded substantial concrete advantages, after all, in terms of greater security and in better international economic conditions. In any case, the authors insisted, the overall global system of interdependence sets certain constraints on the behaviour of even the most powerful players.[38]

Previous concepts of national interest, from this standpoint, had been distorted and 'ideologized'. Only a democratic society, the authors concerned asserted, was capable of correctly defining its interests and, conversely, only that which helped to advance democratization and reform was truly in the national interest.[39] As the dissolution of the USSR advanced, some even argued that there could be no such thing as *Soviet* 'national interests', only interests of the separate nations or republics that made up the union.[40] It was noticeable that some of the strongest argumentation in favour of a sober Western-oriented 'national interest' perspective came from those supporting the development of a strong foreign policy identity for the republics.

New Realists also acknowledged that the USSR had recently lost power and influence in Europe and in international relations generally, but they explained this mainly in terms of the growing importance of non-military factors in international competition, coupled with relative economic backwardness. Far from throwing up barriers against Western exploitation they saw the solution in 'drawing the country into world and European institutions and links', discarding global ambitions, cutting inessential commitments abroad, and concentrating on areas of real importance, principally Europe.[41] In this region the main priorities were defined by one author as: maintaining the current good relations with powerful countries to the West; preventing accidental confrontation and local crises; and building closer economic ties. Germany would be a dominant power in Europe, but this was not a reason for defensiveness, rather for redoubling efforts to keep on good terms with it.[42]

Almost all those individuals who adhered to the New Realist line made a point of defending the withdrawal from Central- and South-Eastern Europe. Even Andrei Kokoshin, Deputy Director of the United States Institute, a man normally careful to take into account military anxieties, was dismissive of the objections of army spokesmen. The regimes in the region, he declared, had been in a state of terminal decay, and had become 'an obstacle to economic, social scientific and technological progress and a brake on the integration process'. 'It is better to have on our borders', wrote Vitaly Zhurkin, Director of the Institute of Europe, 'a set of varied but free states with the prospect of prosperity than an illusory, deceptive monolith made up of ever less reliable allies.'[43] In contrast to the rather alarmist tone of the Party International Department policy document on Central- and South-Eastern Europe, the Foreign Ministry review of policy in 1989–90 produced at around the same time made a point of denying that, whatever the views of 'some segments of the Soviet public', the region in its current state posed any substantial threat to the Soviet Union.[44] In general, then, this tendency defended the broad lines of Soviet European policy in the second half of the 1980s, but in a 'common sense' perspective which answered the prevailing political mood.

Defining Russia's national interests

The months immediately preceding and following the final disintegration of the Soviet Union saw the high tide of Europeanism in Moscow. During a visit to the European Parliament in the summer of 1991, shortly after his inauguration as the first directly elected President of the Russian Republic, Boris Yeltsin had declared his intention 'to correct a 73-year-old injustice and to return Russia to Europe'. During the rest of the year forceful dissent from this line was rare: it would instantly have been interpreted as an indirect expression of sympathy with the organizers of the August *putsch*. Yet by the spring of 1992 the argument over foreign policy had begun again, if anything more violently than before.

Compared with the old Soviet debate, the new Russian one reflected changes in the political context. Most importantly, the final discrediting of 'Leninist' ideology allowed the nationalist core which had so long been present under the surface of thinking about foreign affairs to emerge more explicitly. Issues which could be used to play on national feeling were disputes with the other ex-Soviet states, several of which contained large Russian expatriate communities, and the danger that the Russian Federation would fall prey to the secessionism which had destroyed the USSR. Continued military withdrawals and more and more naked dependence on Western assistance fostered a sense of decline and humiliation.

A second change flowed from disillusionment with internal reforms: wholehearted Westernizing policies backed up by small-scale but much-publicized economic and political support from abroad proved difficult to implement, and the new government failed to produce the improvements that had been expected. Social and economic ills deepened threateningly throughout 1992 and 1993. Discordant voices began to be heard inside the original pro-Yeltsin coalition, and indeed a large segment (the *gosudarstvenniki*, or statists) began to assert that the new Russia needed above all a strong state which would intervene in economic life and act more vigorously to defend the nation's interests abroad.

There were also continuities with 1990–91. As before, the participants tended to divide along Westernist and anti-Westernist lines, with the Ministry of Foreign Affairs at one extreme and the 'national patriots' (as they were christened) at the other. As before, however, only a minority were ready to challenge the view that Russia had to seek its salvation to one degree or another in cooperation with the West; much of the criticism of government policy was directed at its handling of individual issues rather than at its broad strategy.

Joining the Western club

In 1991, as we have seen, the Russian Foreign Minister Andrei Kozyrev had made a point of distancing himself from what he called Shevardnadze's 'utopianism' in foreign policy statements. In 1992 he continued to reject illusions about the possibility of 'a conflict-free, idealistic world', but his official utterances tended to echo the unconditional Westernism of the New Thinking Radicals, minimizing the significance of conflicts of interest between Russia and the advanced Western countries, and emphasizing the connections between rapprochement with the West and internal Westernization. He acknowledged in February 1992 that his aim was to use foreign policy as it had been used under Gorbachev, 'as a sort of locomotive for the Union which hauled it into civilization'.[45]

Pressed repeatedly to provide a 'concept' for the new Russian foreign policy, Kozyrev habitually restricted himself to stating priorities. These were: 'to enter the club of the most dynamically developing democratic countries', the United States, Japan, Western Europe, states with which Russia has no fundamental differences of interest and with which it can form 'relations of friendship, and ultimately of union', on the basis of shared values; and to establish good relations with neighbours, 'again the United States of America, Japan, West and East Europe, and of course the CIS'. He described Russia as 'the missing component of the democratic pole of the Northern Hemisphere'.[46]

The established orientation on Europe was undiminished. 'We have satisfied ourselves', declared the Russian Foreign Minister after a tour of the continent in March, 'that Europe is waiting for us, and we are ready to enter it.'[47] His officials called for Russia to be included in 'a single European economic space', as the first step towards full membership of the European Community.[48] As before, too, involvement with European institutions was seen as part of a wider engagement with Western agencies such as the IMF, the World Bank and the OECD. The Foreign Ministry's spokesman on CSCE matters announced that Russia wanted to see 'the formation of a new type of Euro-Atlantic Community, . . . to guarantee stability from Vancouver to Vladivostok'. It was proposed more than once that Russia could one day become a full member of NATO.[49] 'All our recent diplomatic successes', stated Yeltsin's press secretary in Helsinki in July, 1992, 'are connected with the fact that Europe is acting together with Russia, and Russia together with Europe and the rest of the civilized world. The chain of political solidarity which stretches from Washington via Munich and Helsinki is the result of this new state of European politics.'[50]

In the tradition of New Thinking Radicalism, Foreign Ministry officials repeatedly emphasized how normalization of relations with the West could strengthen domestic reform, welcoming the CSCE's new inspection powers in the human rights field and the CSCE mission to Nagorny Karabakh in March, and declaring that 'Europe must live by a single law'.[51] In answer to criticism from the patriotic wing, they promoted the idea that the civil rights of the Russian population in the Baltic states could best be defended not by muscle-flexing in Moscow but rather through appeals to the Council of Europe, which all the countries concerned aspired to join. In May, applying for full Russian membership of the Council, Kozyrev remarked that 'the young Russian democracy will not be able to flourish without Europe, with its huge democratic experience'.[52] The *Izvestiya* columnist Stanislav Kondrashov argued that international intervention in disputes inside the CIS would be preferable to seeking local settlements: 'This [possibility] is a symptom of the new world we are living in.'[53] So long portrayed as an ever-present threat from outside, the West was now being held out as the source of potential *solutions* to threats arising inside the old Soviet empire.

'Realist' Westernism

In contrast to statements by officials and sympathetic journalists, the general climate of discussion of foreign affairs among specialists, even those who broadly supported government policy, was marked by a deepening of the 'New Realist' trend of 1990–91. While they argued forcefully that the central priorities were to build the closest practicable ties with NATO and the EC, and to encourage the strengthening of the CSCE, commentators characteristically urged Russia to cultivate 'normal state egocentrism', and tried to distance themselves from what they called illusions about the availability of disinterested assistance from the West.[54]

These authors supported a closer relationship with Western institutions not so much on grounds of democratic affinity, as for the concrete advantages Russia could derive from it. Their main focus was on the economic challenge of reversing the country's slide, as one put it, towards the world periphery. Because of the predominant location of Russia's population and infrastructure in the west of the country, Europe was the obvious partner in a drive for economic reconstruction.[55] There was also the need to cope with potential threats from the South and East.[56] Russia might have to resume its historic role as a buffer against dangers to stability in continental Eurasia (this time stemming perhaps from pan-Turkism or Islamic fundamentalism).[57] It was speculated that Russia would become increasingly attractive as a partner for Europe as global competition with the United States and Japan intensified. Some argued that Russia should focus on improving bilateral relations with Germany, the leading power in the region.[58]

A recurrent theme was that Russian diplomats should bargain harder in relations with the West, if the government was not to lose both the support of its own population and the respect of its negotiating partners. 'Senseless eagerness', wrote one critic, 'only closes the door to normal cooperation and invites rejection everywhere.' In an echo of earlier attacks on Shevardnadze, Kozyrev was accused of pursuing an 'ideologized' foreign policy. Even the West, it was argued, would probably prefer Moscow to take a more independent stance: this would give scope for greater flexibility, for example, in dealing with the situation in Yugoslavia and Afghanistan.[59] Such a line became popular with the government's critics in the Supreme Soviet, who criticised it for behaving 'too gently and modestly' in defending its legitimate great power interests.[60] Another danger was signalled, that uncritical Westernism among the intelligentsia would boomerang into hostility as hard reality made itself felt. Several writers referred to the shock delivered to public opinion by press accounts of comments made by the Secretary General of the Council of Europe in March 1992, when she was reported as referring to Russians in Estonia as 'non-indigenous elements'.[61]

Adjusting the balance

In the spring of 1992 there was a growing sense that in view of the transformation in domestic affairs, in East–West relations and in the situation around Russia's borders since the Common European House slogan was first adopted by Gorbachev, a change of geographical emphasis in foreign policy was overdue. Sergei Stankevich, a close political advisor of President Yeltsin, wrote at the end of March:

> Recently two tendencies have become evident in our foreign policy practice. They could be roughly described as Atlanticism and Eurasianism. Atlanticism tends to the following set of ideas and symbols – to become part of Europe, to make a swift and well-organized entry into the world economy, to become the eighth member of the Group of Seven, to concentrate on Germany and the USA as the two dominant members of the Atlantic alliance. This is rational, practical and natural: that is where the credits are, that is where the aid is, that is where the advanced technologies are. The contrary tendency – Eurasianism – is not yet so clear-cut, but it is already knocking at the door of the [Foreign Ministry] building on Smolensk

Square. . . . It is obvious that we shall have to seek a new balance, appropriate to the present-day situation of Russia, between Western and Eastern orientations. Meanwhile the first thing is to strengthen our positions in the East, correcting the evident distortion created by the authors of the Common European House concept.[62]

Stankevich evoked the old notion of Russia's mission as a power reconciling North and South, East and West, Europe and Asia. A most pressing task, he argued, was to deal with 'the arc of crisis' developing on Russia's southern borders, and the complications which had arisen in relations with its own sizeable Muslim population. Russia must develop an active diplomacy to match that being deployed by Turkey, Iran and Saudi Arabia, and forward its national interests more imaginatively and forcefully inside the CIS.

The case for an eastward 'correction of the balance' was made in greater detail by specialists on Asia and the Islamic world employed in the Academy of Sciences foreign policy research institutes. Russia's location, they argued, gave it interests in Asia quite distinct from those of the West: for one thing, it would be much more vulnerable in any North–South confrontation. Taking an uncompromisingly liberal line on human rights, and discussing joint anti-missile defence projects with the United States, they suggested, did little to endear Russia to its Eastern neighbours. This did not mean, wrote the Sinologist Sergei Goncharov, that Russia should turn away from Europe and the West, but rather that it should strive to find the optimum balance: 'Partnership with the West will undoubtedly strengthen Russia in its relations with the East and the South, while partnership with the East and the South will give Russia independence in its contacts with the West.'[63]

As befitted the difficult internal situation of Russia in 1992, this 'pragmatic Eurasianism' implied a more sober appreciation of the country's potential, and of how much change could be achieved (internally as well as externally) in the short term. In the economic sphere, its exponents characteristically emphasized that Russia was too large and beset by problems to be accepted as a member of the European Community and that it would have to make its own special arrangements wherever opportunities presented themselves. More generally, remarked Stankevich for example, Russia would for many years be forced to play the role of junior partner in relations with the world's leading economies; more promising in the meanwhile was interaction with 'second-echelon states' at a similar level of economic development: the Latin American countries, South Africa, Greece, Turkey, India, China and South-East Asia. Another theme was the pressing need to repair economic relations with established partners among the ex-Soviet states.[64]

In terms of foreign policy, the debate between Eurasianists and Atlanticists was in most cases one about where the balance of priorities should rest between the West and the 'near abroad'. The meaning of 'Asia' in the writings of the former group varied from author to author, and was often left vague. Was Russia recommended to align itself with Japan, with South

Korea, with the People's Republic of China, with India or with Iraq? Their opponents were able to point to this weakness and to argue that the economically successful parts of Asia had become so essentially through a process of Westernization.[65]

A separate destiny?

Some critics of 'excessive Europeanism' found geopolitical reasons for Russia's distinctness from Europe. They depicted it as a power destined to bind together the peoples of the Eurasian heartland, to build a state strong internally and externally, one able to resist pressure from the nations of the 'rimland' and beyond.[66] In the writings of more radical critics this argument frequently came together with assertions about Russia's cultural separateness from Europe.

Soviet Common European House rhetoric had put heavy and somewhat one-sided emphasis on Russia's sharing of a common European heritage. Sooner or later even some Westernizers by temperament, like Stankevich, were bound to point out that the Russian state was, in his words, 'a unique historical-cultural alloy of Slav and Turkic, orthodox and Muslim elements'. Those, like Vladimir Razuvaev, who looked forward to the building of 'a European–Russian cultural identity', or Boris Kapustin, who foresaw the gradual integration of Russia in 'a Europeanized world system', nevertheless emphasized the deep-running character of the cultural divisions which separated the Russian and the Western-Christian traditions. It would take time, they argued, for 'all-human values' to take root among the populations of Russia, with their varied and idiosyncratic histories. In any case, 'Russia will remain Russia.'[67]

In the writings of determined opponents of government policy, such arguments were put much more sharply, implying that Western influence represented a threat to the health of Russian society. Citing Dostoevsky, the international relations theorist El'giz Pozdnyakov described the implantation of European practices by Peter the Great and the imposition of socialism by the Bolsheviks as national catastrophes. Russia should remain true to itself, and to its historic role as a great military power able to maintain the political balance in Europe:

> Every attempt to roll the 'European stone' up the 'Russian mountain' by the gigantic effort of the whole nation ended with it rolling back downhill crushing and devastating everything in its way. . . . We are today fulfilling the eternal dream of the West with our own hands, namely to throw Russia back to Asia, to reduce its role to that of a secondary power, to make it dependent on the mercies of the West. As a result, the doors of the 'Common European Home' appear about to be closed, and in quite an unceremonious manner, and for a long while.[68]

As for the neo-communist and 'patriotic' opposition, they developed their own, cruder version of Eurasianism, criticising the unbalanced Westernism of the official reformers, and pointing to the chaos caused by attempts to import an alien way of life.[69] Opposition newspapers like *Sovetskaya Rossiya* suggested that it was vital for Russia to practice an active diplomacy in Asia in order to counteract the deliberate Western policy of driving wedges between the country and its Islamic neighbours inside and outside the former Soviet borders. If not, then intractable ethnic conflicts would be set in motion, and as a result 'the prize sought by the United States', namely the final destruction of the Russian state, would be 'bought with the blood of Russians and Moslems'.[70]

The resurgence of nationalism

As 1992 progressed, the Russian Foreign Minister seemed increasingly at bay. Criticism of his policies continued to mount, both from the 'patriotic' right, and from those 'centrist' democrats whose view was summarized as follows by Sergei Karaganov: 'One could even argue that on the way to modernity Russia will have to live through a period of increased nationalism and statism. This period is already starting. It is not only inevitable, but also necessary in order to resurrect a country so badly damaged by totalitarianism and mismanagement.'[71] In response, Kozyrev complained of the absence of an enlightened public opinion, blaming the newspaper commentators: largely 'still the same old guard', accused the military and security establishments of manipulating the news in order to whip up 'patriotic' feeling, and warned of the danger of another coup attempt.[72]

Yet Yeltsin and his supporters could not ignore that Russian national feeling was an important ingredient in the support which helped them to sweep Gorbachev from power in 1991, nor could they ignore that alternative sources of popularity and authority were running dry, as the market and democracy failed to produce the desired results, as crime and corruption increased, and as the new European order proved unable to guarantee the rights of Russians abroad. Ruslan Khasbulatov, Chairman of the Supreme Soviet, warned openly of the danger of squandering popular backing by pursuing 'irrelevant' foreign policies. Others were even franker:

> If the political situation in the country deteriorates, the only thing that could save the situation would be the personal authority of Boris Yeltsin, and even that may be insufficient, if he fails to tap the popular sources of Russian patriotism, to rekindle their pride in their native land and their army, in Russia's role as a great power in today's world.[73]

The centrist 'Civic Union', with which Yeltsin was being forced to compromise, was an amalgamation of statists (*gosudarstvenniki*), moderate nationalists

and industrialists, who had a common interest in greater state intervention-
ism, protection against foreign competition, and vigorous action to preserve
the integrity of the former Soviet economic space, probably through Russian
hegemony in the region. Their position is better described as pro-Russian
than as anti-Western.

The conservative/nationalist opposition, on the other hand, played avidly
on the popular feelings provoked by the rapidly accumulating evidence of
national military and economic decline. Some appealed to residual anti-
Western sentiment: the newspaper *Den'* routinely referred to Russia as a
country 'under occupation'; Eduard Volodin in *Sovetskaya Rossiya* compared the current 'alliance' with the United States to Stalin's alliance with
Hitler in its foolhardiness; attempts were made to whip up old fears of
Germany.[74] The real value of economic assistance from the West was continually deprecated, and attention was focused on the crippling conditions
supposedly attached to it. The argument was often made that Russia should
play to its traditional (military) strengths, rather than engaging in a quixotic
and unequal disarmament race.[75] The real or imagined plight of Russian
minorities in other parts of the former Soviet Union, particularly in the Baltic
states, was another favourite theme. In the extreme right-wing press anti-
American rhetoric was frequently intertwined with fantastic stories, for
example about an international Jewish conspiracy to destroy Russia, which
was supposedly feared as the natural 'centre of consolidation of healthy
European nations'.[76] Hostility to the West was quite explicitly linked to
hostility to democracy: 'Democracy is profoundly inimical to our national
culture. It tramples down everything that it comes in contact with, in the
name of some world order or other. And in general all these phenomena –
democracy, globalism, Zionism and cosmopolitanism – are identical twins.'[77]

One reaction to unforeseen difficulties was to retreat not so much into
Eurasia as into Russia's 'own' part of Europe. The old theme of Slav solidarity had been exploited by Yeltsin and his colleagues, when they set up the
Commonwealth of Independent States in December 1991 initially as a purely
Slav community. Gennady Burbulis, Yeltsin's State Secretary, issued invitations to Bulgaria and Poland to become members.[78] This initiative no doubt
reflected the broader pro-European orientation of the Russian government,
but later the opposition adapted the idea to their own purposes. During 1992
the notion of Russia as the historic protector of the smaller Slav nations of
Europe became an embarrassment for the government, as the nationalist right
whipped up a campaign of support for Serbia, supposedly threatened by a
Western anti-Orthodox conspiracy similar to the ones being forwarded in
Ukraine, Belarus and Lithuania. Parallels were drawn between the sufferings
of Serbs stranded outside the frontiers of their own state by the break-up of
Yugoslavia, and Russians in the ex-Soviet 'near abroad'. This coincided with
the refusal of the Russian parliament to vote for economic sanctions against
Serbia.[79] In the spring of 1993 Yeltsin was so vulnerable to nationalist criticism

over the Serbian issue that the United Nations was inhibited from taking military action against the Bosnian Serbs partly by Russia's stand in the Security Council.

By the end of 1992 it was clear that growing disorder on the territory of the former Soviet Union and lack of engagement by the West in Russia's problems had resulted in an overall 'Eurasian' shift in the climate of opinion about foreign policy priorities. Even Westernist and liberal intellectuals argued that if Moscow did not shoulder the burden of responsibility for stability and especially for the welfare of Russians in the whole former Soviet area, then public opinion would bring to power a government which would do so in a less civilized way.[80]

In the second half of 1992 the Russian government's drift towards the political centre had begun increasingly to affect foreign policy. The position of the Foreign Ministry on the civil war in Yugoslavia gradually became more distinct from that of its Western counterparts. At the August UN conference on Yugoslavia the outspoken chairman of the Supreme Soviet foreign affairs committee, Evgeny Ambartsumov, was present alongside the Foreign Minister.[81] During a meeting of CSCE foreign ministers in December, Kozyrev shocked his audience by delivering a speech couched in aggressive language and asserting Russia's right to maintain its sphere of influence in Europe, later explaining that it was intended to demonstrate how policy could change should a nationalist regime come to power in the Kremlin. Yeltsin subsequently began to speak of Russia's security responsibilities throughout the whole former Soviet Union. While Moscow indicated that it would prefer to have UN or CSCE sanction for any peace-keeping operations which it decided to undertake there, it was clear that it did not regard this as a precondition for action. During a visit to Seoul in November, the Russian President repeatedly declared that Russia was turning its attention to Asia and the Pacific. One Westernist author complained of 'the striking absence of any interest in European affairs on the part of the top of the Russian foreign policy hierarchy'.[82]

The draft 'Foreign Policy Conception of the Russian Federation' which the Russian Foreign Ministry published at the beginning of 1993 after wide consultation with parliamentarians and experts was a carefully balanced statement expressed largely in 'New Realist' terms, committed to cooperation with the West and to integration in the European and world economic systems, but reflecting also a perception of the competitive dimension of international relations. European matters were allocated the longest single section, but the countries of the 'near abroad' were treated first. The document noted that disarray in Europe and inside Russia created a danger of isolation: it recommended that Russia should do all it could to encourage European unity, and should refrain from trying to achieve short-term advantages by exploiting differences between the European powers. Good relations with Western Europe would encourage improvement in relations with Central- and South-Eastern Europe and the Baltic states, where the main priorities were to prevent the emergence of a buffer zone and to counteract the tendency for Russia to be 'squeezed out'.[83]

The way in which this statement was put together indicates that the Russian government was seeking to build an elite foreign policy consensus, incorporating elements of the centrist opposition platform. This goal was pursued against a background of sharp public disagreements on international issues between leading figures in the state. Kozyrev was openly criticized not only by Vice-President Rutskoi (a leader of Civic Union), by parliamentary and military spokesmen, but also by Yeltsin himself.[84] In sensitive areas such as Eastern Moldova and Crimea, the Ministry of Defence sometimes appeared to be forwarding its own independent policy. On the other hand the hard-line conservatives were themselves divided. In so far as they had a consistent position, it was defined mainly in terms of opposition to particular government policies, and then mainly on emotional grounds: there was no coherent overall alternative strategy. It would be mistaken to confuse the balance of opinion in a public debate which to a large extent fulfilled the functions of a safety valve for wounded national feeling and a subsidiary arena for the forwarding of domestic political goals with the likely balance of judgment among policy-makers or potential policy-makers.[85] Foreign policy consensus is probably more broadly based than it might at first sight appear.

Conclusion

During the period from 1985 to 1993 the debate in Moscow over relations with the rest of Europe changed both in content and in quality. The changes in content are the most immediately striking. When Gorbachev came to power, the impatience of the most educated part of the intelligentsia with decades of enforced isolation from the rest of the world, coupled with their sense that the existing regime had reached a dead end, had generated a powerful Westernism and aspiration to 're-join Europe'. Because the need for radical alterations in the Soviet system and in its external relations was by now very pressing, and was recognized by the ascendant faction in the Party leadership, and because the latter needed intelligentsia support for reform, this Westernism was allowed unprecedentedly full expression. Under the umbrella provided by official New Political Thinking, writers acquired the confidence to stop writing about Western Europe as part of a hostile 'imperialist' alliance to be struggled against, and to start describing it as part of a 'civilized world' to be imitated. At this stage, perhaps because the implications of the new current were not yet clear, opposition to it was weak.

In 1990 and 1991, as the revolutionary implications in practice of the new line became evident, proving false the reformist assumptions of official New Thinking, violent arguments broke out over European matters. Shevardnadze's policy of increasingly bold concessions and rapprochement was supported enthusiastically by Radicalized New Thinkers, who hailed the coming of a new era of cooperative international relations, and in a more measured way by New Realists who perceived relations between states as competitive but not necessarily confrontational. It was opposed by groups that stood to lose from demilitarization and by those who still perceived the West as predatory and hostile to the Soviet Union.

The fiasco of August 1991, by discrediting resistance to reform in all areas of policy, helped to give a boost to the Westernizers, and the passing of Communist rule dispelled the last illusions about a separate socialist, self-sufficient path. In 1992, however, the pendulum swung back somewhat, to the benefit of Russian nationalists. The possibilities and benefits of rapprochement with Europe had been over-sold; the immediate results of domestic reform were mainly unpleasant; and neglect of relations with other ex-Soviet states was already having bad effects. It could not be ignored that Russia was a Eurasian as well as a European power.

The end point of this new tendency could well be no more than a more calculating and cautious version of fundamentally Westernist thinking and a continuing though less ambitious orientation on Europe. Alternatively, given a sufficiently strong wave of injured national feeling, it could swell into a powerful current of Russian self-assertiveness, capable of affecting foreign policy in a direction less welcome to the West. At present, despite the repeated warnings about a 'Weimar Russia', extreme nationalist forces seem to have little support among the informed public. What will be decisive will be the behaviour of those 'centrists' who seek to play the patriotic card, and the reaction of the public: are forces being unleashed which will run out of control, or will the consequences be mainly tactical ones? This issue is discussed below.

Yet the changes in the quality of the discussion are arguably more momentous than the changes in its content. Just as Gorbachev began by using traditional communist methods to reform communism, so the demise of neo-Stalinist foreign policy was ushered in by the kind of campaigning slogans which it itself had made notorious. Instead of fighting to create a Popular Front, forwarding Peaceful Coexistence or Detente, the task this time was to implement New Political Thinking, and to build a Common European House. As before, specialist writers on international affairs moved cautiously, expressing themselves obliquely, testing the boundaries of debate established by the new doctrine. As before, it was understood that the new line, designed as it was to help bring about a gradual change of direction on the part of the lumbering bureaucracies responsible, was deliberately one-sided and over-stated. It was also no doubt expected that in due course an appropriate 'course correction' would be applied in order to stop the change going too far.

This time, however, the old pattern broke down. It was a sign of the decay of the system that it had adopted as unorthodox a doctrine as the New Political Thinking in the first place. Another sign was that it was unable to put a halt to the activities of those specialists and officials who started to take the doctrine with inappropriate seriousness and to employ it to attack core elements of the country's foreign policy ideology.

Finally, when the new ideology had been used to destroy the old one, it in turn came under fire, by those who insisted that foreign affairs be discussed in less utopian, less 'globalist' terms. There was little dispute about policy practice: most of the new generation of self-described realists also argued for the closest possible association with Europe. Yet they advocated this not because of some imagined common cultural identity, or because it might help to expand the nucleus of a peaceful new world order, but rather because in their view it was the most effective way of forwarding Russian national interests.

The emergence in public argument of this conditional, pragmatic Europeanism marked an important shift. Russian intellectuals have commented repeatedly during the last two centuries that the very zeal to imitate Europe (just like the blanket rejection of Europe) is an index of non-Europeanness. As the Russian debates became more transparent and more concerned with real problems than with the manipulation of shibboleths, as the participants began openly to discuss matters such as the order of national priorities in foreign policy, the appropriate balance, for example, between European and Asian concerns, so it began to seem likely that the intellectual life of the country was indeed acquiring a more Western colouring, was becoming more 'European'.

At the same time, it cannot be ignored that the domestic political environment of foreign policy has been radically changed by those very democratizing changes which permitted the emancipation of the intellectual debate. International issues have become pawns in a constant battle by rival political groups to win the support of a wide public opinion. As the contents of the 'patriotic' press demonstrate, there is a serious danger that the currency of discussion of these issues will become debased. The electorate are disorientated by economic and social upheavals at home and the collapse of Soviet power abroad; they are vulnerable to appeals to 'defend' the 25 million Russians who now find themselves living abroad, in the other ex-Soviet republics. The rise of demagogic nationalism could in turn put the fragile beginnings of democracy itself at risk, and suffocate open foreign-policy debate. Coping with that threat is the next challenge facing those Russians who want to keep up the momentum of Europeanization.

Notes

1. Important statements are M. Gorbachev, *Politicheskii doklad Tsentral'nogo Komiteta XXVII s'ezdu KPSS* (Moscow, Politizdat, 1986), pp. 7–27, 80–98 (Gorbachev's speech to the 27th Congress of the CPSU); M. Gorbachev, *Perestroika* (London, Collins, 1987), pt. 2; Gorbachev's speech on the 70th

anniversary of the October Revolution, *Izvestiya*, 3 November 1987. Other authoritative spokesmen were Eduard Shevardnadze, Deputy Foreign Minister Vladimir Petrovsky, Aleksandr Yakovlev, Evgeny Primakov, Aleksandr Bovin, Vadim Zagladin, Georgy Shakhnazarov.

2. Unlike in the Western literature, where it is habitually pointed out that interdependence can be a source of friction and conflict.

3. At first there appeared to be some doubt about its role. In the documents of the 27th Congress of the CPSU in 1986 the growing weight of the region was interpreted as evidence of a trend to greater multipolarity in international affairs, and of tendencies to sharper contradictions between capitalist 'power-centres'. The Common European House likewise was at first conceived of in traditional Soviet terms, as something designed to exclude the United States. Thereafter, however, regional integration was most frequently treated as a component part of global internationalization rather than as an alternative to it, and the USA was welcomed into the European House. N. Malcolm, *Soviet Policy Perspectives on Western Europe* (London, Routledge/RIIA, 1989), chs 2 and 3; N. Malcolm, 'The "Common European Home" and Soviet European Policy', *International Affairs* (London), vol. 65, no. 4 (1989). The initial model was publicised in particular by Aleksandr Yakovlev, for example in his 'Mezhimperialisticheskie protivorechiya – sovremennyi kontekst', *Kommunist*, 1986, no. 17, pp. 3–17. See also Chapter 2.

4. See especially Gorbachev, *Perestroika*, ch. 6.

5. The father of this community was Evgeny Varga, director of Stalin's Institute of the World Economy and World Politics. In 1946 he proposed that capitalism had become more flexible and adaptive, and that its inevitable collapse was some years away. His institute was soon closed down, but the tradition was picked up again in the 1950s in its successor, IMEMO. E. Varga, *Izmeneniya v ekonomike kapitalizma v itoge vtoroi mirovoi voiny* (Moscow, Gospolitizdat, 1946). See B. Parrott, *Politics and Technology in the Soviet Union* (London, MIT Press, 1985); F. Griffiths, 'The Sources of American Conduct: Soviet Perceptions and Their Policy Implications', *International Security*, vol. 9, no. 2 (1984).

6. O. Eran, *The Mezhdunarodniki* (Tel Aviv, Turtledove Press, 1979); A. Brown, 'Political Science in the Soviet Union: a New Stage of Development', *Soviet Studies*, vol. 36, no. 3, pp. 317–44; N. Malcolm, 'De-Stalinization and Soviet Foreign Policy', in Ts. Hasegawa, A. Pravda (eds), *Perestroika: Soviet Domestic and Foreign Policies* (London, Sage/RIIA, 1990).

7. *Washington Post*, 22 May 1988, p. A33, cited in M. MccGwire, *Perestroika and Soviet National Security* (Washington, DC, Brookings, 1991), p. 180. Gorbachev listed Olof Palme as an influence on his own thinking about security (*Perestroika*, p. 207). See too the Palme Commission's Independent Commission on Disarmament and Security Issues, *Common Security: a Blueprint for Survival* (New York: Simon and Schuster, 1982). Even some senior figures in the Party's International Department became agents of infection with the Eurocommunist tendencies which they were formally charged with extirpating. By the end of the 1980s the most significant party-to-party ties of the CPSU in Western Europe were with the PCI and the SPD, and it was trying to institutionalize links with the social-democratic Socialist International. H. Timmermann, 'Die KPdSU Reformer und die Linke in Westeuropa', *Beitrage der Konfliktforschung*, 1990, no. 3, pp. 33–60. O. Norgaard in 'New Political Thinking East and West: A Comparative

Perspective', in V. Harle, J. Iivonen (eds), *Gorbachev and Europe* (London, Pinter, 1990), pp. 51–83, illuminates the role of the SPD in pioneering 'common security' thinking. Examples of campaigning for social democracy can be found in the work of Yury Krasin, head of the Centre for the Study of Social Democracy set up in the CPSU Institute of Social Sciences in 1987, for instance in 'Novoe myshlenie vo vzaimootnosheniyakh kommunistov i sotsial-demokratov', *Mirovaya ekonomika i mezhdunarodnye otnosheniya*, 1988, no. 4, pp. 23–33. See too Yu. Borko, 'O nekotorykh aspektakh izucheniya protsessov zapadnoevropeiskoi integratsii', *Mirovaya ekonomika i mezhdunarodniye otnosheniya*, 1988, no. 2, pp. 35–50; G. Shakhnazarov, 'Vostok-zapad. K voprosu o deideologizatsii mezhgosudarstvennykh otnoshenii', *Kommunist*, 1989, no. 3, pp. 67–78.

8. Michael Sodaro lists early domestic criticisms of Gorbachev's policy in his *Moscow, Germany and the West from Khrushchev to Gorbachev* (London, I. B. Tauris, 1991), pp. 326–7.

9. *Izvestiya*, 15 June 1991.

10. C. Glickham, 'New Directions for Soviet Foreign Policy', *Radio Liberty Research Supplement*, 2/86 (September 1986); J. Checkel, 'Gorbachev's "New Political Thinking" and the formation of Soviet foreign policy', *Radio Liberty Research Report*, 429/88 (September 1988); MccGwire, *Perestroika and Soviet National Security*, p. 208–12.

11. 'The 19th All-Union Conference: Foreign Policy and Diplomacy', *International Affairs* (Moscow), 1988, no. 10, p. 12.

12. *Literaturnaya gazeta*, 5 November 1986.

13. Shevardnadze in *Pravda*, 26 July 1988; Ligachev in *Pravda*, 13 June 1988. See M. Mendras, 'Soviet Foreign Policy – in Search of Critical Thinking', in Hasegawa, Pravda (eds), *Perestroika: Soviet Domestic and Foreign Policies*, pp. 213–4.

14. A. Brown, 'Andropov: Discipline *and* Reform?', *Problems of Communism*, (January–February 1983), pp. 22–3; MccGwire, *Perestroika and Soviet National Security*, pp. 354–9.

15. Rakhmanin wrote over the pseudonym O. Vladimirov, in *Pravda*, 21 June 1985. The debate is summarized in Karen Dawisha, *Eastern Europe, Gorbachev and Reform* (Cambridge, Cambridge University Press, 1990), pp. 203–6.

16. MccGwire, *Perestroika and Soviet National Security*, pp. 357–8.

17. *Moscow News*, 1990, no. 5.

18. In his study of Soviet relations with the Asia-Pacific region, Sergei Solodovnik makes a similar distinction between 'neorealists', 'supercompromisers' and his own 'rational approach'. 'Is there room for us in the APR?', *International Affairs* (Moscow), 1991, no. 3 , pp. 63–4.

19. Some defenders of the official line also described themselves as 'realists', and no doubt would have argued that they had a far better claim to the title than their opponents.

20. A. Prokhanov, 'Tragediya tsentralizma', *Literaturnaya Rossiya*, January 1991. Cited by V. Dashichev in *Moscow News*, 1990, no. 5. No one would describe the 'military-patriotic' author Prokhanov as a 'realist' in the conventional sense, but 'the nightingale of the General Staff' was able to adopt a suitable hard-bitten tone when necessary.

21. Soviet Television, 19 June 1990. *BBC Summary of World Broadcasts*, SU/0797, pp. C1/6, C1/7.

22. *Voennaya mysl'*, 1991, no. 2, p. 16.
23. *Sovetskaya Rossiya*, 15 June 1991. Cited in *The Times*, 17 June 1991.
24. *Pravda*, 21 January 1991.
25. Akhromeev, interviewed in *New Times*, 1991, no. 14, pp. 14–15; N. Karasev, in 'Guest Club', *International Affairs* (Moscow), 1990, no. 5, pp. 143–5.
26. M. Aleksandrov, 'Bezopasnost'. Dva vzglyada na filosofiyu vneshnei politiki', *Literaturnaya Rossiya*, 22 February 1991.
27. S. Kurginyan et al., *Postperestroika: kontseptsual'naya model' razvitiya nashego obshchestva, politicheskikh partii i obshchestvennykh organizatsii* (Moscow, Politizdat, 1990).
28. Akhromeev, *New Times*, 1991, no. 14, p. 15 (on defending socialism); Stanislav Kondrashev in *Izvestiya*, 13 May 1991 (on Western cultivation of Yeltsin as a likely dismantler of the Soviet state); Aleksandrov, 'Bezopasnost'', and Kurginyan, *Postperestroika* (on exploitation).
29. Aleksandrov, 'Bezopasnost''; Kurginyan, *Postperestroika*.
30. A leaked version of the International Department report was published in the *Frankfurter Allgemeine Zeitung*, 7 June 1991. An article by International Department deputy head Valery Mutalibov, very similar in content, was published in *Pravda*, 13 March 1991. This episode is described in Chapter 6. For concern about Germany, see Prokhanov, 'Tragediya tsentralizma'; M. Aleksandrov, 'Ob'edinennaya Germaniya i obshcheevropeiskii dom', *Literaturnaya Rossiya*, 16 March 1990 (echoing French fears).
31. *Moscow News*, 1990, no. 5; see too Smolnikov, *MEMO*, 1990, no. 1.
32. 'Priorities in a Disarming World', *International Affairs* (Moscow), 1991, no. 3, pp. 4, 7. For a discussion of the influence of Kantian thinking on Soviet foreign policy rhetoric after 1985, see S. Kober, 'Idealpolitik', *Foreign Policy*, no. 79 (summer 1990), pp. 3–24.
33. 'Towards a Community of Rule of Law States', *International Affairs* (Moscow), 1990, no. 1, pp. 146–9.
34. Shevardnadze interviewed by Fedor Burlatsky, *Literaturnaya gazeta*, 10 April, 1991. See A. Kozyrev in *International Affairs* (Moscow), 1991, no. 3, p. 13: Russia's task in the 1990s is 'to join the community of civilized countries'.
35. Yury Borko, *Literaturnaya gazeta*, 13 March 1991.
36. A. Kozyrev, 'Russian Diplomacy Reborn', *International Affairs* (Moscow), 1991, no. 3, pp. 130–1; A. Kortunov, *Moscow News*, 1990, no. 19; Kortunov, *Moscow News* (London edition), 1990, no. 15.
37. A. Kokoshin, 'Europe We Need', *International Affairs* (Moscow), 1990, no. 12, pp. 17–18.
38. V. Benevolensky, A. Kortunov, 'Ekonomicheskaya vzaimozavisimost' i vneshnaya politika SShA', *Mirovaya ekonomika i mezhdunarodnye otnosheniya*, 1991, no. 10, pp. 21–2; 28–9.
39. V. Zhurkin, *Izvestiya*, 26 May 1990; S. Karaganov, 'The Problems of the USSR's European Policy', *International Affairs* (Moscow), 1990, no. 7, p. 74; Foreign Ministry review of policy in 1989–90, *Ibid*, 1991, no. 4; Kortunov, *Moscow News* (London edition), 1990, no. 15; A. Likhotal, 'Speaking as Europeans', *International Affairs* (Moscow), 1990, no. 12, p. 72, laments the damage done in the past by 'the divorce between national and state interests' in the Soviet Union.
40. Kozyrev, 'Russian Diplomacy Reborn', *International Affairs* (Moscow), 1991,

no. 3; A. Kortunov, *Moscow News* (London edition), 1990, no. 15.

41. The RSFSR Foreign Minister Andrei Kozyrev ('Russian Diplomacy Reborn', *International Affairs* (Moscow), 1991, no. 3, pp. 128–9) focused particularly strongly on relations with Europe, and 'the great powers of Europe Russia has traditionally looked up to – I mean France and Britain'. Karaganov recommended that the Soviet Union conceive of itself as 'a great European power having interests in Asia'. 'The Problems of the USSR's European Policy', *International Affairs* (Moscow), 1990, no. 7, p. 76.

42. Kokoshin, 'Europe We Need', pp. 19–20; V. Baranovsky, 'Evropa: formirovanie novoi mezhdunarodno-politicheskoi sistemy', *Mirovaya ekonomika i mezhdunarodnye otnosheniya*, 1990, no. 9; V. Zhurkin in *Izvestiya*, 26 May, 1990; 'The Foreign and Diplomatic Activity of the USSR (November 1989 – December 1990)', *International Affairs* (Moscow), 1991, no. 4, pp. 29–40.

43. Zhurkin, *Izvestiya*, 26 May 1990; Kokoshin, 'Europe We Need', p. 75. See too A. Bovin, *Izvestiya*, 11 November 1990; S. Karaganov, 'The Problems of the USSR's European Policy', *International Affairs* (Moscow), 1990, no. 7, pp. 76–7; S. Karaganov, 'Questions Facing the Future of Europe', *International Affairs* (Moscow), 1991, no. 5, pp. 43–4.

44. 'The Foreign and Diplomatic Activity of the USSR, *International Affairs* (Moscow), 1991, no. 4, pp. 13, 29–40.

45. *New Times*, 1992, no. 3, p. 20. The phrase is that of the interviewer, Galina Sidorova. Kozyrev again criticized New Political Thinking 'messianism' at a Foreign Ministry Conference held on 26–7 February 1992. 'A Transformed Russia in a New World', *International Affairs* (Moscow), 1991, no. 4/5 , pp. 85–6.

46. *Nezavisimaya gazeta*, 1 April 1992; 'A Transformed Russia', p. 86. A comprehensive list of goals was contained in a discussion document sent from the Foreign Ministry to the Russian parliament in early 1992. Like the Minister's own statements, it reflected remarkable continuity with the West-oriented line pursued by Shevardnadze. *Interfax* release, 21 February 1992. Summarized by S. Crowe, 'Russia debates its national interests', *RFE/RL Research Report*, 10 July 1992, p. 44.

47. Interview on Radio Rossiya, 12 March 1992, reported in *Foreign Broadcast Information Service*, SOV-92-049 (12 March, 1992).

48. See Kozyrev's speech in Denmark on 6 March. *Foreign Broadcast Information Service*, SOV-92-046 (9 March, 1992). Also V. Sorokin, head of the international economic relations department of the Ministry, in *Rossiiskaya gazeta*, 29 February 1992; and Boris Yeltsin talking to EC Commissioner Andriessen on 25 March (*Summary of World Broadcasts*, SU/1339, A1/1, 26 March, 1992).

49. Particularly explicitly by Yeltsin's State Secretary, Gennady Burbulis, in Brussels in May 1992. *Foreign Broadcast Information Service*, 7 May 1992. The statement quoted is by Evgeny Gusarov, reported in *Rossiiskaya gazeta*, 5 March 1992. See Chapter 2 and Chapter 9 for an analysis of Russia's relations with NATO and the European Community.

50. ITAR-TASS release, 10 July 1992, reprinted in *Summary of World Broadcasts*, SU/1431, C1/2 (13 July 1992).

51. E. Gusarov in *Rossiiskaya gazeta*, 5 March 1992. This was a well-established theme. See S. Kovalev in *Nezavisimaya gazeta*, 21 September 1991; A. Kozyrev in *Komsomol'skaya pravda*, 5 September 1991. Also S. Karaganov, 'Questions

Facing the Future of Europe', *International Affairs* (Moscow), 1991, no. 5 , p. 45; A. Pankin (ed.), 'Speaking as Europeans', *International Affairs* (Moscow), 1990, no. 12, p. 78.

52. ITAR-TASS, 7 May 1992, reprinted in *Summary of World Broadcasts*, SU/1378, A1/2 (12 May 1992). In general Kozyrev described the improved international context as an important factor encouraging the survival of Russian democracy, singling out the 'tactful and discreet support', it had received 'from civilized and democratic nations'. 'A Chance for Russia', *Foreign Affairs*, Spring 1992, pp. 4, 7.

53. *Izvestiya*, 10 July, 1992.

54. E. Agaev, *Moscow News*, 1992, no. 18, p. 12; K. Pleshakov, 'Missiya Rossiya. Tret'ya epokha', *Mezhdunarodnaya zhizn'*, 1993, no. 1, p. 30.

55. A. Zagorsky, 'Rossiya i Evropa', *Mezhdunarodnaya zhizn'*, 1993, no. 1, pp. 55–6. See also A. Zagorsky et al., *After the Disintegration of the Soviet Union: Russia in a New World* (Moscow, Centre of International Studies, Moscow State Institute of International Studies (MGIMO), 1992), pp. 8–13. Zagorsky argues that Russia should aim to associate itself with the more stable 'Baltic Europe', rather than with the conflict-ridden 'Balkan Europe'.

56. V. Kumachev, *Rossiiskaya gazeta*, 9 March 1992.

57. K. Pleshakov, 'Missiya Rossiya. Tret'ya epokha', *Mezhdunarodnaya zhizn'*, 1993, no. 1, p. 26.

58. A. Grachev, *Moscow News*, 1991, no. 27; N. Pavlov in *Izvestiya*, 18 March 1992.

59. V. Kuvaldin, *Moscow News*, 1992, no. 30, p. 12.

60. V. Lukin (then Chairman of the Supreme Soviet Foreign Affairs Committee), in 'A Transformed Russia', *International Affairs*, 1992, no. 4/5, p. 93. See too the contribution (p. 84), by Ruslan Khasbulatov, Chairman of the Supreme Soviet. Ambartsumov, Lukin's successor as head of the Foreign Affairs Committee of the Supreme Soviet, declared: 'The West . . . respects a strong and not a defeatist position. It despises the weak and is never generous to them.' *Moscow News*, 1992, no. 8.

61. For a particularly trenchant contribution, see V. Razuvaev, *Nezavisimaya gazeta*, 5 March 1992; also S. Stankevich, 'A Transformed Russia', p. 100.

62. *Nezavisimaya gazeta*, 28 March 1992. A shorter version in English appears in 'A Transformed Russia', pp. 98–101.

63. *Izvestiya*, 25 February 1992. See also A. Vasiliev in *Izvestiya*, 19 February 1992, and other authors cited in A. Rahr, '"Atlanticists" versus "Eurasians" in Russian Foreign Policy', *RFE/RL Research Report* 29 May 1992, pp. 17–22; P. Ferdinand, 'Russia and Russians after Communism: Western or Eurasian?', *The World Today*, December 1992. Later contributions to the debate by Nodari Simoniya (IMEMO) and Vladimir Lukin (ex-chairman of the Supreme Soviet foreign affairs committee and formerly an expert on Pacific affairs) are summarized by Jonathan Steele in *The Guardian*, 4 January 1993. Kozyrev and his adviser Ednan Agaev both rejected the criticism that the Ministry had neglected Asian affairs, the former in *Nezavisimaya gazeta*, 1 April 1992 ('a myth'), the latter in *Moscow News*, 1992, no. 9.

64. Stankevich in *Nezavisimaya gazeta*, 28 March 1992; Lipsky, *Moscow News*, 1991, no. 52; Goncharov, *Izvestiya*, 25 February 1992; R. Khasbulatov, *Rossiiskaya gazeta*, 6 March 1992.

65. A. Zagorsky, 'Rossiya i Evropa', *Mezhdunarodnaya zhizn'*, 1993, no. 1, pp. 52–5.

Zagorsky emphasizes that nations like Korea and Japan have been able to modernize themselves without sacrificing their cultural identity.

66. An early thorough exposition of this geopolitical view, from a fairly Westernist perspective, can be found in A. Malashenko, 'Russia: the Earth's Heartland', *International Affairs* (Moscow), 1990, no. 7, pp. 46–54. See also Malashenko's article in *Nezavisimaya gazeta*, 22 February 1992. Similar arguments are used to justify a strongly anti-Westernist position by E. Pozdnyakov, in 'Returning the Soviet Union to European Civilization', *Paradigms* (University of Kent), 1991, vol. 5, no. 1/2, p. 47.

67. Stankevich in *Nezavisimaya gazeta*, 28 March 1992; V. Razuvaev in *International Affairs* (Moscow), 1991, no. 7, p. 48; B. Kapustin in *Mirovaya ekonomika i mezhdunarodnye otnosheniya*, 1992, no. 4 , pp. 43–50. See too K. Pleshakov ('The Russian Dilemma', *New Times*, 1992, no. 2, pp. 14–15), who envisages Russia joining 'the planetary civilizational current' as a distinct cultural entity.

68. Pozdnyakov, 'Returning the Soviet Union', pp. 50–51; later, in 'We must rebuild what we have destroyed with our own hands', *International Affairs* (Moscow), 1992, no. 4/5, pp. 134–5, Pozdnyakov argued that the West would seek to keep Russia in its current enfeebled state. See also his 'Rossiya – velikaya derzhava', *Mezhdunarodnaya zhizn'*, 1993, no. 1, p. 15 ('Russia has never been Europe, she has never been Asia, and neither has she been Eurasia – she has always been RUSSIA.') Also V. Krupin, 'If Russia is saved, the world will be saved', *Sovetskaya Rossiya*, 4 July 1992.

69. See, for example, S. Zyuganov, previously a secretary of the Russian Communist Party and by that time chairman of the Coordinating council of the People's Patriotic Forces of Russia, in *Vestnik*, March 1992, pp. 34–5.

70. E. Volodin in *Sovetskaya Rossiya*, 24 March, 1992. See also the account of the meeting organized by the leader of the Rossiya faction in the Russian parliament, E. Baburin, for the Iraqi ambassador on 18 March. *Kommersant*, 16–23 March 1992. Accounts of the debates are provided in V. Tolz, 'Russia: Westernizers Continue to Challenge National Patriots', *RFE/RL Research Report*, 11 December 1992, pp. 1–9; I. Torbakov, 'The "Statists" and the Ideology of Russian Imperial Nationalism', *RFE/RL Research Report*, 11 December 1992, pp. 10–16.

71. S. Karaganov, *Russia – the New Foreign Policy and Security Agenda* (London, Centre for Defence Studies, London University, 1992), p. 31. See too 'Strategiya dlya Rossii. Nekotorye tezisy dlya doklada Soveta po vneshnei i oboronnoi politike', *Nezavisimaya gazeta*, 19 August 1992. The Council on Foreign and Defence Policy, organized by Karaganov, brings together a large number of eminent specialists, politicians and officials from various parts of the political spectrum. Also A. Vladislavlev, S. Karaganov, 'The Idea of Russia', *International Affairs*, 1992, no. 12, pp. 30–7. Vladislavlev is a leading figure in the centrist Civic Union.

72. *Nezavisimaya gazeta*, 1 April 1992; *Izvestiya*, 30 June 1992.

73. V. Kurochkin, *Rossiiskaya gazeta*, 27 March 1992. Khasbulatov's statement is in *Rossiiskaya gazeta*, 6 March 1992.

74. On Germany see E. Popov, *Sovetskaya Rossiya*, 14 July 1992; on the USA, E. Volodin in *Sovetskaya Rossiya*, 24 March, 1992. See also, for example, Yury Glukhov's article ('Washington on the Moscow River') in *Pravda*, 23 April 1992; A. Baryshev in *Sovetskaya Rossiya*, 18 April 1992; B. Zanegin in *Sovetskaya Rossiya*, 25 June 1992.

75. V. Kurochkin, *Rossiiskaya gazeta*, 27 March 1992; A. Demchenko, *Krasnaya zvezda*, 5 March 1992.
76. A. Bakashov, 'Era Rossii', *Den'*, 17–23 May 1992.
77. V. Krupin, *Sovetskaya Rossiya*, 4 July 1992. *Sovetskaya Rossiya* is not, strictly speaking, an organ of the extreme right, but it is catholic in what it prints. 'Cosmopolitan' is a Stalinist code-word for 'Jewish'.
78. Russian Television (*Vesti*), 9 December 1991. Cited by A. Rahr, '"Atlanticists" versus "Eurasians"', p. 17.
79. V. Rasputin, *Den'*, 5–11 April 1992; V. Buzuev, *Rossiiskaya gazeta*, 25 February 1992; several articles in *Den'*, 7–13 June; 14–20 July 1992.
80. K. Pleshakov, 'Missiya Rossii. Tret'ya epokha', *Mezhdunarodnaya zhizn'*, 1993, no. 1, p. 30; A. Chereshnya, *Rossiya*, 1992, no. 41 (7–13 October) (cited in Tolz, 'Russia: Westernizers Continue to Challenge National Patriots', p. 7).
81. *Trud*, 3 September 1992. Kozyrev is reported to have told Ambartsumov that he would have the opportunity of introducing adjustments in Russian foreign policy. S. Crowe, 'The Fragmentation of Russian Foreign Policy Decision-making', Draft Occasional Study, RFE/RL Research Institute, Munich, 1993.
82. A. Zagorsky, 'Rossiya i Evropa', *Mezhdunarodnaya zhizn'*, 1993, no. 1, p. 53.
83. 'Kontseptsiya vneshnei politiki Rossiiskoi Federatsii', *Diplomaticheskii vestnik*, January 1993 (special issue), pp. 1–23. A report on the compilation of the final version of this document appeared in *Nezavisimaya gazeta*, 29 April 1993.
84. Yeltsin himself blamed the Foreign Ministry for not keeping control of policy, in a critical speech to the Ministry collegium in October 1992. *Radio Mayak*, 27 October 1992. Cited in S. Crowe, 'The Fragmentation of Russian Foreign Policy Decision-making'.
85. John Vincent warned against too heavy a focus on national culture as a factor in international relations, as likely to give 'a harsher view of the clash of cultures in world politics than is justified by the reality of their mutual recognition'. R. J. Vincent, 'The Factor of Culture in the Global International Order', *The Yearbook of World Affairs* (London, Stevens and Sons, 1980), vol. 34, p. 259. See also Iver Neumann, *The Russian Debate About Europe 1800–1991*, Doctoral Thesis, University of Oxford, 1993, p. 8.

8 Economic Relations with the Rest of Europe
David Dyker

As the political and military problems in Russia's relations with the rest of Europe have receded, the economic ones have come relentlessly to the fore. Two preliminary points need to be made. First, in this sphere the connections between internal reform and restructuring of external relations are particularly direct. To take two examples, it is, as economists would put it, impossible to achieve equilibrium in the external balance of payments without achieving internal macro-economic balance, and marketization of the domestic economy demands marketization and multilateralization of foreign trade. Economic reform is only as strong as its weakest link. It is futile to talk about a 'realistic' rate for the rouble, as the former Prime Minister Yegor Gaidar did, as long as Russian economic policy-makers cannot solve key budgetary and systemic reform issues.

Second, a Russian–European economic partnership cannot be planned or ordered. In a true market, deals will be made on the basis of profitability, irrespective of whether they involve the EC, Central- and South-Eastern Europe, North America, the Third World or indeed CIS fellow-members. Under a comprehensively reformed system Western Europe would no doubt remain the main trading partner in the developed world of the successor states to the Soviet Union. But it would do so for reasons of geography and the logic of international specialization. Before we explore the implications of these remarks, we must consider briefly the Soviet legacy in economics and foreign economic relations.

The Soviet disease: a profile

In the 1970s economists identified what they christened the 'Dutch disease'. By this they meant the economic consequences of too heavy a dependence on exploiting a non-renewable resource, gas in the case of the Netherlands. It hardly needs saying that the 'Soviet disease' involved fundamental problems

Table 8.1   The commodity structure of Soviet foreign trade (calculated in terms of current prices)

	1975	1988	1989	1990
Imports				
Machinery and equipment	33.9	40.9	38.5	44.8
Fuel and energy	4.0	4.4	3.0	2.6
Ores and metals	11.5	8.0	7.3	5.1
Chemicals	4.7	5.0	5.1	4.1
Timber and paper	2.2	1.2	1.2	1.0
Textiles	2.4	1.6	1.6	1.1
Foodstuffs	23.0	15.8	16.6	15.8
Consumer durables	13.0	12.8	14.4	17.7
Total	100	100	100	100
Exports				
Machinery and equipment	18.7	16.2	16.4	18.3
Fuel and energy	31.4	42.1	39.9	40.6
Ores and metals	14.3	9.5	10.5	11.2
Chemicals	3.5	4.0	4.0	4.6
Timber and paper	5.7	3.5	3.5	3.7
Textiles	2.9	1.6	1.6	1.2
Foodstuffs	4.8	1.7	1.6	2.0
Consumer durables	3.1	2.8	2.6	3.6
Total	100	100	100	100

Source: *Vneshnyaya torgovlya SSSR v 1975 godu* (Moscow, Statistika, 1976); *Vneshnie ekonomicheskie svyazi SSSR v 1988 godu* (Moscow, Finansy i statistika, 1989); 'Vneshnyaya torgovlya SSSR v 1990 godu', *Ekonomika i zhizn'*, 1991, no. 18.

of the economic and political system, and was immeasurably more serious than the Dutch case. Nevertheless, the argument that the USSR's vast hydrocarbon reserves were a poisoned chalice, permitting the Brezhnev leadership to block desperately needed reforms in the planning system for so long as to actually pre-empt the option of such reforms for subsequent leaderships, is a powerful one.

It seems clear that the enormous windfall gain to the Soviet Union occasioned by the first oil shock of 1974 helped to persuade Brezhnev that the economic reform programme initiated by Prime Minister Kosygin in 1965 and already getting bogged down could finally be abandoned. It is striking that one of Gorbachev's early (apparent) successes as Soviet leader was to

Table 8.2   Soviet oil production (average annual percentage rates of growth)

1971–5	1976–80	1981	1982	1983	1984	1985	1986	1987	1988	1989	1990	1991
6.8	4.2	1.0	0.7	0.5	-0.5	-2.9	3.0	2.0	–	-3.0	-6.0	-10.0

Source: Official Soviet statistics

reverse the downward trend in Soviet oil output which had set in during the early-mid 1980s. But he did so at the cost of driving the Soviet Union further and further down the curve of diminishing returns, which directly contradicted the perestroika goal of making the Soviet economy a more cost-conscious one. And it was, of course, ultimately all in vain, as Table 8.2 shows. It is noticeable that the year when the downward trend in oil production returned with a vengeance, 1989, was the year in which perestroika started to fall apart.

The most obvious symptom of the 'Soviet disease' was the failure to develop a powerful impetus in the export of manufactures of the kind observable in Japan and in the highly successful, resource-poor newly industrializing countries of the Pacific Rim: Korea, Taiwan, Hong Kong and Singapore. Even in a period of sharply falling Soviet oil output, over half of total Soviet exports in 1990 comprised energy and raw materials, while engineering products accounted for just over one-fifth (see Table 8.1). The picture is particularly clear-cut in Soviet trade with the West. In the Brezhnev era the Soviet Union expanded arms deliveries to the Third World as a major export item, but there were increasing problems in obtaining full payment, even where it was envisaged in the first place.

It was a constant theme of the perestroika period that the acknowledged technical merit of the Soviet military-industrial complex could and should be exploited by exporting for hard currency to the West. Ambitious plans were published during the last years of the Soviet Union, including proposals to sell space stations,[1] and recent Western research based on recomputations of the Soviet price structure suggests that machine-building was in general an area of comparative advantage to the Soviet Union, probably mainly because of the military priority.[2] Yet Soviet specialists were increasingly pessimistic towards the end about the possibility of converting actual production facilities, and tended to lay more and more stress on the scope for converting the *human capital* involved, retraining and redeploying, on a 'dispersion rather than conversion' model, the highly skilled work-forces of the defence and space industries. The idea of the military-industrial complex as a section of the economy immune from the Soviet disease and ready to be switched over to any area of technology-based manufacturing the leadership targeted seems to have been largely wishful thinking.

The Soviet disease affected the importing side as much as the exporting. The mistake made by Moscow in the 1970s was to imagine that with large oil export earnings at its disposal, it could substitute technology imports for economic reform. Soviet imports of machinery from West Germany, for instance, nearly doubled between 1974 and 1975.[3] In practice (as was demonstrated even more dramatically in Poland at the end of the decade), sharp increases in the rate of inward technology transfer, not backed up by sustained, general economic reform, merely serve to accentuate many of the chronic weaknesses of central planning: excessive lead-times, the inadequacy of the construction sector, and the absence of any mechanism to ensure that the machinery, licenses and so on purchased did indeed represent the most efficient use of hard-currency resources.

The structural and institutional background

The external context of these developments was a predominantly European one. In 1988 nearly 60 per cent of Soviet trade was with European CMEA partners, and the bulk of the rest was with Western and Southern Europe. European countries occupied five of the top six places in the league table of Western trading partners of the Soviet Union (Japan was the remaining one). Grain shipments from the USA, worth over 2 billion dollars in 1988, represented the only major single Soviet trade flow that was extra-European.[4] But the Europe of the pre-1990 period was, of course, two Europes, nowhere more obviously than in the economic field, and trade with the two parts of the continent was organized in contrasting ways.

Under the established Soviet state monopoly of foreign trade, which survived until 1986, trade with Western Europe, as with the West in general, was based on a 'USSR Incorporated' model. The Ministry of Foreign Trade was the only Soviet organization licensed to deal with capitalist firms. It did so on an essentially commercial basis, calculating in deutschmarks and dollars rather than in roubles. The foreign-trade rouble in which hard-currency trade figures were eventually published represented nothing more than a basket of Western currencies multiplied by an arbitrary coefficient. The Ministry bought cheap and sold dear, and was generally very successful in using its countervailing power, as one of the biggest trading corporations on the world market. It was, of course, much less effective at ensuring that the Soviet economy used efficiently that which it bought cheap, or indeed ensuring that that which was sold dear had not cost even more to produce. In other words, when the Ministry of Foreign Trade turned to face the domestic economy, it was as vulnerable to all the essential systemic weaknesses mentioned above as any other Soviet organization.

The model for trading with Central- and South-East European CMEA partners contrasted sharply with the one just described. Where the latter model was multilateral, the CMEA model was bilateral. Where trade with the West was based on hard currency, the CMEA model was based on no currency, with clearing agreements imperfectly filling the gap. (There was an attempt in 1964 to introduce a 'transferable' rouble into the CMEA system, but, in the event, the transferable rouble remained obstinately untransferable.) As a result, price criteria in intra-CMEA trade remained at best implicit, at worst totally obscure. There was a mechanism for pegging CMEA prices to world prices on a five-year moving average basis, and this worked well enough for primary products like oil, though even here the volatility of world market prices in the 1970s and 1980s meant that CMEA prices were usually significantly above or below the world level. For manufactures, quality discrepancies made the world-price rule largely useless. For primary products and manufactures alike there was the additional problem that since surpluses or deficits could not be cashed in, those countries which ran persistent deficits within the CMEA were effectively bending the bilateral terms of trade in their favour. (Before 1990 a large proportion of Soviet trade with Finland and Yugoslavia was also on a bilateral, clearing-account basis.)

In both Eastern and Western Europe, then, Soviet trading patterns cast the world's second most powerful state in an essentially colonial role, exporting raw materials and importing manufactures and also food staples when the harvest was poor. Yet to describe matters in this way is misleading as far as relations with the CMEA were concerned. Not only was the Soviet Union the unquestioned metropolis of the East European region in political terms, but the trading patterns themselves in practice gave Moscow the whip hand. Commodities that the USSR delivered to her allies were predominantly 'hard' goods which could equally well have been sold on Western markets, while the Central- and South-East European countries gave in return mainly 'soft' goods, low-tech or low-quality consumer goods which were simply not saleable for hard currency. (Hungarian and Bulgarian foodstuffs represented an obvious exception.) Thus Moscow could always argue that, whatever the apparent price relationships, whatever the pattern of surpluses and deficits, the Soviet Union was always doing Central- and South-Eastern Europe a favour by supplying it with energy materials. Behind that lay the notion that the energy-poor satellite states were in some sense 'naturally' dependent on the Soviet Union.

Capital deficit and international debt

There is a powerful argument that the smaller Central- and South-East European countries, as former colonies of the great pre-1914 empires, with few natural resources and other advantages, were in no position to finance

Table 8.3 The Soviet hard-currency external balance (US$bn)

	1983*	1984*	1985*	1986*	1987*	1988*	1989*	1990	1991
Balance of trade	1.3	2.2	-0.8	-3.9	0.4	-2.7	-6.5	-1.6	1.1
Balance of payments, current account	1.5	3.0	1.0	-1.0	1.5	-2.5	-7.5	-5.1	-1.8

Source: Economist Intelligence Unit, *USSR Country Report*, no. 1, (1991);
    'Platezhnyi balans SSSR i Rossii', *Ekonomika i zhizn'*, no. 6 (1992).
Note: * Trade and settlements with Western industrialized countries only.

their own economic development. In the interwar period most of them had chronic trading deficits,[5] and the re-emergence of serious debt problems in the 1970s and 1980s cannot be interpreted simply as a consequence of their systemic shortcomings. The Soviet case is quite different. Tsarist Russia certainly did borrow abroad to finance industrialization, and at least some of the Soviet leaders of the 1920s would have done the same if they could have. Stalin, it may be argued, was able to impose capital self-sufficiency on the Soviet Union in the period of the early five-year plans only at the cost of depressing living standards below a 'reasonable' level. The fact remains that he was able to raise the ratio of investment to national income from 13 per cent to 26 per cent between 1928 and 1937,[6] despite the handicap of a disastrous rural collectivization campaign which destroyed a good part of the potential for savings and investment. That 1937 figure is well above the comparable figure for the present-day UK or the USA.

The figures provided in Table 8.3 show that the Soviet balance of payments shifted during the final years of Communist rule. The USSR moved, it seems, from being a capital-surplus to a capital-deficit country. External borrowing increased sharply, with total gross foreign debt rising from 35 billion dollars in 1986 to some 81 billion dollars in 1991,[7] and the Soviet hard-currency debt service ratio was approaching the danger zone of 25 per cent well before the final collapse of the USSR. By late 1991 the Soviet government was having to make repeated requests to Western creditors for stays on debt service. Since the formation of the CIS, and despite agreement in principle that the old Soviet debt should be serviced collectively, there have been virtually no debt service payments, and it seems unlikely that there will be any rapid resumption of full servicing of interest payments and repayments of principal.

On the other hand, during the last years of its existence the Soviet Union did manage to reduce its current-account deficit quite sharply. Indeed, the hard-currency trade balance actually came back into surplus. This was done largely by cutting back sharply on imports, which could certainly only have been a temporary strategy, in view of the importance of imports of equipment and technology for economic restructuring. Yet the Soviet Union showed that it was quite capable, even as it entered the stage of final dissolution and systemic collapse, of taking effective short-term measures to bring its current account balance under control. It is true that the capital investment requirements of a comprehensive programme of rebuilding the CIS economies are colossal. But the Soviet Union still managed during 1991 to finance 245 billion roubles (some 13.6 per cent of national income) of fixed capital formation in the state sector, predominantly from domestic sources. The central problem of investment under Gorbachev-era perestroika was in fact not one of volume. It arose rather from a failure to deal with one of the key sources of Brezhnev-era stagnation, namely a pitifully low rate of return – for some sectors and projects below zero – on the investments made. It would be a mistake, therefore, to assume that effective reconstruction of the post-

Soviet economies (and particularly the Russian economy) is critically dependent on a large-scale inflow of capital investment from abroad.

The restructuring of the foreign trade system

In 1986 the Leninist central monopoly of foreign trade was liquidated. This was one of a series of measures that signalled the beginning of Gorbachev's attempt to introduce the key principles of economic perestroika: decision-making autonomy, self-financing and the primacy of prices. The Ministry of Foreign Trade lost most of its traditional directive powers. It was abolished altogether a couple of years later, and replaced by a new Ministry for External Economic Affairs shorn of explicit powers of command, but still with substantial prerogatives. It was responsible for vetting organizations wishing to engage in foreign trade, and for determining the complex system of 'coefficients' on the basis of which world prices were converted into roubles for domestic accounting, and incentive, purposes. In addition, the new ministry was intended to play an important part in articulating long-term strategy.

Under the 1986 legislation a specified group of ministries and enterprises gained the freedom to enter into direct contractual links with foreign companies. They would be at liberty to export goods, including equipment, surplus to planned needs at home, at prices agreed by them with the foreign purchaser. They would also be permitted to retain a fixed proportion of their hard-currency export earnings to spend freely on imports of equipment, to provide hard-currency incentives for their work-force, or indeed to lend at a fixed rate of interest to other Soviet organizations wanting to finance imports. Direct state control was maintained over the key strategic areas of energy exports and food imports, but by early 1988 about a quarter of Soviet trade was being carried on under the new dispensation. A decree of December 1988 in principle extended the right to trade directly on the world market to all Soviet enterprises. In March 1989 a tight procedure was introduced for registering enterprises engaged in foreign trade, but the principle of universal access was preserved. By 1 April 1991 more than 30,000 Soviet organizations were registered for foreign trade activity.[8]

The final years of Soviet power saw the growth of a complex and clumsy system of export licensing, which proved highly vulnerable to hijacking by populist leaders eager to jump on the bandwagon of 'export nothing that we need ourselves' and departmental bosses seeking to neutralize potential competition. This trend strengthened after the dissolution of the USSR, with export duties emerging as the main foreign trade policy instrument of the Russian Federation. Import and export licenses and quotas are also widely used in post-Soviet Russia. They were slated for abolition on 1 July 1992 as part of the internal convertibility package (see below). In practice, little changed at that point, and the October 1992 *Medium-Term Programme of*

Economic Reforms of the Russian Government merely lists abolition of quantitative restrictions as a medium-term goal. The Russian government has replaced the old system of registration of foreign trade participants with one that is at least as complex, and possibly less consistent. Trends in other republics have been similar. At the time of writing, then, foreign trade was still only just beginning to emerge from the no man's land, neither planned nor market-led, into which it strayed in the late Gorbachev era.

An equally momentous piece of legislation was passed in 1987. The joint venture law of that year permitted foreign ownership of equity in the Soviet Union for the first time. The maximum foreign share in a joint venture was initially limited to 49 per cent, but it was raised to 80 per cent at the end of 1988, and 100 per cent foreign ownership was subsequently permitted. Joint ventures were in principle subject to both profits tax and repatriation tax, but with a tax holiday for foreign partners from the date on which profits were first generated. In practice, joint venture regimes turned out to be one of the major battlefields of the 'War of Laws' that developed as republics, and even lower-level authorities, started to try to assert their sovereignty, promulgating their own joint venture regulations, often in a competitive spirit. For individual foreign firms it came down in the end to a matter of negotiating the best deal they could with Soviet, republic or local governments, as the case might be. By the middle of 1991 more than 3,000 joint ventures had been agreed with foreign partners, the bulk of them from Western countries. Since the dissolution of the Soviet Union there have been no great changes in principle, although with the republics replacing the union, at least one level of legal confusion over joint ventures has been removed.

There was also substantial discussion of special economic zones (SEZs). Clearly modelled on Chinese experience, the Soviet SEZ was envisaged essentially as an enclave of the world economy on Soviet territory, based on market principles and hard-currency settlements, and allowing for private property. Early candidates for SEZ status included Novgorod, the old Hansa town of the Russian Baltic region, and Kaliningrad *oblast'*, representing the greater part of the previous German province of East Prussia.

Foreign trade reforms in practice

The measures of 1986 and 1987, together with their subsequent glosses, failed to revolutionize the pattern of Soviet foreign trade. Nor has the disappearance of the USSR produced any dramatic change in the situation. Despite unfavourable production trends, particularly in oil, Russia continued in 1992 and 1993 to export predominantly Ricardo goods. It continued to export manufactures on only a small scale, and to import grain on a massive scale. It appeared likely to continue in the medium term, if not in the short term, to spend large volumes of hard currency on equipment imports and technology transfers. There is as yet no guarantee that these will be better assimilated than the equipment imports and technology transfers of the late Soviet period.

While the number of joint ventures set up in the last years of the USSR looks impressive, the amount of capital and volume of business involved does not. By February 1990 joint ventures had attracted just 1.5 billion dollars of international equity capital,[9] and that figure had probably not risen much by 1991. They did not emerge as major vehicles for technology transfer into the Soviet economy, or as major stimulators of Soviet exports. In 1989, the most recent year for which figures are available, the net effect of joint ventures on the Soviet balance of trade was substantially negative.[10]

It is not difficult to find specific technical reasons for this lack of impact in the period up to the dissolution of the USSR. The tax regime for joint ventures was unattractive, repatriation of profits uncertain, and the whole question of converting roubles into hard currency hopelessly confused for everyone involved in foreign trade. While in principle joint ventures were autonomous of (what was left of) the planning system, their activity was still in practice obstructed because state organs retained the right, under Gorbachev's half-reformed system, arbitrarily to pre-empt resources, whether imports or potential exports, on the basis of 'state orders' (the *gosudarst-vennyi zakaz*).

The position for Soviet trading enterprises was even less satisfactory. The erratic pluralization of authority in the foreign trade sphere that occurred from 1990 onwards was based on administrative fiat rather than on the market mechanism. It is significant that Boris Yeltsin's Russian government is still maintaining the prerogative to pre-empt resources through the placing of priority state orders. The general absence of joint venture activity in 1992, it must be added, was largely a function of uncertainty over political prospects and anxieties about the international payments position, rather than about the details of regulatory or planning regimes.

Nothing more clearly reflected the fundamental tensions and contradictions, both economic and political, of the Soviet perestroika process than the history of attempted implementation of the Special Economic Zone idea up to the end of 1991. Throughout 1990 the idea of turning Kaliningrad *oblast'* into an SEZ was strongly canvassed by the local civilian authorities, and on 1 January 1991 the province was opened up to foreigners for the first time, by decision of the Soviet government. But Kaliningrad remained a key base for the Soviet military. With the collapse of the Warsaw Pact it became the most westerly salient of the Soviet Union, with the added advantage, compared to, say, the Baltic republics or Western Ukraine, of being populated largely by Russians. As an ice-free port, Kaliningrad was particularly important for the Soviet navy. It seems clear that at some point in late 1991 the Soviet military imposed a kind of veto on rapid progress towards the setting up of a Kaliningrad SEZ.

While the Novgorod proposal hung fire, plans to set up a SEZ were also maturing in Leningrad (now St Petersburg), just a hundred miles north of

Novgorod and, like Kaliningrad, a Baltic port. But these plans, pressed by the radical mayor of Leningrad, Anatoly Sobchak, represented more a manoeuvre in domestic Soviet politics than an element in foreign trade policy. What Sobchak was seeking was effective economic independence for Leningrad (the SEZ would be coextensive with the city), including the right to do separate, bilateral deals with the independence-minded, and soon to be independent, Baltic republics.

The one proposed SEZ that was actually set up before the collapse of the Soviet Union was at Nakhodka, in the Soviet Far East. Construction of factory and warehouse space began at the end of 1990, with the actual building work being done, it seems, by mainland Chinese, and sites were already being rented out in early 1991. Even here, however, the War of Laws took its toll, with the Russian Federation taking the early initiative, the Union then failing to follow up, the local government of the Maritime Province in which Nakhodka is located subsequently taking matters into its own hands, and the Russian Federation government then coming back and seeking to reimpose its authority.

The demise of the Soviet Union has not changed the basic orientation of the SEZ policy initiative. It has certainly accelerated its implementation, and given it some real content in the European part of the Russian Federation. By 1992 Kaliningrad had joined Nakhodka as a functioning special economic zone, with calls from local leaders for the region to be set up as an independent 'fourth Baltic republic'.[11] SEZs were also reported to be operational in Novgorod, Vyborg (on the Finnish border), Sakhalin and the Kuriles (next to Japan), and in a number of other Russian far eastern regions. But by early 1993 even the fully operational SEZs had failed to achieve the total commercial autonomy of their Chinese counterparts, and SEZ administrators viewed the prospects for their zones as critically dependent on *general* trends in economic policy.

The question of convertibility

As noted above, much of the weakness of the CMEA as an instrument of division of labour stemmed from the absence of a universally accepted means of settlement. One of the factors that hindered the effective implementation of late-Soviet foreign trade reforms was the continued absence of a unified formula for translating export earnings into domestic purchasing power. A convertible rouble would, of course, have solved all these problems, and many more, at a stroke.

In the past economists have tended, perhaps, to be too pessimistic about the feasibility of introducing a degree of convertibility into medium-developed economies with weak manufacturing export bases. Experience with *internal convertibility*, introduced in Poland in 1989 and Yugoslavia in 1990, demonstrates that such economies can tolerate (in balance of trade terms), and indeed benefit from (in more general macro-economic terms), a degree of convertibility. Internal convertibility, based on fixed exchange rates, limits convertibility to the sphere of current transactions, and restricts it largely to the citizens of the country in question. Its immediate effectiveness depends on pitching the exchange rate at a level which if anything errs in the direction of undervaluing the local currency. Its continued effectiveness depends on maintaining a degree of control over the domestic money supply tight enough to stop the emergence of a strong inflationary trend which would inevitably push the exchange rate out of line, and ultimately create pressures for devaluation, which could unleash waves of destabilizing speculation. The Polish and the Yugoslav experience demonstrated both how well the package can work when these conditions are fulfilled, and how vulnerable it is when they are not fulfilled.[12]

Rouble convertibility was cited as one of the key medium-term goals of perestroika from the middle-late 1980s onwards, and developments from late 1989 through 1990 and early 1991 seemed to be preparing the ground for convertibility. The old, wholly unrealistic parity of around one rouble to the pound sterling was effectively abandoned in October 1989, with the introduction of a new tourist rate fixed at just 10 per cent of the old rate. On 3 November 1989 the first Soviet foreign-exchange auction was held. It generated rates of exchange two to three times lower than the new tourist rate. In the course of 1990 both foreign-exchange auction and black-market rates tended increasingly to the bottom end of that range. In April 1991 the Soviet authorities gave their blessing to the trend, devaluing the tourist rouble to a rate of around 30 to the pound sterling. By June, the rate had gone to 50 to the pound. Meanwhile, in late 1990, a commercial rate, for use in business transactions, was introduced at a rate of about three to the pound sterling.

At the beginning of 1992, Boris Yeltsin's Russian Federation government introduced a system which established convertibility at a market-determined rate for private transactions by residents, but required that businesses sell a fixed proportion of their hard-currency earnings to the Central Bank of Russia at an exchange rate set by that bank, normally half the market rate. The Central Bank had no corresponding obligation to supply would-be importers with the necessary foreign exchange, though foreign exchange auctions made some hard currency available to the business sector. This regime did not, of course, amount to full internal convertibility. Internal convertibility was promised as part of the 1 July 1992 package. In the event that package failed to deliver internal convertibility, though it did unify the exchange rate, thus ending the penalization of importers and reducing the incentive for them to try to cheat the Central Bank. The October 1992 *Medium-Term Programme* of the Russian government merely reiterates the commitment to internal convertibility without giving a timetable. In view of the ever-worsening problem of budgetary deficit, and the consequent slide into hyper-inflation, there seems to be no immediate prospect of this commitment being realized.

Prospects for a new role for Russia in the European division of labour

But let us assume that the rouble achieves partial convertibility, that quantitative trade restrictions are removed, and that a chain of SEZs emerges in the European part of Russia. The ultimate aim would be to generate a new pattern of international trade which would kill the Soviet disease at the roots, and which would reflect the emergence of a new division of labour within Eastern Europe, and between Eastern Europe and Western Europe, based on comparative advantage. The model most often cited is, of course, the European Community, not only because it is a European organization, but also because it has shown how much can be achieved with an incomplete package of economic integration measures, backed up by a minimal degree of political integration.

Yet it is not at all clear that the experience of West European integration is helpful in identifying likely trends in the East, and at the continental level. For the unique success of the EC among contemporary customs-union experiments is based on the fact that the core countries of the Community display an extraordinary degree of *similarity* in their economic structures. They are all heavily industrialized, with very large engineering sectors, but with highly developed service sectors as well. In each of them technology, in the broadest sense, is a key source of economic growth. The reason why they find trade so profitable is the degree of micro-specialization which has developed between advanced industrial countries since the Second World War. This phenomenon is by no means limited to Western Europe, but the provisions of the Treaty of Rome have encouraged its growth. Micro-specialization arises because a growing proportion of sophisticated engineering and engineering services activities is most efficiently carried out in highly specialized, medium-sized organizations.

Of course the history of the EC is not just one of the painless deepening of micro-specialization. There has been a tendency for Germany to dominate the process to an extent which other Community members have sometimes found uncomfortable. Many sectors, moreover, have remained untouched by micro-specialization, notably agriculture, textiles and footwear, but also vehicle production. In the case of the first, there is simply no common market, nor any stable common external tariff. The CAP is a clumsy and expensive way of preventing – perhaps for perfectly good reasons – the deepening of agricultural specialization within Europe and between Europe and the rest of the world. The Multi-Fibre Agreement, and numerous 'voluntary' export restraints (VERs) – effectively export quotas – have been imposed by the governments of EC-member countries on East European and East Asian producers precisely in order to arrest the 'natural' evolution of the international division of labour. The track-record of the EC, in a word, is of huge success in developing micro-specialization, which is based on similarities in resource endowments, and of substantial failure when it comes to macro-specialization, based on differences in resource endowments.

It is instructive to look at what happened in the case of another customs union, the Latin American Free Trade Area, which covered a region of the world more similar to Eastern than to Western Europe in terms of its general level of economic development.[13] While the EC stands out as a great triumph of integrationism, the history of the LAFTA was largely one of failure. The most obvious reasons were political. But behind the political disagreements lay substantial economic issues. In a continent which does not possess the technology and human capital to develop intra-regional micro-specialization on a large scale, the only possible basis for integration was traditional comparative advantage. And here LAFTA ran into precisely the same problems as Khrushchev had in the late 1950s and early 1960s, in his largely unsuccessful attempts to put some real content into the idea of 'the international socialist division of labour'. Just as Romania under Gheorghiu-Dej simply refused point-blank to have anything to do with a programme for deepening the intra-CMEA division of labour which consigned Romania to the role of food-producer, so heavily agrarian countries like Bolivia found unacceptable programmes which would have reinforced their own agricultural orientation while facilitating the further industrial development of countries like Brazil.

The record of free-trade areas in the development of macro-specialization is poor the world over. However, for the time being, macro-specialization is the only kind of specialization available to the successor states of the Soviet Union, whether in relation to Eastern or Western Europe. The implementation of the Single European Act in 1992 should act to reduce the incidence of, for instance, VERs in relation to imports into Western Europe. But it would be over-sanguine to expect that the EC is simply going to open its doors to imports of foodstuffs and low-tech manufactures. (See Chapter 9 for an analysis of Russia's relations with the European Community.) In the East, the combination of ethnic-territorial tensions and acute worries about the impact of radical restructuring on employment levels is bound to place very serious obstacles in the way of a deepening of the regional division of labour.

Is there anything the outside world can do to help?

Against this somewhat pessimistic background, can we pick out any levers that the individual countries and international organizations of the industrialized world could bring to bear on the task of adjusting Russia's position in the international division of labour? Maximal liberalization of all quantitative restrictions on the import of agricultural and industrial products is an obvious one, but it would have much more purchase in relation to the smaller countries of Central- and South-Eastern Europe, with their food surpluses and manufacturing export bases of sorts, than in relation to Russia. Abolition of the security related COCOM restrictions would target Russia much more specifically, by facilitating access to the kinds of technology which would permit that country to re-employ the stock of human capital and know-how accumulated in the defence and space industries. It would also make things easier for the joint ventures which in the future could provide a vehicle for the kind of effective continuous technology transfer which the Soviet Union never knew. In September 1991 there was an across-the-board 40 per cent reduction in the product-by-product coverage of COCOM. But it continues to impose significant restrictions in relation to trade in advanced materials, electronics, computers, lasers and sensors, navigation equipment and means of propulsion, and those on all successor states of the Soviet Union. At the same time COCOM has laid down fairly clear conditions on which ex-Warsaw Pact countries may hope eventually to be 'deproscribed', as indeed Hungary has already been. The main general consideration is the status and effectiveness of the export controls imposed by the country seeking deproscription in relation to the sensitive product groups. At the first meeting of the COCOM Cooperation Forum, held in November 1992, the principle was established that countries will benefit from relaxation in restrictions as they impose their own controls, so that the process will be of a gradual, rather than an all-or-nothing character. Continuing concern about the volatility of the CIS region may, however, induce governments to take a very cautious approach to the whole process in the Russian case.

As far as economic aid is concerned, it is important to make a clear distinction between Russia and the rest of Eastern Europe. As was said earlier, there is no reason to treat Russia as an innately capital-deficit region. The problem has been, and still is, one of the efficiency with which fixed capital formation is carried out. Another powerful argument against open-ended industrial aid is that it would almost certainly be diverted, to one degree or another, to the defence of existing industrial structures and employment patterns, in effect to help maintain the system of soft budget constraints. (Chapter 9 provides details of aid so far.)

But there may be an argument for extending specific forms of aid in the area of infrastructure. Environmental aid, for instance, could be directed towards specific ecological disaster areas, like the Chernobyl fall-out zone and the Aral region. Perhaps even more important, educational and technical aid could be organized in specific programmes in such a way as to remove the need for indefinite recurrent financial commitments. Such programmes would address the underlying problem of how to create a new Russian know-how complex, capable of linking up with other know-how complexes and ultimately of generating its own innovatory dynamism. In so doing, they would address the critical medium- to long-term problem of how to bring about Russia's participation in the European pattern of micro-specialization of the next century.

There is also a powerful argument that for a country saddled with huge debts contracted in the pre-1989 period, and minimal foreign exchange reserves, liquidity support may be enormously valuable. The great danger in Eastern

Europe as a whole is that political obstacles to trade, against the background of the breakdown of the clearing-account system, might push the countries of the region into a new autarky more damaging even than the autarky of the CMEA period. In 1991 Soviet trade with former CMEA partners contracted by around 60 per cent.[14] In 1992 Russia's trade with the ex-CMEA area fell by 43 per cent compared with a notional figure for 1991.[15] As we have seen, by the end of 1991 the Soviet Union had encountered severe hard-currency payments problems. The contraction of the rouble zone, as more of the former Soviet states start to issue their own currency, means that liquidity shortages begin to affect an ever greater proportion of what was intra-regional trade under the old regime. It is true that Russia and some other former Soviet states retain a significant capacity to produce gold (300–350 tons a year). But gold is a Ricardo good like oil, and in post-Soviet conditions the law of diminishing returns applies as much to the production of the one as to that of the other. By making other sources of liquidity available, the West would be reducing the chance of a reversion to the Soviet disease.

Proponents of the ecu monetary standard system[16] argue that the ecu has three main advantages as a means of hard-currency settlements between the Central- and South-East European countries and former Soviet states. First, as an international unit, it has an attractive quality of political neutrality. Second, the fact that it is based on a basket of the currencies of the main extra-regional trading partners of the East European countries gives it the advantages of stability and appropriateness in real trading terms. Third, use of the ecu as a monetary standard would represent some kind of initial, informal association with the European Monetary System. At the level of domestic monetary policy, a crucial variable in general restructuring policies, 'shadowing the deutschmark' would give way to 'shadowing the ecu'.

The proposal would only operate painlessly if each country were more or less in trade balance with all the others together, taking one year with another. In the event of persisting structural deficits within the region it would break down, unless backed up by some element of long-term capital transfer. But it is quite improbable that any such structural deficits would be generated by hydrocarbons-producing states such as Russia.

The European and Western institutional setting: possible patterns of assistance

The strength of an international trade and finance liberalization strategy is that it requires very little institutional development and has no financial implications. That is why abolition of COCOM and relaxation of EC trading restrictions could be so important. It is equally why Russia's entry to full membership of the IMF in April 1992 could have important medium-term implications. While the Russian Federation's continuing macro-economic difficulties may, for instance, ensure that the promised 6 billion dollar stabilization fund for the rouble is never delivered, membership of the 'club' could have considerable value in helping Russia to break down trade discrimination. In that regard, of course, full membership of GATT, still but a distant prospect, would be a much greater prize.

What kind of overall aid package would be appropriate, in the light of what has been said so far? When it comes down to hard cash for specific purposes, the World Bank, and possibly also the European Bank for Reconstruction and Development (EBRD), are surely appropriate sources for loans on preferential terms for environmental and training/technical assistance programmes. The EC will no doubt continue to extend its direct support for technical assistance programmes for the successor states. Liquidity support for intra-East European trade could be provided by a consortium of commercial banks, such as the Ecu Banking Association (EBA). The EBA hosted a meeting on 23 April 1991 in Turin, attended by central bankers from the Soviet Union, Poland, Hungary and Czechoslovakia, devoted to an initial practical assessment of the ecu monetary standard system. Such a system would, of course, only work if there were some organization in the background willing to provide an ultimate guarantee that finance would be made available to compensate for persistent payments imbalances. It seemed in 1992 that the Group of Seven might in principle be prepared to fulfil this role. It is still not clear, however, what specific institutional form such support might take. In the past, the IMF has not engaged in financing structural deficits; historically its role, too, has tended to stop at liquidity support. The World Bank has followed the practice of extending Structural Adjustment Loans to individual countries, but under very specific conditions which would be difficult to impose in this case. Perhaps this is where the EBRD, which is still trying to define its role vis-à-vis the former Soviet Union and Central- and South-Eastern Europe, could play a key role.

In formulating European and wider Western policy responses, it is clear from what has been said so far that five main points should be borne in mind. First of all, it is not obvious that the goal of an internally convertible rouble is feasible in the foreseeable future. But unless a critical degree of convertibility is achieved for the rouble zone, the rate of integration of Russia and the other former Soviet states into the European and world economy in the short to medium term will be severely hampered. Second, there is no general argument that large-scale capital transfers are a necessary condition for effective restructuring in Russia. Indeed such transfers could hold up the process by lifting some of the pressure towards energetic industrial adjustment. Third, the collapse of intra-regional trade in Eastern Europe is one of the biggest single short-term problems affecting all the countries of the region, including Russia and the other former Soviet states. The idea of an ecu-based payments system to provide a sound foundation for a reexpansion of the trade is realistic, and would represent a valuable bridgehead for the extension of European Community influence throughout the region. In order to work properly it would require some public institution, possibly the EBRD, to provide last-resort cover in the event of the emergence of serious structural deficits. Fourth, a general dismantling of Western trading restrictions in relation to Russia and the other former Soviet states would be an effective and cost-free way of helping to lock the region into the European and world trading systems. Finally, existing EC initiatives in the area of financial support for training and in general adapting Russia's human capital should be developed, within the framework of overall Western strategy. They should be granted a degree of exemption from short-term political pressures, but should be tied to the principle of hard budget constraints.

Notes

1. A. Tarasov, 'Orbital'nyi zavod', *Pravda*, 17 May 1990, p. 3.
2. G. Duchêne, C. Senik-Leygonie, 'Prices liberalization and redeployment in the USSR. The Soviet economy at world prices', *European Economy* (forthcoming).
3. *Vneshnyaya torgovlya SSSR v 1975 godu* (Moscow, Statistika, 1976); 'Vneshnyaya torgovlya SSSR v 1990 godu', *Ekonomika i zhizn'*, 1991, no. 18 , pp. 10–11.
4. *Vneshnie ekonomicheskie svyazi SSSR v 1988 godu* (Moscow, Finansy i statistika, 1989).
5. R. Nötel, 'International Credit and Finance', in M. C. Kaser and E. A. Radice (eds), *The Economic History of Europe*, vol. 2 (Oxford, Clarendon Press, 1986).
6. P. Gregory, R. Stuart, *Soviet Economic Structure and Performance*, 4th edn. (New York, Harper & Row, 1990).
7. Economist Intelligence Unit, *USSR Country Report*, 1991, no. 1, p. 17.
8. 'Ekonomika SSSR v pervom polugodii 1991 goda', *Ekonomika i zhizn'*, 1991, no. 30, special supplement, p. 18.
9. B. Kheifets, 'Joint entrepreneurship in the USSR and prospects for Soviet-South Korean cooperation', Moscow, 1990, unpublished.
10. Ibid.
11. *The Baltic Independent* (Riga), 28 February–5 March 1992, p. 2.
12. D. A. Dyker, *Can Systemic Reform Survive National Disintegration?* (Bala Cynwyd, WEFA, 1991); A. Kondratowicz, J. Michalek, 'Polish trade adjustment under convertibility', University of Sussex working paper, 1991.
13. P. T. Ellsworth, J. C. Leith, *The International Economy*, 6th edn (New York, Macmillan, 1984).
14. 'Ekonomika stran-chlenov sodruzhestva nezavisimykh gosudarstv v 1991 godu', *Ekono-mika i zhizn'*, 1992, no. 6, pp. 13–16.
15. 'Sotsial'no-ekonomicheskoe polozhenie i razvitie ekonomicheskikh reform v Rossiiskoi Federatsii v 1992 godu', *Ekonomika i zhizn'*, 1993, no. 4, p. 15.
16. P. Zaino, 'East–West financial issues', in *The Central and East European Economies in the 1990s: Prospects and Constraints*, NATO, Economics Directorate and Office of Information and Press, 1990.

9   Russia, the CIS and the European Community: Building a Relationship

Perdita Fraser

Ever since its foundation, the European Community has declared its role to be one of building peace and reconciliation through the development of closer relations between European states. The treaties establishing the European Community clearly state that all European countries have the right to be included ('any European state may apply to become a member of the Community', Article 237, EEC Treaty), with the aim of laying 'the foundation of an ever closer union among the peoples of Europe'.[1] In the 1960s some political scientists were already beginning to speculate about the eventual inclusion of Central- and South-Eastern Europe and a no longer hostile USSR in a single interdependent Europe.[2] By the late 1980s, as the Soviet leaders sought an exit from the Cold War, and called for the building of a 'Common European House', it had begun to look conceivable that there could be a peace-building role for the Community, this time on a larger scale. (For an account of changing Soviet and Russian perceptions of the European Community, see Chapter 3.)

Yet the very success of the European Community, the advances in integration and economic development which made it so attractive to the East, meant that the East–West gulf was by then much deeper than the divisions which separated the original six. There was no evident external threat to stimulate decisive action and to make sacrifices seem worthwhile. While some progress was made in building formal ties with Poland, Hungary and Czechoslovakia, relations with the USSR and Russia developed slowly, and in a piecemeal way. Although the relationship between Brussels and Moscow improved and deepened markedly after 1989, it is still an arm's length one, and the prospects are by no means clear. This chapter looks at developments so far, and options for the future.

199

EC policy towards the USSR and Russia under Gorbachev and Yeltsin

Soon after he came to power Mikhail Gorbachev conceded the principle, long resisted by his predecessors, that the individual European member states of the CMEA could establish direct ties with the EC. The accelerating thaw which followed culminated in the opening of diplomatic relations with Brussels by all the countries concerned. In December 1989 a comprehensive Trade and Cooperation Agreement was signed by the Community and the USSR. The provisions of this agreement are still largely in force, pending the reaching of new agreements with the separate former Soviet states.

The agreement resembled others concluded between the EC and the Central- and South-East European countries in that it constituted a necessary but not a sufficient condition for the expansion of trade. Specific quantitative restrictions on EC imports from the USSR were to be abolished by 1995, with the exception of some sensitive products. The USSR, for its part, undertook to grant non-discriminatory treatment to EC exports as regards quotas, licences and the necessary currency allocations. Apart from these provisions the trade arrangements contained little beyond a mutual granting of most-favoured nation treatment, with the usual safeguard clauses. The agreement also contained undertakings to promote economic development, and trade and business interaction, through cooperation in areas such as management training, joint ventures, statistics, standardization, environmental protection, financial services, transport and commercial law as well as in key sectors of the economy. A joint committee, meeting annually, was established to oversee the agreement and act as a forum to increase dialogue and cooperation between the EC and the USSR.

One year after the signing of the Trade and Cooperation Agreement, the European Council, meeting in Rome in December 1990, asked the Commission to start negotiations for a broader agreement, intended to parallel the agreements being negotiated with the other European ex-CMEA countries. The initiative came from the French and German governments, which proposed very wide-ranging cooperation measures, together with a gradual liberalization of trade, leading to the establishment of a free-trade area. It was proposed that Article 238 of the EEC Treaty should be used as the legal basis for the new agreement. This was a controversial suggestion because Article 238 refers to the conclusion of Association Agreements. It had been taken as the basis for the Europe Agreements then under negotiation with Poland, the CSFR and Hungary, which refer to eventual full membership of the Community. The EC Commission was extremely reluctant to take up this suggestion, in view of the unstable political and economic situation in the USSR. It had reservations, too, about many other aspects of the Franco-German proposal. In particular the idea of a free trade area, which was strongly supported by the Soviet government, provoked considerable debate, since the USSR was not even a member of the GATT and still operated commercially under traditional state-trading regulations.³ Current prospects for a new agreement are discussed below, in the section on Institutional Relations.

In the late 1980s most of the political initiative in EC–Soviet relations had come from President Gorbachev, with his talk of a Common European House, his arms reductions and his non-interventionist policy in the satellite states. The Community for its part often found it difficult to react in a coherent way. This was not only due to the manifest uncertainties within the USSR, but also to differences of opinion between the EC member states. West Germany, which had its own special reasons, was pushing hard for greater concessions and the development of closer relations with the East. Some other EC member states, such as Britain, pursued a similar although less active policy. Meanwhile France and most of the southern member states tended to adopt a more cautious, wait-and-see approach. Policy-makers in EC states had to balance a wide range of considerations. Not only was it undesirable to leave the Soviet leadership to define the agenda alone, but also the EC's relations with the USSR were of key importance to the future of the Central- and South-East European countries. Attractive commercial opportunities were offered by the opening up of a vast new market in the Community's back yard, and particularly a market whose products were mostly complementary to the EC's, unlike those of former satellite states. Towards the end of the 1980s, the Community states were also concerned that the upheavals in Central-Eastern Europe should not derail Soviet perestroika: the 'Prague Spring' and events in the CSFR in 1968 had been an important factor in terminating Kosygin's Soviet economic reform project in 1969. Finally, the greatest fear in Western Europe was that increased instability and economic distress in the USSR would lead to mass emigration and, even more worryingly, nuclear weapons falling into unsafe hands.

As the crisis deepened in the Soviet Union during 1990, the EC offered food and medical assistance (largely in the form of credits, see below), and a technical assistance package with a budget of 400 million ecu was activated in 1991. Apart from these actions, it was primarily in the framework of general Community/Western assistance to the East European region that the USSR began to benefit, for example with the creation of the European Bank for Reconstruction and Development, and the signing of the European Energy Charter (see below). Although, for the reasons outlined above, assisting the USSR had become a priority concern for the Community, the Central- and South-East European countries were the main focus of attention: a framework for relations with these countries was already being constructed, whereas the role of the USSR in the future European architecture was still unclear. Gradually, however, the West began to become more deeply involved. President Gorbachev was invited to attend the Group of Seven summit in July 1991, and associate membership of the IMF was approved in October 1991, giving the USSR access to the technical assistance and advisory services of the IMF (although not yet to macro-economic assistance).

By the time the Soviet Union finally fell apart, in December 1991, the economies of its constituent republics had undoubtedly reached crisis point, and the West, and Western Europe in particular, was faced with difficult decisions about what it should (or could) do to promote recovery. The break-up of the USSR failed to resolve the uncertainties surrounding the future of the region. Indeed it created new ones. Policy-makers in Western Europe continued to react with caution. This chapter looks in turn at the issues which face them in the areas of trade, institutional relations, and assistance, and reviews the progress made to date. The concluding section considers the longer term prospects for relations between the European Community, Russia and the other former Soviet states.

Trade relations

During the Soviet period, members of the CMEA were forced into an inefficient system of bilateral trade, essentially based on barter arrangements (see Chapter 8). Prices of goods traded within the CMEA were denominated in the transferable rouble and bore little resemblance to world prices. Input prices and exchange rates were set unilaterally by the individual countries concerned, and vast inefficiencies were inherent in the system: normal trading practices were rendered effectively impossible. Only specialized foreign trade organizations had access to foreign markets, and the CMEA trading environment was sheltered from world market forces, leaving the productive units ill-equipped to face a competitive environment. As a result only a limited number of enterprises could successfully redirect their products towards Western markets.

After the dissolution of the CMEA in June 1991, although the Soviet authorities pushed hard for the establishment of a successor organization, no viable acceptable alternative could be found. Together with the introduction of hard-currency trade at world prices, the disappearance of the CMEA had a very damaging effect on economic relations between its former members. The worst consequences were experienced by the former satellite states, which in the early 1980s had conducted only 22 per cent of their total trade between themselves, relying heavily on the USSR as an export market. The latter emerged in a position of *relative* strength, because of its wealth in natural resources, particularly energy products (which unlike many CMEA goods could be redirected to the developed world to earn much-needed hard currency), and a productive structure which provided many of the investment goods for the other economies. Subsequently the break-up of the USSR brought with it a slow-up in trade relations between its former members, and in some areas caused severe economic dislocation. The new states began to introduce quantitative restrictions and excise duties, intended to curb exports rather than to prevent imports. Most of the natural resources turned out to be in Russia.

Table 9.1 Summary of Quantitative Restrictions imposed in 1990 by EC member states on Soviet exports by product category

	Number of products	Value of products covered by QRs (1990, Ecu mn)	Value of EC imports from USSR (1990, Ecu mn)	Imports covered by QRs (%)	Number of QRs applied by one MS	Number of QRs applied by two MS	Number of QRs applied by more than two MS
Agriculture	329	44	234	19	253	52	24
Raw Materials	193	39	11,791	0	102	91	0
of which base materials	75	38	1,387	3	75	0	0
Primary manufactures	101	2	379	1	40	56	5
incl. textiles/apparel	0	0	288	0	0	0	0
Chemicals	18	3	656	1	3	0	0
Other manufactures	576	359	578	62	400	118	58
Total	1,217	447	13,638		798	317	102

Source: European Commission

Notes: The total value of EC imports from the USSR in 1990 differs from the amount shown in Table 9.2 since the Not specified and non-reported ('Confidential') category of products (2,528 million ecu) is not included in this analysis.

In 1990, there were French QRs covering 34 oil, gas and mineral exports (amounting to 8,399 million ecu). However, these were so large that they never formed a trading constraint. They were removed in January 1993.

Table 9.2 Summary of the trade balance between the USSR, the former USSR and the EC (all figures in million ecu)

	1986	1987	1988	1989	1990	1991	1991*	1992*
EC imports from (ex-) USSR	13,158	13,128	12,988	15,166	16,167	18,477	14,022	12,774
EC exports to (ex-) USSR	9,875	9,189	10,113	12,603	11,184	14,228	9,906	10,072
(ex-)USSR trade balance with EC	3,283	3,939	2,875	2,563	4,983	4,249	4,116	2,702

Source: Eurostat
Note: *First nine months

Table 9.3 EC trade with the former USSR in the first nine months of 1992

	EC exports			EC imports			EC trade balance
	Ecu mn	Growth compared first nine months 1991 (%)	% of total	Ecu mn	Growth compared first nine months 1991 (%)	% of total	
Agricultural goods	2887.2	164.5	28.7	291	29.7	2.3	2596.2
Raw materials	792.9	-22.9	7.9	8171.2	-5.3	64.0	-7378.3
incl. base metals	407.9	-44.1	4.0	1548.7	12.0	12.1	-1140.8
oil, gas, minerals	65.4	68.1	0.6	5701.9	-14	44.6	-5636.5
Primary manufactures	1238.1	44.2	12.3	492.9	41.2	3.9	745.2
incl. textiles/apparel	397.1	86.4	3.9	408.0	48.6	3.2	-10.9
Chemicals	771.8	-8.2	7.7	569.7	4.2	4.5	202.1
Other manufactures	4033.6	-22.9	40.0	593.7	-24.2	4.6	3439.9
incl. transport vehicles	1222.1	15.7	12.1	435.8	-27.9	3.4	786.3
(Not specified, mainly 'confidential')	348.4	15.7	3.5	2655.3	-4.7	20.8	-2306.9
Total	10072	1.7	100	12774	-8.97	100	-2702

The West's ability to provide preferential market access for Russia and the other former Soviet states is constrained by GATT most-favoured-nation and non-discrimination provisions. Moreover, although the EC has verbally committed itself not to use anti-dumping procedures against the ex-CMEA states,[4] current GATT provisions on anti-dumping are open to interpretation by the EC in such a fashion that it could use anti-dumping duties to limit import competition from these countries, as they strive to export using their main competitive advantage, namely a cheap and skilled labour force.[5]

It is true that the GATT Uruguay round negotiations, together with the implementation of the EC's Single Market Programme, appear to promise a very favourable exporting environment, given that VERs (Voluntary Export

Table 9.4 Share of each member state in Soviet exports to the EC, 1991

	Proportion of EC imports from the ex-USSR accounted for by member state (%)	Proportion of EC imports from the ex-USSR accounted for by member state (oil, gas and mineral imports)(%)
France	16.0	11.7
Belgium, Lux.	7.5	3.0
Netherlands	10.5	8.4
Germany	32.3	18.6
Italy	17.1	9.2
UK	8.1	4.7
Ireland	0.4	0.3
Denmark	1.2	0.5
Greece	2.0	0.8
Portugal	0.3	0.0
Spain	3.7	1.7
Total	100.0	58.7

Source: Eurostat
Note: Totals may show small discrepancies due to rounding.

Table 9.5 Share of each member state in EC exports to the USSR, 1991

	Proportion of EC exports to the ex-USSR accounted for by member state(%)
France	8.6
Belgium, Lux	2.4
Netherlands	3.6
Germany	62.8
Italy	14.1
UK	3.1
Ireland	0.6
Denmark	1.2
Greece	0.5
Portugal	0.1
Spain	2.3
Total*	100.0

Source: Eurostat
Note: *Small discrepancy in total due to rounding.

Restraints) and other non-tariff barriers are to be phased out. Unlike Central-and South-Eastern Europe, Russia and several of the other former Soviet states specialize in the kind of export commodities, mainly raw materials and industrial inputs, which, except in the case of coal and steel, do not meet high tariff barriers. Furthermore, in their imports from the EC, they have benefited considerably from Community surpluses (for example, of butter). In reality, however, exports from Russia and the other former Soviet states will still face protected markets, through the special protocols for so-called 'sensitive' products[6] and through the global Multifibre Arrangement (MFA). The MFA has been negotiated between all the principal exporters and importers of textiles, so that bilateral VERs exist for each pair of participating countries. Even if the current Uruguay Round of GATT succeeds, and the MFA is eventually phased out, there will still be intense protectionist pressures from textile and clothing manufacturers inside the Community. In addition, the EC's commitment to the non-application of anti-dumping procedures is certainly not binding, and the EC could at any point break its commitment without incurring legal sanctions. A total of 1,058 quantitative restrictions (QRs) are still imposed on a transitional basis by the member states of the EC, but most QRs are applied in only one or two member states. These QRs do not always represent substantial barriers to trade, because in practice foreign goods may enter a member state that does not apply the QR and then freely circulate within the EC, but they do represent administrative barriers. Table 9.1 summarizes the Community QRs imposed on imports from the Soviet Union in 1990. These are still in place today, with the exception of the QRs, mentioned in the note to Table 9.1, which were lifted in early 1993. The European Council is currently (May 1993) discussing a proposal to scrap *all* QRs in trade with third countries, with the exception of some Far Eastern state-trading countries, such as China.

Although the dissolution of the USSR and the current political upheavals and economic decline affecting its successor states have disrupted old trade patterns, and although the restructuring which is planned will, if it succeeds, have far-reaching effects on external economic relations, it is nevertheless instructive to examine the pre-1992 state of trade relations with the EC countries (see Table 9.2).

The overall Soviet trade balance experienced a marked improvement between 1990 and 1991, from a trade deficit of almost 17 billion dollars to a trade surplus of 2 billion dollars. This can largely be attributed to the collapse of imports from the ex-CMEA countries, which dropped from 68 billion dollars during 1990 to 24 billion dollars during 1991. The EC has constituted the most important trade partner for the USSR and its successor states. In 1991 Soviet exports to the EC accounted for 42 per cent of total Soviet exports, while Soviet imports from the EC accounted for 39 per cent of total imports.

The USSR historically enjoyed a trade surplus with the EC due to its energy exports, although this contracted from approximately 3 billion ecu during 1990 to just over 1 billion ecu during 1991, excluding trade in non-specified and non-reported products.[7] The deterioration in the trade balance can largely be attributed to a surge in Soviet imports of vehicles and equipment, which rose from 0.3 billion ecu in 1990 to 1.7 billion ecu in 1991. The first nine months of 1992 witnessed a further increase of nearly 16 per cent in this category of imports, although overall imports from the EC to the former

USSR rose by only 1.7 per cent, while exports to the EC contracted by 8.9 per cent, reflecting the economic disruption in the region.

Table 9.3 reveals that raw materials accounted for 64 per cent of former Soviet exports to the EC during the first nine months of 1992, down from 67 per cent in 1991 as a whole. The bulk of these raw material exports (45 per cent of total exports in 1991) was accounted for by oil, gas and minerals, which were uniformly distributed across the EC countries. The only other significant items were base metals, which accounted for 12 per cent of exports in the first nine months of 1992 (the German market absorbed nearly 60 per cent of this export) and non-specified products (21 per cent of total EC imports). In the case of Soviet exports of transportation vehicles and equipment, Germany was the destination of over 60 per cent. Overall, Germany absorbed over 32 per cent of all Soviet exports to the EC (see Table 9.4), and accounted for over 60 per cent of EC exports to the USSR, in 1991 (see Table 9.5) Manufactured products made up over 60 per cent of EC exports to the Soviet Union. This reflected the increasing demand for consumer goods, coupled with a strong demand for investment products necessary to replace the largely inefficient inherited productive capacity.

Russia, which accounted for the bulk of Soviet raw material exports, is thus a complementary trading partner for the EC, because of the latter's relative scarcity of natural resources. Compared with most of the other former Soviet republics, Russia emerges in a position of potential strength, since raw materials continue to find relatively unrestricted trading conditions in global markets. It could in theory exploit its comparative advantages in more labour-intensive sectors such as agriculture, apparel and textiles, but the current trading relationship with the EC means that a massive expansion of exports of these products is unlikely. The real threat to the trade balance with the EC is the huge potential demand in Russia for more sophisticated capital goods and consumer products, which will not be satisfied domestically. A lack of hard currency has restricted imports of these products, but it is clear that foreign grants and credits, together with any increased hard currency earnings in the medium to long term, will lead to an acceleration of such imports, with the EC, and in particular Germany, poised to benefit. As Chapter 8 argues, if the structure of trade is to be changed, and a new balance created, improved trade access to the West for a broader range of goods is vital. This is needed as an incentive for Western investors, who will be deterred from major industrial investment if it is not clear that the goods produced will have relatively free entry to Western markets.

Institutional relations

Following the disintegration of the USSR, it was decided, as we have seen, that the provisions of the EC's 1989 Trade and Cooperation Agreement with the USSR should stand until replacement agreements with each of the new states were concluded. This was done promptly only in the case of the Baltic republics. Letters formalizing the interim arrangements were sent to all the other states with the exception of Russia, which adopted the position of legal successor to the USSR. Negotiations on the replacement agreements have only begun with a few of the former Soviet states, and only with Russia have talks substantially begun to address all the issues.

Initially the EC's goal was to negotiate agreements similar (but less extensive) to those signed in 1992 with Albania and the Baltic states. These were wide-ranging trade and cooperation agreements regarded by the states concerned as a first step towards Association Agreements and eventual membership. The Russian government was keen to achieve something close to the Association Agreements, and it proposed that Russia (along with some of the other Soviet states) could be part of a future European economic space.[8] Meanwhile the EC, and in particular the Commission, felt unable to agree to any such suggestion, since the concept of a European economic space presupposed a common market with extensive policy coordination. Others continue to argue that a new European economic space, to be instituted in some ten or fifteen years time (by which time the EFTA states, or most of them, would presumably have joined the EC) could form a useful goal to offer the CIS states, which would constitute the outer ring in the Europe of 'concentric circles'. Several member states, in particular the UK, Germany and Holland, expressed considerable interest in such ideas.

Negotiations on an agreement with Russia began in late 1992. As far as the Community was concerned, the objective of these new agreements was to support the transition process, and to assist the integration of Russia and the other former Soviet states into the 'wider European area of cooperation'. Since it was not envisaged in Brussels that these states would join the EC in the foreseeable future, there was a reluctance to match the scope of the Association Agreements. But Russia and the other former Soviet states were pressing for more commitment than was implied in the traditional (or even new Baltic-style) trade and cooperation agreements.

The talks continued for several months in this vein until early April 1993, when the EC eventually agreed to persistent Russian requests that the scope of the agreement be broadened to include as a stated goal the gradual establishment of the 'four freedoms of movement' (goods, persons, services and capital) between the participating states. Although some had opposed the inclusion of such a clause in any agreement with Russia, the member states appeared to have reached a consensus view that more commitment was necessary to support the transition process in Russia. There is still some disagreement over the exact wording of the clause, with some member states, led by Germany, pushing for a fairly definite promise of eventual participation for Russia in a European free trade area (subject to certain conditions), and other member states holding out for a more cautious, non-committal reference to the four freedoms. Of course, neither the timing nor the arrangements for achieving such an objective will be outlined in the agreement, and any future free trade agreement between the EC and Russia could only be implemented when Russia had completed its transition to a market economy. However, even the general commitment to a free trade area will bolster foreign investor confidence, and although Russia's export potential is low at the moment, it must surely increase. Furthermore, having made such a commitment, the EC is now free under the provisions of the GATT to provide more trade concessions in the intervening period. The GATT states that countries may give exceptions to MFN treatment principally in three cases: where a free trade area is to be established, without prejudice to third countries (Article 24); in the context of concessions to developing countries (Article 18), for instance by means of the Community's Generalized System of Preferences (GSP);[9] and, by inference, where a specific product or group of products is liberalized for all trade partners.

The Community itself, as well as the European Economic Area Agreement and the Association Agreements, are all established under Article 24 of the GATT, which requires that substantially all trade must be covered by the agreement. Admittedly, in the past the Community has reached preferential trade agreements with third parties under this article,[10] but the Community is anxious to differentiate between the deal gained by the Central- and South-East European countries in their Association Agreements in view of their future membership, and the provisions that can be offered to the former Soviet states. It is not clear at the time of writing whether the new agreement with Russia will be explicitly established under Article 24.

As for the category of concessions to developing countries, it must be noted that all the Central- and South-East European countries (including the Baltic states) have been granted GSP treatment, although not within the context of an agreement, since most of them cannot be technically defined as developing countries. The Community has also granted GSP treatment to the former Soviet states, from 1 January 1993. The purpose is largely political, to signal that they are being treated on an equal footing with their Western neighbours. The commercial impact is likely to be limited in the medium term, only materially stimulating the import of industrial goods, which because of the slow rate of economic recovery is unlikely to increase substantially. Nuclear issues remain outside the province of the new agreement, although negotiations are expected to start on a specific agreement between Russia and Euratom (the European Atomic Community).

It is likely that, as Trade Commissioner Leon Brittan has proposed, there will be a provision for regular review of a future EC–Russian agreement every two or three years. The planned agreement includes a paragraph on respect for human rights and democratic principles as defined in the Helsinki Final Act and the Charter of Paris for a New Europe, accompanied by a suspension clause which would be activated if the condition should be broken. There is also an expression of commitment to market economy principles. Other provisions of the treaty will include enhanced cooperation measures, embracing financial assistance (although there is no contractual commitment on the part of the community) and cooperation in crime prevention; Russian workers are to be entitled to non-discriminatory treatment within the EC, although this does not mean the de facto free movement of persons; EC companies operating in Russia will be able to choose between the most-favoured-nation clause and national treatment, while Russian companies established in the EC will benefit from national treatment in the country of establishment; with regard to services, national treatment will generally be provided; and there are provisions on competition and investment. Germany, Holland and the Benelux countries have been supporting the idea of access to the European Investment Bank (a concession not accorded to the Central- and South-East European states), but it is not clear at the time of writing whether there will be any mention of this in the final version of the agreement, especially since France and most of the southern EC member states are supporting a much-watered down version of the financial provisions.

The initial schedule, according to which Russia would sign the new agreement in June 1993, seems unlikely to be adhered to, since there are still unresolved issues. These include Russian opposition to the human rights clause. The EC is unwilling to concede on this point, since following the meeting of the European Council at Maastricht in December 1991, the Commission explicitly stated that all future agreements with the CSCE partners would be conditional on the inclusion of such a clause. The Commission is also concerned about the bad state of relations between the Russian government and the Russian Central Bank authorities, and the impact this could have on EC investments in Russia.

Assistance from the European Community

What forms of direct assistance are appropriate for the former USSR is a thorny problem for the West. The first difficulty is one of size. It has been estimated that if Russia were to receive aid on a similar scale to that received by the former GDR (approximately 100 billion dollars annually), it would require some 1.8 trillion dollars every year, in view of the size of its population and its economy.[11] The 24 billion dollar aid package[12] for Russia which was announced by the G7 on 1 April 1992 in fact contained little actual resource transfer, and much of it was in the form of loans on marginally favourable terms, which the CIS states would have had access to anyway and would have to repay at a later date. In the event, very little of the aid package was actually utilized. The aid package announced in Tokyo in April 1993 appears to be more effectively structured. At every stage the assistance process has been complicated and hindered by the difficulty of setting appropriate conditions – of a kind which will stimu-

Table 9.6   Breakdown of EC technical assistance programmes to the former Soviet states in 1992 (Ecu mn.)

Baltic states	25
Total for the other 12 former Soviet states	425
minibudget	5
nuclear specialists	30
regional projects	73
coordination units	12
other	5
indicative programmes	300
of which:	
Armenia	10
Azerbaijan	12
Belarus	12
Kazakhstan	18
Kyrgyzstan	10
Moldova	10
Russia	120
Tajikistan	12
Turkmenistan	10
Ukraine	54
Uzbekistan	22
Georgia	10

Source: European Commission

late the reform process without being politically unacceptable to the recipients – and by problems of administration and implementation. Transport networks are poor, communications inadequate, there is an absence of Western-style norms, standards and accounting practices, and the division of authority, for example between local and national levels, is ill defined.

Nevertheless, tangible aid programmes have been got under way, and the EC is channelling considerable technical assistance and other forms of help to Russia and the other former Soviet states. Indeed the EC and its member states have contributed the lion's share of credits (70 per cent of the world total by April 1993; see below, Table 9.7). The Community also played a leading part in setting up the European Bank for Reconstruction and Development, and promoting the European Energy Charter.

In December 1990 the EC governments decided that, rather than including the USSR in the existing PHARE programme of assistance to Central-Eastern Europe, a separate technical assistance programme would be established for it, which would take into account the special requirements of the region. Some 400 million ecu was allocated in 1991, of which 375 million ecu was actually available for commitments, with a further 450 million ecu allocated in 1992, 610 million ecu in 1993 and a similar amount expected in 1994. Following the collapse of the USSR at the end of 1991, the technical

Table 9.7 Distribution of global assistance to the ex-USSR to March 1993, million ecu (excluding aid to the Baltic states committed under the EC's PHARE programme)

	Food and medical aid (grants)	Credits and credit guarantees including untied balance of payments support	Strategic assistance	Technical assistance	Others or non-available	Total
EC	466.5	1750	0	1310	0	3526.50
Member states	1415.92	37450.02	8768.9	519.59	1535.26	49689.69
EFTA countries + Nordic Council	48.28	1009.34	0	128.99	3.07	1189.68
Other countries	1240.72	13348.71	676.55	712.46	3491.79	19468.74
International institutions	0	1478.92	0	58.69	0	1537.60
TOTAL[4]	3171.42	55036.99	9444.45	2729.72	5030.12	75412.21

Source: European Commission

Notes: 1 The table includes estimates of commitments made by the Community, its member states, other countries and international institutions (IMF, World Bank and EBRD) between September 1990 and 8 March 1993. These commitments may cover several years. Commitments made by international institutions are not included under those of their member states. Figures do not take rescheduling or private grants into account.

2 Figures do not include the commitments made during or after the Vancouver summit of 3–4 April 1993, and the Tokyo G7 Ministerial Meeting on 14–15 April 1993, since most of these are still subject to approval by the competent authorities. Furthermore, some measures announced include money already pledged. The following commitments were made in Vancouver and Tokyo:

USA: $6.5 billion, including $1.6 billion announced in Vancouver, $1.8 billion announced in Tokyo, $2 billion in Eximbank guarantees for oil and gas equipment, $700 million in the budget for 1994 and $400 million under the Nunn/Lugar provisions for nuclear dismantling.

EC: Ecu3.47 billion for the CIS, of which Ecu2.082 billion is for Russia. This includes Ecu1.02 billion for TACIS across 1993 and 1994, the Ecu1.25 billion loan financing the imports of food and medical supplies presently under implementation, as well as Ecu1.2 billion of Euratom loans. Part of this package is subject to Council approval.

Japan: $1.82 billion, consisting of $100 million for humanitarian assistance, $120 million for technical assistance and exchange programmes, $30 million for SMEs in the Far East, $100 million for denuclearization and $1.5 billion of loan assistance.

UK: £320 million in additional credits, as well as £60 million for the Know-how Fund.

Canada: C$200 million, covering grants for technical assistance and a new credit for health assistance. The resumption of a credit line to finance 500,000 tonnes of wheat shipments has been decided.

3 Figures for commitments giving rise to legal obligations for disbursements are not available for most donors. Proportions may be different in these cases.

4 Totals may show small discrepancies due to rounding.

assistance programme was christened TACIS (Technical Assistance for the Commonwealth of Independent States).

Despite numerous problems, the Commission succeeded in committing all the available funds in 1991, across five priority areas: management training (103 million ecu), financial services (37.5 million ecu), energy (115 million ecu), transport (45.8 million ecu) and food distribution (74 million ecu), with 6.2 million ecu set aside for the funding of small multidisciplinary projects. Its policy priorities in 1992 were to reduce CIS dependence on food aid and to encourage cooperation between the former Soviet states, by directing assistance towards projects that necessarily involved more than one of them, for example, improvements to the rail and water transport networks. Although the implementation of the budget was reasonably effective given the constraints, companies and institutions attempting to obtain contracts under the technical assistance programme found the process frustrating: only 40 per cent of the 1991 programme had actually been contracted out by the end of May 1992 (see Table 9.6).

The 1992 budget for technical assistance was set at 450 million ecu, of which 120 million ecu was specifically allocated to Russia.

The Rome EC Council meeting in December 1990 also decided in principle to grant food aid to the USSR, with 250 million ecu in the form of grants and 500 million ecu in the form of a credit guarantee. The distribution of the 250 million ecu food aid grant was held up by the general suspension of assistance following the Soviet crackdown in the Baltic states in January 1991, and eventually began only in the summer of 1991. By the end of May 1992, some 85 per cent had been delivered, with the shortfall largely in the unstable Transcaucasian republics. Meanwhile the 500 million ecu credit was made available to guarantee a loan granted to the Soviet Vneshekonombank by a consortium of banks led by the Deutsche Bank. The loan was initially designed to finance imports from the EC only, but was extended to included products from the Central- and South-East European countries and the Baltic states, up to a ceiling of 25 per cent of the total. These triangular trade operations were designed not only to support traditional trade links, but also to ease pressure from Central- and South-East European food exporters on the EC market. The implementation of the credit was held up because a responsible interlocutor could not be found to meet the requirements of the Western banks, and by the end of 1991 the credit had still not been activated. Following the disintegration of the USSR, the European Council decided in February 1992 to transfer this guarantee to benefit the Russian Federation exclusively, with the share of other former Soviet states in a subsequent 1.25 billion ecu credit (see below) to be adjusted accordingly. Thereafter, letters of credit were finally approved, and the credit was disbursed by the end of May 1992. Of this 16 per cent was used in triangular trade operations with East European countries. A further food grant of 200 million ecu was announced by the Maastricht Council in December 1991. This was intended principally

Table 9.8 Membership of the EBRD

Country	Capital subscription (Ecu mn)	% of capital stock	Country	Capital subscription (Ecu mn)	% of capital stock
Members of the EC			**Recipient members**		
Belgium	228	2.3	Albania	10	0.1
Denmark	120	1.2	Armenia	5	0.1
France	852	8.5	Azerbaijan	10	0.1
Germany	852	8.5	Belarus	20	0.2
Greece	65	0.7	Bulgaria	79	0.8
Ireland	30	0.3	CSFR	128	1.3
Italy	852	8.5	Estonia	10	0.1
Luxembourg	20	0.2	Georgia	10	0.1
Netherlands	248	2.5	Hungary	79	0.8
Portugal	42	0.4	Kazakhstan	23	0.2
Spain	340	3.4	Kyrgyzstan	10	0.1
UK	852	8.5	Latvia	10	0.1
EEC	300	3.0	Lithuania	10	0.1
European Investment Bank	300	3.0	Moldova	6	0.1
			Poland	128	1.3
Other European Countries			Romania	48	0.5
Austria	228	2.3	Russian Federation	400	4.0
Cyprus	10	0.1	Slovenia	1	0.0
Finland	125	1.3	Tajikistan	10	0.1
Iceland	10	0.1	Turkmenistan	1	0.0
Israel	65	0.7	Ukraine	40	0.4
Lichtenstein	2	0.0	Uzbekistan	21	0.2
Malta	1	0.0			
Norway	125	1.3	Unallocated former USSR	44	0.4
Sweden	228	2.3	Unallocated former		
Switzerland	228	2.3	Yugoslavia	127	1.3
Turkey	115	1.2	Capital subscribed by		
			members	9884	98.8
Non-European Countries			Non-allocated shares	116	1.2
Australia	100	1	Authorized share capital	10000	100
Canada	340	3.4			
Egypt	10	0.1			
Japan	852	8.5			
Republic of Korea	65	0.7			
Mexico	30	0.3			
Morocco	10	0.1			
New Zealand	10	0.1			
USA	1000	10			

Source: Annual Report of the Bank for European Reconstruction and Development 1992

Notes: Shares totalling Ecu15.5 million, which were originally allocated to the German Democratic Republic, were added to non-allocated shares.

Albania was admitted in December 1991. Estonia, Latvia and Lithuania were admitted in February 1992. In March 1992, the Board of Governors reallocated for Moscow, St Petersburg, and three other cities. The products purchased with this second food grant were sold through the existing commercial networks, with the proceeds contributing towards a counterpart fund intended to help the least privileged sections of the population.

At the end of the summer of 1991, the Soviet government had presented a detailed request for further food assistance, originally amounting to 15 billion dollars and later reduced to 10.2 billion. The Western response was announced in early October 1991, when the Group of Seven nations pledged to provide a 6 billion ecu credit facility for the USSR to buy food and medicine abroad. The EC undertook to provide one-third of this credit, with the remaining 4 billion ecu coming from the US, Japan and Canada. However, by no means all of the 6 billion ecu was new money. The EC's contribution included the 250 million ecu food aid grant, as well as the 500 million ecu credit guarantee. The new element was an 1.25 billion ecu medium-term loan intended to finance the import of agricultural, food and medical supplies. Up to 50 per cent of the loan was to be used to purchase goods from Central- and South-Eastern Europe and the Baltic states. Conditions (a commitment to market economy and democratic principles) were attached to the credit line, although these were to be dropped in cases of hardship, for example in relation to food and drug deliveries to orphanages, hospitals and old people's homes. Access to the loan was subject to further conditions. First, a traditional waiver of sovereign immunity was required, which Russia has yet to sign. Second, the former Soviet states had to sign the memorandum of 28 October 1991 regarding the Soviet debt legacy, although much of this agreement has not yet been implemented,[13] and they had to be generally regarded as current with debt servicing.

All this must be seen in the context of the wider assistance effort mounted by the EC member states and by other industrialized countries, which between September 1990 and mid-March 1993 comprised commitments of nearly 75 billion ecu.[14]

The Community did not take the lead in coordinating assistance to Russia and the other former Soviet states, as it had in the case of Central- and South-Eastern Europe. After Russia's entry to full membership of the IMF in June 1992, the latter seemed more likely to take on that role.

---

the Ecu600 million capital subscription of the former USSR among the 12 CIS states, with Ecu44 million remaining unallocated. In September 1992, the Board recognized that the Republic of Yugoslavia had ceased to exist and decided that its share could be reallocated among the countries previously forming part of Yugoslavia. By early 1993 only Slovenia had been formally admitted as a member. In December 1992, the Board of Governors decided that the shares of the former CSFR should be divided on a two-to-one basis between the Czech Republic and the Slovak Republic, and that their individual membership should be regarded as effective from 1 January 1993, subject to the completion of membership procedures.

Another mechanism for assisting Central- and South-Eastern Europe and the USSR appeared with the founding of the European Bank for Reconstruction and Development (EBRD) in April 1991. The initial proposal for such a bank was made by President Mitterrand of France in October 1989. The twelve member states of the European Community and two EC institutions (the Commission and the European Investment Bank) were founder members of the Bank, along with twenty-seven other countries (see Table 9.8). Community member states, together with the Commission and the EIB hold 51 per cent of the EBRD's capital stock. The EBRD was initially mandated to operate in the seven East European countries which were founder members of the Bank, namely Bulgaria, Czechoslovakia, Hungary, Poland, Romania, the USSR and Yugoslavia. The list was subsequently extended to include Albania and the three Baltic states. At the end of March 1992 most of the shares of the former USSR were redistributed among its constituent republics, with the exception of Georgia, which joined later in the year.

EBRD activities in the then USSR were initially limited by the bank's statutes to a total amount not exceeding the Soviet Union's paid-in capital. This restriction was lifted in March 1992, but no more than 40 per cent of total bank lending can go to the former Soviet states. Several technical assistance projects have been initiated, chief among which are the Moscow City Council privatization programme (1.23 million ecu), and the setting up of an International School for Banking and Finance in Moscow (2.30 million ecu) and in St Petersburg (1 million ecu). The latter are being established in cooperation with European Bank Training Network, and with financial support from the EC Commission.

Although the mandate of the Bank stipulates that not less than 60 per cent of its financing activities must be directed to the private sector, the EBRD is keen to increase its involvement in areas associated with the public sector, such as defence conversion. However, this idea has met with resistance from some shareholders, notably the United States, who want the Bank to stick to its brief. Theo Waigel, the German Finance Minister and chairman of the EBRD board of governors, nevertheless held open the possibility that soft loans might be made to finance urgent safety work on nuclear reactors in the beneficiary countries. Problems are also caused for the EBRD by West European fears of trade competition. Sectors such as food, textiles, steel and the automotive industry are the areas with the most short-term potential for restructuring and privatization. Unfortunately these sectors are also those in which the EC is most protectionist.

Unlike other institutions involved, the EBRD has a specific mandate to establish the framework for a market economy in Central- and South-Eastern Europe and the former Soviet states, and unlike commercial banks its lending is conditional on evidence of moves to pluralist democracy and a market economy. The Bank's pattern of activities, and the involvement of large companies such as Nestlé, General Motors and GEC–Alsthom in the co-financing of projects, has reassured its early critics. The EBRD has also probably benefited from the reluctance of many Western governments to provide further export credit guarantees, forcing investors to look to it to provide some security for their activities in the uncertain post-Soviet environment.

The European Energy Charter was signed at the Hague on 17 December 1991, by all the countries of Europe, the European Community, and nine of the fifteen former Soviet states (the remaining six signed subsequently), together with the USA, Japan, Canada and Australia. The Charter represented a political commitment[15] to establishing greater cooperation in the energy field. Its ultimate goal is a single integrated energy market in Europe. However, the initial aim is more modest: to improve 'security of energy supply and [to maximize] the efficiency of production, conversion, transport, distribution and use of energy, to enhance safety and to minimize environmental problems, on an acceptable economic basis'.[16] The initiative, launched by the Dutch Prime Minister, Ruud Lubbers, in March 1990, was taken up nine months later at the European Council meeting in Rome, which requested the Commission to prepare a draft text to present at a special international conference. Subsequently the European Community, especially under the Dutch presidency during the second half of 1991, played a leading part in organizing negotiations for the Charter.

The European Energy Charter emphasizes that East European energy inefficiency is a continent-wide problem. It acknowledges that 'account must be taken of the problems of reconstruction and restructuring in the countries of Central and Eastern Europe and in the USSR'[17] and it calls for the signatories 'to participate in joint efforts aimed at facilitating and promoting market-oriented reforms and modernization of the energy sectors in these countries'. The benefits of this arrangement are also, it declares, likely to accrue to the West Europeans, through an increase and diversification of supplies, particularly desirable in view of their current dependence on the Middle East.

The Charter describes three main areas for cooperation. The first is energy trade. The goal is to build an open competitive market, with unrestricted access to energy resources, markets, capital and technologies, to remove barriers to trade in energy, to modernize services and fixtures relating to the energy sector, to develop energy transport infrastructure and to facilitate access to it, and to promote and protect investment. The second is coordinating energy policies and safety standards, formulating stable and transparent legal frameworks, and facilitating exchanges of technology and know-how. The third is promoting energy efficiency and environmental protection, together with appropriate education and training. The Charter calls on private industry to invest, acknowledging that public sector involvement, although necessary to the development of the energy market, will be largely auxiliary. The success of the Charter relies largely on the willingness of Western industry to operate in the East and bring investment, technology, management and other skills with it. The document simultaneously stresses 'the sovereign rights over their energy resources' of the participating states.

The Energy Charter also provided for the negotiation of a legally binding Basic Agreement to implement the cooperation established by the Charter. The Agreement covers the following areas: affirming the principle of sovereignty over energy resources; international trading regulations, establishing the progressive liberalization and non-discriminatory nature of trade in energy; rules regarding access to resources, technology, market and capital; provisions for technology transfer; the regulation of competition; the banning of aid, other than in exceptional cases; public procurement policies (with transitional arrangements protecting Eastern markets); transport and transit regulations; environmental protection; providing for and regulating investment; rules for the settlement of disputes; the establishment of a secretariat. Negotiations on the Basic Agreement between the 50 contracting parties began in December 1991, and proved more difficult than was foreseen, due to the sensitivity of energy policy in the countries concerned. It is hoped that it can be concluded by July 1993. In parallel to the Agreement, negotiations were opened on a number of sectoral protocols: on nuclear energy, oil and gas, energy efficiency, clean coal, electricity, and new and renewable energy sources.

The future shape of relations between Russia and the European Community

The key question for the future is whether any of those involved seriously envisage full membership of the European Community for Russia or any other of the former Soviet states (apart from the Baltic states, which will have separate, more favourable treatment), and, if not, what kind of relationship can be envisaged.

The first thing that must be said is that a great deal will depend on the way that the Community itself evolves, and how relations in the global economy develop. The future shape of Europe is clouded for the time being. However, it can be assumed that the Community will constitute a broader single market incorporating the four freedoms, at the very least, with most if not all of the EFTA countries acceding to membership. It is likely that the Central-East European and South-East European countries (Poland, Hungary, the Czech and Slovak republics, Romania and Bulgaria, and most probably the Baltic states, Albania and the former Yugoslav republics) will subsequently join, and possibly Malta and Cyprus. Moreover, although the Maastricht Treaty on European Union has encountered significant obstacles in the ratification process, we can expect that even if the treaty in its current form is eventually dropped, a replacement treaty containing some of the Maastricht provisions will eventually be signed by a significant number of the member states. While it is generally held that 'deepening' of the Community should be seen as a prerequisite for, rather than as an alternative to, any substantial 'widening', the kind of drastic widening represented by the entry (even in the long term) of a state such as Russia cannot but be perceived by advocates of deeper union as incompatible with their plans.

Of course the world has changed, partly because of the changes which have occurred in the former Soviet Union in the last three years, and it would be unwise to refuse to consider, if only in passing, more far-reaching changes. It is easily conceivable, for instance, that the Community as a whole may fail to advance towards any kind of European Union, although a core group may proceed along a fast track. In such circumstances internal resistance to expansion would be less, and the hurdles to wider membership would be lower. It is also conceivable that progress in GATT might be blocked and that trading blocs would grow up in America, the Pacific Rim and Europe. For a 'fortress Europe', Russia, Ukraine and some of the other former Soviet states, with their wealth of natural resources, their population and their agricultural potential, would represent a valuable hinterland. In particular, dependence on energy supplies from the Middle East would be sharply reduced.

On the other hand, many of the trading benefits could probably be secured through arrangements falling short of full membership. The arguments against full incorporation into the Community in the foreseeable future seem in general too numerous and too powerful. They revolve around instability, incompatibility, size and boundary-drawing problems.

It is true that EC membership has been justified in the past for countries such as Portugal and Spain precisely in order to counteract trends to instability in a period of transition to democracy. Western Europe certainly has a large stake in maintaining civil peace and progress towards stable democracies in the East: it cannot ignore the likely effects of large-scale population movements or environmental catastrophes. The problem is that the sources of instability (ethnic, cultural, economic) in Russia and its neighbours are so numerous that the situation appears unpredictable and difficult to control. There is, in other words, not sufficient evidence yet to bet on a successful transition, even with sizeable assistance from outside. The gamble would be expensive, and if it were to fail possibly destructive for the Community itself.

There is also the question of the substantial cultural, (political and economic) institutional differences, and differences in level of economic development, relative to the EC, of the former Soviet states. These are less striking in the case of Russia and Ukraine, and are a hindrance which to one degree or another also affects the Central-East European and especially the South-East European states, but they seem more daunting when taken in the context of the other obstacles.

The sheer size of the former Soviet territory acts as a multiplying factor for all the other negative ones (membership would entail a quadrupling of area and a 50 per cent increase in population). A severe strain would be placed on the Community's administration and on its budget. Huge contributions would be required from the wealthier states for development purposes, and existing relatively less-developed areas would have resources diverted away from them. The Community would also have to consider the response of its global partners, in particular the United States and Japan, to its rapid expansion across northern Eurasia, and the possible effects on progress in GATT.

The issue of size is related to the final obstacle, which concerns the difficulty of defining 'Europe'. Under the founding treaties of the European Communities, it is clearly established that *all* European countries have the right to belong to the Community. But where should the cut-off line be drawn in the East? How much should a shared culture and history weigh in the balance? Should all the Turkic peoples and Slav lands be counted as European? What about the Islamic former Soviet republics? At present the potential boundary of the Community is drawn along the eastern border of the Baltic states, and then south to include Poland, the Czech and Slovak republics, Hungary, Romania and the Balkans, ending with a question mark at Turkey. Any discussion of redrawing that line unavoidably raises difficult questions concerning Turkey's position. The EC concluded an Association Agreement with Turkey in 1963 in which eventual membership was explicitly mentioned. The Turks have been continually pressing for full membership, with a formal application presented in 1987. The Community's answer to Turkey was that it could not consider any new applications for membership until its Single Market programme was completed, although it is now planning to start accession negotiations in early 1993 with Austria, Sweden, Finland, Switzerland (all of whom presented membership applications considerably later than Turkey) and possibly Norway. The Turkish issue is still a subject of great controversy inside the EC.

Recently Turkey has begun to be discussed as a pole of attraction and stability for Azerbaijan and the Central Asian states (Turkmenistan, Uzbekistan, Kyrgyzstan, Kazakhstan and Tajikistan), with which, to varying degrees, it shares linguistic, cultural and religious traditions. In so far as this opens up a new mission for Turkey it is capable of diverting attention there away from the vexed issue of EC membership. Yet such a new role would only entangle more closely the questions of policy towards Turkey and towards the former Soviet states. Any discussion of EC membership for the former Soviet states in Europe leads into discussion of a closer relationship for those in Asia, and consequently for Turkey.

A related boundary-drawing problem concerns the fate of the admittedly tenuous but still very interdependent community of states grouped around Russia in the CIS. For the time being it seems to be considered impractical to plan to separate off individual republics or groups of republics as potential EC members, leaving others out in the cold. This is both because of the residual economic integrity of the CIS and because of the political implications. Admitting Belarus and/or Ukraine to the Community and not Russia, for instance, would undoubtedly risk provoking a dangerous reaction from Moscow; separating the Slav from the Muslim republics might pour fuel on the flames of any incipient anti-Western tendencies in Central Asia. This factor makes the states concerned appear all the more indigestible, and encourages the perception of Russia and the other former Soviet states as a separate 'Eurasian' entity.

Yet, however unlikely the accession of Russia and the other non-Baltic former Soviet states to the European Community in the foreseeable future, it is clear that for reasons of security and economic advantage the member states have powerful interests in building closer relations of one kind or another with them. They will accordingly seek to tread a path between the risk of over-hasty, financially wasteful and politically risky involvement on the one hand, and on the other the risks of neglect and alienation. Clearly a special place will have to be found for Russia and its neighbours in some kind of wider European framework.

Even in immediate material terms, the European Community can only benefit from closer relations with Russia. In terms of trade, the gains from lower world energy prices for the Community which assistance could bring about will, according to Gros, exceed the total aid the Community is providing.[18] And the Community has little to fear in opening its own market, since in the medium term, even in some of the so-called sensitive sectors, where Russia has a latent comparative advantage, the volume of exports will continue to be relatively small for some time to come. In return the Community is gaining access to nearly 150 million potential new customers with a thirst for Western products limited only by lack of hard currency. Furthermore, access to the country's vast mineral resources, possibly through the kind of debt-for-equity swaps proposed by President Yeltsin at the Munich G7 summit, offers very interesting prospects for Western business. If closer relationships led to a loosening of border controls, the threat of mass migration as a result of escalating instability would worsen. On the other hand a policy of disengagement and isolation would, it could be argued, be even more risky in this respect.

How things will develop is uncertain. The implications of the new partnership and cooperation agreement which is under negotiation are still unclear. Since neither the Community, nor indeed the West as a whole, can expect to meet all Russia's financing needs, the best they can do is to target their assistance carefully. In the long run, Russia has ample hard-currency-earning potential, but it must be unlocked. At this stage the importance of stabilization financing and technical assistance cannot be overemphasized, as a means of creating certain vital preconditions for progress across the board. Stabilization financing is vital in order to assist the achievement of currency convertibility and monetary stabilization, while attempting to sustain trade between Russia and the other former Soviet states. Technical assistance is necessary in order to rebuild the economy, not only through the introduction of essential Western practices, customs, standards and norms, but also through access to Western human resources, management and training. This is an area where realistic sums of money can be made to reap real dividends, and where assistance can encourage greater involvement on the part of Western business. As for conditionality, it is likely that all assistance will continue to be tied to perceptible moves towards the establishment of a market economy and pluralist democracy, but the stringency of these conditions will be toned down as the limits of the possible become clearer. Indeed, as the political and economic crisis in Russia deepens, the Community and its member states will have to display considerably greater flexibility, imagination and commitment than they have done so far.

Notes

An earlier version of sections of this chapter appeared in P. Fraser, *The Post-Soviet States and the EC* (London, RIIA, Post-Soviet Business Forum, 1992). The author would like to thank Dr Mary Buckley and Richard McAllister of the University of Edinburgh.

1. Preamble of the Treaty of Rome establishing the European Economic Community in 1957.
2. Ernst Haas, *Beyond the Nation State* (Stanford, CA, Stanford University Press, 1964), pp. 452, 496.
3. Nearly two-and-a-half years later, the Council has finally mandated the Commission to negotiate an agreement to establish 'the four freedoms' of goods, services, capital and labour with Russia. See below.
4. P. Holmes, Geng Su, *EC Anti-Dumping Policy and the Emerging Market Economies of Eastern Europe*. Paper presented to the Hellenic Economic Association Conference, 18–20 December 1991.
5. With the exception of strawberries (Poland), and uranium, plutonium and steel (Russia).
6. 'Sensitive' products are agricultural goods, textiles and coal and steel. Special protocols for these sectors are annexed to almost all Community trade agreements with third countries.
7. A significant proportion of trade appears not to have been reported in statistics until 1993. See Table 9.3.
8. Although in reality the Association Agreements are not the key to membership that it was once hoped they would be. See J. M. C. Rollo, J. Batt, B. Granville, N. Malcolm, *The New Eastern Europe: Western Responses* (London, RIIA/Pinter Publishers Ltd, 1990). Furthermore, conditions for membership will be tighter if the Maastricht Treaty or something like it is ratified.
9. This is a UN sponsored scheme, introduced by the EC in 1971, under which developed countries (and in this case the EC) have agreed to give tariff concessions to all developing countries (over and above MFN treatment under GATT regulations) and to seek to make continuous improvements to them.
10. A quick glance at the Community's relations with the Mashreq and Maghreb

countries (in the Mediterranean Basin) confirms this. Agreements have been signed with all these countries, with the stated aim of eventually establishing a free trade area in industrial goods. However the arrangement is asymmetrical, with no concessions expected from the partner countries for the foreseeable future, largely due to United States objections to the idea of the Community establishing a Commonwealth-style network of preferential trade agreements around it. Obviously the objections were carefully worded with reference to the developing nature of these economies.

11. Talk by Dr Ruben Yevstigneyev, Deputy Director, Institute for International Economic and Political Studies, Moscow, at the Royal Institute of International Affairs on 30 June 1992.

12. Of which: 6 billion dollars for a rouble stabilization fund, together with 18 billion dollars in credits from the IMF (4 bn), the World Bank (1.5 bn), the EBRD, and export credit guarantees and food credits from the G7 and Scandinavian countries.

13. Foreign debts already amounted to 65 billion dollars in 1992 (*Financial Times* 30 June 1992), excluding debt owed to former CMEA member states. At the G7 summit in July 1992, Russia obtained a 1 billion dollar credit package from the IMF (which was finally approved in mid-August 1992), together with an assurance that the G7 would back rescheduling of official debts of 2.5 billion dollars, through the Paris Club of Western creditor countries, with new loans to be made available by other financial institutions such as the World Bank (a total of 1.7 billion dollars was proposed in loans to support the Russian balance of payments assistance) and the EBRD (see below). The rescheduling is expected to be under normal Paris Club regulations, with a five-year grace period and repayments over the subsequent ten years. Although part of the G7 24 billion dollar support package was disbursed rapidly (some 4–5 billion of the total 11 billion dollars expected in bilateral flows), some of the credits were blocked due to the growing arrears on existing debts.

14. The 24 billion dollar (19.35 billion ecu) package announced by the G7 on 2 April 1992, and confirmed by the G7 summit on 8 July 1992, is not included in this 75 billion ecu.

15. The Charter itself was not legally binding.

16. From the preamble to the European Energy Charter, signed in the Hague on 17 December 1992.

17. The USSR was still in existence on the day the Charter was signed.

18. Daniel Gros, *The EC and Central and Eastern Europe: Issues for Discussion*, paper presented to Economic Policy Group in the Centre for European Policy Studies, March 1992.

10 Russia and Europe: Possibilities for the Future

Sergei Karaganov

Again Russia is faced with the recurrent agonizing question: where does it belong? Is it a European, Asian – culturally and politically non-European, or Eurasian – neither a European, nor an Asian country? It is, indeed, a sad irony that this question is put now, at a time when Soviet and Russian Westernizers and modernizers have achieved the political and cultural opening up of the country to Europe.

Only two or three years ago, when the Moscow elite was propagandizing the concept of the Common European House, all doubts concerning the 'Europeanness' of the Soviet Union were adamantly dismissed. The Common European House concept implied a large agenda, both open and hidden. It was aimed at overcoming the system of military confrontation, at thawing the Western front of the USSR, at dismantling an 'outer empire' that in political terms was costly to control, and in economic and military terms was virtually useless, at opening the country up to European democracy, to European socially responsible capitalism. For many Soviet-Russian Westernizers the Common European House was a device to return Russia to where, as they believed, it belonged, and from where it was cast adrift and shut out after 1917.

Almost all their hopes were fulfilled. The system of military confrontation does not exist any more. It has become almost indecent to talk about military threats, at least in the old sense. Political systems have become much closer. A common cultural and information space has been created. It has become easier for people to communicate and to travel. The situation in many spheres of human rights has changed for the better.

But the Common European House has fallen out of favour in Moscow. This has happened not just because it eventually became a banality, and people tired of it. The vanishing of most of the external barriers which separated the USSR/Russia from Europe brought to the fore the deep internal obstacles preventing Russia's return to Europe. In addition a few new barriers emerged, barriers which were not foreseen a few years ago. The revolution has brought to the surface a great deal of untapped energy and talent. But it has also focused attention on certain cultural peculiarities, and revealed the depth to which the totalitarian disease had penetrated into the mental fabric of society. The communist ideology may have gone, but totalitarian thinking reproduces itself in the pronouncements and actions of reputedly democratic politicians. But above all it is the unclear future of Russia and the former Soviet Union that puts in question and slows up the return to Europe. The relationship of Russia and Europe is almost totally scenario-dependent.

At this juncture four scenarios of the development of the former Soviet Union look plausible. First, the coming to power of a national fundamentalist neo-fascist regime or regimes. Second, an attempt at a military *coup d'état*. Third, the slide of parts of the former Soviet Union into a series of Yugoslav-style conflicts and civil wars, and further disintegration of its major republics into even smaller units, with all the accompanying repercussions for the fate of the military forces, including weapons of mass destruction; eventual Lebanonization and collapse of order on the territory of what was called the Soviet Union. Fourth, the major republics, independent states, and above all, Russia, muddle through, and, avoiding civil war and fascist degeneration, move slowly from crisis to crisis along the road of gradual societal and economic modernization. To be sure, this relatively optimistic scenario will, most probably, include some elements of the previous three, but catastrophe will be avoided.

One could of course posit a fifth, optimistic scenario, envisaging relatively swift modernization and democratization without authoritarian detours. Unfortunately, realism forbids belief in the feasibility of such a scenario. In this chapter I shall focus on the possible repercussions for Europe, and for relations between Russia and other European countries, of the four scenarios outlined above.

If the position before August 1991 in the country could be described as 'pre-Weimar', the *putsch* and the events that followed it, especially the December 1991 Minsk agreement, transformed it into an unmistakably 'Weimar' situation. The cumulative effect of rapid inflation during the whole of 1991, and the liberalization of prices in 1992 effectively did away with people's savings. The accelerating deterioration of living standards propels more and more groups of the population into poverty. And that is before the massive unemployment resulting from radical reforms and economic restructuring even starts, probably in the second half of 1993 or in 1994.

The break-up of the country is creating a feeling of national humiliation and/or insecurity among the population of the republics. Many strata of society are psychologically prey to a syndrome of national defeat. It could be objected that the country did not in fact suffer a defeat. What is more, it proved capable of starting out on its own to overcome the totalitarian heritage, and achieved some remarkable successes along that path. But during the preceding seventy years this heritage had become part of the fabric of the country, and uprooting it causes psychological, political and economic after-effects of dangerous proportions. Growing economic deprivation provides a fertile ground for populist and outright fascist ideologies. This is helped by the absence of responsible political parties which could represent and channel the grievances of the deprived masses of the population and, especially, of blue collar workers. The most obvious gap in the political spectrum is now on the left, because of the absence of social democracy. This yawning gap could well be filled by left-wing or right-wing populists, now almost indistinguishable from each other.

Yet so far no significant elite groups in Russia have put their stake on a national-socialist regime, and those groups which previously supported the neo-fascist leader Zhirinovsky lost power after the failure of the August coup. Fortunately, the factors listed above do not bring about fascism automatically. This is not to deny that its day could come, given a combination of bad luck, grave mistakes by political leaders, feelings of unfair treatment by the outside world and ill-treatment of national minorities, which amount to something close to one third of the population of the former Soviet Union. Any significant internal migration would form a social milieu which would almost inevitably create movements of a fascist nature, sucking in and merging with the urban poor and other disgruntled groups. Hunger, or at least severe malnutrition of a large stratum of the population, especially in the big cities, would exacerbate the situation. After the winter of 1992–3, it may be hoped that at least the agricultural sector will start to take off, and that the population will start to adapt to the new conditions.

A lot will depend on the policies of the Russian leadership. By a combination of strong-arm tactics and co-optation of less extreme Russian nationalist tendencies it could succeed in marginalizing the neo-fascist and neo-communist – the so-called red-brown – forces. Over the next three years much will depend also on whether the West can organize itself for a constructive engagement with the internal situation in Russia, whether it is able to provide funds for currency stabilization and to make available the necessary seed money for restructuring the economy.

If these conditions are not fulfilled, scenario one could become a reality, most likely in one-and-a-half to three years at the earliest. The new regime would inevitably try to shut off the country, at least partly, from the 'poisonous West', would resort to xenophobic propaganda, and would halt, if only temporarily, the reduction in size of the military machine. Such a government, to hold on to power, would have to be supported by at least a part of the military.

But apart from verbal hostility towards the West, aimed mostly at Westernizers inside the country, such a regime would be unlikely to pursue belligerent policies towards the world outside the former USSR. First, it would discover very rapidly how limited were the political, economic and military resources at its disposal. Second, its philosophy would most probably be isolationist rather than expansionist, just as the Soviet one initially was. Third, it would have too many problems at home or very close to home to be able to afford to engage in more than hostile rhetoric. And, finally, if it wished to engage in adventurist strong-arm policies, it would have quite a few targets to choose from closer to home, namely the former Soviet republics. A 'red-brown' government would almost inevitably pursue a revanchist policy, in the sense of trying to recreate the former Soviet Union by force. Most probably the first targets of such a policy would be Ukraine, Belarus and Moldova. The Baltic states would escape such a fate, provided the level of tensions was not too high by that time. Of course, they would come under pressure, but they are already increasingly written off as possessions: there is a growing acknowledgment by even the most conservative elements that these states have never really been a part of the USSR, and that reintegrated they could become more of a liability than an asset. However, by the time of such a coup, tensions would run high, and the Baltic states could become the first targets, because they are a relatively easy prey.

Europe's reaction would be relatively predictable. NATO would provide guarantees of one sort or another to the Central-East European nations. The latter would form the first line of a new *cordon sanitaire*. Then the Western countries would most probably try to provide support, although without any formal obligations, to the Baltic states, Ukraine, Belarus and Moldova. The latter would play the part of a 'soft' *cordon sanitaire*. Russia would find itself in a state of complete geopolitical isolation, exacerbated by geoeconomic isolation. It would be 'thrown out' of Europe. The country's situation could then become much worse than it was in the 1920s and the 1930s, when the geostrategic situation of the USSR was more advantageous. Most of Ukraine and Belarus with their ports and railways were under Moscow's control, the West was disunited and provided opportunities for playing on disagreements in the political field and over trade and economic issues, and the country was not dependent to the same extent on spare parts and materials for its industry. Now large portions of industry cannot function without these and the credits which facilitate their supply.

So the coming of the 'red-browns' to power would spell not only tragedy for the Russian people, but also geostrategic tragedy for Russia.

In Europe outside Russia the decline in military spending would be reversed. Most probably, due to inevitable political tensions among European Community member states, the advance to political union would be slowed down. (The new challenge could have strengthened political cohesion if this process had been more advanced, but not at the present stage, when it is still too fragile.) NATO would regain its prominence in the Western system and, with the inevitable widening of the geographic scope of its activities to Central-Eastern Europe, could become an even more influential actor in European politics. The system of deterrence and containment would be recreated, but on much less favourable terms for Russia than previously.

Thus for Europe outside the former Soviet Union the situation would at first sight be tolerable. However, such a regime would be unable to stay in power unless it unleashed massive 1930s-style bloodshed. It is difficult to see where it would find the forces which would have to be mobilized to carry that out, or what ideology could be implanted which would provide it with even partial legitimacy. Most probably such a regime would provoke a string of conflicts, and finally the disintegration of Russia itself. The consequences of that for Europe and Russian–European relations will be discussed later, in connection with scenario three.

A scenario similar in some repects to a 'red-brown' coup would be a military coup. A military coup could have happened at some point during the winter of early 1992 because of the desperation provoked among the military by the prospect of disintegration of the armed forces. But after February and March 1992 the chances of an 'all-union' coup taking place receded. The military share many of the democratic values of other groups of the elite and are generally more law-abiding than most. In addition they are disorganized, and they are aware that they cannot deliver a better life for the population. Some of the most reactionary elements have been excised from their ranks. The partial 'nationalization' of the armed forces of Ukraine has further decreased the chances of a concerted, large-scale coup.

What is more likely is a series of coups or semi-coups, in the course of which different commanders try to achieve their goals by taking power or by threatening to do so, or – more likely – in which different governments on the territory of the former Soviet Union rely on the military to hold on to power or to keep order. The inevitable price to be paid would be to hand over additional political influence to the military.

The international consequences of a full-scale military coup, if it nevertheless happened, would most probably be almost identical to those described in the preceding scenario. However, there could be slight differences. If the leaders who came to power as a result of the coup stopped short of trying to recreate the Soviet Union by force, and devoted themselves to establishing law and order, preventing further disintegration of Russia and thus loss of control over chemical, and especially nuclear installations (both civilian and military), any negative Western responses would likely be more a matter of rhetoric than action. After initial condemnations, and a strengthening of security ties with the Central-East European states, many elements of cooperation would be restored. It is feared by some Russians that there are those in the West who would sigh with relief at such a turn of events.

However, it is clear that such a regime could not last for long and would have to yield power to someone else, most probably to authoritarian modernizers. If it tried to hold on to power, sooner or later economic disintegration would threaten the disintegration of Russia itself.

The third, civil war scenario could become a reality even without a preceding neo-fascist or military coup. Relatively small-scale civil-war-type conflicts are indeed already in progress on the territory of the former Soviet Union. So far they have occurred mainly in the Caucasus. But the disease is spreading. Moldova has moved in the same direction, and threatens to suck in Ukraine and Russia.

The core problem as regards the future security of what was the Soviet Union as well as international peace and stability is, of course, how relations develop between the Russian Federation and Ukraine. If historical analogies, including the recent fate of Yugoslavia, were to be used as a basis for prognostication, the chances of conflict between these two newly emerging states would seem high, and current political and economic developments confirm this.

Both countries are in a period of state formation. They are undergoing deep societal transformation and crisis. Their economic plight is deepening. Under such circumstances elites cultivate an enemy image in order to build up their own popularity, and such an image is already being fostered in Ukraine. There is no consistent policy of that kind in Russia, but anti-Ukrainian feelings and sentiments are very evident. As the economic reforms in Russia and Ukraine develop at different speeds, they will most probably give rise to sharp tensions over protectionism and price adjustment, which could exacerbate political relations. Political assertiveness will further damage economic ties. One could add to this list the intangible but potentially dangerous psychological malaise afflicting most of the population of Russia and many citizens of Ukraine, who previously believed themselves to be living in a single country and all of a sudden find themselves being torn apart.

This list of problems is incomplete. But it indicates clearly enough that in order to live through the transitional decade peacefully, political leaders in both states will have to demonstrate unusual ingenuity, flexibility, and above all wisdom. The new revolutionary or quasi-revolutionary elites are by and large not likely to demonstrate such traits.

The situation is of course not as ominous as our catalogue might suggest. The two republics are so closely interdependent that economic separation is virtually impossible. Even the most zealous separatists will have to accept this fact, although the lesson may be a costly one. Unlike the Serbs and Croats, moreover, the two nations concerned do not have a history of wars and hatred.

With good luck, wisdom and help from outside, conflicts and wars can be avoided. However, the possibility of such a development exists. If tensions start to grow and to deteriorate into open conflicts, that will most probably provoke further disintegration of Russia, and then Ukraine, into smaller units. A process of 'feudalization' will begin throughout the territory of the former Soviet Union.

The slide of this vast area into 'Lebanonization' and then, almost inevitably, into further disintegration of Russia, Ukraine, Kazakhstan and certain other republics, would most probably spell the end of the Europe we know. At first, most likely, the West would try a sealing-off strategy, using Central-

Eastern Europe and Turkey as a buffer to absorb the waves of immigrants, stray troops, terrorists of various kinds, and so on. The Central-East European countries would not only be provided with security guarantees, but would probably be admitted as full members of NATO. One could even envisage deployment of NATO troops on their territory. However, the natural inclination of the current generation of Western politicians would be to keep as far away as possible from the conflict.

But relatively soon this tactic of non-involvement would most probably prove counterproductive. It would not prevent the weakening or even total loss of control over nuclear and chemical arsenals, nuclear power stations, chemical plants, etc. The outside world would be faced with an unprecedented challenge: the need to play an active (and probably a military) role in a whole string of countries and territories simultaneously, many at war with each other. The diplomatic games of the seventeenth and eighteenth centuries would be resurrected, and the outcome could take the form of a large part of the European continent slipping into the category of Third World states. It is impossible to predict whether even the West's efforts could avert catastrophic outcomes, such as the accidental firing of weapons of mass destruction or their acquisition by irresponsible or desperate groups. The situation would be inherently unpredictable.

One could try to envisage, though, the impact of such a scenario on inter-Western affairs. The still very weak edifice of the European Union would start to crumble, as would the CSCE. The latter is far too weak to withstand shocks of the kind to which it would be exposed, or to prove useful under the political pressures which would come into play. The United Nations and NATO would regain their prominence in European affairs. Most probably UN and not CSCE mechanisms would be used for peacekeeping. Germany, already inward-oriented and preoccupied with the tasks of unification, would withdraw into itself even further, ceasing to play the role of the main economic locomotive in Central-Eastern Europe.

Gradually the Central-East European countries would be sucked into the conflicts, their economic reconstruction would be stalled, and their populations would be drawn towards more radical political options. The West would have to spend additional political, economic and military resources on preventing Balkanization and 'Third-Worldization' of this area, too. That would put the kind of additional strain on resources which would threaten to erode the social fabric of Western societies.

The weakening of the EC would not be matched by a strengthening of NATO. The United States, to judge by current trends in public opinion, would most probably not choose to take up the burden of saviour of Europe for the second time, and would opt, at least initially, for a limited, nuclear-oriented involvement. How and whether the vacuum thus created would be filled is unclear. It is possible that the disease of disintegration could start to spread throughout Europe, bringing in new, as yet unforeseen realignments.

The fourth, 'normal', scenario is a continuation of the slow and painful modernization of Russia. It includes elements of the previous three scenarios, but in less dramatic and less catastrophic proportions. Indeed, it is along these lines that the former USSR and then Russia have moved since the late spring of 1991. The coup speeded up the reforms, cleared the way for them, but also created a more unstable and dangerous environment. It appears that in the summer of 1992 a conservative retreat from the radical reform line of the first part of the year got under way. Most probably, and barring disasters, in due course radical reform will get under way again. This scenario would entail several waves of market-oriented reforms, gradually creating a more propitious environment and preconditions for the modernization of the economy. Politically it would mean continued instability, frequent changes of government, a combination of regionalization of Russia, Ukraine and some other republics, and increasingly authoritarian methods of government in the capitals and in the provinces. A certain degree of authoritarianism looks virtually inevitable. The question will be how far this trend goes, whether some democratic control over the executive is preserved. If not, the existing presidential republics will slide into authoritarianism and then will degenerate into some kind of dictatorship.

From a socio-economic point of view the country would gradually develop according to a corporate-state-capitalist model, neither socialism, nor modern capitalism. Riots and local *putsches* would also most probably form part of the picture, along with an increase in the political influence of the military.

The 'normal' scenario is the only one which would permit other countries to plan policy towards the former Soviet states with any confidence that their actions would have relatively predictable outcomes. According to this scenario the foreign policy positions of the heirs to the Soviet Union, and first of all Russia, would probably be characterized by the following features.

The first would be semi-isolation of Russia and most of the other former members of the Soviet Union. This relative isolation is already coming about as a result of the collapse of foreign trade, and because of certain unpleasant aspects of the behaviour of most of the new regimes. Another factor which makes the semi-isolation of Russia and most other former member states of the USSR virtually inevitable is the 'provincialization' of their policies. They are obliged to concentrate on solving the most acute and immediate security and foreign policy problems, and these lie mainly inside the boundaries of the former USSR. From one point of view this provincialization is healthy, but if it were to be coupled with a feeling of being cold-shouldered, and shut out of Europe, it could become dangerous, and it could weaken the position of the reformists. In foreign and defence policy a neo-conservative retrenchment has begun. There is a feeling that Moscow has given away too much and too easily, and that the government should defend Russia's national interests more diligently. This retrenchment will bring a less flexible line on arms control, especially on nuclear matters.

This scenario would pose, then, quite a few problems for policy-makers in the West. They would be faced not with a relatively stable and predictable partner, as with the USSR under Mikhail Gorbachev, nor with a clear-cut enemy, but with a number of difficult partners. They would find it hard to ignore some of these governments' less attractive characteristics. On the one hand they would understand the counterproductiveness of reacting to these unpleasant features by adopting policies of ostracism and isolation. On the other, they would see the dangers of condoning the non-democratic and anti-reform behaviour of some of the regimes concerned.

Another complication the outside world would be faced with would be the virtually inevitable growth of Russian patriotism, national consciousness and nationalism. The growth of national feeling is not just inevitable. It is also, one could argue, a necessary step in the moral resurrection of the people. It is impossible without it to accomplish the rebuilding of the country on the economic and ideological ruins of totalitarianism. To date this rise of national feeling has been slow, and has taken mainly civilized forms. There are some ugly manifestations of nationalism, but these are the work of minority, marginal groups. Yet the upsurge has begun, and the West will have to try to devise a reasonable policy response. The tendency to label every manifestation of Russian nationalism or patriotism as 'imperial', and to condemn it, only strengthens xenophobic and anti-Western tendencies. Attempts to ignore or to appease such tendencies are equally counterproductive, as the experiences of many of the republics of the former USSR demonstrate.

The turn to neo-conservatism – not so much in the old Soviet as in the traditional Western sense – will manifest itself in a partial retreat from the optimistic, one-sidedly pro-Western orientation of the Gorbachev and especially the early Yeltsin administrations. This partial retreat stems from at least three sources. First, from the coming to power of more pragmatic politicians, who reflect the interests of and the climate of opinion among traditional power groups, especially industrialists. Second, from the growing disillusionment even among liberal politicians concerning the capability and willingness of the West to come forward with massive assistance. Third, from a realistic reassessment of Russian interests, which due to the unavoidable facts of geography tie Russia to Asia almost as closely as to Europe.

But this partial retreat will not signify a turn to an anti-European or an anti-Western orientation. Most elites are still interested in close cooperation with the West, at least in economic and technological terms, and are emotionally drawn to European cultural values (though these are not always correctly understood). They are aware of the deep dependence of economic progress in Russia on continuous cooperation with the West, as well as of the virtual impossibility of modernizing of the country without at least an initial infusion of credits and technology, without an opening-up to Western markets.

Russia is pushed towards cooperation with Europe also by its new geostrategic interests. Russia is scarcely more than half the size of the USSR in terms of GNP and population. Its economy for quite some time will be in deep crisis. This alters the significance of the Chinese factor. The economic and political balance between the two countries has drastically shifted and is continuing to change. It is necessary not only to develop good relations with China, but also to build up a geostrategic alliance with Europe and the USA. The uncertain situation in Central Asia pushes Russia in the same direction. Indeed (unless a 'red-brown' regime should be installed) Russia is fated to be deeply interested in close cooperation and good political relations with Europe.

In the fourth scenario the future of Russian–European relations will to a very large extent be dependent on the policy choices made by Western states. Of course, Western governments are not completely unconstrained in making these policy choices. If the shift towards authoritarian methods goes far enough, for example, such choices could be swayed by movements in public opinion.

At present it is not clear what their choice will be. There appear to be two tendencies in Western policy. One is to get involved in supporting reform in Russia and the former Soviet states, and to help the new countries politically and economically. The other is to 'forget about' the former USSR. After all it is not threatening the West any more, it holds out no large new economic opportunities in the near future, and it threatens to become a significant drain on resources. The outcome of this contradiction is a flurry of contacts, especially with Americans, but very small-scale, possibly even decreasing, political and economic involvement, especially on the part of the Europeans.

On the one hand, grand sounding schemes, such as multi-billion dollar IMF support packages, are proposed. On the other, even according to such plans, relatively small sums of money would actually be transferred. And it is not really evident that they are properly thought through and designed to suit Russian realities.

Above all, there is no evidence that there exists a coherent and comprehensive policy for helping to manage the triple transition in the former Soviet Union to new state structures, to the market and to democracy. So far, despite all the problems and conflicts which have arisen, this transition has been remarkably smooth. But tensions are growing, and a geostrategic gap – an almost completely unregulated security space – is emerging on the territory of the former USSR. Most of those who have come to power have not been trained and prepared for the new responsibilities which history has imposed on them. There is a growing need not so much for aid as for deep involvement – advice, pressure, mediation between elites in order to manage inter-state relations – schemes to prevent the economic situation from becoming intolerable for the mass of population, to guide the process of economic reform. Without such a deep involvement the modernization of Russia and the other former Soviet states has much less chance of success. The outcome could well take the form described in one of the first three scenarios, with all the unpredictable consequences this would have for Europe as a whole.

Index

Adomeit, Hannes viii, 10, 16, 20, 22
Afghanistan 6, 38, 93, 128, 134
Akhromeev, Marshal Sergei 37, 44, 46, 48,
    154, 158
Aleksandrov, Mikhail 158
Ambartsumov, Evgeny 171
Alexander I, Tsar 5
Alexander II, Tsar 6
Alexander III, Tsar 6
Andreeva, Nina 103
Andropov, Yury 35, 37, 38, 127, 156
Antall, Jozsef 71
Arbatov, Aleksei 49, 52, 112
Arbatov, Georgy 153, 156
Armenia 51, 83, 88-93 passim
arms control 16-17, 19, 20, 21, 134
    conventional arms ix, 19, 86
    under Gorbachev 79-88
    post-Gorbachev 88-93
    of nuclear weapons see main heading
        nuclear arms
    verification measures 17, 81-2
    see also Mutual Balanced Force Reduc-
        tions
Asian-Pacific region x, 40
Atlantic alliance ix, 17, 31, 69
    Russian interest in 33-4, 47-53
    Soviet perspective of viii, 9-11, 32-3, 34-
        8, 42-3, 46, 79, 99
        and collapse of Warsaw Pact 43-7
        and German unification 41-3
        and Gorbachev revision of 31, 36,
        37-40, 41-3
Austria 69-70
Azerbaijan 50-1, 84, 88-93 passim

Baker, James 52, 88, 107
Balkans 7
Baltic states 2, 20, 47, 51, 73, 75, 92, 143, 156,
    157, 165, 208, 216, 227

Baranovsky, Vladimir viii, 10, 21, 152
Belarus 25, 82, 84, 88, 90-2 passim, 145, 170,
    227
Berlin 9, 10, 79, 100, 102, 103, 105
    Berlin Wall 20, 45, 105
    blockade of 35
Bessmertnykh, Aleksandr 45
Bismarck, Prince Otto von 6
Black Sea Fleet 51, 85, 90
Bogomolov, Oleg 156
Bovin, Aleksandr 156
Brandt, Willy 115
Brezhnev, Leonid 14, 35, 38, 63, 79, 86, 94,
    113, 115, 153, 182-3, 184
    Brezhnev Doctrine 31, 46, 81, 104, 134
    detente policy of 12, 37, 123, 124
    and Eastern Europe 123, 124, 127, 132
    and NATO 32, 33, 36, 37
    Tbilisi signal 32, 33, 36, 37
    on US relationship 10, 36
Britain 85, 106, 107, 201
Brittan, Leon 209
Bulgaria 170, 216
    CFE allocation 89. 91, 92
    relations with Russia 146
    revised USSR relations 46, 130, 135, 136,
        142
Burbulis, Gennady 170
Burlatsky, Fedor 156
Bush, President George 42, 83, 85, 108, 115

Canada 36, 79
Catherine II, Empress 4
Ceauşescu, Nicolae 136
Central-Eastern and South-Eastern Europe
    2, 11, 35, 37, 123-47, 153, 154, 159,
    227, 229-30
    collapse of Soviet position in 45, 104, 144,
        163
    EC and 199, 200, 211, 215, 217, 218-9

economic decline in 12
emergence of democratic and market
  orientation in 31
Freedom of Choice 39, 125
and NATO 48, 146
revision of Soviet policy in 15, 17, 18-20,
  21-2, 25, 27, 33, 41, 44, 123-47, 156,
  157, 159
    stages of implementation 132-42
relations with successor states 143-6
trade with USSR 184-7
withdrawal of Soviet troops 41, 42, 80-1,
  134, 140-1, 146
Charter of Paris 20, 109, 115, 209
Chernenko, Konstantin 32, 35, 37, 38
Chernyaev, Anatoly 128
Chervov, Col.-Gen. Nikolai F. 44
China 25, 233
CMEA (Council for Mutual Economic
  Assistance) 11, 12, 17, 19, 31, 41, 46,
  99, 102, 124, 126, 133, 185, 186, 191,
  196
dissolution of 70, 125, 143, 146, 202
EC relations 63, 64, 66, 68, 69, 137, 197-8
trading pattern 202-4
COCOM 194-5, 196
Cold War, end of viii, 11-14, 20-1, 25
Cold War period 34, 42
Common European House concept viii, 14,
  15-21, 39, 41, 65, 151-5, 157, 173, 199,
  224
criticisms of 140, 158, 159, 160
Gorbachev and 16, 38, 39, 130, 138, 157,
  166, 201
role of US and NATO 32, 39
Commonwealth of Independent States (CIS)
  50, 51, 164, 170, 220
Agreement on Strategic Forces 83, 84
arms control policy in 93
deteriorating internal relations 85
EC TACIS programme for 213
formation of 83, 84, 112, 144
NACC membership 22
redistribution of armaments in 51, 88-94
Communist rule 7, 8, 18
collapse of 11-12, 15, 16, 41, 151, 173
Conference on Security and Cooperation in
  Europe see CSCE
conventional armaments ix, 46, 69
Conventional Forces in Europe talks 19, 21,
  43, 44
CFE Treaty 21, 43, 46, 141
  arms quotas 22
  CIS and 89-94
  Soviet attempts to renew terms of
    87-90
Council for Mutual Economic Assistance see
  CMEA

Council of Europe, Gorbachev visit to 20
Craxi, Benedetto 66
CSCE (Conference on Security and Cooperation in Europe) 17, 19, 20, 21, 22, 37,
  52, 79, 81, 86, 109, 143, 157, 160, 164-5
Paris Conference and Charter 21, 39, 109,
  115
Czechoslovakia 50, 105, 123, 141, 216
1968 events in 128, 144, 201
approaches to NATO 45
CFE allocations 89, 91, 92
EC relationship 199, 200
relations with Russia 145
revised Soviet relations 46, 130, 135, 136,
  142
Soviet withdrawal from 18, 19, 81, 141, 146

Dashichev, Vyacheslav 157, 160
De Gaulle, President Charles 36-7
Defensive Realist Thinking 142, 158, 160
Delors, Jacques 66, 68, 74
Diderot, Denis 4
Dienstbier, Jiří 45
Dobrynin, Anatoly 154
Dombrowski, Polish adviser 146
Dostoevsky, Fyodor 168
Dubček, Alexander 128
Dumas, Roland 41, 84
Dyker, David ix, 22, 23

East Germany 8, 99-100
  see also German Democratic Republic
Ecu Banking Association 197
Emerson, Michael 75
European Atomic Community 209
European Bank for Reconstruction and
  Development (EBRD) ix, 72, 197, 198,
  201, 211, 216-17
European Coal and Steel Community 61
European Common Market 61, 63
European Community 3, 9, 10, 12, 14, 17, 31,
  63, 125, 164
aid for USSR and successor states 196-7,
  201, 207-15
basis of economic success of 193-4
Common Agricultural Policy 193
ecu monetary system 196
enlargement and expansion of 23, 70-1
Europe 1992 67, 68
Multi-Fibre Agreement 193, 206
PHARE Programme 211
Quantitative Restrictions 203, 206
relations with CMEA countries 63, 64, 66,
  68-9, 137, 200, 202
relations with Russia viii, ix, x, 3, 63, 66-7,
  199, 207-10
relations with Turkey 220
Single European Act 194

Single Market programme 204, 220
Soviet impression of 25, 60-72, 152
Soviet relationship viii, 22, 66, 199-202
    Trade and Cooperation Agreement
    200, 207-8
    trade with 204, 205-7
TACIS (Technological Assistance for
    CIS) programme 213
European Defence Community 33, 36, 48, 60
European Energy Charter 201, 211, 217-8
European Energy Community 72
European Free Trade Association (EFTA)
    states 208, 212, 218
European Investment Bank 210, 216
European Monetary System 196
European Political Cooperation 63, 68
Europeanization 4-7, 14, 20, 123, 155-7
    in defence policy 101

Falin, Valentin 111, 155
Finland 2
First World War 7
Fischer, Oskar 45
France 11, 36, 37, 38, 42, 76, 106, 107
Fraser, Perdita ix, 22, 23
Freedman, Lawrence 9
Freedom of Choice 39, 41, 125, 130, 135, 138
Friedrich Wilhelm IV, of Prussia 5
Frolov, Ivan 128

Gaidar, Yegor 182
GATT (General Agreement on Tarifs and
    Trade) 197, 204, 209, 219, 220
Genscher, Hans-Dietrich 44, 101, 102, 105,
    107, 111, 112
Georgia 51, 88, 89, 90, 91, 92
    events of 1956 128
German Democratic Republic 34, 35, 36, 133
    collapse of communism in 41, 42
    reaction to new Soviet policies 103, 104,
        105, 135, 136-7, 139
    refugees from 104, 139
    relations with Soviet Union 100, 104, 105
    Soviet policy on 99, 101, 104, 105
    unification question 9, 33, 94, 107
    withdrawal of Soviet troops 20, 42-3, 106,
        110, 111, 114, 115
Germany ix, 7-10, 14, 20, 60-1, 76, 99-122,
    230
    'final settlement' with USSR 110, 111
    immigration to 112, 113
    NATO membership 19, 20, 33, 34, 42, 43,
        109, 110
    new treaties with Soviet Union 110
    relations with Soviet Union 111-12, 115
    unification of 9, 20, 21, 31, 32, 41-3, 69,
        102, 106-10, 114, 157
Germany, Federal Republic of 10, 33-4, 35, 99

economic aid for Soviet Union 106-7,
    111-12, 115, 117
NATO membership 36-7
Soviet attitude to US troops in 79
Soviet relationship with 17, 18, 20, 21,
    101, 102-3, 115
and unification question 9, 31, 32, 41-2,
    47, 69, 70
Gheorghiu-Dej, Gheorghe 194
Giscard D'Estaing, Valéry 22
Goncharov, Sergei 167
Gorbachev, Mikhail 13, 16, 18, 21, 37, 38, 39,
    45, 60, 100, 101, 112, 139, 155, 156,
    157, 164, 172, 173, 232
    acceptance of NATO by 32, 38-40
    and arms control viii, 79, 80-1, 86, 94, 95,
        201
    and 'Common European House' viii, 16,
        38, 39, 130, 139, 157, 166, 201
    criticisms of 21, 88, 94, 104, 111
    and German unification 32, 33, 70, 80,
        105, 108, 109, 115
        and German NATO membership
        34, 42
    German visit 103
    on Hungary 104
    intelligentsia support for 13
    loss of power 169
    new approach to Eastern Europe 125-38
    new approach to Germany 101-3, 115
    and New Thinking viii, 15, 18, 25, 65, 66,
        125, 151, 153, 155
    and new Union Treaty 22
    on nuclear disarmament ix, 38, 81, 82, 83
    October 1987 speech 14
    on Poland 104
    relations with EC 66, 67, 68, 200, 201
    relations with Kohl 20, 43, 68, 105, 109-
        10, 112
    relations with US 38, 80, 100-1
    self-determination abroad 19
    Soviet military and 20, 21
    summit meetings 17, 18, 19, 38, 39, 42, 81,
        82, 108, 201
    and Western Europe integration 17, 66,
        172
Grechko, Marshall Andrei 127
Gromyko, Andrei 34, 79
Group of Seven x, 22, 111, 166, 197, 201, 210,
    215

Havel, President Václav 46, 71
Helsinki Conference on Security and
    Cooperation in Europe, Final Act 11,
    20-1, 124, 209
Holg Alliance, of 1815 5
Honecker, Erich 102, 103, 104, 112, 115,
    136-7, 139

Hungary 46, 100, 104, 127-8, 133, 141, 144, 216
    agreements with successor states 144
    attitude to NATO 45, 46, 47, 48
    CFE allocations 89, 92
    decline of communism in 19
    and East German refugees 139
    EC relationship 71, 199, 200
    events of 1989 in 138-9
    revised relations with USSR 46, 130, 131, 136, 143
    Soviet withdrawal from 19, 81, 141, 146
Husák, Czech leader 136

IMF (International Monetary Fund) 164, 196, 201, 215
INF (Intermediate range nuclear forces) agreement 17, 18, 81, 93
Inozemtsev, Nikolai 153

Jakeš, Milos 136, 139
Japan x, 11
Jaruzelski, General Wojciech 135, 138

Kádár, János 136
Karaganov, Sergei ix, 25, 48, 57
Kazakhstan 82, 83, 84, 88, 90, 92, 113, 143, 220, 229
Khasbulatov, Ruslan 169
Khrushchev, Nikita 14, 128, 153
    and Berlin crises 10, 35, 79
Kissinger, Henry 40
Klaus, Václav 146
Kochemasov, USSR ambassador to GDR 105
Kohl, Chancellor Helmut 18, 20, 38, 104, 108, 109
    and German unification 41, 105
    on Gorbachev 73, 101
    meeting with Gorbachev 43, 109, 111
    Moscow visit 103, 109, 117
Kokoshin, Andrei 162
Kondrashov, Stanislav 165
Kortunov, Andrei 161
Kosygin, Alexei Nikolayevich 183, 201
Kozyrev, Andrei ix, 22, 24, 48, 50, 161, 164-5, 166, 169, 171
Kravchuk, Leonid 84, 90
Krenz, Egon ix, 104, 115, 139
Kurginyan, Sergei 159
Kvitsinskg, Yuly 34, 111
Kyrgyzstan 113, 220

Latin America Free Trade Area 194
Legvold, Robert 10
Lenin, Vladimir Ilyich 7, 25, 59, 152, 153
Leninism 10, 163
Ligachev, Egor 103, 155
Lithuania 170

Lobov, General 158
Lubbers, Ruud 217

Maastricht Treaty 218
Makashov, Albert 158
Malcolm, Neil 142
Malenkov, Geory 32
Mansfield, Senator Mike 37
Marxisnm-Leninism 1, 8, 31, 101
Mazowiecki, Tadeusz 44, 138, 141
Medvedev, Roy 13
Mitterrand, President François 108, 147, 216
Modrow, Hans 106
Moldova 83, 88-92 passim, 144
Moreton, Edwina 9
Morozov, General Konstantin 85
Mutual Balanced Force Reductions (MBRF) 34, 37

Nagorny Karabak issue 51, 93, 165
NATO viii, 11, 12, 19, 141, 142, 158
    conventional arms control 86, 88-90
    German unification conference 108
    London summit 20, 43, 108
    meetings with Warsaw Pact 45, 49
    nuclear arms control 82-3
        see also main heading nuclear arms
    original role of 52
    possible future attitude to Russia 227, 230
    response to Gorbachev policies 80, 81, 157
    role in Europe 10, 19, 43, 49-50
    Soviet attitude to 31-6, 38, 39, 40
    united Germany membership question 19, 34, 42, 106
    US role in 127
Nazarbayev, President Nursultan 82, 83
New Political Thinking ix, 15, 18, 25, 172, 173
new realism 24, 158-61, 165-6, 171, 173
New Thinking 39, 40, 46, 103, 125, 128, 134, 140
    and approach to EC 59, 65, 66, 68
    implementation of 155-7
    on Moscow and Europe 151-74
        Common European House 151-5
        crisis of 151, 157-63
    Europeanization 155-7
    and Russian national interests 151, 163-72
    origins of 152-5
    and security 18, 19, 152
Nicholas I, Tsar 5
Nicholas II, Tsar 6
North Atlantic Cooperation Council (NACC) 22, 32, 48, 50, 146
    role in intra-CIS security issues 51
North Atlantic Treaty Organization see NATO

nuclear armaments ix, 9, 15, 22, 38, 46, 81-6,
    101
    allocation process 22, 50-1
    Cruise and Pershing-2 missiles 17, 38, 103
    denuclearization aim 81, 82
    deployment in republics 82-3, 84
    dismantling of 84-5, 94
    intermediate range 10, 17, 37, 81-2, 103
        see also main heading INF
    nuclear proliferation 83-4, 201
    'reasonable sufficiency' 126
    START treaties 46, 51, 80, 81, 82, 84-5

OECD (Organization for Economic
    Cooperation and Development) 164
Oldenburg, Fred ix, 14

Pankin, Boris 143
pan-Slavism 6, 7
Peter the Great, Tsar 4, 168
Petrovsky, Vladimir 160
Poland 2, 3, 12, 36, 44-5, 50, 104, 127, 133,
    170, 216
    CFE allocations 89, 92
    cooperation with USSR 44-5
    decline of communism and elections in 19
    EC relations 199, 200
    events of 1989 138
    and German unification 141
    relations with Russian republics 143,
        145-6
    relations with Ukraine 145
    revised relations with USSR 45-6, 130,
        131, 135, 142-3
    Solidarity 19, 138
Ponomarev, Boris 154
Poszgay, Imre 136, 139
Pozdngakov, El'giz 168
Pravda, Alex ix, 19

Rakhmanin, Oleg 158
Rapacki, Adam 36
Rapallo Treaty, 1922 7
Razuvaev, Vladimir 168
Reagan, President Ronald 81, 101
'Realist Westernism' 165
Reykjavik summit 17, 81
Romania 46, 130, 135, 136
    CFE allocations 89, 92
Rome, Treaty of 22, 75
Roosevelt, President F. D. 34
Rougemont, Denis de 1
Russia,
    arms control 79, 88-93 passim
    democratization, results of 24, 32
    division of forces and equipment 50-1
    economic position ix, 22-3, 25-6, 48, 114,
        146-7, 167, 225-6

inflation and unemployment 225
joint ventures 195
see also relations and trade with
    Europe below
Europeanness of x, 1-2, 164, 168, 170, 171,
    174
formation of CIS 83, 84
future place in Europe ix, 25, 50, 94, 164,
    224-33
    possible scenarios,
        gradual modernization 225,
            231-3
        internal conflicts 225, 228-
            30, 232, 233
        military coup d'état 225,
            228-30, 232, 233
        neo-fascist regime 225-8,
            233
        sources of instability 219,
            225-6
        swift modernization 225
future relations with EC 218-22
    membership question 208, 218-22
inherits USSR's place at UN 83
military reactions to changes ix, 33, 90, 92,
    93
nuclear status of 82-4, 85
participation in NACC 22, 32
'Realist Westernism' in 165
relations with Atlantic alliance/NATO
    viii, 22, 24, 32, 47-52
relations with
    Bulgaria 146
    EBRD ix
    EC ix, 22, 23
relations and trade with Europe viii, ix, x,
    1-26, 171, 182-98, 199, 204-6, 207-10
    aid in transition period 23, 195,
        196-7
    economic barriers 20-3
    end of Cold War period 11-15
    historical background 4-8
    new European trade patterns 193-6
    patterns of assistance 196-8, 210-18
    Soviet legacy 182-91, 208
    underlying factors in 2-4
relations with Germany 113-14
    Volga Germans 113
    troop withdrawals 114
relations with
    Poland 144, 145-6
    Ukraine 85, 229
    United States 170
and Westernization x, 26, 163-4, 165-6
Russo-Japanese war 6
Rutskoi, Aleksandr 172
Ryzhkov, Nikolai 107

Sadykov, A. 75
Sakharov, Andrei 13, 134
Schumann Plan 60
Segal, Gerald, 9
Shakhnazarov, Georgy 128, 129, 134, 156
Sharipov, Yu 75
Sharp, Jane viii, 10, 19, 21, 22
Shevardnadze, Eduard 34, 66, 71, 72, 164, 172
  antipathy to use of force 126, 128
  criticisms of 21, 24, 88, 111, 140, 142, 157, 166
  disarmament and restructuring 18, 81, 82, 87
  Eastern European policy 125, 126, 129, 133, 137, 140
  on European integration 20, 67, 160
  and German question 44-5, 104-8 *passim*, 114, 140
  and New Thinking ix, 23, 24, 154, 155
  resignation 21, 45, 88, 142
Shmelev, N. 7
Single European Act 66
Skubiszewski, Krystof 45, 109
Slavophilism, 6
Soviet Academy of Sciences 39, 61, 75, 167
Soviet Union,
  1954 bid to join NATO 32, 35, 36
  attitude to NATO/Atlantic alliance *see under* Atlantic alliance
  attitude to Unites States 12, 16, 17, 63, 79
  and Common European House 224
  coup of August 1991 16, 21, 33, 47, 73, 112
    effects of 143-4, 173, 231
  dissolution and demise of ix, 31, 33, 47, 73, 112, 113, 144, 151, 162, 163, 206
  de-Stalinization in 61
  economic situation 11-13, 25, 72, 75, 182-91
    capital deficit and international debt 186-8
    convertibility question 191-2
    credits from FRG 107, 108, 110, 114-15, 117
    democratization and market experiments 16, 103-4, 155
    EC aid for 72, 108 *passim*
    joint ventures 189, 190
    oil production and export 182-4, 207
    restructuring foreign trade 188-91
    special economic zones 189, 190-91, 193
    trade with Western Europe 17, 19, 22, 67, 184-5, 204-5, 206-7
  foreign policy x, 7-11, 15, 18-19, 23, 42, 43, 47, 64, 65, 79
    'Common European House' 65, 224

and Germany 78, 101-18
  NATO membership of 45, 107, 108, 140
  unification question 9, 18, 20, 32, 69, 101-2, 106, 115, 140, 156
  on United States 10, 16, 17, 63-4
former republics of viii, 32, 73, 76, 82, 83
influence of military in 80-1, 83-4, 87, 88, 89, 94, 108, 111, 157-8
international affairs specialists 153
political disarray in 25, 73, 75
reform of armed forces 45-6, 79-88, 93-4
relations with
  Balkan states 46
  Czechoslovakia 46, 128
  East Germany 100, 104, 105
  EC viii, 22, 66-8
  Germany ix, 101-1, 112
  Hungary 46, 128
  West Germany 17-18, 19, 20, 101
  Western Europe 8-11, 17-19, 59-65, 68, 69, 74, 94, 100, 170
relations with Central-Eastern and South-Eastern Europe 79, 123-8
policy flaws 129-40
post-coup position 143-7
salvaging efforts 140-2
security aims of 80, 99, 106, 107, 152
Westernization in 13, 155
Späth, Lothar 103
Stalin, Iosif 13, 113
  and Berlin crises 10, 35
  and Eastern Europe 123
  and NATO 32, 33
  regime of 7, 8
Stankevich, Sergei 166, 167, 168
START negotiations 46, 81
  treaties 51, 80, 83, 85
Strauss, Franz-Josef 103

Tajikistan 85, 90
Teltschik, Horst 104, 107
Timofeev, Ivan 1
Transcaucasus states 85
Trofimenko, Genrikh 37
Trotsky, Leon 7
Turchin, Valentin 13
Turkey 23, 220
Turkmenistan 90, 220
Two-plus-four talks 107-11 *passim*, 115

Ukraine 25, 50, 51 *passim*
  CFE allocations 88, 89, 90, 91
  independence and formation of CIS 83, 84, 144
  nuclear status of 82, 83, 84-5
  position vis-à-vis Central, E. and S. E.

Europe and Russia 144-5
relations with Poland 144-5
relations with Russian Federation 85, 229
United Nations 51, 52, 230
United States x, 8-13 *passim*, 25, 46, 107, 230
and arms control negotiations 17, 82-3, 85
presence in Europe 31-40 *passim*
Reagan administration 11, 100, 115
role in NATO 127
SDI programme 46, 101
Soviet attitude to 13, 17, 63, 79, 100
support for reformed Soviet Union 115
Uzbekistan 143, 220

Van den Broek, Dutch Foreign Minister 52
Višegrad triangle grouping 142, 145
Volodin, Eduard 170

Waigel, Theo 216
Wałęsa, Lech 145, 146
Warsaw Pact 9, 11, 17-21 *passim*, 34, 35, 36,
42, 86, 99, 107
attitude to NATO/US 34, 35, 36, 37
CFE talks 86
collapse of 21, 31, 33, 35-6, 43, 47, 71, 81,
125, 141, 157
consequences of 43-7, 94
intra-Pact arms talks 87-8
Soviet control over 79, 101, 133
Weizsäcker, President Richard von 102
Western Europe 9, 11-12, 152
NATO/US relationship 31, 39, 40

Soviet reaction to integration 8-11, 59-70,
74
Western European Union (WEU) 36, 142
World Bank 164, 197
World Economy and International Relations,
Institute of the (IMEMO) 61
Wörner, Manfred 52

Yakovlev, Aleksandr 126, 128, 155, 156
Yalta Conference 34
Yanaev, Gennady 47
Yeltsin, Boris viii, 112, 142, 165, 166, 169,
170, 171, 172, 232
and Baltic states 88
control of nuclear arsenal 83, 84, 85
as CIS leader 84
and Europe 22-6, 73, 112, 163, 221
and Central, E. and S. E. European states
144, 145
as leader of Russian Federation 73, 169,
171, 190, 192
on Russian membership of Atlantic
alliance viii, 22, 32, 45-6
and Volga Germans 113
Yugoslavia 25, 72, 85, 171, 216, 229

Zagladin, Vadim 128
Zaykov, Lev 93
Zhirinovsky, Vladimir 226
Zhivkov, Todor 136
Zhurkin, Vitaly 163